# Shipping & Commercial Case Law

**Albert Badia**

# Shipping & Commercial Case Law

**Albert Badia**

*250 leading cases of the High Courts of England
and the European Court of Justice*

*Collection:* GESTIONA
*Director:* David Soler


SHIPPING & COMMERCIAL CASE LAW
First edition, 2003
Second edition, 2013




*Publisher:* Marge Books
València, 558, ático 2.ª - 08026 Barcelona (Spain)
Tel. +34-932 449 130 - marge@marge.es - www.marge.es

*Managing editors:* Hèctor Soler, Ana Soto, Laura Martínez, Neus Piñol
*Editing:* Natalia Echezuría, Rosa Serra
*Make-up editor:* Mercedes Lara


ISBN: 978-84-15340-84-3
Legal deposit: B-22.067-2013

*To Elisabeth, Pilgrims and Voltaire*

# Index

Preface

**Table of Cases**

# Preface

This book contains summaries of 250 cases related to international trade and carriage of goods by sea. Each case is presented with an abstract of the factual background and the key findings of the court. All the cases relate to disputes decided by the High Courts of England or by the European Court of Justice, the knowledge of which is a must for any practitioner in this area.

The issues referred to in the cases relate to contracts of carriage on bills of lading, waybills and charterparties, as well as to international trade instruments like sale contracts, letters of credit, performance bonds, indemnities and agency. There is also wide reference to ship arrests, limitation of liability, injunctions, choice of law, arbitration and jurisdiction. Full consideration is given to the Hague-Visby Rules, the Carriage of Goods by Sea Act, the Sale of Goods Act, Incoterms and UCP for Documentary Credits.

Albert Badia is a practicing solicitor in England and Wales. He has acted as Counsel in many disputes and has been appointed as arbitrator in commercial matters. Special thanks are given to James Sonsalla for his contribution to the 2nd edition.

ALBERT BADIA
AACNI (Partner). Solicitor (England and Wales). Abogado (Spain)
PhD (Dundee). LLM (Southampton). FCIArb (London)
albertbadia@aacni.com

## 1
## Actis Co. Ltd. v. The Sanko Steamship Co.
*(The Aquacharm)*
1982, 1 Lloyd's Rep. 7 (C.A.)

The vessel *Aquacharm* was time chartered for a carriage of coal from Baltimore (USA) through the Panama Canal to Tokyo (Japan). The charterparty incorporated the Hague Rules and included an off-hire clause stating that in the event of loss of time by "any other cause preventing the full working of the vessel, the payment of hire shall cease for the time thereby lost". The charterers ordered the vessel to load up to the draught "permissible by the Panama Canal Company of 39 feet 6 inches TFW (Tropical Fresh Water)". The master took on board 43,000 tonnes of coal which was read as exceeding the amount that could safely pass through the Canal. Subsequently, the Panama Canal Co. refused to allow the vessel to pass through the canal because she exceeded the permitted draught. To overcome this difficulty, 636 tonnes of coal were discharged onto a lighter and reloaded again once the Canal had been crossed. This delay held up the vessel for 9 days. The charterers refused to pay the hire for such period invoking the off-hire clause; alternatively, they claimed damages caused by unseaworthiness.

*Held:* The off hire clause was not applicable to the nine days the vessel was delayed due to off loading and reloading. The deciding factor is whether the "full working of the vessel" was prevented, not the assignment of fault for the vessel's delay. Accordingly, the court ruled that the ship was "fully working" at all times irrespective of the nature of the work (i.e. reloading the cargo into the lighter). Hence she was not off-hire. **ii)** Considering that the cause of the delay was the result of the master overloading the vessel, the question arose whether the charterers can recover damages from the owners; such damages being the hire for the nine days. The answer depends on whether the vessel was seaworthy or not when she left Baltimore. If she was unseaworthy and the shipowners failed to prove that they exercised due diligence, shipowners would be liable under art. III (1) and IV of the Hague Rules. If, on the contrary, the vessel were seaworthy, they would be exempted by virtue of art. IV (2.a) insofar the loss arose from the neglect of the master in the "management" of the ship. Based on the evidence, the court ruled that when the vessel left Baltimore she was seaworthy because she was fit to carry the cargo safely and to encounter the ordinary perils on that voyage, and thus Art. IV (2.a) of the Hague Rules exempting the vessel owners applied.

## 2
## ADAMASTOS SHIPPING CO. V. ANGLO-SAXON PETROLEUM CO.
### 1959, A.C. 133 (H.L.)

An oil tanker was time chartered for eighteen months. The charterparty contained a clause providing that the vessel "being tight, staunch and strong and every way fitted for the voyage, and to be maintained in such condition during the voyage…". There was a further clause incorporated by a slip stating: "Paramount clause. This bill of lading shall have effect subject to the Carriage of Goods by Sea Act of the United States 1936[1]…which shall be deemed to be incorporated herein, and nothing herein contained shall be deemed a surrender by the carrier of any of its rights or immunities or an increase of any of its responsibilities or liabilities under said Act. If any term of this bill of lading be repugnant to said Act to any extent, such term shall be void to that extent, but no further". The owners, exercising due diligence, selected and appointed adequate engine-room staff, but that staff proved incompetent. Such incompetence (amounting to unseaworthiness) led the vessel to break down on the first voyage from Baltimore to her loading port. The charterers lost the services of the vessel for over three months. Charterers subsequently brought a claim against the owners for unseaworthiness and for the resulting damages they suffered. The owners contended that their obligations as to seaworthiness were limited by the Act to their due diligence to make the ship seaworthy at the beginning of the journey and properly man, equip and supply the ship, as provided in section 3(1) of the Act. The charterers argued that the Act was not applicable since Sec. 5 stated "*The provisions of the Act shall not be applicable to charterparties*".

***Held (for the owners):* i)** (Lord Somervell of Harrow) "*The first point taken by the charterer is based on the opening words of the Paramount clause 'This bill of lading…' I agree with the learned judge that the answer to this point is an application of the principle falsa demonstratio non nocet. I have nothing I wish to add to his conclusion on this point. The opening words of the Paramount clause are to be read as if they were: 'This charterparty…'*" **ii)** (Lord Reid) "*As the parties have chosen to incorporate in a charterparty provisions which are designed to apply, and only to apply, to bills of lading, one must, I think, infer that they intended these provisions to be incorporated mutatis mutandis; and in order to see what this involves I would begin by trying to read references to bills of lading in the Act as if they were references to charterparties. That necessarily involves the rejection as insensible of the provisions of section 5 of the Act that its provisions shall not be applicable to charterparties…*"[2] **iii)** The provisions of the Act

---

[1] The 1936 Act incorporated the Hague Rules into US law.

[2] The inclusion of a Paramount clause into a charterparty generally seeks to import to the contract between owners and charterers the same standard of rights and duties as exists between the carrier and the shipper under the Hague Rules. "*When a Paramount clause is incorporated into a contract, the purpose is to give the Hague Rules contractual force; so that, although the bill of lading may contain very wide exceptions, the Rules are Paramount and make the shipowners liable for want of due diligence to make the ship seaworthy and so forth.*"

affected the rights and liabilities of the parties in connection with (a) non-cargo carrying voyages as well as cargo carrying voyages, and (b) voyages other than those to and from U.S. ports, as well as such voyages.[3] Therefore the Act did apply to the ballast voyage from Baltimore to the loading port. (Viscount Simonds) *"The contractual subject matter was the whole period during which the vessel was under charter, and, it is to that period that the parties agreed that the statutory standard of obligation and immunity should relate."* **iv)** By incorporating the Act, the owners have the obligation to exercise due diligence in providing a seaworthy vessel, but no more than that. That duty arises at the beginning of each consecutive voyage under the charter.[4] **v)** The words 'loss or damage' in section 4 of the Act, relating to the immunity of the carrier, refer not only to the physical loss or damage to the goods but also covered the charterer's loss in only being able to complete fewer voyages than they would otherwise have done. The claim in relation to loading and carriage of goods also fails.

**3**

**AECTRA REFINING AND MARKETING INC. V. EXMAR N.V.**
*(The New Vanguard)*
1995, 1 Lloyd's Rep. 191 (C.A.)

In 1987-1988 Exmar N.V. (the owners) time chartered two ships, the *Pacifica* and the *New Vanguard*, from Aectra (the

charterers). Both charterparties led to disputes, which were referred to arbitrators. The arbitration relating to the *New Vanguard* was settled and the owners agreed to pay USD 120,000 to the charterers on Jan. 7, 1988. In the *Pacifica* arbitration the owners claimed USD 297,156 for unpaid hire and for bunkers supplied, but only USD 42,070 was awarded the balance remaining in dispute. The charterer's position was that nothing was due for bunkers since the *Pacifica* was allegedly off-hire. The owners requested that the USD 42,070 be offset from the USD 120,000 due under the *New Vanguard* settlement. The arbitrators granted the request and therefore only USD 77,930 was left outstanding relating to the *New Vanguard* arbitration. The owners then requested that they refrain from paying the USD 77,930 due under the *New Vanguard* arbitration pending final resolution of their remaining claim for bunkers in the *Pacifica* arbitration. The charterers objected to that request. They served a writ and applied for summary judgment to recover the money due. The owners, in turn, (i) pleaded their petition in the *Pacifica* arbitration as a legitimate set-off, and (ii) asked for leave to defend i.e. the right to have their cross-claim adjudicated by the court.

***Held (for the charterers):*** **i)** The set-off pleading: The owners' claims for hire and bunkers in the Pacifica arbitration were liquidated claims capable of being set-off at common law. (Hirst, L.J.) *"In the present case the pleaded set-off is undoubtedly one for a liquidated debt for the stipulated daily rate of hire..."* **ii)** The leave to defend: Although generally independent

---

[3] Lord Morton of Henryton and Lord Reid dissenting.
[4] See also *The Kriti Rex.*

set-off enable the parties to have their various disputes tried in one action instead of two or more, the owners' claims for hire and bunkers in the *Pacifica* arbitration cannot be pleaded as independent set-off. (Hoffmann, L.J.) *"If the defendants' object was to obtain security for those claims they could, as they had suggested, have applied for a Mareva injunction. No doubt for good reason they did not. They could have applied for a stay of execution of the plaintiffs' judgment. Again they did not."* Leave to defend was dismissed.

**4**

**Aegean Sea Traders Corp. v. Repsol Petroleo S.A. and Another**
*(The Aegean Sea)*
1998, 2 Lloyd's Rep. 39 (QBD)

The *Aegean Sea* was chartered by her owners to ROIL, a wholly owned subsidiary of a company at the time owned by the State of Spain known as Repsol. The charter was on the Asbatankvoy form dated Nov. 17, 1992. The charter covered a carriage of crude oil to "one or two United Kingdom-Continent (Gibraltar/Hamburg range) or, one or two safe port(s) European Mediterranean...". Clause 9 of the charterparty stated, "the vessel shall... discharge at any safe place or wharf... designated and procured by the charterer, provided the Vessel can proceed thereto, lie and depart therefrom always safely afloat...". A further clause stated that "the Master shall not be required to sign Bills of Lading for any port which the vessel cannot enter, remain at and leave in safely and always afloat nor for any blockaded port". After loading, Repsol telexed a letter of indemnity dated Nov. 26, 1992, to the owners. Two bills of lading were issued, one naming Mobil North Sea Oil as shipper and the other Sun Oil Great Britain Ltd. as shipper. Both mentioned "port of Spain" as the port of discharge. ROIL had purchased the cargo covered by the Sun Oil bill of lading f.o.b. from Louis Dreyfus and sold it to Repsol ex ship terms. It happened that Louis Dreyfus endorsed the bill of lading to Repsol instead of to ROIL. Louis Dreyfus acknowledged they had made an error and, following return of the bills, voided the endorsement made to Repsol and re-endorsed the bills to ROIL on Dec. 24, 1992. Repsol, as holders of the Sun Oil bill of lading, nominated La Coruña as discharge port. On Dec. 3, 1993, while proceeding to berth at La Coruña, the *Aegean Sea* grounded. Attempts to refloat her failed and within hours she broke in two and exploded, resulting in the total loss of the vessel and most of her cargo, as well as in significant pollution of the coastal and marine environment. The owners sought the following: (1) the value of the vessel and, (2) her bunkers, (3) the freight earned, (4) an indemnity against all liabilities (property damage, clean up costs, loss of fishing profits,...) arising under Spanish legislation giving effect to the Civil Liability Convention, (5) potential liability to Cristal Ltd., a company created by oil companies to provide additional compensation for oil pollution, and (6) salvage fees. The owners claimed against ROIL as first defendants and against Repsol as second defendants. Their claim against ROIL was based on breach of the safe port provision contained in the charterparty, and alternatively, for failure to comply with charterers' orders which – they contend- were covered by an implied indemnity in the charter. The owners claims against Repsol were based on reasons similar to those against ROIL on the ground that Repsol was the intermediate holder of one bill of lading and, as such, –according to owners- Repsol was subject to liabilities under the Carriage of Goods by Sea Act, 1992. The main issues before the Court were: (i) Is ROIL, as charterer, entitled to limit its liability under art. 1 of the 1976 Convention on Limitation of Liability for Maritime Claims? and (ii) Is Repsol, as intermediate holder of the bill of lading, subject to liability under S. 3 of COGSA, 1992, or alternatively, (iii) is Repsol liable under s. 3(1)(c) due to the letter of indemnity it had issued to the owners?

***Held:*** (Thomas, J.) **(i)** *"It follows from the development of limitation prior to the 1976 Convention and the way in which the 1976 Convention is structured and its language that, in my view, it does not provide (and is not intended to provide) an entitlement to charterers to limit where the shipowner brings the type of claim I am concerned with against the charterers. Such claims cannot in principle, in my view, be reasonably brought within its language; It cannot have been intended that either the limitation amount or the fund be reduced by direct claims by the owners against charterers for the loss of the ship or the freight or the bunkers; it was intended for claims by cargo interests and other third parties external to the operation of the ship against those responsible for the operation of the ship. To permit claims of the type advanced by owners against the charterers for the direct losses they suffer to come with-in the scope of the limitation amount or the fund would diminish what was available to others."* **(ii)** *"I do not consider that a person satisfies the requirements under s. 5(2)(b)[5] and becomes the holder of a bill of lading if that person obtains the bill of lading merely in consequence of someone endorsing it and sending it to him; Moreover, the bill of lading was never delivered to Repsol by Louis Dreyfus; Louis Dreyfus sent the bill to ROIL under cover of a letter addressed to ROIL as principals; it was not delivered by Louis Dreyfus to ROIL to receive as Repsol's agents as it was intended for ROIL and the covering letter was addressed to them; There was never any delivery of the bill of lading by Louis Dreyfus to Repsol to complete the endorsement; It cannot have been intended by the draftsman of the Act that a person to whom a bill of lading is endorsed and sent in error has then to act as if he was a person entitled to endorse the bill of lading as a pre-condition of the person who made the mistake being enabled to rectify his error by re-endorsing and delivering it to the correct party; the person to whom it was sent was not the lawful holder and not therefore entitled to endorse it."* **iii)** *"Although the letter of undertaking was …provided by Repsol, even if in the context of ROIL's obligations under cl. 13 of the charter-party, I (Thomas, J.) do not consider it was a demand for delivery. The letter of undertaking was on its terms an undertaking that, if delivery was made to the order of Repsol, then Repsol would indemnify the owners against any claim that might be made under the bills of lading. It did not oblige Repsol to take*

---

[5] Section 5(2)(b) of COGSA 1992 defines the scope of the term "holder of a bill of lading".

*delivery or oblige the owners to deliver to the order of Repsol. It was in short an agreement to indemnify that took effect only if delivery was made to the order of Repsol. On its terms the letter of indemnity was therefore not a demand for delivery; The claims under the bill of lading against Repsol can not…succeed because Repsol never became subject to the liabilities under the bills of lading; even if they had, the bills of lading did not contain the implied terms on which the owners' claim is based."*

# 5
## AET Inc. Ltd. v. Arcadia Petroleum
*(The Eagle Valencia)*
[2009] EWHC 2337 (C.A.)

The MT *Eagle Valencia* was chartered on a Shellvoy 5 Form, as amended, with Shell Additional Clauses (SAC). Clause 13 of the charterparty provided for laytime to start counting six hours after (a) the vessel was in all respects ready to load or discharge and written notice had been tendered, or (b) the vessel was securely moored at the specified berth, whichever first occurred. Additionally, SAC 22 provided that the Notice of Readiness (NOR) would not be valid if owners failed to obtain free practice within the six hours period. At the time the original NOR was presented, the berth was occupied and the vessel was required to wait at anchorage. The port health authorities granted the vessel free practice, but that occurred more than six hours after the NOR was tendered. Right after free practice was granted, the Master sent two emails "repeating" the NOR. Once the voyage was completed, owners claimed demurrage. Charterers argued that the NOR was invalid by the failure to obtain free practice within the six hours time. Alternatively, they said that owners' claim for demurrage was time-barred under the demurrage clause of the charter, which provided that any demurrage claim should be notified within sixty days and full supporting documentation provided within ninety days from discharge.

***Held (for charterers):*** The Court of Appeal took a different view. The SAC invalidated the original NOR, but did not prevent the owners from tendering a fresh NOR, which would start running the laytime after a further six hours. Do the master's emails "repeating" the NOR constitute a fresh NOR? Yes. The Court held that, as the emails were sent after free practice was granted, they constitute a valid NOR. However, owners could not rely on that finding because the time-bar clause required a "fully and correctly documented" demurrage claim to be submitted within 90 days after completion of discharge. So, as the original NOR was invalid, it was ineffective for the purpose of supporting the owners' claim for demurrage.

# 6
## AIC Ltd. v. Marine Pilot Ltd.
*(The Archimidis)*
2007, 2 Lloyd's Rep. 101 (Q.B.)

Marine Pilot Ltd. (the owners) let their vessel *Archimidis* to AIC Ltd. (the charterers) for three consecutive voyage for the carriage of gasoil from "1 safe port

Ventspils" with "discharge ½ safe ports" in the "UK Continent Bordeaux/Hamburg range". The charterparty contained the following provisions inter alia: "(3) DEADFREIGHT Should the charterer fail to supply a full cargo, the Vessel may, at the Master's discretion, and shall upon request of the charterer, proceed on her voyage, provided that the tanks in which cargo is loaded are sufficiently filed to put her in seaworthy condition. In that event, however, deadfreight shall be paid at the rate specified in Part 1 hereof on the difference between the intake quantity and the quantity the essel would have carried if loaded to her minimum permission freeboard for the voyage. ... Special provisions... Minimum 90,000 metric tones always consistent with 45 feet fresh basis arrival Northwest Europe. No deadfreight to be for charterer's account provided minimum quantity supplied. ... AIC TERMS ... (11) LIGHTERING CLAUSE ... If charterers request vessel to load/discharge via lightering/ship-to-ship transfer (weather permitting and always subject to master's approval which [is] not unreasonably to be withheld) at anchor of any load/discharge port". The vessel arrived at Ventspils to take on the cargo, but as a result of previous poor weather, the dredged channel had silted up. Subsequently, the master served a notice of readiness stating that he expected to take on a reduced cargo of "approximately 67,000 mt" due to draft restrictions caused by the silt. Charterers tendered for loading a quantity of 93,410 mt even though they had notice that the vessel could not take on this amount. The master loaded 67,058 mt. Owners subsequently sought damag-

es in arbitration for deadfreight based on the difference between 90,000 mt and the 67,058 mt actually loaded before an arbitral. Owners argued that charterers were in breach of the safe port provision and that the charterers could have loaded the remaining 33,000 mt by ship-to-ship. The issues before the court were (i) whether the charterers fail to supply the minimum amount of cargo by tendering an amount of cargo that was "without legal significance" and whether, even if the tender would have prima facie satisfied the charterers' obligations, whether the charterers could not escape liability because the option to load the balance of the cargo per ship-to-ship pursuant clause 11 was not exercised, (ii) whether the safe port provision constituted a warranty on the part of the charterers as opposed to an agreement by the parties that the port was safe; and (iii) whether draft restrictions at the load port rendered it as a matter of law prospectively unsafe because characteristics of the load port might mean that a vessel "could not proceed to, load the contractual cargo at and depart from the port".

***Held (Gloster, J.):*** **(i)** *"The mere fact that both parties knew that such a quantity could not be loaded does not, in the absence of some express contractual provision, mean that the tender of performance had no legal finding. By finding that the charterer had tendered for loading the minimum quantity, the tribunal was concluding that the charterer had indeed indicated that it was ready and willing to perform its part of the contract. The obligation under clause 3 to pay deadfreight is only triggered in the event that the charterer fails to supply a full car-*

*go.*" Here, because the charterer had tendered and were ready to supply the full cargo, they were not in breach of clause 3 and thus not liable for deadfreight. Under the tribunal's finding the charterer was effectively bound to exercise its option to load ship-to-ship to avoid any liability for deadfreight which the judge held was incorrect. *"There had been no 'failure' on its [charterers'] part to supply. It was the owner which had in effect refused, because of the draft restrictions, and no doubt justifiably, to load more than 67,058 mt at the berth."* **(ii)** The language in the charterparty, "1 safe port Ventspils" was more than simply a mutual agreement between charterers and owners that the port was safe. The words were not part of the standard printed Asbatankvoy form, but were rather expressly agreed to by the parties. When parties insert chosen words into standard printed terms, it is resumed to have meant that the parties agreed that those words would have some effect. And furthermore, *"In the context of charterparties, the authorities clearly demonstrate that (absent express provision to the contrary) the words 'safe port' or 'safe berth' usually connote a warranty of safety".* **(iii)** There is authority for the view that a port can be unsafe because of a need for lightering to get into or out of it and, subsequently, a determination whether Ventspils was in fact unsafe was left for further determination by the tribunal whether the whether and silting of the channel at the port at the relevant time was an "abnormal occurrence", since only in cases where events resulting in the need for "lightering" are normal would the charterers be liable for damages resulting from an unsafe port.

# 7

## AKTIESELSKABET REIDAR v. ARCOS LTD.
### 1927, 1 KB 352 (C.A.)

The vessel *Sagatind* was chartered to load a full and complete cargo of 850 standards of timber at a White Sea port and proceed to an English port for discharge. The freight was calculated at a fixed sum per standard. Cargo was to be loaded at the rate of 80 standards per weather working day for deals and battens and 60 standards for other goods. Demurrage was to be paid at 25% per day and pro-rata for any part thereof should the ship be detained beyond the stipulated time. Early in Oct. the vessel reached the port of loading. Had the vessel loaded within the time stipulated in the charter she would have taken the 850 standards by Oct.17, but by Oct. 23 she had loaded no more than 544 standards and the charterers failed to provide the balance to bring the load up to the contracted for quantity of 850. The vessel left part-loaded on Oct. 24. The owners claimed dead freight in respect to the 306 standards missing.

***Held (for the owners):*** (Atkins L.J.) *"… in a contract fixing a number of lay days and providing for days at demurrage thereafter, the charterer enters into a binding obligation to load a complete cargo within the lay days subject to any default by the shipowner or to the operation of any exceptions, matters which do not arise in this case. If the lay days expire without a full cargo having been loaded the charterer has broken his contract. The provisions as to demurrage quantify the damages, not for the complete breach, but only such damages as arise from the detention of the vessel. For correlative to* *the ship's right to receive the agreed damages is the charterer's right to detain the ship for the purpose of enabling him, if possible, to perform his broken contract and so mitigate any further damage. If however, for reasons other than the shipowner's default, the charterer becomes unable to do that which he contracted to do -namely, put a full and complete cargo on board during the fixed lay days, the breach is never repaired, the damages are not completely mitigated, and the shipowner may recover the loss that he has incurred in addition to his liquidated demurrage or his unliquidated damages for detention".* The charterers, upon payment of demurrage, were not entitled to detain the ship beyond the time stipulated for loading; by doing so, they committed a breach of the charterparty. In this case, the charterers were found liable for dead freight in addition to the sums due for demurrage.

**8**

**ALAN (W.J.) & CO. LTD. V. EL NASR EXPORT & IMPORT CO.**
1972, Q.B. 189 (C.A.)

By two contracts egyptian buyers purchased from kenyan sellers two lots of 250 tons of coffee f.o.b Mombasa. Payment was agreed by confirmed irrevocable letters of credit to be opened at sight one month prior to payment. Kenyan shillings was stipulated as the currency of payment. The contracts incorporated the London Coffee Trade Federation form, which included an express choice of English Law. Under the first contract, shipment was to be effected in 1967 "during September/October", and "during October/Novem-

ber" under the second contract. For the September/October shipment, the buyers opened the credit in pounds sterling instead of shillings. The sellers accepted the confirmation on those terms and began to operate with the letter of credit presenting invoices expressed in sterling. The buyers, in turn, sold the coffee to their sub-buyers who also opened an irrevocable letter of credit in sterling. In the meantime, the value of sterling fell. The sellers then demanded the price of the second shipment to be in kenyan shillings, and sought to recover the difference in currency from sterling pounds to shillings, which they had lost in the first shipment.

***Held (for the buyers):*** **i)** Although the sale contract provided payment in kenyan shillings, the sellers waived or accepted a variation of the terms of the contract of sale (i.e. their right to be paid in shillings) by accepting payment in sterling. (Lord Denning MR) *"If one party, by his conduct, leads another to believe that the strict rights arising under the contract will not be insisted upon, intending that the other should act on that belief, and he does act on it, then the first party will not afterwards be allowed to insist on the strict legal rights when it would be inequitable for him to do so."* **ii)** (Stephenson, L.J.) *"Where, as here, the letter of credit by which the buyer's liability to pay was to be discharged did not conform to the contract, it only became binding on the sellers if they accepted or agreed to it. Alternatively, they could reject the letter of credit or insist on its amendment to conform with the sale contract. But if the sellers wanted to accept the letter of credit and payment under it without prejudice to their right to the full price (in the curren-*

*cy of account) from the buyers, they must say so and not allow buyers and sub-buyers, issuing and confirming banks to act upon it.*" **iii)** (Lord Denning MR) "*When the contract of sale stipulates for payment to be made by confirmed irrevocable letter of credit, then, when the letter of credit is issued and accepted by the seller, it operates as conditional payment of the price. It does not operate as absolute payment.*" Such conditional payment was found analogous to the mechanism of a bill of exchange or a cheque: "*if the letter of credit is honoured by the bank when documents are presented, the debt is discharged; if it is not honoured, the debt is not discharged, and the seller has a remedy in damages against both banker and buyer*". The letter of credit constitutes absolute payment only if the seller so stipulates it in the contract.

# 9

## ALDEBARAN COMPAÑÍA MARITIMA S.A. v. AUSSENHANDEL A.G. ZÜRICH
### *(The Darrah)*
### 1977, A.C. 157 (H.L.)

The ship *Darrah* was chartered under a port voyage charterparty on the Gencon form. The charterparty stated Tripoli (Libia) as the discharging port and included two clauses stating: (cls. 4) "Time lost in waiting for berth to count as laytime" and (cls. 20) cargo to be discharged by the charterers per weather working days, Fridays and holidays excepted". While entering the port (and being thereby an "arrived ship"), the vessel gave notice of readiness to discharge immediately, but because of congestion, she was delayed from reaching her discharging berth for

seven days. The shipowners, relying on the "time lost waiting for a berth" clause, claimed that the 7-day delay counted against the laytime allowed for discharge and that 14 days' demurrage was due to them.

***Held (for the shipowners):*** **i)** "*Time lost in waiting for berth' in the context of the adventure contemplated by a voyage charter, as it seems to me* (Lord Diplock), *must mean the period during which the vessel would have been in berth and at the disposition of the charterer for carrying out the loading or discharging operation, if she had not been prevented by congestion at the port from reaching a berth at which the operation could be carried out. The clauses go on to say that that period is to count as loading time or as discharging time, as the case may be… In a berth charter the effect of the clauses is to put the shipowner in the same position financially as he would have been if, instead of being compelled to wait, his vessel had been able to go straight to her berth and the obligations of the charterer to carry out the loading or discharging operation had started then. In a port charter the clauses are superfluous so far as concerns time spent in waiting in turn within the limits of the port. This counts as laytime anyway; it is laytime.*" **ii)** "*In the computation of time lost in waiting for a berth there are to be excluded all periods which would have been left out in the computation of permitted laytime used up if the vessel had actually been in berth.*" From the above it is clear that the exceptions stipulated for the laytime period should apply equally to the "time lost" period. Therefore, the period spent in waiting for berth must exclude Sundays, Fridays and legal holidays, as well as days on which working was prevented by inclement weather.

**10**

**ALLIANZ SPA AND GENERALI ASSICURAZIONI GENERALI SPA V. WEST TANKERS INC.**
*(The Front Connor)*
Case C 185/07, Feb. 10, 2009
(European Court of Justice)

There was a collision involving the vessel *Front Connor* and a jetty at an oil refinery in Syracuse (Italy), operated by Erg Petroli Spa. Erg claimed against the owners for the resulting loss and damage under a charterparty, which provided for London arbitration. Erg was partly indemnified for the loss by its own insurers, Allianz and others (the Insurers), but in the meantime London arbitration proceedings were commenced as between Erg and the owners to recover the loss suffered in excess of its insurance coverage. Subsequently, the Insurers launched their own recovery proceedings against the owners, pursuant to their subrogation rights, in the Italian court. The result was that the same claim was being pursued in two separate venues, in the London arbitration on the one hand, and by way of litigation pursued by the Insurers in the Italian court. In response, the owners issued an application in the English court for an injunction to restrain the Italian litigation. Initially, the English court considered itself competent to grant such an injunction, but the House of Lords referred the matter for determination by the European Court of Justice (ECJ).

***Held:*** Only the court first seized of the matter (in this case the Italian Court) could decide on the proper allocation of jurisdiction under the EC Regulation 44/2001. The English court, therefore, could not issue an anti-suit injunction in support of an English arbitration. In the absence of an injunction, both sets of proceedings continued in parallel: the London arbitration on the one hand and the Italian litigation on the other. The main issue was whether the proceedings brought by Allianz and Generali against West Tankers before the Tribunale di Siracusa themselves came within the scope of EC Regulation 44/2001 and, if they did, what was the efficacy of the English anti-suit injunction under EU law. The anti-suit injunction was found not compatible with the Regulation on various grounds. Amongst others, the ECJ held that "*the objection of lack of jurisdiction raised by West Tankers before the Tribunale di Siracusa on the basis of the existence of an arbitration agreement, including the question of the validity of that agreement, comes within the scope of Regulation No 44/2001 and that it is therefore exclusively for that court to rule on that objection and on its own jurisdiction, pursuant to Articles 1(2)(d) and 5(3) of that regulation*". Accordingly, "*the use of an anti-suit injunction to prevent a court of a Member State, which normally has jurisdiction to resolve a dispute under Article 5(3) of Regulation No 44/2001, from ruling, in accordance with Article 1(2)(d) of that regulation, on the very applicability of the regulation to the dispute brought before it necessarily amounts to stripping that court of the power to rule on its own jurisdiction under Regulation No 44/2001*".

# 11
## ANDRE & CIE. S.A. V. ORIENT SHIPPING (ROTTERDAM) B.V.
*(The Laconian Confidence)*
1997, 1 Lloyd's Rep. 139 (Q.B.)

The vessel *Laconian Confidence* was chartered on a time-trip charter from Yangon (Birmania) to Bangladesh. The charterparty was on the New York Produce Exchange form and incorporated an off-hire clause no. 15 which read: "That in the event of the loss of time from deficiency of and/or default men or stores, fire, breakdown or damages to hull machinery or equipment, grounding, detention by average accidents to ship or cargo, dry-docking for the purpose of examination or painting bottom, or by any other cause preventing the full working of the vessel, the payment of hire shall cease for the time thereby lost". The Laconian Confidence shipped a cargo of rice and sailed to Chittagong (Bangladesh) where the cargo was partially discharged. When she was to make sail for another port, the Bangladesh port authorities refused to allow her to proceed because of fifteen tonnes of rejected residues remaining on board. The vessel was delayed for eighteen days while awaiting permission to discharge the residues. The charterers refused to pay hire for those eighteen days arguing that the vessel was off-hire during that period. The owners referred the dispute to arbitration and received a favourable award. The charterers subsequently appealed.

***Held (for the shipowners):*** (Rix, J.) **i)** *"The delay was due to the authorities. There was no 'average accident' to the cargo... the arbitrators were clearly right to say that an average 'accident' must involve a fortuitous occurrence, and the arbitrators were entitled to form the view...that there was no element of fortuity in the presence of residues. The assumption of breach of contract is then beside the point."* **ii)** *"Above all, the charterers cannot, in the light of the findings, assert 'detention' by average accident to the cargo. Equally they cannot assert the presence of residues to be itself 'any other cause' either causing 'loss of time' or causing the prevention of the full working of the vessel; In my judgment, the qualifying phrase 'preventing the full working of the vessel' did not require the vessel to be inefficient in herself: A vessel's working may be prevented by legal as well as physical means and by outside as well as internal causes."* **iii)** With regard to the words "any other cause", Rix, J. said: *"[I]t is well established that those words, in the absence of 'whatsoever', should be construed either ejusdem generis or at any rate in some limited way reflecting the general context of the charter and clause; I would suggest that if the clause had been amended to contain the word 'whatsoever', then the position would probably have been otherwise".*[6]

# 12
## ANTIPAROS ENE V. SK SHIPPING CO. LTD. AND OTHERS
*(The Antiparos)*
2008, Lloyd's Rep. 237 (Q.B.)

The MV *Antiparos* was chartered on an amended Asbatankvoy form for a single voyage from the Arabian Gulf to South Korea or Japan on 9 Mar. 2007. Clause

---

[6] See *The Aquacharm.*

4 of the charterparty provided: (a) Charterer should name the loading port(s) "at least 24 hours prior to the vessel's readiness to sail from the last previous port of discharge, or from bunkering port for the voyage, or upon signing this charter if the vessel has already sailed…". (c) "Any extra expense incurred in connection with any change in loading or discharging ports (so named) shall be paid for by the charterer and any time thereby lost to the vessel shall count as used lay-time." The vessel was discharging at Daesan (South Korea), at the time the charterparty was concluded. She then left that port on 10 Mar. 2007 bound for Fujairah (Arab Emirates) with an ETA of 26 Mar., 2007. On 21 Mar. the the owners received voyage instructions from the charterers, the load ports of Ras Laffan (Qtar) for loading on 28-29 Mar. and Mina Al-Ahmadi (Kuwait) for loading on 29-31 Mar. being nominated. On that day, the owners arranged to bunker the vessel at Mina Al-Ahmadi for USD 301 per mt. Five days later the charterers altered their voyage instructions and required that the vessel load at Ras Laffan and Ras Tanura. The bunkers to be supplied at Ras Tanura happened to be more expensive than those initially agreed. Owners then claimed the difference of price in bunkers.

***Held (for the owners):*** **The Court rejected charterers'** argument that they had a right to revise the original nomination. Nothing in the Asbatankvoy form or the charterparty expressly confers upon the charterers a right to revise their nomination. Charterers were thus not entitled to change their original nomination. The compensation due under cl. 4(c) was not limited to compensation for deviation type losses. *"Clause 4(c) is designed to transfer from the owner to the charterer "extra expenses" because, although it is of a kind that the owner would usually bear, it is incurred as a result of the charterer revising its choice of loading or discharge port." "There is nothing in the wording of clause 4(c) that indicates that it is to be confined to expenses arising by way of deviation resulting from a change of nominated port: if the first limb of clause 4(c) dealing with expenses were so restricted, consistency would require that the second limb regarding time be similarly restricted but nothing in either limb supports this interpretation."*

**13**

**APIOIL LTD. V. KUWAIT PETROLEUM ITALIA SPA**
1995, 1 Lloyd's Rep. 124 (Q.B.)

In June 1992, a cargo of fuel oil of Russian origin designated E-4 was purchased by the plaintiffs c.i.f. Falconara or Naples. Clause 10 of the contract of sale provided: "10. Determination of Quality: …as per certificate issued at loadport by shippers to be final and binding upon both parties, unless it can be proved that testing and/or sampling was incorrectly performed". As the Russian supplier had run out of E-4 fuel oil, the parties subsequently agreed on the sale of M-40 instead of E-4 oil. The revised agreement, the "M-40 agreement" provided, inter alia, the following clause: "Where not inconsistent with the above all other terms and conditions shall be as per the existing contract…" There was also a price adjustment clause whereby the agreed price was fixed basis 3-4 degrees of viscosity and, in the event of actual viscosity between 4-5, price should be reduced by USD 0.40 for each 0.1 degree. A further clause of the M-40 contract entitled the buyers to reject the cargo if viscosity exceeded the maximum as per an SGS certificate to be issued in Istanbul (Turkey). Following SGS analysis the samples were determined to have a viscosity of 3.91 degrees. That result proved to vary considerably from other tests of samples drawn at Odessa whose results ranged between 4 and 5.1 degrees. The buyers paid the contracted for price for the oil to the suppliers based on the SGS certificate stating 3.91 degrees. Buyers subsequently claimed that they had overpaid in view of the other viscosity results and sought repayment on the basis of the price adjustment clause. The main issue before the Court was whether the SGS certificate was final and binding on the parties.

***Held:*** (Colman J.) **i)** The original obligation on the seller to provide a final certificate would be included into the M-40 agreement only if it was not inconsistent with the terms of such agreement. However, it was found that, as per the terms of the M-40 agreement, the establishment of the quality was to be achieved by the SGS certificate at Istanbul and not by the shipper's certificate of quality at Odessa. The incorporation clause contained in the M-40 agreement overrode clause 10 of the original sale contract. *"[T]he obligation on the seller to provide a shipper's certificate of quality and the mutual assent to that document being final and binding unless based on an incorrectly-performed sampling or testing could not be terms which were incorporated by the incorporation clause into the… M-40*

*contract because the establishment of the cargo quality was to be achieved by quite different means, in particular,…analysis by SGS, and there was therefore to be no shippers' certificate of quality; Although the contract telexes did not expressly state that the SGS certificate was to be final for the purposes of the price adjustment clause as well as for the purpose of the rejection clause, there was a compelling commercial purpose requiring the implication that it was final for both purposes."* **ii)** There was no implied term in that the oil so supplied had the same degree of viscosity as that on which the invoice was calculated. The sellers did not warrant the accuracy of the degree stated in the invoice. Furthermore, the existence of the price adjustment clause showed that there were no implied terms as to the viscosity of the oil.

**14**

**ARAMIS, THE**

1989, 1 Lloyd's Rep. 213 (C.A.)

Two parcels of linseed expellers were shipped from Buenos Aires (Argentina) to Rotterdam (Netherlands) on board the vessel *Aramis*. They were commingled with other bulk cargoes of the same goods that had previously loaded in Necochea (Argentina). Two bills of lading were issued in respect to the two parcels, one for 204,000 kilos and the other for 255,000 kilos. The two bills were signed by the master "to order" and contained the words "said to weigh" and "weight unknown". The vessel called to intermediate ports to discharge the other parcels of the bulk linseed expellers. On arrival at Rotterdam the indorsees presented the bills of lading to the ship's agent. It was found that there were substantial shortages of cargo for each parcel: the parcel of 204,000 kilos had exhausted and that of 255,000 kilos turned to weigh only 11,500 kilos. Subsequently, the indorsees of the bills of lading claimed loss of cargo against the shipowners. However, regarding the parcel of 204,000 kilos the receivers did not possess a sales contract issued in writing nor any other evidence of title. As a result, they based their right to sue on the implied contract that came into being by presenting the bill of lading and taking delivery from the vessel. The shipowners challenged the receivers' suggestion that the parcel of 204,000 kilos had been reduced due to an overdischarge at a previous port, and contended that the full quantity had failed to be loaded. The evidence showed that no cargo remained on board at Rotterdam.

***Held (for the shipowners):*** **i)** Regarding the receivers' rights against the shipowners, Bingham L.J. said: *"When property in the goods passes upon or by reason of an endorsement, contractual rights of suit and contractual liabilities are transferred to the endorsee. When property does not so pass, there is no such transfer; but here it is (necessarily) accepted that property did not pass in the goods the subject of this bill because they formed part of a single undivided bulk cargo".* Property did not pass to the buyers/receivers because the requirement of ascertainment contained in sec. 16 of the Sale of Goods Act 1979 had not been fulfilled. The buyers/receivers did not come within section 1 of the Bills of Lading Act 1855 and, therefore, they had no right to sue the carrier. The buyers had no claim in tort either as they did not have property in the goods at the time the loss occurred.[7] **ii)** As to the implied contract under which the receivers claimed to sue the shipowners, the mere production of the bill of lading followed by part delivery did not constitute sufficient evidence to find an implied contract between the carrier and the receivers. The mere tender of the bill of lading can not be understood as an offer to enter into a contract on the bill of lading terms as between the carrier and the receivers, as well as the reception of the same document cannot reasonably be regarded as an acceptance to that offer. There would have been an implied contract if the conduct of the parties were different than expected under the original contract. There is no need to imply a contract where the parties acted exactly as they would have acted in the absence of a contract. (Bingham, L.J.) *"...I think it is impossible to imply a contract on the bare facts of this case. Nothing that the shipowners or the bill of lading holders did need have been different had their intention been not to make a contract on the bill of lading terms. Their business relationship was entirely efficacious without the implication of any contract between them. Although the bill of lading holders had no title to any part of the undivided bulk cargo they had a perfectly good right to demand delivery and the shipowners had no right to refuse or to impose conditions."*[8]

---

[7] See *The Aliakmon*, 1986, 1 Lloyd's Rep. 1 (H.L.). See now the Sale of Goods Act 1979 (as amended, 1995), section 20A.

[8] Contrast with *Brandt v. Liverpool, Brazil and River-Plate S.N. Co. Ltd., The Captain Gregos* and *The Dona Mari*. See also the subsequent Carriage of Goods by Sea, 1992, sections 2(1) and 5(2).

## 15
### ARDENNES, S.S. (CARGO OWNERS) V. ARDENNES, S.S. (OWNERS)
*(The Ardennes)*
1951, 1 KB 55 (K.B.)

The plaintiffs were exporters of fruit from Spain. By an oral contract, they agreed with the agents of the defendant shipowner to load on board the vessel *Ardennes* a cargo of mandarin oranges for a direct carriage to London (England). At that time, the vessel was loading at several Spanish ports (Tarragona, Barcelona, Valencia and Gandia) some additional goods for Antwerp (Belgium) and London. When the *Ardennes* arrived at Cartagena (Colombia), the plaintiffs' cargo was loaded and a bill of lading was issued with a general clause allowing the vessel to call at any port for any purpose whatsoever before London. The vessel sailed to Antwerp prior to London. Other shipments of mandarins had been discharged in London prior to the *Ardeness's* arrival there, resulting in a fall in the market price for that fruit. As a result, the shippers claimed damages against the shipowners resulting from the loss of profits due to the change in market price.

***Held (for the plaintiffs):*** **i)** The contract of carriage was actually concluded before the bill of lading was issued. The shippers loaded in reliance of the oral promise consisting of a direct transit to London and that oral agreement was binding on the shipowners. The liberty clause in the bill of lading does not discharge the shipowners from that oral agreement since the bill of lading is not in itself the contract, but the evidence of the pre-existing oral contract. The prior oral warranty overrides the general terms of the bill of lading. Lord Goddard L.J., distin-guished the present case from Leduc Co. v. Ward on the ground that the latter was *"a case between shipowner and endorsee of the bill of lading, between whom its terms are conclusive by virtue of the Bills of Lading Act 1855, so that no evidence was admissible in that case to contradict or vary its terms"*.[9] **ii)** Because the bill of lading is handed to the shipper once the goods are shipped, it would be uncommercial to demand the goods back regarding such a variation of the contract. The shipper was not a party in the preparation of the bill of lading nor did he sign it. It cannot be said that the shipper waived his claim by taking delivery of the bill of lading and paying for the freight. What he did, in fact, was merely to sell the cargo to avoid losses given the perishable nature of the goods. **iii)** Damages were fixed by the difference between the actual sale price and the market rate price of the goods on the date at which the ship would had arrived London if no intermediate port had been called.

## 16
### ARMAR SHIPPING CO. LTD. V. CAISSE ALGERIENNE D'ASSURANCE ET DE REASSURANCE
*(The Armar)*
1981, 1 WLR 207 (C.A.)

The plaintiff shipowners chartered the ship *Armar* to a Cuban company for a

---

[9] This is established only in relation to bills of lading in hands of the shipper. Where the bills are indorsed to third parties, then they become conclusive evidence of the terms of the contract of carriage and no other agreements (either oral or written) are binding. See *Leduc Co. v. Ward* and also *Hain Steamship Company Ltd. v. Tate and Lyle Ltd.*

carriage of sugar from Habana to Mostagenem (Algeria). The charterparty included a London arbitration clause and a provision that general average would be settled and adjusted in London according to the York-Antwerp Rules 1950. Bills of lading were issued containing a clause (clause 10) which provided that general average should be adjusted and settled according to the York-Antwerp Rules, except rule XXII, at the place which might be selected by the shipowners. There was no incorporation of the charterparty terms into the bills. During the voyage the vessel grounded and the shipowners declared general average to enable the adventure to be completed. At Mostagenem, a Lloyd's average bond in English was issued by the shipowners and signed, albeit with reserves in French, by the defendant consignees. The bond contained neither a choice of law nor jurisdiction or arbitration clauses. Pursuant to cl. 10 of the bills of lading, the shipowners placed and published the adjustment in London showing that a contribution was due from cargo. They issued a writ against the consignees in London for contribution to general average. Leave was set ex parte to serve notice of the writ on the defendants. The defendant consignees applied for the order to be set aside. They challenged English law and London as the place for adjustment on the grounds that the bond contained no such agreement.

***Held (for the consignees):*** (Megaw, L.J.) According to the R.S.C., Ord. 11, r. 1(1)(f)(iii), *"Leave may be given to serve out of the jurisdiction… where the action is brought on a contract which 'is by its terms, or by implication, governed by English law'. The contract here in question is contained in a Lloyd's average bond which was signed on behalf of the plaintiffs and the defendants… The Lloyd's average bond contains no express provision as to the law which is to govern the contract contained therein; nor is there any provision for arbitration in London or for submission to the jurisdiction of the English courts…"* Their lordships found that English law did not apply either by implication as neither the fact that the bond was written in English nor the use of the word "Lloyd's" were sufficient to incorporate English law by implication. In words of Megaw L.J., *"There must be a governing law from the outset: not a floating absence of law, continuing to float until the carrier, unilaterally, makes a decision; If… the fact of the carriers' subsequent designation of England as the place of the general average adjustment cannot operate to crystallize a therefore 'floating' proper law (or to fill the gap of a therefore non-existent proper law), the most that can be said in this case is that, when the contract was made, there was a possibility that English law might be the place of the general average adjustment. But that…cannot, in my opinion, have the effect of making English law the governing law of the contract".*[10] Accordingly, the order for leave to serve notice of the writ out of the jurisdiction was set aside.

---

[10] See *The Iran Vojdan* and *Compagnie Tunisienne de Navigation S.A. v. Compagnie d'Armement Maritime S.A.*

# 17
## ATHANASIA COMINOS, THE
### 1990, 1 Lloyd's Rep. 277 (Q.B.)

The vessels *Athanasia Cominos* and *Georges Chr. Lemos* were time chartered to a company for several shipments of coal. During her third voyage under the charterparty, the *Athanasia Cominos* suffered an explosion in two of her holds two days after clearing the loading berth in Sydney (Australia). The *Georges Chr. Lemos* also suffered a minor explosion in one hold during her second voyage the day following her loading at Sydney. In both cases the explosions arose as a result of the ignition of explosive mixtures of air and the methane gas emitted by the coal. Both ships were severally damaged but were able to arrive at their destinations and completed discharge. The shipowners claimed against the time charterers and against the consignees in contract. The issues before the Court were, inter alia, (i) whether the consignee incurred a potential liability by virtue of an implied contract arising when the cosignee tendered the bill of lading and took delivery at the destination; (ii) whether the consignees succeeded to the shippers' liabilities in respect to any dangerous characteristics of the goods by virtue of sec. 1 of the Bills of Lading Act 1855; and, (iii) whether the loading of such cargo constituted a breach of the contract of carriage by the charterers in their condition of shippers.

**Held:** *(Mustill J)* **i)** *"…it cannot automatically be assumed that such a (implied) contract involves the consignee in all the obligations to which the shipper becomes subject, when he ships the goods and becomes party to the bill of lading. To my mind the reported cases[11] from which this notion of an implied contract is derived, make it clear that the consignee, by taking delivery of the goods under the bill of lading, assumes only those rights and liabilities created by the contract of carriage which concern the carriage and delivery of the goods, and the payment therefore. I can, however, see no ground for extending this implication to embrace a warranty by the consignee as to the fitness of the goods for carriage. In the ordinary case, the person named as consignee stands in no relation to the goods at the moment of shipment."* **ii)** *"It may well be that in the main a transfer of the document, satisfying the requirements of the Bills of Lading Act 1855 (sec.1), operates to transfer away many of the shipper's contractual obligations, but the Act cannot in my judgement have been intended to divest the shipper of responsibility for the consequences of loss, arising from the act of shipment itself."*[12] **iii)** The shipowners argued that the present cargo fell outside the range of the emission characteristics of the contractual cargo. The Court admitted that carriage of coal involves hazards greater than those associated with inert goods, but insisted on the fact that such hazards should have been overcome if the shipowner had had the necessary knowledge, skill and equipment. The shipowners contended that the present cargo involved a degree of risk which was higher than average coal cargoes and that they never contracted to bear such particular risk. However, they failed to prove this particular point to the satisfaction of the Court.

---

[11] See *Brandt v. Liverpool and River Plate Steamship Navigation Co.*
[12] See *The Giannis NK.*

## 18
### ATKINS INTERNATIONAL H.A. v. ISLAMIC REPUBLIC OF IRAN SHIPPING LINES
*(The A.P.J. Priti)*
1987, 2 Lloyd's Rep. 37 (C.A.)

A voyage charterparty was agreed for the hire of the vessel *A.P.J. Priti* on the Gencon form. The charter provided for a carriage from Damman (Saudi Arabia) to 1/2 safe berths Bandar Abbas (Iran), 1/2 safe berths Bandar Bushire (Iran), 1/2 safe berths Bandar Khomeini (Iran) in charterer's option. The vessel "...shall proceed to the discharging port...or so near thereto as she may safely get and lie always afloat". When she proceeded from Bandar Bushire to Bandar Khomeini, a missile damaged the vessel. The owners claimed that the charterers were in breach as Bandar Khomeini was unsafe due to the ongoing Iran-Irak war.

***Held (for the charterers):* i)** It was inferred that the parties were aware at the time of the charter that the safety at the discharging ports was at least in doubt since the three ports were located within Iran. Given that inference, the charterparty lacked an express safe port warranty. The provisions as to freight and as to extra war risk insurance indicate the owners' acceptance of such risk. There was no express warranty or promise that the nominated ports were prospectively safe.[13] Parker L.J. said: *"From cl. 18 above there is in my view some infer-*

*ence that the parties were aware at the time of the charter that the safety of Bandar Bushire and Bandar Khoomeini was at least in doubt...There being no express safe port warranty, the question whether there was any implied safe port warranty might in some cases call for consideration, but it does not do so in the present case".* In this case, the omission of an express warranty was found to be deliberate, because such an implied term was not necessary for the business efficacy of the charterparty and also because inferring such an implied term would contradict other terms of the charterparty (i.e. extra freight, war insurance risk).[14] (Charterparty, safe port warranty).

## 19
### BALLI TRADING LTD. v. AFALONA SHIPPING CO. LTD.
*(The Coral)*
1993, 1 Lloyd's Rep. 1 (C.A.)

By a time charter the bulker *Coral* was let for the carriage of steel sheets. The charterparty provided, inter alia, the following: *"2. [line 45] charterers are to provide necessary dunnage and shifting boards, also any extra fitting requisite for a special trade or unusual cargo, but owners to allow them the use of any dunnage and shifting boards already aboard the vessel",* and *"8. ... charterers are to load, stow and trim and discharge the cargo at their expense under the supervision of the Captain...".* After loading, a set of three bills of lading was issued to the order of the charterers' agents. Each bill was

---

[13] Bingham L.J.: *"... a safe port is one which, during the relevant period of time, the vessel can reach, remain and depart from without, in the absence of some abnormal occurrence, being exposed to danger which cannot be avoided by good navigation and seamanship."*

[14] But see *The Evaggelos TH,* where the courts did imply an express safe port warranty in a time charter.

stamped "clean on board freight pre-paid" and they all incorporated the Hague-Visby Rules in a general Paramount clause. There was also a clause no.1 saying: *"All terms and conditions, liberties and exceptions of the charterparty, dated as overleaf, are herewith incorporated. The carrier shall in no case be responsible for loss of or damage to cargo arisen prior to loading and after discharging".* The vessel encountered stormy weather and some cargo suffered damage. The cargo-owners sued the shipowners in reliance of art. III (2) of the Rules. The shipowners alleged that the charterparty and the bills of lading had the effect to allocate the responsibility for the stowage to the charterers and, alternatively, to the shippers or subsequent holders of the bills by verbal manipulation of the terms of the charter.

***Held (for the shipowners):*** **i)** The incorporation clause in the bills of lading was wide enough to effectively incorporate, inter alia, clause 8 of the charterparty. As to the contents of the clause, Beldam L.J. said: *"I do not think that there is anything inconsistent, surplus or insensible in incorporating into a bill of lading provisions regulating the responsibility for loading or stowing of cargo".* **ii)** Beldam, L.J. went on adding: *"It is now settled that art. III(2) does not impose upon the carrier an obligation to load, handle, stow, carry, keep, etc. the goods carried;[15] It goes without saying that the agreement between the owner and charterer that the latter should undertake responsibility for loading, stowing and discharging, etc., could not affect the obligations which the defendant owner had undertaken by the bills of lading".*

In so far the charterers -by necessary implication- undertook such obligations, no others than the charterers warranted to use reasonable skill in performing them. The charterers were thus responsible for bad stowage. **iii)** (Beldam, L.J.) *"The question for decision is the effect of incorporating cls. 2 and 8 of the charterparty on the scope of the obligations the defendant had undertaken in the bill of lading. It is accepted that, subject to questions of compatibility and construction, the language of cls. 1 of the bill of lading is wide enough to incorporate cls. 2 and 8 of the charterparty into the bill of lading. The clauses were 'directly germane to the shipment, carriage and delivery of goods.'"*[16]


## 20
### BANCO SANTANDER S.A. v. BAYFERN LTD.
### 2000 WLR 191098 (C.A.)

Banque Paribas issued a deferred payment letter of credit (deferred 180 days) in favour of Bayfern Ltd., which, at Pariba's request, Banco Santander confirmed. Santander discounted the credit and, as found by the Court, took an assignment off Bayfern's rights under it. Subsequently, but still before maturity (which was on 27.11.98), Paribas advised Santander that the documents presented and accepted by Santander were false or forged. Paribas refused to reimburse Santander and, as a consequence, a claim was filed by the latter against Bayfern and Paribas. It was argued by Santander that that payment to Bayfern amounted to a discharge of Paribas' and Santander's joint and several

---

[15] See *Pyrene Co. Ltd. v. Scindia Steam Navigation Co. Ltd.*

[16] See *The Miramar* and *The Varenna*.

liability under the letter of credit and that there was nothing preventing Santander from making payment to the beneficiary prior to maturity. On the evidence, it was assumed that Bayfern had committed a fraud of which Santander had the relevant knowledge prior to the maturity date.

***Held:*** Walter L.J. posed the question as follows: *"Ultimately the question to be asked is what precisely the issuing bank has requested the confirming bank to do, and what the issuing bank has promised to do if the confirming bank does what is requested of it. The answer, as it seems to me, is that the Issuing Bank has requested the Confirming Bank to give its own undertaking to pay on 27th Nov. 1998, in addition to that of the Issuing Bank, and has promised to reimburse the Confirming Bank when it pays on that deferred payment undertaking i.e. pays $20,315,796.30 on 27th Nov. 1998. There is no request from Paribas that Santander should discount or give any value for the documents prior to 27th Nov. 1998, and albeit it may not be a breach of mandate for Santander to do so, it is up to Santander whether it does so or not".* The Court concluded that Santander had no actual or implied authority to make payment before maturity and doing so was for their own account and upon the risk of the discovery of fraud between the discount date and maturity date.

**21**

**BANKERS TRUST CO. V. STATE BANK OF INDIA**

1991, 2 Lloyd's Rep. 443 (C.A.)

The plaintiffs issued a confirmed, irrevocable letter of credit without recourse in respect to cargo being sold from indian sellers to english buyers. The expiry date for the presentation of the documents was 21 Sept. 1988. The UCP 400 (1983 Rev.) were incorporated into the credit. On 9 Sept. the documents were presented to the confirming bank. The confirming bank forwarded the documents to the plaintiffs (i.e. issuing bank) on 21 Sept. The plaintiffs accepted the documents and paid the confirming bank, which, in turn, authorized payment to the sellers and beneficiaries of the credit. On 28 Sept. the plaintiffs alerted the confirming bank about certain discrepancies in the documents, but nonetheless sent the documents to the buyers for review, the result being that several more discrepancies were found. On 30 Sept. the confirming bank received a further message from the plaintiffs with a larger list of discrepancies. A telex and a demand of reimbursement was sent to the confirming bank the following day, but no mention was made of the documents, which still remained in the possession of the plaintiffs. The confirming bank refused to refund the money and was sued by the plaintiffs.

***Held***[17] ***(for the confirming bank):* i)** Article 16 of the UCP 400 (1983 Rev.) entitles only to ask the buyer for a waiver of the discrepancies found by the bank, but not for a second check of the documents. By no means a bank should be allowed time to enable the buyer to re-examine the documents for the purpose of discovering further discrepancies. **ii)** The same article 16 UCP 400 provides that,

---

[17] Lloyd L.J. dissenting.

as soon as documents are rejected, they must be put back in circulation. But here, the plaintiffs' notice of rejection was not given within a "reasonable time".[18] **iii)** In addition, neither art. 16 UCP 400 nor the special terms of the credit allowed the plaintiffs to retain the documents as security for repayment by the confirming bank. It is the obligation of the plaintiffs, as issuing bank, to give notice that the documents are at the disposal of the confirming bank before being entitled to claim any refund from the latter. A conditional holding at the bank's disposal is not authorised under art. 16.

# 22

## Banque de l'Indochine et de Suez S.A. v. J. H. Rayner (Mincing Lane) Ltd.
### 1983, 1 Lloyd's Rep. 228 (C.A.)

The confirming bank advised the beneficiaries of an irrevocable credit opened by the applicants at the issuing bank in Djibouti. The 1974 Revision of the UCP governed the letter of credit. Upon the tender of documents, the confirming bank found several discrepancies. After an agreement reached with the beneficiaries, the confirming bank made payment under reserve and forwarded the documents to the issuing bank in Djibouti. The issuing bank rejected the documents and refused to reimburse the confirming bank, which then sought to recoup the amount from the beneficiaries. The main questions on appeal were: (1) whether the reserves made under the agreement so reached between the confirming bank and the beneficiaries entitled the bank to recover the money from the beneficiaries after the issuing bank's rejection or, on the contrary, only upon a court's ruling that the documents were actually defective; and (2) whether the discrepancies by themselves entitled the bank to reject the documents.

***Held (for the confirming bank):*** **i)** Payment under reserve means that the bank reserves his right to get the money back from the beneficiaries in case the documents be rejected by the issuing bank (whether on his own initiative or upon the applicants' instruction) on the same grounds on which the confirming bank had originally relied upon. This is a conditional payment that consists of a binding agreement between the confirming bank and the beneficiaries to resolve the impasse so created by the uncertainty of their respective legal positions. In the words of Kerr L.J., payment under reserve means *"that payment was to be made under reserve in the sense that the beneficiary would be bound to repay the money on demand if the issuing bank should reject the documents, whether on its own initiative or on the buyer's instructions".* **ii)** The letter of credit called for "shipment to be effected on vessel belonging to a member of an Int. Ship. Conference": As the credit concerns documents and not mere facts,[19] the condition so stated in the credit was a wrongful one in so far that it consisted of a fact and not a document. Therefore,

---

[18] See *The Royan.*

[19] See art. 13 of the UCP 500 (1993 Rev.).

the bank was not entitled to reject based on this particular ground. **iii)** The letter of credit called for documents covering shipment "cost and freight liner out Djibouti", which meant that the collected freight should cover all costs up to and including discharge at Djibouti. However, the bill of lading so tendered included a "portmarking clause" providing that all charges outside Djibouti were to be paid by the consignee. This clause was inconsistent with the terms of the letter of credit and so does constitute a specific prohibition under the UCP rules.[20] **iv)** The third discrepancy was based on the absence of linkage between the documents. Whilst there was only a commercial invoice, there were two certificates of weight, quality and packing, and three EUR 1 certificates. Regarding the documents other than the invoice, the identification of the goods was confusing: while the bills of lading indicated the goods were loaded onto the vessel "Markhor", one of the certificates of origin referred to "vessel Markhor or substitute" and another to "transport mixed at destination Djibouti Port in Transit Yemen". The court ruled that the necessary linkage between the documents meant that each document should refer unequivocally to the same goods. The UCP rules[21] give certain latitude in the description of the goods, but not as far as their identification is concerned: however general the description may be, the identification must be unequivocal. Therefore, the necessary link-

age between the bills of lading and the certificates of origin was missing. This very last discrepancy constituted a valid ground for rejection.

**23**

**BARCLAYS BANK LTD. V. COMMISSIONERS OF CUSTOMS AND EXCISE**
1963, 1 Lloyd's Rep. 81 (Q.B.D.)

A hundred cartons of washing machines were bought c.i.f. Cardiff by a company called Buitrix Electric Co. Ltd. Delivery was agreed against acceptance of bills of exchange payable thirty seven days after shipments. The consignment was shipped in Rotterdam (Netherlands) by a Dutch firm and a bill of lading was issued to the order of the shipper or their assigns. On the face of the bill of lading, Buitrix Electric Co. appeared as Notify party. The documents (namely, the bill of lading and the invoice) were forward and transferred to Buitrix against bills of exchange. On Feb. 18, 1961, the goods were discharged in Cardiff (Wales) and remained in the transit warehouse as no steps to obtain delivery or entry of customs clearance had been taken by Buitrix. On June 2, 1961, Buitrix pledged the bills of lading with Barclays Bank Ltd. as security for advances made by the bank on overdraft. On Aug. 22, 1961, the Customs and Excise Department recovered judgment against Bruitix Electric Co. for arrears of purchase tax and seized the goods. One month later, the bank gave formal notice of the pledge to the shipowners who then requested payment for their warehousing charges. Upon the bank's presentation of the bill of lading the shipowners issued

---

[20] See art. 16(d) of the UCP 500 (1993 Rev.).
[21] See art. 37(c) of the UCP 500 (1993 Rev.).

delivery orders. The bank took the delivery orders to the warehouse seeking dock warrants in respect to the goods. At that time, however, the Sheriff had already taken walking possession of the goods on behalf of the Customs and Excise Department as judgment creditors. The bank then filed an action against the Customs and Excise Department claiming possession as pledgees of the goods. The main question to resolve was whether on June 2, 1961, the bill of lading was still a document of title for the goods, and if so, whether the pledge of the goods by the bank was valid.

***Held (for the bank):*** (Diplock, L.J.) *"The contract for the carriage of goods by sea, which is evidenced by a bill of lading, is a combined contract of bailment and transportation under which the shipowner undertakes to accept possession of the goods from the shipper, to carry them to their contractual destination and there to surrender possession of them to the person who, under the terms of the contract, is entitled to obtain possession of them from the shipowners. Such a contract is not discharged by performance until the shipowner has actually surrendered possession…to the person entitled under the terms of the contract to obtain possession of them. So long as the contract is not discharged, the bill of lading in my view, remains a document of title by indorsement and delivery of which the rights of property in the goods can be transferred. It is clear law that where a bill of lading to the order is issued in respect of the contract of carriage by sea, the shipowner is not bound to surrender possession of the goods to any person whether named as consignee or not, except on production of the bill of lading;[22] In the present case, the contract of carriage evidenced by the bills of lading, had not been discharged on June 2, 1961, when Buitrix purported to pledge the goods to the bank by deposit of the bills of lading as security for advancement of money to them; The shipowners were under no obligation to surrender their constructive possession and control to deal with the goods, except on production of the bill of lading…"[23]*

## 24
## BAUMWOLL MANUFACTUR, THE V. FURNESS, CHRISTOPHER
### 1893, A.C. 8 (H.L.)

The vessel *Asia* was sold and demise chartered as finance security for a term

---

[22] See also *Lickbarrow v. Mason* and *The Stettin.*

[23] See Bowen L.J. in *Sanders Brothers v. Maclean & Co.* [1883] 11 Q.B.D. 327, at p. 341: *"The law as to the indorsement of bills of lading is as clear as in my opinion the practice of all European merchants thoroughly understood. A cargo at sea while in hands of the carrier is necessarily incapable of physical delivery. During this period of transit and voyage the bill of lading by the law merchant is universally recognised as its symbol, and the indorsement and delivery of the bill of lading operates as a symbolical delivery of the cargo. Property in the goods passes by such indorsement and delivery of the bill of lading, whenever it is the intention of the parties that the property should pass, just as under similar circumstances the property would pass by an actual delivery of the goods. And for the purpose of passing such property in the goods and completing the title of the indorsee to full possession thereof, the bill of lading, until complete delivery of the cargo has been made on shore to some one rightfully claiming under it, remains in force as a symbol, and carries with it not only the full ownership of the goods, but also all rights created by the contract of carriage between the shipper and the shipowner. It is a key which in the hands of a rightful owner is intended to unlock the door of the warehouse, floating or fixed, in which the goods may chance to be".*

of four months. The charterparty provided, inter alia, that the master, officers and crew were to be paid by the charterers and were also under his orders as regards employment, agency or other arrangements. Under the charterparty, the demise charterers were to indemnify the owner for all liabilities arising from the master's signing of bills of lading. The owners were obligated to maintain the ship in a thoroughly efficient state in hull and machinery and pay for the insurance of the ship. When the charterers took possession of the vessel they appointed the master, officers and crew, but not the chief engineer who was appointed by the owners in exercise of an option contained in the charterparty. Under the charter, a consignment of cotton was shipped at New Orleans (USA) and bills of lading were issued and delivered to the shippers. Some of the bills were signed by the master and some others by the charterers' agents at that port. In all bills of lading reference was made to the charterparty. It occurred that the goods were lost during transit and the shippers sued the owners on the ground that the vessel was unseaworthy. The owners alleged that neither the master nor the charterers' agents had authority to sign bills of lading on their behalf, and therefore the bills were not binding upon the owners.

***Held (for the owners):*** Pursuant to the terms of the demise charterparty, the owners demised or handed over the possession and control of the vessel to the charterers, and the charterparty did not confer the charterers or the master any right to sign bills of lading on behalf of the owners. (Lord Watson) *"The master who signed the bill of lading was the servant and agent of the charterers and not the servant and agent of the respondent Furness* (the owners)*; No doubt, when a shipowner who enters into a charterparty without parting with the possession and control of his ship seeks to limit the powers assigned by law to his captain, the limitation will be altogether ineffectual in any question with shippers who are ignorant of the terms of the instrument. That, however, is a question as to the limitation of the powers of an actual agent who has known powers according to law. Notice of the limitation must be given to those who deal with the agent in order to disable them from contracting with him.*[24] *But I know of no principle of authority which requires that notice must be given when an owner parts, even temporarily, with the possession and control of his ship in order to prevent the servant of the charterer from pledging his credit."* The House of Lords applied here the general rule that a man is not liable upon contracts made by persons who are neither his agents nor his servants. The fact that the shippers were unaware of the terms of the charterparty could not be an exception to that rule.


**25**

**B**AYERISCHE **V**EREINSBANK V. **N**ATIONAL **B**ANK OF **P**AKISTAN

1997, 1 Lloyd's Rep. 59 (Q.B.)

The plaintiffs acted as confirming bank and the defendants as issuing bank under an irrevocable letter of credit opened

---

[24] See *The Jalamohan* and *The Berkshire*.

in favour of an english firm (the beneficiary). The credit was available against presentation by the beneficiary of the drafts drawn on the confirming bank at fifteen days' sight following the date of the bill of lading and within the credit facility period, which expired on July 30, 1994. As London banks were closed on July 30 and 31 (Saturday and Sunday, respectively), the beneficiary presented the documents to the confirming bank on Aug. 1, and was paid three days later. The confirming bank forwarded the documents to the issuing bank in Pakistan, which in turn passed them to the applicant. The applicant presented a number of discrepancies and returned the documents to the issuing bank. The documents were finally rejected and returned with a list of discrepancies to the confirming bank by courier. The confirming bank then disposed of their interest in the goods by selling them at a low price back to the beneficiary and sought damages against the issuing bank. The issuing bank justified his rejection on two grounds: (1) the confirming bank did not provide the statement of art. 44(c) of UCP 500 (1993 Rev.) which is required when the credit expiry date is extended until the following banking day by virtue of art. 44(a); and (2) the weight certificates tendered among the documents did not comply with the terms of the credit.

***Held (for the confirming bank):*** (Mance, J.) **i)** Compliance with art. 44(c) is not a condition precedent to a confirming bank's right to reimbursement from the issuing bank. The statement required would do no more than confirm what was already implicit in the transmittal of the documents by the plaintiffs. A failure to provide such notice could give rise to damages by the issuing bank only if, for example, they had faced difficulties or delays in persuading the applicants that the documents were taken during the validity period of the credit. But in the present case, however, there was no such loss. The breach of art. 44(a) does not discharge the issuing bank from its obligation under the contract. If the bank had suffered any loss due to such a breach, they would be entitled to recover, but only by way of damages; not by rejecting the documents. **ii)** Although the weight certificates were irregular, the issuing bank failed to raise any objection in accordance with art. 14(d) of UCP 500 (1993 Rev.). In doing no more than returning the rejected documents to the confirming bank, they failed to "give notice by telecommunication or, if that is not possible, by other expeditious means, without delay but not later than the close of the seventh banking day following the day of receipt of the documents". A failure to comply with the requirement of art. 14(d) resulted in the loss of the defendants' right to reject the documents. **iii)** The court also found that the issuing bank acted merely as a "postbox" between the confirming bank and the applicants of the credit without forming their own independent judgement. The issuing bank failed to independently check the documents and merely relied upon the representations of the applicant. Therefore, the bank was also precluded under art. 14(c) UCP 500 (1993 Rev.) from claiming that the weight certificates failed to conform with the terms of the credit.

## 26
### BERGECO USA v. VEGOIL LTD.
1984, 1 Lloyd's Rep. 440 (Q.B.)

Five hundred tones of Alaskan green peas were sold C. & F. Bombay on liner terms. The sale contract incorporated the terms of GAFTA Form No. 28, which contained a clause 10 stating, *"Shipment to be made direct or indirect"*. Payment was agreed through letter of credit, the final shipment date being Oct. 31, 1978. The contractual date of shipment was not observed by the sellers. The buyers consented to grant an extension up to Nov. 15 provided that "the ship sails direct from port of loading to Bombay…". Further exchanges between the parties led to a further extension until Nov. 30. The cargo was finally loaded on Nov. 10. The sellers were paid by the bank against Inter Alia, a direct bill of lading and a ship's agent certificate confirming direct transit to Bombay. Before the arrival, the buyers discovered that the vessel had not sailed directly to Bombay, but rather had called to four previous ports. Once at Bombay harbour, the vessel was delayed for two months because of port congestion. Four days before she berthed on May 18, the market for the cargo had dropped and the buyers decided to reject the goods and claimed a full refund of the price. The GAFTA arbitrators found in favour of the buyers. The sellers appealed.

**Held (for the buyers):** (Hobhouse, J.) The court considered a number of issues in holding for the buyers. **i)** Was the "direct shipment" provision contemplated by the contract? The final agreement has to be construed taking into account not only the contract originally agreed but also the further exchanges and communications held between the parties. Accordingly, the direct shipment clause was indeed part of the contract as a whole. **ii)** Was the "direct shipment" clause a condition or merely an innominate term? Whether or not a term is a condition is a matter of construction of the contract. In this case the "direct ship" term is a condition as it becomes part of the definition terms of the acceptance by the buyers.[25] **iii)** Did the buyers waive their right to reject the goods? There is a right to reject documents and a right to reject goods, being both rights separate and distinct. *"The exercise of the right to reject the goods is one which the buyer is entitled to postpone until the goods arrive. He can make up his mind then to exercise the right as it suits him best. He may lose his right meanwhile if he deals with the goods or documents so as to disable himself from restoring title to the sellers or by actual waiver, but nothing of that kind happened in the present case. The buyers still had a right of rejection they could exercise on May 14. I therefore agree… that the rejection was valid and there was no waiver or election not to reject."*[26]

## 27
### BERKSHIRE, THE
1974, 1 Lloyd's Rep. 185 (Q.B.D.)

A cargo of compressed bales of cotton was shipped on board the ship *Lancashire* in Houston (USA) for a carriage to Massa-

---

[25] See *The Ardennes*.

[26] See *James Finlay v. Kwik Hoo Tong Handel Maatschppij* and also *Kwei Tek Chao v. British Traders and Shippers Ltd.*

wa. The ship was operated under a time charter and the charterers' agents were Ocean Wide Shipping Co. of Monrovia (Liberia). They employed Ayers Steamship Co. of Houston as their sub-agents at loading. Before loading, the master wrote a letter to Ayers Steamship authorising them to sign bills of lading in the name of the *Lancashire*. After loading, a bill of lading was issued under Ocean Wide's printed form and signed by Ayer Steamship "as agents" of Ocean Wide Shipping. The bill of lading contained a demise Clause drafted in these terms: *"If the Ship is not owned or chartered by demise to the company or line by whom this Bill of Lading is issued (as may be the case notwithstanding anything that appears to the contrary) the Bill of Lading shall take effect as a contract with the owner or demise charterer as the case may be as principal made through the agency of the said company or line who act as agents only and shall be under no personal liability whatsoever in respect thereof".* In the course of the voyage, the charterers instructed the master to discharge the cargo at Jeddah (Saudi Arabia) for transhipment to Massawa. Following those instructions, the goods were discharged at Jeddah and transferred in sound condition to the ship "Star of Mariam" for on-carriage to Massawa. The Star of Mariam was owned and operated by a different shipowner. When the receivers took delivery from the MV "Star of Mariam at Massawa" the goods appeared damaged by sea water. An action *in rem* was brought by the receivers against another ship owned by the shipowners of the Lancashire. The main question was whether the bill of lading evidenced a contract made between the receivers and the ship-

owners, or between the receivers and the time-charterers. The issues for decision were: (i) whether by virtue of the demise clause the shipowners were bound by the bill of lading issued by Ocean Wide; (ii) whether the bill of lading was issued with the authority of the shipowners; and, alternatively, (iii) whether the shipowners were entitled to rely on the exemptions contained in clauses 1 and 11 of the bill.

***Held (for the receivers):*** (Brandon, J.) **i)** *"Despite arguments to the contrary put forward by the shipowners, I see no reason not to give effect to the demise clause in accordance with its terms. The company or line by whom the bill of lading was issued, within the meaning of that clause, is clearly in this case Ocean Wide; …the ship was not owned or chartered by demise to that company, but was on the contrary owned by the shipowners. It follows that the bill of lading is, by its express terms, intended to take effect as a contract between the shippers and the shipowners made on behalf of the shipowners by Ocean Wide as agents only. The circumstance that Ayers signed the bill of lading as sub-agents for Ocean Wide does not affect the position, which is the same as if Ocean Wide had signed it themselves."* Accordingly, by virtue of the demise Clause, the bill of lading was intended to be a shipowners' (and not a charterers') bill of lading. **ii)** With regard to the question whether the bill of lading was issued with the authority of the shipowner, Brandon J. called the terms of the time charterparty which, in its clause 8 of the New York Produce Exchange form, provided that the master was obliged to sign bills of lading on the shipowners' behalf as presented by the charterers. *"In either case, whether the master signs on the* *directions of the charterers, or the charterers short-circuit the matter and sign themselves, the signature binds the shipowners as principals to the contract contained in or evidenced by the bills of lading;[27] [t]he charter-party entitles the charterers to present to the master for signature by him on the shipowners' behalf, or to sign themselves on the same behalf, bills of lading of that kind."* As to the fact that it was Ayers Steamship (the sub-agent) and not Ocean Wide (the charterers' agent) who signed the bills of lading, Mr. J. Brandon said: *"On the footing that the charterers had authority, under cl. 8 of the charter-party, to sign the bills of lading on the shipowners' behalf, they were in my view entitled to appoint Ocean Wide as agents to do this for them and Ocean Wide were entitled to appoint Ayers as sub-agents to do it for them. The signing of a bill of lading is a ministerial act and I do not consider for this and other reasons that the principle 'delegatus non potest delegare' applies to such an act".* Besides that, *"...the authority given in any case by the charter-party was reinforced or confirmed by a letter written by the master to Ayers when the ship was in Houston".* **iii)** Concerning the alternative pleading of the shipowners, Brandon J. took the view that they were not exempted from liability on the basis of clauses 11 and 1 of the bill of lading. Clause 11 provided that the carrier was entitled to tranship the goods "whenever the goods are consigned to a point where the ship does not expect to discharge...; this Carrier, in making arrangements for any transhipments or forwarding vessel... not operated by this carrier shall be considered solely the forwarding agent of the shipper and without any other responsibility whatsoever...". Clause 1 said that "The Carrier shall not be liable in any capacity whatsoever for any delay, nondelivery or misdelivery, or loss of or damage to the goods occurring while the goods are not in the actual custody of the Carrier". To that respect the judge considered that, on its true construction, clause 11 did not give the shipowners the right to discharge and tranship the goods at Jeddah and, by doing so, they were in breach of the bill of lading contract. With regard to clause 1, Mr. J. Brandon said: *"By discharging the goods at Jeddah and transhipping them into another ship not owned or operated by them, the shipowners were making a fundamental departure from the method of performing the contract contemplated by the parties at the time it was made. In these circumstances I have no doubt that the 'four corners' rule, as explained in the Suisse Atlantique case above,[28] applies so as to prevent the shipowners from relying on the exception concerned".* Accordingly, judgment was for the receivers.

# 28

## BLANDY BROTHERS & CO. LDA. V. NELLO SIMONI LTD.
## 1963, 2 Lloyd's Rep. 393 (C.A.)

Blandy Brothers were shipping agents in Funchal in the Island of Madeira (Portugal). They had been appointed as ship agents by Nello Simoni, who had chartered five ships to be loaded at Funchal. In all five charterparties the freight was

---

[27] See *Knutsford Ltd. SS. v. Tillmanns & Co.*

[28] *Suisse Atlantique Societe d'Armement Maritime v. Rotter-damsche Kolen Centrale* [1967] 1 AC 361.

described as FIOS (i.e. free in out stowage) and included the following clause: *"Cargo to be put on board, stowed and discharged free of expense to the vessel. Vessel to supply steam of power, winches and winchmen (from ship's crew) if required by charterers and provided permitted by port regulations in both loading and discharging, otherwise winchmen, if required to be supplied by charterers at their own expense".* It was also stipulated that the charterers should appoint ship agents at the port of loading and the port of discharge. In arranging for the loading of the ships, Blandy Brothers engaged and paid for the stevedores who took the goods from alongside and loaded and stowed them in all five ships. When Blandy Brothers invoiced Nello Simoni for the stevedoring expenses, these refused to pay alleging that they had not given any instruction to engage and pay stevedores on their behalf.

***Held (for Blandy Brothers):*** **i)** As to the responsibility of loading and stowage L.J. Willmer said: *"If the charter-party is silent as to the responsibility for loading and stowage, or if it puts the responsibility expressly on the shipowner, the ship's agent, as agent for the shipowner, has authority, and a duty to his principal, to make the necessary arrangements. If the charter-party, as here, transfers the responsibility from the shipowner, then, as between the shipowner and the charterer, the responsibility rests with the charterer and no one else".* **ii)** As to the authority of the ship agents, L.J. Willmer took the view that the agents engaged and paid the stevedores for the charterer and not for the shipowner: *"The arrangement for, and the payment for, the stevedoring on ship and the stowage were within*

*the plaintiffs' authority, and indeed duty, as agents for the charterers. They are entitled to be indemnified by their principals, the defendants, for the stevedoring expenses which they claim, in relation both to loading and stowage, and in relation to all five vessels".* **iii)** In connection with the effect of the FIOS clause, L.J. Willmer found generally that *"the responsibility of shippers in relation to the operation of loading ceases when the goods concerned reach the ship's rail. It is prima facie the duty of the ship to take over the cargo from there, to load it and stow it;[29] In those circumstances it can hardly be denied that it is within the ordinary authority and duty of a ship's agent, in discharge (in the normal case) of his duty to the shipowner, to arrange for and pay for the work of stowage of the cargo on board the ship; It appears to me that the only effect of the provision in the charter-party that these goods were to be FIOS, is that the plaintiffs, as ship's agents, when rendering their accounts, must look to the charterers for reimbursement rather than to the owner, which would normally be the case".* Accordingly, the charterers had to reimburse the ship agents for the stevedoring expenses.

**29**

**BOREALIS A.B. v. STARGAS LTD. AND OTHERS**
*(The Berge Sisar)*
2001, 1 Lloyd' Rep. 663 (H.L.)

Borealis purchased from Stargas some 43,000 tones of Field Grade quality fully refrigerated propane on terms C. & F.

---

[29] See the Hague Rules, art. III (2).

Stenungsund. The contract prescribed that the cargo be free of corrosive compounds detectable when analysed by the corrosion test method ASTM D-1838. The cargo was loaded at Yanbu (Saudi Arabia) on board the vessel *Berge Sisar*, which had been chartered to Stargas by her owners Bergesen D.Y. Bills of lading were issued naming the firm Saudi Aramco as shippers. When the ship arrived at Stenungsund (Sweden), samples were taken and analysed. The analysis showed that the quality of the cargo failed the corrosion test prescribed under the contract. Borealis requested delivery of the cargo, but, after the analysis results, decided to reject the cargo and sold it to Dow Europe on terms c.i.f. Terneuzen. Borealis sought damages from Stargas on the contention that the cargo did not meet the quality required before loading. Stargas then claimed an indemnity from Bergesen in respect to any liability Stargas may be exposed to by Borealis. Bergesen, in turn, counterclaimed for damages caused by the corrosive cargo to the ship against Stargas under the charterparty. Bergesen also made similar claims against Saudi Aramco as shippers, and against Borealis as holders of the bills of lading who initially had requested delivery at Stenungsund. The main question for the appeal was whether Borealis, as lawful holder of a bill of lading who demanded delivery of the goods within the terms of sec. 3(1) of the Carriage of Goods by Sea Act 1992, was discharged from liability by endorsing the bills of lading and transferring the goods to a third party (i.e. Dow Europe). Bergensen appealed to the House of Lords, the issue for decision being 1) whether Bergesen had a good arguable case in

contract against Borealis; a) whether Borealis had ever become liable to Bergesen pursuant s. 3 of the and if the answer was in the affirmative, (b) whether Borealis's liability to Bergesen had ceased upon Borealis's endorsement of the bills of lading over to Dow Europe on 20 Jan., 1994. Appellants took the position that Borealis became liable to Appellants when they received the endorsed bills of lading from Stargas on 19 or 20 Jan. 1994. Furthermore, Appellants asserted once Borealis became liable it remained liable under s. 3(1) of the Act[30] regardless of the fact that Borealis had endorsed the bills of lading over to another party. There was a difference of opinion in the Court of Appeal regarding this last point.

***Held (for the respondents):*** The principle of mutuality is contained within section 3(1) of the Carriage of Goods by Sea Act 1992, and it mandates that a holder of the bill of lading enforces rights conferred on him under the contract of car-

---

[30] Section 3(1) of the Act provides: *"Where subsection (1) of section 2 of this Act operates in relation to any document to which this Act applies and the person in whom rights are vested by virtue of that subsection — (a) takes or demands delivery from the carrier of any of the goods to which the document relates; (b) makes a claim under the contract of carriage against the carrier in respect of any of those goods; or (c) is a person who, at a time before those rights were vested in him, took or demanded delivery from the carrier of any of those goods, that person shall (by virtue of taking or demanding delivery or making the claim or, in a case falling within paragraph (c) above, of having rights vested in him) become subject to the same liabilities under the contract as if he had been a party to that contract. (3) This section, so far as it imposes liabilities under any contract on any person, shall be without prejudice to the liabilities under the contract of any person as an original party to the contract".*

riage in exchange for the assumption of liabilities imposed upon him under the contract. Delivery, or a demand for delivery, must occur for the holder of the bill of lading to be subject to liability under section 3(1), which involves a full transfer of the possession of the relevant goods by the carrier to the holder of the bill of lading. (i) Did Borealis make a "demand" for delivery of the cargo as endorsees of the bill of lading, establishing its liability towards the carrier Bergesen under the contract of carriage pursuant to sec. 3(1)? Per Lord Hobhouse of Woodborough: *"The vessel was under charter to Stargas. It was Stargas (or their agents) who gave orders to Bergesen. It was Stargas who offered and then gave the letter of indemnity to Bergesen against their agreement to deliver to Borealis without production of the bills of lading. The only thing done by Borealis appears to have been to direct the master to their import jetty and then, having allowed her to berth there, to take the routine samples from the cargo tanks before clearing the vessel for discharge into their terminal. These are exactly the type of co-operative acts, assisting the shipowners and charterers... which cannot on any view be treated as a demand by Borealis to deliver". "What occurred did not get even as far as the stage of Borealis expressing their willingness to receive this cargo into their terminal. It fell a long way short of amounting to any demand or request that it should be. Once Borealis knew what true characteristics of the cargo were, they refused to accept it from the ship. It follows that, as a matter of fact, Bergesen have failed on the agreed primary facts to make out even an arguable case that Borealis demanded the delivery of cargo."* Subsequently, because Borealis made no demand for delivery, Borealis cannot be caught by sec. 3(1) and thus it was not liable to the carrier Bergesen. (ii) When an endorsee who has both had transferred to and vested in him all the rights of suit under the contract of carriage pursuant to s. 2(1) and become subject to the liabilities under that contract pursuant to sec. 3(1), does he cease to be so liable when he endorses over the bill of lading to another so as to transfer his rights of suit to that other? Their lordships relied on two principles in answering the second issue in the affirmative. First, the lord was of the opinion that the drafters of the Act wished to preserve the decision in Smurthwaite v. Wilkins, (1862) 11 C.B. (N.S.) 842 which interpreted the corresponding section in the Bill of Lading Act, 1855, by holding that, "...the assignee who receives the cargo shall have all the rights and bear all the liabilities of a contracting party; but that if he passes on the bill of lading by indorsement to another, he passes on all the rights and liabilities which the bill of lading carries with it". Second, it was held that the principle of mutuality is preserved by an answer of the second issue in the affirmative. *"Section 3(1) is drafted following this principle [mutuality] because it makes it fundamental that, for a person to be caught by s. 3(1), he must be the person in whom the rights of suit under the contract of carriage are vested pursuant to s. 2(1). The liability is dependent upon the possession of the rights. It follows that, as there is no provision to the contrary, the Act should be construed as providing that, if the person should cease to have the rights vested in him, he should no longer be subject to the liabilities."*

## 30
### BORROWMAN, PHILLIPS & CO. V. FREE & HOLLIS
### 1878, 4 Q.B. 500 (C.A.)

The plaintiffs agreed to sell american maize to the defendants. The contract provided "bill of lading to be dated between the 15th of May and 30th of June inclusive. Payment by cash in London (England) in exchange for shipping documents...or by the buyer's acceptance at sixty days' sight from the date of arrival of bill of lading in London". The plaintiff sellers offered for the cargo to arrive on board the vessel *Charles Platt,* but stated that they had not yet received the shipping documents. The defendants refused to accept the documents without the shipping documents. An arbitrator awarded in favour of the buyers. Subsequently, the plaintiffs offered a second vessel within the time limited by the contract, and in their message stated "bill of lading to hand today and dated about the 24th of June". The buyers refused to accept the cargo and then the sellers claimed for damages. The buyers alleged that (1) the cargo did not belong yet to the sellers at the time of tender; and (2) the sellers could not lawfully tender the cargo of the second vessel because they had already tendered that of the *Charles Platt* and so cargo had been already appropriated.

***Held (for the plaintiffs):* i)** Per Bramwell, L.J.: *"It is quite competent to a man to sell what does not belong to him: before the time of performance he may have bought it or procured the assignment of it, and be ready to fulfil his contract. The contention for the defendants is not maintainable either in the shape taken at the trial or in the form urged before us".* It is clear that the performance of the contract did not strictly depend upon the sellers' possession at the time of tendering the documents. **ii)** The question as to whether the plaintiffs are barred by the doctrine of election was answered in negative too. It is true that, where goods that fulfil the terms of a contract are appropriated for sale in performance thereof, there is an irrevocable election by the vendor. In the present case, however, since the first offer was rejected on the basis that the goods did not fulfil the terms of the contract, there was not a binding election of the goods and thus the sellers were at liberty to offer another cargo. A seller, who has tendered goods not in accordance with the contract, may cancel the original tender and make a new tender provided that he is still within the time stipulated in the contract.

## 31
### BOUKADORA MARITIME CORP. V. SOCIETE ANONYME MAROCAINE DE L'INDUSTRIE ET DU RAFFINAGE
### *(The Boukadora)*
### 1989, 1 Lloyd's Rep. (Q.B.)

Under a voyage charter, the tanker *Boukadora* loaded a cargo of fuel oil at Yanbu (Saudi Arabia). The charterparty provided inter alia: "20(a) Bills of Lading shall be signed by the master as presented...the charterer shall indemnify the owner against all consequences or liabilities which may arise from any inconsistency...which may arise from any irregularity in papers supplied by the charterer or its agent...". After loading was completed, hoses were disconnected. There was a difference of view as to the quantity loaded. The owners' P&I survey showed a 1% difference from the quantity stated in the bills of lading as presented by the shippers. The master issued a letter of protest and refused to sign bills of lading. He agreed to sign the bills of lading only if he could endorse them with the ship's figures. As a consequence of the dispute, there was a substantial delay in the ship's departure and the owners claimed demurrage. The charterers challenged the ship's figures and the reasonableness of the master's conduct.

***Held (for the owners):*** (Evans, J.) **i)** *"The master's conduct has to be seen against the background of the situation in which he found himself, his instructions from his owners as to how he should deal with it, and his legal obligations in respect of signing bills of lading presented to him; …the master acted reasonably throughout, conversely that he did not cause or contribute to the delay by any unreasonable act or omission on his part."* **ii)** *"Apart from the requirements of the Hague Rules…there is, in my judgment, a basic and implied requirement that the bills as presented shall relate to goods actually shipped and that they shall not contain a misdescription of the goods which is known to be incorrect; Here, the charterers through the shippers presented a bill which was inaccurate as to the quantity loaded and they refused to accept the master's signature if it was qualified with regard to the shore figure."* **iii)** *"I hold, therefore, that the shipowners are entitled to recover compensation under the express terms of cl. 20(a). Also, in my judgment, the charterers were in breach of an implied warranty that the bill of lading figure was accurate."*

# 32
## BOWES, E. AND OTHERS V. SHAND, C. AND OTHERS
### 1877, 2 App.Cas. 455 (H.L.)

A contract was concluded for the sale of 300 tons "of Madras rice, to be shipped at Madras (India)…during the months of March and/or Apr., 1874". The nominated vessel arrived at Madras in February, and in that month, 300 tons were loaded and a bill of lading dated February was issued. The buyers refused the cargo on the ground that the goods had not been shipped according to the contract, i.e. "in March and/or April". The sellers claimed the price and obtained a favourable decision from the Court of Appeal. The buyers appealed to the House of Lords.

***Held (for the buyers):*** The contract stated that the cargo should be "shipped" during the two specified months, which means neither before nor after those months. Subsequently, the rice should have been loaded within March and/or April. It cannot be accepted by the sellers' submission that their contractual duty was to make a continuous shipment to be concluded in its whole within those two months. Lord Blackburn said: *"If an article sold is described, the description amounts to a warranty or a condition precedent that it shall be an article of the kind described. The buyers were entitled to reject the documents since the shipment date is part of the description of the goods; What is sold is not 300 tons of rice in gross or in general. It is 300 tons of Madras rice to be put on board at Madras during the particular months".*

## 33
### BP Oil International Ltd. v. Target Shipping Ltd.
### [2012] EWHC 1590 (Q.B.)

Overage freight is freight on cargo loaded in excess of the minimum quantity agreed in the charterparty. In this case, the charterers sought repayment of overage freight that they had allegedly paid by a mistake of their demurrage department. The charter was for a minimum cargo of 80,000 m of fuel oil, but the recap, which incorporated BPVoy 4 Form, included a provision whereby overage freight was "50% applicable for Euromed discharge only". The total loaded was of 112,843.5 m, which, for a number of reasons, was discharged at Galveston and Houston in the USA. The main questions were as follow: (a) Was overage freight due and in what amount? (b) Were charterers entitled to claim back the moneys paid? Owners alleged that freight was payable for the total cargo loaded and that the 50% rate did not apply because discharge did not take place in any Euromed port. charterers' interpretation was that freight was payable only up to 80,000 m, with overage freight (at 50%) being payable only for Euromed discharge and 0% for discharge elsewhere. The Court rejected both parties' contentions.

***Held:*** On a true construction of the charter, the parties did not reach an agreement as to the applicable overage rate for the carriage to the USA. Andrew Smith J. decided to apply Section 15 of the Supply of Goods and Services Act 1982, which provides that: "Where, under a contract for the supply of a service, the considera-

tion for the service is not determined by the contract...there is an implied term that the party contracting with the supplier will pay a reasonable charge". Under Section 15, owners became entitled to "reasonable" overage freight. Andrew Smith J. directed an inquiry of what a reasonable overage freight was. Yet, were charterers entitled to claim back the moneys paid? Charterers were allowed to recover the overage freight paid in excess of what was reasonable. The judge took into consideration the fact that the charterers' employee who made the payment, did so purely by mistake, without awareness or suspicion that liability for overage freight was an issue.

## 34
### Brandt v. Liverpool, Brazil & River Plate Steamship Navigation Co.
### 1924 K.B. 575 (C.A.)

A cargo of zinc ashes in bags was shipped at Buenos Aires (Argentina) for a carriage to Liverpool (England). The shipowners issued a bill of lading stating that all bags were shipped in apparent good order and condition. Some of the bags were exposed to rain before shipment and the upper layers of bags in one of the holds became heated. To avoid damage to the vessel and the other cargo, the master ordered to discharge the wet bags at Buenos Aires and to place them in a warehouse. The bags were reconditioned and shipped aboard another vessel for Liverpool at an additional expenditure of about 748l. At that time, the buyers had paid only ninetenths of the cargo value to the sellers. The second vessel arrived at Liverpool three months after the first. In the meantime, the market value of zinc ashes had fallen considerably. The bill of lading was endorsed to pledgees who presented it to the shipowners and paid the freight, but the goods were not released until they had paid, under protest, the 748l. The indorsees sued the shipowners for damages and repayment of the 748l. The shipowners contended that the indorsees lacked a property in the cargo, and that therefore they were not entitled to sue by virtue of section 1 of the Bills of Lading Act 1855.

***Held (for the indorsees):* i)** The plaintiffs, to whom the full property of the goods did not intend to pass within the meaning of section 1 of the Bills of Lading Act 1855, were nevertheless entitled to sue the shipowner under an implied contract that is established from the acts of presenting the bill of lading, paying the freight and taking delivery of the goods specified in the bill of lading. The implied contract made all the terms contained in the bill of lading as between the shipowners and the indorsees enforceable.[31] **ii)** The shipowners were estopped from denying that the goods were shipped in poor order and condition. They put into circulation a document which they knew contained untrue statements as to the condition of the goods. All persons taking the bill of lading in good faith were entitled to rely on the statements contained therein. In view of that, the indorsees were allowed to enforce the terms of the bill of lading as against the shipowners by virtue of an inferred contract, and thus were entitled to the benefit of estoppel created by the statement in the bill of lading.[32]

# 35
## BRASS V. MAITLAND
### 1856, 6 E & B 470 (Q.B.)

A cargo of bleaching powder was shipped on board the vessel *Regina* from London (England) to Calcutta (India). The powder contained chloride of lime, which corroded the casks and allowed the contents and fumes to leak and damage other cargoes. The shipowner compensated the other cargo-owners who had been victims of damages and sought damages from the shippers of the bleaching powder. The shippers alleged that they had been unaware of the dangerous nature of the goods since they had shipped them as received from a third party, and that no time had been available for an intermediate inspection.

***Held (for the shippers):*** (Lord Campbell CJ) **i)** *"Although those employed on behalf of the shipowner have no reasonable means during the loading of a general ship to ascertain the quality of the goods offered for shipment, or narrowly to examine the sufficiency of the packing of the goods, the shippers have*

---

[31] In situations where the requirements of sec. 1 of the Bills of Lading Act 1855 were not fulfilled, the courts, considering the circumstances of each case, decided as necessary to imply a contract between the consignee or assignee of the bill of lading and the carrier. That new contract was separate and distinct from the original one concluded between the shipper and carrier, but still subject to the same terms and conditions to that one.

[32] See *Compañía Naviera Vascongada v. Churchill & Sim.*

*such means; and it seems more just and expedient that, although they were ignorant of the dangerous quality of the goods or the insufficiency of the packing, the loss occasioned by the dangerous quality of the goods and the insufficient packing should be cast upon the shippers than upon the shipowners."*[33]
**ii)** The shippers were held not liable insofar the shipowner, the master or their servants, ought to have known, and had, in fact, means of knowing, that the powder contained chloride of lime and was insufficiently packed. (Lord Campbell) *"On this supposition the loss which has happened is to be imputed to the careless and misconduct of the master and those employed by the plaintiffs in stowing the casks where they were likely to injure other goods; the shippers were justified in acting upon the supposition that the master to whom the goods are alleged to have been delivered did know what 'he reasonably might and could and ought to have known'; ...the master received these casks knowing the degree to which they were dangerous, in the same manner as if he had received carboys of vitriol, universally known to be most dangerous."* Therefore, the shippers were not liable.

**36**
**BROWN, JENKINSON & CO. LTD. V. PERCY DALTON (LONDON) LTD.**
1957, 2 Lloyd's Rep. 1 (C.A.)

A hundred barrels of orange juice were shipped at London (England) for a carriage to Hamburg (Germany). The shippers were aware that the barrels were old, weak and leaking at the time of shipment. When delivered at the London dock for loading, the actual order and condition of the barrels were noted by the shipowners. As the shippers were anxious to obtain clean bills of lading to satisfy the documentary credit, they undertook to indemnify the shipowners for issuing bills of lading describing the goods as received "in apparent good order and condition". Under the terms of the guarantee, the shippers acknowledged the actual condition of the barrels prior to shipment, and undertook to indemnify the master, the vessel, the shipowners and their representatives against all losses or damages arising from the issuance of clean bills whoever the claimants may be. Subsequently to delivery in Hamburg, the ship agents were sued by the consignees for loss in transit and were held liable for short-delivery. The ship agents sought to recover from the shippers by enforcing the terms of the letter of indemnity. The shippers contended that the indemnity was unenforceable since it had been issued in pursuance of a conspiracy and fraud to misrepresent the actual condition of the barrels.

***Held (for the shippers):***[34] **i)** The bills of lading contained the words "in apparent good order and condition" the meaning of which proved, upon the evidence, utterly false. Those words when inserted in the bill of lading do not contain a contractual statement but a representation of fact on which third parties may probably rely.[35]

---

[33] See *The Giannis NK.*

[34] Lord Evershed, dissenting.

[35] See *Compañia Naviera Vascongada v. Churchill & Sim.*

Therefore, the shipowner is estopped, as against those third parties (purchasers, holders of the bills of lading, banks…), from proving that the goods were not "in apparent good order and condition" when loaded.[36] **ii)** (Pearce, L.J.) *"In the last 20 years it has become customary, in the short-sea trade in particular, for shipowners to give clean bills against an indemnity from the shippers in certain cases where there is a bona fide dispute as to the condition or packing of the goods. This avoids the necessity of rearranging any letter of credit, a matter which can create difficulty where time is short. If the goods turn out to be faulty, the purchaser will have his recourse against the shipping owner, who will in turn recover under his indemnity from the shippers. Thus no one will ultimately be wronged. This practice is convenient where it is used with conscience and circumspection, but it has perils if it is used with laxity and recklessness. It is not enough that the banks or the purchasers who have been misled by clean bills of lading may have recourse at law against the shipowner. They are intending to buy goods, not law suits."* On the facts of the case, all the elements of the tort of deceit were present. The Court applied the rule "ex dolo malo non oritur actio" and held that the indemnity was illegal and void on the ground of fraud. **iii)** Notwithstanding that, Pearce, L.J. remarked *"The evidence seemed to show that in general the practice is kept within reasonable limits. In trivial matters and in cases of bona fide dispute where the difficulty of ascertaining the correct state of affairs is out*

---

[36] See *Brandt v. Liverpool, Brazil and River Plate S.N. Co.*

*of proportion to its importance, no doubt the practice is useful".*

37

**BROWNER INTERNATIONAL LTD. v. MONARCH SHIPPING CO. LTD.**
*(The European Enterprise)*
1989, 2 Lloyd's Rep. 185 (Q.B.)

Freight hauliers agreed to carry a consignment of meat from Cork (Ireland) to inland destinations in France. They entered into a contract of carriage with the owners of the Ro-Ro ferry European Enterprise to cross the Channel from Dover (England) to Calais (France). The meat went packed in a refrigerated tractor-trailer unit. It was loaded on deck under a non-negotiable consignment note (or waybill). It was customary for cross channel operators to issue waybills instead of bills of lading in the Ro-Ro ferry trade. The waybill incorporated the Hague-Visby Rules but subject to a particular provisions relating to the one-package/unit limits on the carrier's liability. Such provisions were fully contractual and substantially less generous than that contained in art. IV(5) of the Hague-Visby Rules. During heavy weather the goods overturned and were severally damaged. The carrier admitted liability under art. III(2) of the Rules but subject to the contractual limits of the waybill. The freight hauliers relied on the integral statutory liability regime of the Hague-Visby Rules and claimed their applicability to the waybill by virtue of sec 1(6.b) of the Carriage of Goods by Sea Act 1971.

***Held (for the shipowners):* i)** The Hague-Visby Rules are not mandatorily applicable to non-negotiable receipts. The parties are free to negotiate their own terms and to decide whether or not to incorporate the Rules, in whole or in part, into their contract. (Steyn J.) *"Shipowners, if they are in a strong enough bargaining position, can escape the application of the Rules by issuing a notice to shippers that no bills of lading will be issued by them in a particular trade."* **ii)** With regard to the question whether a partial incorporation of the Rules may result in the statutory application of all the Rules, Steyn J. clarified: *"…it is only when the receipt expressly provides that the whole Convention, as amended by the Protocol, is to govern the contract, that section 1(6.b) comes into operation; it would be curious if a voluntary Paramount clause, which effected only a partial incorporation of the Rules, had the result that a statutory binding character was given to all the Rules, even where there was no primary contractual bond. It must be right that in enacting section 1 (6.b) the legislation did not intend to override the agreement of the parties when the parties had freedom of choice whether or not to incorporate the Rules into their contract".* **iii)** Furthermore, for the Rules to acquire the force of law by virtue of a Paramount clause inserted in a non-negotiable receipt, it is necessary to fulfil the two requirements contained in sec. 1(6.b): first, the receipt must be marked as "non-negotiable" on its face and, secondly, it must expressly provide that the Rules are to govern the contract "as if the receipt were a bill of lading". Failure to comply with the second requirement resulted in the non-applicability of the Rules in the present case. **iv)** Turning to the right of the carrier to apply the limits

of liability, Steyn J. added: *"The received view is that rule 5(e) of the article IV of the Hague-Visby Rules refers to the carrier himself, and does not include his servants or agents, except in so far as employees are to be regarded as constituting part of the alter ego of the company;*[37] *It follows that I (Steyn J.) have come to the conclusion: -(a) that the limitation provision of the non-negotiable receipt are not invalidated by section 1(6.b) of the 1971 Act; and (b) art. IV(5.e) of the Hague-Visby Rules, refers only to the misconduct or recklessness of the carrier himself or his alter ego".*

## 38
## B.S. & N. LTD. (BVI) v. MICADO SHIPPING LTD. (MALTA)
*(The Seaflower)*
2000, 2 Lloyd's Rep 37 (Q.B.)

Defendant owners chartered their vessel *Seaflower* to the claimants for a period of eleven months, maximum twelve months at the charterers' option by a charterparty dated 20 Oct. 1997. Contained within the charterparty was a major approvals clause which provided inter alia: *"Vessel is presently MOBIL (expiring 27/1/98), CONOCO (expiring 3/2/98), BP (expiring 28/1/98) and SHELL (expiring 14/1/98) acceptable. Owners guarantee to obtain within sixty days EXXON approval in addition to present approvals. On delivery date hire rate will be discounted USD 250 (two*

---

[37] "…on the basis of the principle enunciated in *Lennard's Carrying Co. Ltd. v. Asiatic Petroleum Co. Ltd.*, 1915, AC 705 and reaffirmed in *Grand Champion Tankers v. Norpipe A/S ("The Marion")*, 1984, 2 Lloyd's Rep. 1; 1984, AC 563."

*hundred and fifty) for each approval missing, i.e. MOBIL, CONOCO, BP, SHELL, EXXON. If for any reason, during the time-charter period, owners would lose even one of such acceptances they must advise charterers at once and they must reinstate same within thirty days from such occurrence failing which charterers will be at liberty to cancel charter party or to maintain same at reduced rate as stipulated above. Hire rate will be reinstated once owners will show written evidence of approvals from Major Oil Companies".* The vessel was delivered to the charterers on 5 Nov. 1997, at which time the Exxon approval had not been obtained. On 30 Dec. 1997 the charterers fixed the vessel "on subjects" to load a cargo of Exxon products and charterers' brokers contacted owners' brokers to confirm Exxon's approval pursuant the charterparty approvals clause. The owners' brokers responded that the proper schedule of vetting inspection will take place within January-February 1998. In a telex dated 30 Dec., 1997, charterers responded by terminated the charter and redelivered the vessel. Both owners and charterers sought damages and the main issues before the court were (1) whether the owners' breach in failing to obtain an Exxon approval by 17 Dec. was a repudiatory breach, and (2) whether owners' damages should be limited based on an inevitable event resulting in an early end to the contract prior to the termination date.

**Held:** (1) In deciding whether the owners' failure to obtain Exxon approval was a repudiatory breach of contract, Walter J. laid out the test as one which requires to *"... look at the events which had oc-* *curred as a result of the breach at the time at which the charterers purported to rescind the charter-party and to decide whether the occurrence of those events deprived the charterers of substantially the whole benefit which it was the intention of the parties as expressed in the charter-party that the charterers should obtain from the further performance of their own contractual undertakings".*[38] It was found that the failure to obtain Exxon approval failed to meet that test and thus the charterers were not deprived of substantially the whole benefit of the contract. This is because the financial consequences of the failure to obtain the approval were never advanced in evidence. Besides that, despite the failure the charterers were still able to continuously employ the vessel. Most importantly, the charterers knew the vessel lacked Exxon's approval when they formed the contract with the owners and the contract itself expressed the intention of the parties to reduce the daily hire rate of only 3% if there was no approval from Exxon. Subsequently, no automatic right to cancel had been agreed to between the parties and the charters were not entitled to terminate on 30 Dec., 1997 for breach of what was ultimately an innominate term. (2) Regarding the measure of owners' damages for early redelivery of the vessel, the judge ruled that, *"If the contract would inevitably have come to an end earlier than its due date anyway, it is right that the damages should be limited accordingly, regardless of whether or not the event was predestined*

---

[38] Per Lord Justice Diplock in *Hongkong Fir Shipping v. Kawasaki Kisen Kaisha*, [1961] 2 Lloyd's Rep. 478 at p. 495.

*at the date of repudiation"*. The judge ultimately determined that the charterparty would have inevitably come to an end on 26 Feb., 1998, because the owners would have lost and been unable to timely regain the Mobil approval, allowing charterers to cancel the contract as per the agreed terms. Subsequently, owners were allowed damages for early return of the vessel only up to the time of 26, Feb. 1998 instead of the full duration of the charterparty.

**39**

**BUNGE CORPORATION V. TRADAX EXPORT S.A.**
1981, 2 Lloyd's Rep. 1 (H.L.)

In Jan. 1974, Bunge Corp. (the buyers) purchased from Tradax Export (the sellers) 15,000 tons of soya bean meal f.o.b. one U.S. Gulf port at sellers' option. The buyers, in turn, had sold part of that cargo to a third company. The contract stated that the buyers were to give fifteen days' loading notice. GAFTA Form No. 119 was generally incorporated providing, inter alia, clause 7: "Period of delivery: During --- at buyers' call. Buyers shall give at least --- consecutive days notice of probable readiness of vessel(s) and of the approximate quantity required to be loaded". On June 17 at 08:46 hours, the buyers forwarded the loading notice to the sellers immediately after having received it from their on-buyers in string. The message said: "For the contract in object we nominate the ss. Sankograin ETA US Gulf 23/25 June for T 5,000 5% M/L U.S. Soyabean meal. Waiting for shippers name/loading port". The sellers replied on June 20 saying that the loading notice was

late, and thereby terminated the contract declaring the buyers in default. The main question for the appeal was whether cl. 7 was a condition whose breach entitled the sellers to terminate the contract.

***Held (for the sellers):* i)** (Lord Lowry) *"A condition is a term the failure to perform which entitles the other party to treat the contract as at an end. A warranty is a term, breach of which sounds in damages but does not terminate, or entitle the other party to terminate, the contract. An innominate or intermediate term is one, the effect of non-performance of which the parties expressly or (as more usual) impliedly agree will depend upon the nature and the consequences of breach; Unless the contract makes it clear, either by express provision or by necessary implication arising from its nature, purpose, and circumstances,…that a particular stipulation is a condition or only a warranty, it is an innominate term, the remedy for a breach of which depends upon the nature, consequences, and effect of the breach."*[39] **ii)** *"After some hesitation, I (Lord Lowry) have concluded that the clause was intended as a term, the buyer's performance of which was the necessary condition to performance by the seller of his obligations. The contract, when made, was…'synalagmatic', i.e. a contract of mutual engagements to be performed in the future,…an 'executory' contract. The seller needed sufficient notice to enable him to choose the loading port: the parties were agreed that the notice to be given him was 15 days: this was a mercantile contract in*

---

[39] See *Hong Kong Fir Shipping Co. Ltd. v. Kawasaki Kisen Kaisha Ltd.*

*which the parties required to know where they stood not merely later with hindsight but at once as events occurred.*[40] *Because it makes commercial sense to treat the clause in the context and circumstances of this contract as a condition to be performed before the seller takes his steps to comply with bargain, I would hold it to be not an innominate term but a condition.*"

# 40
## BUNGE S.A. V. NIDERA BV
### [2013] EWHC 84 (Q.B.)

The case concerned a contract for the sale of 25,000 m of russian milling wheat to be delivered on f.o.b. Novorossyisk terms between 23 and 30 Aug. 2010. The contract incorporated GAFTA Contract No. 49, which included

the following Prohibition Clause: "*in case of prohibition of export, blockade or hostilities or in case of any executive or legislative act done by or on behalf of the government of the country of origin of the goods, or of the country from which the goods are to be shipped, restricting export, whether partially or otherwise, any such restriction shall be deemed by both parties to apply to this contract and to the extent of such total or partial restriction to prevent fulfilment whether by shipment or by any other means whatsoever and to that extent this contract or an unfulfilled portion thereof shall be cancelled...*". On 5 Aug. 2010, the russian government issued a resolution prohibiting the export of wheat between 15 Aug. and 31 Aug. 2010 (therefore covering the entirety of the contractual delivery period). On 9 Aug. 2010, sellers purported to declare the contract as automatically cancelled under the Prohibition Clause. Buyers treated the sellers' act as a wrongful repudiation and decided to terminate the contract. The appeal concerned the construction and application of the GAFTA Prohibition Clause.

***Held (for buyers):*** The Prohibition Clause did not cancel the sale when the prohibition was enacted, but only if it remained in place until the end of the delivery period. For a party to rely on the Prohibition Clause, it was necessary to establish a causal connection between the prohibition and the restriction of export of goods of the particular contractual description during the particular contractual shipment period. The Court also had to consider the application of the GAFTA Default Clause, according to which dam-

---

[40] In the same judgment, Lord Roskill quoted paragraphs 481 and 482 of the 4th edition (1974) of Halsbury's Laws of England concerning the rules to be applied on time stipulations like the present one: 481. "*The modern law, in the case of contracts of all types, may be summarised as follows. Time will not be considered of the essence unless: (1) the parties expressly stipulate that conditions as to time must be strictly complied with; or (2) the nature of the subject matter of the contract or the surrounding circumstances show that time should be considered to be of the essence; or (3) a party who has been subjected to unreasonable delay gives notice to the party in default making time of the essence.*" 482. "*Apart from express agreement or notice making time of the essence, the court will require precise compliance with stipulations as to time wherever the circumstances of the case indicate that this would fulfil the intention of the parties. Broadly speaking, time will be considered of the essence in 'mercantile' contracts and in other cases where the nature of the contract or of the subject matter or the circumstances of the case require precise compliance.*"

ages are to be based on, but not limited to, the difference between the contract price and the actual or estimated value of the goods at the date of default. sellers argued that, on the facts, buyers had suffered no loss. However, the Court held that the parties had agreed that their damages would be based upon the measure set out in the Default Clause alone, and it was only such measure which should be applied here.

**41**

**C**ALCUTTA **S**TEAMSHIP **C**O. **L**TD. V.
**A**NDREW **W**EIR **&** **C**O.
1910, 1 KB 759 (K.B.)

The vessel *Calcutta* was chartered to proceed to Busreh to load any lawful cargo and sail to a safe port in the U.K. for discharge. The freight was agreed on a lump sum basis. The charterparty incorporated a clause saying: *"The captain to sign bill of lading at any rate of freight without prejudice to this charterparty, but not below charterparty rate, but should the charterers or their agents be unable to have or not have ready for signature all or any bills of lading at any port or ports by the time the ship is otherwise ready to sail, it is agreed that this charter shall constitute owners' authority for charterers' agents to sign in the captain's name all unsigned bill of lading in conformity with mate's receipts, which shall be granted in due course…"*. At Busreh a shipper loaded a cargo of dates and received a bill of lading signed by the charterers' agent in accordance with the charterparty. The bill of lading contained several exceptions of liability not contemplated in the charterparty. While the vessel was on her way

to U.K. the charterers made an advance payment to the shipper, who endorsed his bill of lading to them as security for the advance. At the port of discharge the charterers took delivery of the goods and found them damaged. The charterers, as holders of the bill of lading, deducted from the lump sum freight a sum equal to the depreciation in value suffered by the goods. The owners claimed the freight balance unpaid and invoked the exclusions of liability contained in the bill of lading. The main question was whether the charterers' claim should be ruled by the terms evidenced in the bill of lading or by those of the charterparty.

***Held (for the owners):*** (Hamilton, J.)
**i)** The words "without prejudice to this charterparty" must mean that, whatever the terms of the bill of lading may be, the contract contained in the charterparty could not to be altered or superseded by them. *"It follows that, if the bill of lading, whether by indorsement or otherwise, comes into the hands of the charterers, they are entitled to say that as between themselves and the shipowners the bill of lading cannot alter the terms of the charterparty to their prejudice."* In that regard, the bill of lading could not prejudice the charterparty. **ii)** The two instruments operated independently: whilst the bill of lading dealt with the carriage of the goods, the charterparty governed the hire for the use of the ship. Since the goods were not shipped by the charterers themselves under the terms of the charterparty, but by the transferors of the bill of lading, it is the bill of lading (and not the charterparty) that contained the terms of the contract of carriage. In that contractual

framework, assuming that the goods were damaged by causes for which the bill of lading (as distinguished from the charter-party) exempted the owners from liability, the charterers were liable to pay the lump sum freight in full.

**42**

CIE. GROUPE CONCORDE AND OTHERS
v. THE MASTER OF THE VESSEL
SUHADIWARNO PANJAN AND OTHERS
*(European Court of Justice)*
28.09.1999, Case C-440/97

Cartons containing bottles of wine were shipped in containers on board the vessel *Suhadiwarno Panjan* in Le Havre (France) for a carriage to Santos (Brazil). On arrival at Santos the cargo was found to be short and damaged. Under the terms of the policy, the receivers were paid by the insurers who then commenced subrogation proceedings in Le Havre against the master of the vessel and the carrier. The Tribunal de Commerce of Le Havre declined jurisdiction and the Cour d'Appel of Rouen upheld the judgment on the ground that Le Havre was not the place where the contract of carriage was performed. Under art. 5(1) of the Convention of 27 Sept. 1968 on Jurisdiction and Enforcement of Judgments in Civil and Commercial Matters[41] (the "Brussels Convention"), "A person domiciled in a Contracting State may, in another Contracting State,

be sued: 1. In matters relating to a contract, in the courts for the place of performance of the obligation in question; in matters relating to individual contracts of employment, this place is that where the employee habitually carries out his work…" The insurers appealed to the Cour de Cassation and the following question was referred to the European Court of Justice for a preliminary ruling: "With a view to the application of Article 5(1) of the Brussels Convention…, must the place of performance of the obligation, within the meaning of that provision, be determined in accordance with the law which, pursuant to the rules on conflicts of law of the courts seized, governs the obligation at issue, or should national courts determine the place of performance of the obligation by seeking to establish, having regard to the nature of the relationship creating the obligation and the circumstances of the case, the place where performance actually took place or should have taken place, without having to refer to the law which, under the rules on conflict of laws, governs the obligation at issue?". In other words, the question was whether the place of performance of the obligation at issue was to be determined according to the law applicable to the contract as specified by the conflict of law rules of France (i.e. the forum seized), or whether it was to be determined according to an independent interpretation (e.g. as in reference to employment contracts).

***Held:*** (after the opinion of the General Advocate D. Ruiz-Jarabo Colomer) **i)** *"As regards the expression 'place of performance of the obligation in question', the court has*

---

[41] As amended by the Convention of 9 Oct.1978 on the Accession of Denmark, Ireland and the United Kingdom, and by the Convention of 26 May 1989 on the Accession of Spain and Portugal.

*repeatedly ruled that this expression is to be interpreted as referring to the law which governs the obligation in question according to the conflict rules of the court seized."* **ii)** *"It is true that, in the case of contract of employment, the court has ruled that the place of performance of the relevant obligation should be determined by reference, not to the applicable national law in accordance with the conflict rules of the court seized, but to uniform criteria which it is for the court to lay down on the basis of the scheme and the objectives of the Brussels Convention. These criteria lead to the choice of the place where the employee actually performs the work covered by the contract with his employer."* **iii)** Notwithstanding that, the court held that, where the obligation is not directly referred to a contract of employment (as it was the case), the place of performance of the relevant obligation should be generally determined according to the applicable law as ascertained by the conflict of law rules of the place of the courts first seized. *"It should be added that there is no risk that the law applicable to the determination of the place of performance will vary depending on the court seized, since the conflict rules enabling the law applicable to the contract to be determined have been standardised in the Contracting States by the Convention of 19 June 1980 on the Law applicable to Contractual."*[42] On these grounds, the court ruled as follows: *"On a proper construction of Article 5(1) of the Convention the place of performance of the obligation, within the meaning of that provision, is to be determined in accordance with the law governing the obli-*

gation in question according to the conflict rules of the court seized".

---

**43**

**CEVAL ALIMENTOS S.A. V. AGRIMPEX TRADING CO. LTD.**
*(The Northern Progress)*
1996, 2 Lloyd's Rep. 319 (Q.B.)

Brazilian sellers sold c.& f. free out Rijeka/Koper (ex Yugoslavia) 26,000 tonnes of soya bean meal in bulk. The contract of sale incorporated the words "All terms, conditions and exceptions as per Charterparty". Bills of lading were to be issued also incorporating the charterparty terms. For carrying the goods the seller voyage-chartered the vessel *Northern Progress* from Paranagua (Brazil) to Koper/Rijeka/Kardeljevo. The charterparty contained a clause whereby the charterer was to nominate an alternative port within Italian Adriatic in the event that ex Yugoslavian ports were closed to merchant shipping or subject to an insurance premium due to war-like conditions; any insurance premium or deviation was to be for the account of the charterers. The sale contract was amended stating Hamburg (Germany) and Ravenna (Italy) as other optional ports in addition to the prior agreed ones. It was contemplated that the nomination of the discharge port was at the election of the buyers two days before the vessel passing Gibraltar. The war in ex Yugoslavia had not yet started, but the London insurance market announced war-risk additional premiums in all Yugoslavian ports. In the event the buyers declared Rijeka as discharging port. The sellers/charterers did not want to pay additional

---

[42] Commonly known as the Rome Convention 1980.

premiums in Rijeka under the charter-party and otherwise decided to nominate Hamburg. The buyers took delivery at Hamburg under protest and claimed damages. They contended, inter alia, that the incorporation clause of the sale contract was ineffective because, at the time the contract was issued, the charterparty had not yet fixed.

***Held (for the buyers):*** (Rix, J.) **i)** *"The sale contract itself contemplates that a charterparty may be fixed only after the sale contract has been made; the incorporation clause… contemplates a future contract. Indeed, that is typical of c.i.f. contracts, under which a seller is obliged to procure a contract of carriage for the sale: such carriage contracts must regularly be entered into only after the sale contract in question."*[43] **ii)** The charterparty clause which allowed the shipowners to sail elsewhere than to the contract port depending on any additional premium announced was found unreasonable and in conflict with other clauses concerning renomination of the discharging port. The incorporation of such a clause into the bills of lading was uncontractual and improper.[44] **iii)** The sellers were in breach of the (amended) contract of sale. The buyers expressed that they wanted bills of lading to be issued naming a ex Yugoslavian port. The amendment of the sale contract meant that it was open to them to nominate, at their convenience, one port out of the five alternative ones two days be-

fore Gibraltar. It cannot be concluded that they were bound to accept Sellers' bills of lading naming Hamburg as unique port of discharge.

44

### CHEIKH BOUTROS SELIM EL-KHOURY V. CEYLON SHIPPING LINES LTD.
*(The Madelein)*
1967, 2 Lloyd's Rep. 224 (Q.B.D.)

A vessel called *Madelein* was hired under a time charterparty, which provided that she had to be delivered to the charterers at Calcutta (India). It also contained a cancelling clause that said: *"Should the vessel not be delivered by 6 p.m. on 10ᵗʰ May, 1957, the charterers to have the option of cancelling".* On May 9, the owners informed the charterers that the ship would be delivered on the morning of the following day, i.e. May 10. She had been freshly inspected by the port health authority and ordered to be fumigated. The fumigation tasks could not be completed before midnight of the same day. In view of that, the charterers purported to cancel the charter at 8 a.m. of the same day by sending a message to the owners declaring them in breach.

***Held (for the charterers):*** (Roskill, J.) **i)** As the time (i.e. 6:00 p.m. on May 10) mentioned in the cancellation clause had not been yet reached, the purported cancellation was of no effect. *"It is clear law that there is no contractual right to rescind a charter-party under the cancelling clause unless and until the date specified in that clause has been reached. In other words… there is no anticipatory right to cancel under*

---

[43] See *OK Petroleum A.B. v. Vitol Energy Ltd.* Contrast that case with *Gill & Duffus S.A. v. Rionda Futures. Ltd.*

[44] See *Miramar Maritime Corp. v. Holborn Oil Trading Ltd.* and *S.I.A.T. di dal Ferro v. Tradax.*

*the clause.*"[45] **ii)** Nonetheless, although the charterers had no *contractual* right to cancel under the cancellation clause, they were not prevented from seeking to rescind the charter *at Common Law* by alleging frustration or anticipatory breach of the contract. *"Of course, the fact that there is no contractual right to cancel in advance does not prevent a charterer seeking to claim the right to rescind in advance of the cancelling date, as the learned editors of Scrutton put it 'at Common Law'; Where the charterer seeks to say that the contract has been frustrated or that there has been an anticipatory breach which entitled him to rescind, then he has such rights as are given to him at Common Law."*

**45**

**C**HS **I**NC **I**BERICA **S.L.** AND **A**NOTHER V. **F**AR **E**AST **M**ARINE **S.A.**
*(The Devon)*
[2012] EWHC 3747

A consignment of corn was loaded on board *The Devon* in Varna (Bulgaria), for discharge at Tarragona (Spain). Three hours after she sailed from Varna, the vessel suffered a main engine breakdown and had to be towed back to Varna, where repairs were carried out. There was extensive damage to the engine and the repairs took more than fourty five days to complete. As a result, the intended voyage

took fifty nine days instead of eight days. At the time the vessel arrived in Tarragona, part of the cargo had turned mouldy and caked. A salvage sale was organized for 21% of the cargo at a value substantially lower than the purchase price. The cargo owners, CHS Inc. Iberica S.L., sued the ship-owners for the reduction of value, stevedore costs, warehousing costs, the loss adjuster's charges for arranging the salvage sale and their surveyor's costs. Most likely, the breakdown had been caused by an overheating of the engines due to a failure of the cooling systems, which, in turn, caused a breakdown of the lube oils viscosity. The contract of carriage incorporated the Hague Rules. The ship-owners failed to advance an explanation for the failure of the lubrication system. In addition, they seemed to have disclosed very little information themselves about the incident and the subsequent repairs. The inference was that the ship-owners were hiding documents essential to progress the case.

***Held (for the cargo owners):*** One of the questions was if the vessel was unseaworthy at the beginning of the voyage. The cargo owners accused the ship-owners of the ship of failing to exercise due diligence when they supplied the vessel for the voyage. The Court agreed. It held that *The Devon* was unseaworthy upon the commencement of her voyage. The ship-owners were denied the defence of "latent defect not discoverable by due diligence" contained in Article IV(2) of the Hague Rules article. Several factors contributed to this decision: the cooling system's partially blocked state, together with the absence of any monitoring sys-

---

[45] Roskill J. recalled the passage in the 7th ed. (1964) of *Scrutton on Charterparties* at p. 110: *"A charterer is not entitled to cancel (semble under the clause as distinct from any right he may have to rescind at Common Law) before the cancelling date even though it is clear that the owner will be unable to tender the ship in time".*

tem for the efficacy of the cooling system and the inadequate and slow monitoring system for tracking the temperature of the lube oil.


## 46
## CLEA SHIPPING CO. V. BULK OIL INTERNATIONAL LTD.
*(The Alaskan Trader, No. 2)*
1983, 2 Lloyd's Rep. 645 (Q.B.)

The ship *Alaskan Trader* was chartered for a period of 24 months 15 days more or less. She was an old gas oil tanker built in 1954. She was delivered on Dec. 20, 1979 but on Oct. 19, 1980 suffered a serious engine breakdown. Considering that repairs would take several months, the charterers indicated that they had no further use of her. The market turned against them: the market rate was USD 4-5 lower than the charter rate. Throughout the period of repairs the vessel was off-hire and, once completed, the owners informed the charterers that the vessel was again at their disposal. The charterers ratified their prior decision and refused to give orders to the master. Curiously, the owners did not treat such conduct as a repudiation of the charterparty, but kept the vessel anchored with a full crew on board ready to sail, but idle, until the charterparty expired on Dec. 5, 1981. Then she was sold for scrap. The Ooners claimed the hire for the whole period. On the opposite, the charterers argued that the owners should have accepted their conduct as repudiatory and offered only remedial damages.

**Held:** (Lloyd, J.) **i)** A charterparty cannot be performed without the co-operation of the charterers. A time charter is more analogous to a contract between master and servant than a simple debt. *"Thus it can be said with force that bankers need to know where they are when accepting an assignment of charter hire as security for their loan."* In sought of some certainty, Lloyd J. held that the charterparty had truly come to an end as a result of the charterers' repudiation. **ii)** That did not necessarily mean that the owners were entitled to rely on their own conduct and claim the hire for the whole period. They truly could have mitigated their own damages, but they did the opposite. *"There comes a point at which the Court will cease, on general equitable principles, to allow the innocent party (the owners) to enforce his contract according to its strict legal terms."* **iii)** Furthermore, the owners had no legitimate interest, financial or otherwise, in performing the contract. Being a one-ship company, they decided to keep the charterparty in order to protect their parent company from possible claims under the charter. The owners were entitled to damages, but not to the full hire period.


## 47
## COASTAL (BERMUDA) PETROLEUM LTD. V. VTT VULCAN PETROLEUM S.A.
*(The Marine Star)*
1993, Lloyd's Rep. 329 (C.A.)

A cargo of oil was sold c.i.f. on July 19, 1991. The contract provided that the vessel's nomination was to be given by the sellers at the time the vessel passed Gibraltar 31 July, 1991, the latest. There was a force majeure clause saying: "Neither party shall be liable for any breach, delay or non-performance…which directly or indirectly results from…impairment or interference with seller's means of supply… or which directly or indirectly results from any cause beyond sellers…control". Delivery was agreed on an outturn basis Aruba 4-10 Aug.1991. The day before passing Gibraltar, the sellers nominated the Vessel: MT *Marine Star/substitute* and it was so was accepted by the buyers. Later on that day a further telex was sent by the sellers informing that the *Marine Star* was to be substituted. The reason of the withdrawal of such vessel was that the shat they could be able to perform their contract with Aruba buyers engaging a different vessel, but at the end of the day no substitute vessel was nominated. On Aug. 2, 1991, the buyers treated the sellers' inability to perform as a breach of contract. They cancelled the contract and claimed for damages. The sellers contended that they were entitled to substitute the vessel provided that the delivery date was not beyond Aug. 10, 1991. Alternatively, the sellers alleged force majeure.

***Held (for the buyers):*** **i)** (Hirst L.J.) *"Certainty is of particular importance in the oil market, where, as is very well known, chains of back to back contracts are commonplace, so that the buyer, in his capacity as a sub-seller in the next contract down in the chain, will frequently need to pass nomination to his sub-buyer."* In order to preserve such principle, the nomination of the *Marine Star* should stand as firm and binding to all the relevant parties unless immediately replaced by another contractual vessel with a contractual cargo which may enable the Buyer to pass this infor-

mation down the string in time.[46] **ii)** The force majeure clause did not apply here. The sellers' inability to perform their obligation (i.e. to nominate another vessel before 31 July, 1991) was due to a mere commercial decision, i.e. to switch the *Marine Star* to Exxon. It is not applicable the principle ex post facto by which a seller, being prevented to perform his duties by force majeure, has to allocate in a reasonable manner all the available goods between competing buyers. But that is not the case. The sellers here were not conditioned by force majeure and their preference for Exxon was due to mere commercial interest, which by no means falls within the scope of the force majeure clause.

<h3 align="center">48<br>COBELFRET N.V. v. CYCLADES SHIPPING CO. LTD.<br>(The Linardos)<br>1994, 1 Lloyd's Rep. 28 (Q.B.)</h3>

The vessel *Linardos* was chartered for a carriage of coal from Richards Bay (South Africa) to Antwerp (Belgium). The charter was on the standard Richards Bay Coal Charter form, which provided, inter alia, the following clause 4: *"Time commencing 18 hours after notice of readiness has been given by the master certifying that the vessel has arrived and is in all respects ready to load whether in berth or not…"*; the clause went on saying *"Any time lost subsequently by vessel not fulfilling requirements for readiness to load in all respects, including Ma-*

---

[46] See *The Playa Larga and Marble Islands.*

*rine Surveyors Certificate or for any other reason for which the vessel is responsible… shall NOT count as notice time or as time allowed for loading".* The vessel arrived at Richards Bay and the master gave notice of readiness of loading, but no berth was available for three days due to congestion. Once berthed, the local surveyor inspected the vessel and certified that the holds were not fit since they contained water and rust. The vessel's hatches were cleaned and thereafter the cargo was loaded. The shipowners claimed demurrage contending that the laytime started to run the day where the master gave the notice of readiness. The charterers contended that, since the vessel was not ready to load on that day, the laytime should be counted from the date when the vessel was, in fact, fit for loading the coal.

**Held:** (Colman, J.) **i)** From the second part of cl. 4 the parties agreed that laytime would start at the waiting place even if the holds were later rejected. Any time subsequently lost as a result of the owners' failure (to present the vessel in an acceptable condition) would not count against the charterers, but the accrued waiting time would. Laytime included, as contended by the shipowners, the three days of berth waiting. In that respect, the judge said: *"I do not accept that (the second part of cls. 4) should be construed as confined to loss of time due to events occurring after the giving of notice of readiness because the common law rule is that valid notice of readiness can be given only if the vessel is indeed ready".* **ii)** The judge took the view that this argument might give the shipowners a license to tender notices of readiness on

arrival regardless of the knowledge that the ship was not in fact ready. *"The natural meaning of (the second part of cls. 4) in this commercial setting is as a matter of construction inconsistent with the normal requirement that notice of readiness can validly be given only when the vessel is in all respects physically ready to load. Accordingly, the effect of cl. 4 is to contract out of the normal rule requiring that the vessel must be ready at the time of giving the notice."* **iii)** *"A notice of readiness proved to be given by the master or chief officer with knowledge that it was untrue, that is to say in the knowledge that the vessel was not then ready would be ineffective to start time running. There must by implication be a requirement of good faith".*[47]

## 49

### COLONIAL BANK V. EUROPEAN GRAIN & SHIPPING LTD.
### (*The Dominique*)
### 1989, 1 Lloyd's Rep. 431 (H.L.)

By an assignment under seal of Apr. 14, 1982, the Owners of the "Dominique" assigned to the Colonial Bank all the earnings of the ship, including but not limited to freight. On June 16, 1982, the owners let her to the charterers, European Grain & Shipping Ltd., for a carriage of agricultural products in bulk from Kakinada (India) to European ports. The charterparty was made under the Gencon form and provided, inter alia, the

---

[47] But see *The Jay Ganesh* where, in a similar situation, the notice of readiness was found as valid since the master was unaware of the actual unreadiness of the ship's holds.

following clause 16: *"Freight shall be prepaid within five days of signing and surrender of final Bills of Lading, full freight deemed to be earned on signing Bills of Lading, discountless and non-returnable, vessel and or cargo lost or not lost…"*. On July 14, 1982, the ship completed loading and bills of lading were signed and surrendered to the shippers. After sailing towards Colombo for bunkers, the bank learnt that the P&I Club's entry would be cancelled and gave notice to the charterers of the assignment mentioned earlier. When she arrived at Colombo on July 19 she was arrested by a third party creditor. The owners indicated that they were unable to lift the arrest and continue the voyage. On July 22, the charterers treated the owners' conduct as a breach. They terminated the charter and transhipped their cargo to another vessel at a cost higher than the freight. The bank claimed payment of USD 223,767 for freight allegedly due. The charterers refused payment as –they said– freight never became due and counter-claimed for damages.

**Held *(for the bank/owners)*: i)** The owners' (or rather, his assignor's) right to freight accrued before the termination of the charterparty. The effect of clause 16 was that the owners' right to the freight accrued on completion of the signing of the bills of lading, but that payment was postponed until five days after the signed bills were delivered to the shippers. (Lord Brandon) *"The postponement of payment was an incident attaching to the right acquired, but it was not a condition of its acquisition. It follows that… the owners' right to the freight, having*

*been unconditionally acquired before the termination of the charter-party, was not divested or discharged by such termination. I would therefore answer… by saying that the owners' right to the freight survived the termination of the charter-party."* On those grounds, as the owners' right to freight accrued on July 14 and the charter was terminated on July 22, the freight did become legitimately due. **ii)** It is an established rule that a cargo-owner is not entitled to set up, as a defence to a claim for freight, damage suffered by reason of some breach of the contract of carriage by the owners. In that regard, Lord Brandon said: *"[W]hen an owners' breach of charter-party is of a non-repudiatory character, such as partial loss of or damage to cargo, it does not give rise to an equity in favour of the charterers sufficient to override the established rule against deduction; and a repudiatory breach is no more capable of giving rise to a defence of equitable set-off than is a non-repudiatory breach"*. **iii)** The charterers' counterclaim for damages resulting from transhipping the goods failed too. They were not entitled to rely on their counterclaim as a defence of equitable set-off as against the bank to the extent that they would not be either, but for the assignment, as against the owners.

**50**

**COMPAÑÍA NAVIERA TEDELKA S.A.** v.
**TRADAX INTERNACIONAL S.A.**

*(The Tres Flores)*

1973, 2 Lloyd's Rep. 247 (C.A.)

The vessel *Tres Flores* was chartered for a voyage to Varna (Bulgaria) to load a cargo of maize in bulk, and for a subsequent voyage to Famagusta (Cyprus) for discharge. The charterparty was on the Synacomex form and provided the following clause: *"Before tendering notice (of readiness), master has to take necessary measures for holds to be clean, dry, without smell and in every way suitable to receive grain to shippers/charterers' satisfaction"*. On Nov. 22, 1970, the vessel reached the loading port of Varna and gave notice of readiness, but no berth was available. Because of bad weather, the inspectors of the authorities were unable to reach the vessel (anchored) to survey her hatches. Five days later, the inspectors made the survey and found pests in the hatches. On Dec.1, 1970, when the fumigation was finished and the vessel was, in fact, ready, the charterers accepted the notice of readiness as valid. The dispute was whether laytime commenced on the date the master gave the notice (as suggested by the shipowners) or contrary when the charterers had accepted it as valid.

***Held (for the charterers):*** **i)** The MV *Tres Flores* was an "arrived ship" but it was unready to load at the time the notice of readiness was given. The relevant clause of the charterparty was to be treated as a condition precedent to the validity of the notice. It was held that the notice of readiness was not validly given since, at that time, the holds were unfit to receive the cargo. (Lord Denning MR) *"One thing is clear. In order for a notice of readiness to be good, the vessel must be ready at the time that the notice is given, and not at a time in the future. Readiness is a preliminary existing fact which must exist before you can give*

*a notice of readiness."*[48] **ii)** Even in the absence of the clause, the result would have been either the same: laytime would not commence to run if it is discovered that the notice was given when the vessel was unready. Laytime started to run only after the fumigation was finished. That is to be understood irrespectively of the fact that the fumigation took a couple of hours only and the vessel had waited for berth several days.

<h1 style="text-align:center">51</h1>

COMPAÑÍA NAVIERA VASCONGADA V.<br>CHURCHILL & SIM.<br>1906, 1 KB 237 (K.B.)

Shippers of timber chartered the vessel *Virgen de Lourdes* to carry goods bound for London (England). The charterparty provided that the bills of lading should be prepared by the shippers in the form indorsed on the charterparty, and should be signed by the master upon presentation only in that form. The prescribed form contained the clauses "shipped in good order and condition" and "quality and measure unknown". The American "Harter Act" was incorporated into the bills of lading imposing, in its section 4, the duty to deliver merchantable bills of lading stating

---

[48] Lord Denning MR although admitted at p. 249 that: *"…notice of readiness can be given even though there are some further preliminaries to be done, or routine matters to be carried on, or formalities observed. If those things are not such as to give any reason to suppose that they will cause any delay, and it is apparent that the ship will be ready when the appropriate time arrives, then notice of readiness can be given; fumigation was not a mere preliminary or routine matter, not a formality at all".*

"the apparent order and condition" of the goods. The goods became stained and saturated with petroleum whilst waiting on the quay at shipper's risk. The master received the stained goods on board and signed a set of "shipped in good order and condition" bills as stated under the charterparty, but at the foot of the bills wrote the words "quality and measure unknown". The bills of lading were indorsed by the shippers to the buyers, who became indorsees under section 1 of the Bills of Lading Act 1855. The buyers took delivery of the stained timber at London and claimed thereafter against the shippers in arbitration under the sale contract. They were awarded with the difference between the contract price of the timber and its depreciated value as stained by petroleum. However, the buyers did not manage to enforce the award against the shippers, who were a foreign firm. The buyers then decided not to pay the freight to the shipowner, who in turn sued them. The buyers counter-claimed for damages at an amount equal to that awarded by the arbitrator plus the expenses incurred owing to the marks on the timber having become obliterated.

***Held (for the buyers):*** (Channell, J.) **i)** The terms "shipped in good order and condition" *"are not words of contract in the sense of a promise or undertaking. The words are an affirmation of fact, or perhaps rather in the nature of an assent by the captain to an affirmation of fact which the shipper may be supposed to make as to his own goods".* In the present case, that representation was untrue and made negligently. The Harter Act, as incorporated to the bill of lading, in its section 4 imposes a duty upon owners and masters to state in the bill of lading the true apparent order and condition of the goods. **ii)** *"The defendants …are entitled to sue the shipowner for damages for breach of the contract to deliver the timber in good order and condition. The words 'quality and measure unknown' do not qualify the words 'shipped in good order and condition'"* as they do not relate to the order and condition at all, but to quality and measure only. *"I think that 'condition' refers to the external and apparent condition, and 'quality' to something which is usually not apparent, at all events to an unskilled person; I think the captain is expected to notice the apparent condition of the goods, though not the quality".* But, even if the words were related to condition (e.g. "order and condition unknown"), they would still be unable to qualify what had been an admission of the contrary. The cause of action was therefore based on estoppel (not on breach of contract) in so far the shipowners were estopped as against the indorsee from denying the truth of that statement. **iii)** It was alleged by the owners that the master had been compelled by the charterparty terms to sign the bills of lading in the form indorsed, which indeed contained the words "good order and condition". Channell, J., however, held that the master was not bound by the charterparty to sign an untrue statement in the bills of lading; *"He was… at liberty to qualify the words according to the truth, without departing from the form".* **iv)** As to whether the master had authority to make that statement on behalf of the shipowners, the judge found that *"the statement is within his authority, and, whatever its effect may be, it binds the owner and not merely the master personally".*[49]

---

[49] See *Grant v. Norway, 1851, 10 CB 665.*

## 52

### COMPAÑÍA PORTORAFTI COMMERCIALE S.A. v. ULTRAMAR PANAMA INC. AND OTHERS

*(The Captain Gregos No. 2)*
1990, 2 Lloyd's Rep. 395 (C.A.)

About 800,000 barrels of crude oil were purchased by Ultramar Panama Inc. to Amoco. They subsequently on-sold the cargo to the second defendants (PEAG) f.o.b. Ras Shukheir. Payment was to be made thirty days from the bill of lading date against documents, which were to include the original bill of lading. Should the original bill were not available at the moment of discharge, it was agreed that a letter of indemnity countersigned by Ultramar was admissible. Title and risk were to pass as the oil passed the ship's intake at the port of loading. The cargo was shipped on board the *Captain Gregos*, which had been chartered by a sister company of PEAG. The charter was on the Asbatankvoy form and contemplated discharge against a letter of indemnity issued by a P&I Club. PEAG happened to sell the cargo to the third defendants (British Petroleum), who as ultimate buyers took delivery at Rotterdam. As per their contract, risk and property were to pass to BP when the documents were delivered or at the moment the ship entered dutch waters. Discharging the goods at BP's refinery complex in Rotterdam required the active co-operation of the crew. The documents were not available at that time and the shipowners (Compañía Portorafti) accepted to release the cargo against a letter of indemnity furnished by BP. On June 17, 1985, there were claims for short-delivery shortly after discharge, but the official complaint was not lodged until later on that year. On June 28, 1987, the shipowners issued a summons seeking a declaration that the cargo claims were time-barred under art. III(6) of the Hague-Visby Rules. The question was whether the cargo owners were parties to the contract evidenced by the bill of lading (which indeed incorporated the Rules), or they were parties to a bailment to the shipowners.

***Held:*** **i)** Taking into account that the discharge was carried out with the active co-operation of both BP and the crew of the vessel, Bingham, L.J. said: *"Against the background we have described there would seem to us very powerful grounds for concluding that it is necessary to imply a contract between BP and the shipowners to give business reality to the transaction between them and create obligations which, as we think, both parties believed to exist; As between the shipowners and BP we are of the opinion that in all the circumstances it is appropriate to imply a contract"*. On that ground, their lordships concluded that: *"…if a contract is to be implied its terms must be those of the contract of carriage which, by operation of law, incorporated the Hague-Visby Rules"*.[50] **ii)** The

---

[50] See *Brandt. v. Liverpool, Brazil and River Plate S.N. Co.* and *The Dona Mari (No.2)*. Bingham, L.J.: *"…the position of BP differs from that of the plaintiffs in The Aramis in at least two respects relevant when considering whether a contract should be implied: first, BP were the Owners of the cargo before discharge began; and, secondly, BP have clearly and explicitly consented to the carriage of the goods on terms incorporating any of the charterparty conditions normally in use for tankships, which would include the Hague-Visby Rules"*.

submission that PEAG became assignees of Ultramar's rights and duties under a contract of bailment in the bill of lading was rejected by the court. Bingham, L.J. said: *"[T]itle passed to PEAG on shipment, at which time the bills had not yet been issued and Ultramar had not become the named consignee and had no rights against the shipowners to assign, at any rate under the bills; Since nothing passed between Ultramar and PEAG on shipment, any assignment could only have been by operation of law"*. As a conclusion, BP was bound by the terms of the bill of lading and thus was subject to the one-year time bar of the Hague-Visby Rules, but PEAG was not.


## 53
## COMPTOIR D'ACHAT ET DE VENTE V. LUIS DE RIDDER LIMITADA
*(The Julia)*
1949, A.C. 293 (H.L.)

Under "c.i.f. Antwerp" terms contained in Form no. 41 of the London Corn Association, a cargo of grain was sold by argentine sellers/charterers to belgian buyers. The contract stipulated payment "on first presentation of and in exchange for bill of lading…and/or delivery order, and policy/certificate of insurance". It was agreed that the sellers were to pay for any deficiency in the condition and quantity of the goods occurred up to the arrival, and that sellers were responsible of all cargo averages. The buyers paid against tender of an insurance certificate and a delivery order at Antwerp issued by the sellers. Although it referred to a c.i.f. sale, the delivery order stated "release

after payment of the freight", so that the buyers decided to deduct the freight from the total c.i.f. price invoiced. The charterparty recognised no other port than Antwerp. While the vessel *Julia* (on which the goods were shipped) was still en route, the germans invaded Belgium and occupied the town. With no consent from the buyers, the sellers/charterers and the shipowners agreed to discharge at Lisbon, where the grain was sold by the formers to a third party. It became obvious that the delivery order could not be implemented by the buyers at Antwerp. The buyers claimed the total reimbursement of the sum paid.

***Held (for the buyers):*** **i)** (Lord Porter) *"The obligations imposed on a seller under a c.i.f. contract are well known, and in the ordinary case, include the tender of a bill of lading covering the goods contracted to be sold and no others, coupled with an insurance policy in the normal form and accompanied by an invoice which shows the price and, as in this case, usually contains a deduction of the freight which the buyer pays before delivery at the port of discharge. Against tender of these documents the purchaser must pay the price. In such a case the property may pass either on shipment or on tender, the risk generally passes on shipment or as from shipment, but possession does not pass until the documents which represent the goods are handed over in exchange for the price. In the result, the buyer, after receipt of the documents, can claim against the ship for breach of the contract of carriage and against the underwriters for any loss covered by the policy. The strict form of c.i.f. contract may, however, be modified. A provision that a delivery order may be sub-*

*stituted for a bill of lading or a certificate of insurance for a policy would not, I think, make the contract be concluded on something other than c.i.f. terms."* **ii)** The main question here was whether the buyers paid for the documents as representing the goods or for the delivery of the goods themselves. Their lordships held that the buyers were entitled to the return of the purchase price on the ground that *"payment was not made for the documents but as an advance payment for a contract afterwards to be performed"*. The property and possession of the goods remained on the sellers and the delivery order did not confer any contractual rights against the carrier.[51] Furthermore, the sellers expressly made themselves responsible in the contract for all the risks until delivery to the buyers. The contract was in law an arrival contract, or more accurately, a contract for delivery of the goods in Antwerp.[52] The sellers were not capable to deliver the goods to the buyers and thus were not entitled to the price. The rule "res perit domino" should be applied against the sellers.

---

[51] A *cargo delivery order* does not give the buyer a direct right against the carrier, nor does render the buyer liable to the shipowner for demurrage (*see Tradax Internacional S.A. v. Pagnan, R. & Fratelli*, 1968, 1 Lloyd's Rep. 244). On the contrary, a *ship's delivery order* generally gives the holder a direct right of action against the carrier and therefore is within the scope of true c.i.f. contracts. In this regard, see the Carriage of Goods by Sea Act 1992, sections 1(4), 2(1) and 5(1).
[52] See *The Aliakmon*, where an original (shipment) c. & f. contract turned into an ex warehouse (arrival) contract by a further agreement of the parties. See also *Holland Colombo Trading Society Ltd. v. Segu Mohamed Khaja Alawdeen*, 1954, 2 Lloyd's Rep. 45 (P.C.).

## 54
## Congimex Companhia Geral de Comercio Importadora e. Exportadora v. Tradax Export S.A.
### 1983, 1 Lloyd's Rep. 250 (C.A.)

The plaintiffs purchased 16,500 tons of soya bean meal c.i.f. Lisbon (Portugal) free out from the defendants. The cargo was to be shipped in four monthly instalments, three of which were each payable by letters of credit and the last one by cash against documents in New York (USA). The price was agreed on an outturn basis according to the weighing and sampling at Lisbon. The contracts incorporated GAFTA Form No. 100 and were subject to english law. The initial two shipments were performed and paid. It happened that the Portuguese Ministry of Agriculture issued a directive whereby the imports of soya bean were restricted and subject to the state concern. As a result, the buyers were unable to obtain an import license (i.e. B.R.I., Boletin de Registro de Importaçao) even though they made their best efforts to. The sellers tendered documents for the balance of the cargo but the buyers rejected them. The sellers then declared the buyers in default on the ground that the buyers had failed to open the letter of credit and had refused to take delivery. The buyers contended that (i) they were excused from further performance, (ii) the contract had been frustrated under portuguese law, and (iii) the commercial object of the contract had been destroyed.

***Held (for the sellers):* i)** Although the buyers' submitted that they were excused from further performance because as –they said-there was an implied term that they would use due diligence to obtain all necessary licenses, their lordships found that they were not indeed as no such term could be implied in the contract. **ii)** Concerning the allegation of frustration, Sir John Donaldson, M.R. said: *"It is important to bear in mind the nature of a classic c.i.f. contract. It is a contract for the sale of documents representing goods which are (a) laden upon a vessel and (b) the subject matter of a contract for their carriage to the contractual destination. It is not a contract for the sale of goods at or guaranteed to arrive at the contractual destination. Given that the sale contract was governed by English law and that payment was to be in New York, if this had been a classic c.i.f. contract the only aspect which could be affected by Portuguese law was the performance of the contract of affreightment; However these sale contracts were not in fact on classic c.i.f. terms. There was the modification that the price was to be related to delivered weights and that there should be weighing and sampling at Lisbon. Whilst it is quite clear that the change in the Portuguese import regulations made it impossible for either weighing or sampling to take place after importation, it is not found that either was prohibited if delivery at Lisbon was for the purpose of reshipment or transhipment to a non-Portuguese destination".* **iii)** (Sir John Donaldson, M.R.) *"This leaves only the submission that the whole commercial object of the contracts had been destroyed. The short answer to this is that frustrated expectations and intentions of one party to a contract do not necessarily or indeed usually lead to the frustration of that contract and that the board's findings that the buyers should have considered reselling the goods impliedly negatives this submission."*

## 55
## CONTIGROUP COMPANIES INC. V. GLENCORE A.G.
### 2005, 1 Lloyd's Rep. 241 (Q.B.)

In this action the claimant, Contigroup Companies, Inc. (Contichem') claims the unpaid balance of the price of a cargo of butane that it sold to the Defendant, Glencore A.G. (Glencore) in 2002. Glencore resold the cargo to an associated company, Glencore International A.G. (Glencore International') which, in turn, resold it to Petrochina Zhejiang Huadian Resource Co. Ltd. (Petrochina'). Under the terms of the sale contract (and the sub-sale to Glencore International) the cargo should have reached Wenzhou in Eastern China by 10 June 2002; and under the sub-sale contract with Petrochina delivery was to take place by 12 June 2002. In fact the cargo reached Wenzhou and started unloading on 15 June 2002. Petrochina claimed against Glencore International in respect of the delay, and that claim was settled for US$172,899.67. The question for me is whether Glencore is entitled to a like sum in damages against Contichem, which it can set off against Contichem's claim.

***Held:*** (Glick, Q.C.): In determining whether Glencore could recover a loss resulting from late delivery by Contichem, the Court first determined whether there was an available market for butane on 10 June 2002 for it would be difficult for Glencore to argue that its loss could have been any more than the additional cost of obtaining that substitute. The Court accepted the strenuous efforts Glencore and Glencore International had made to acquire a substitute cargo and Contichem's expert evidence failed to establish that there were cargoes of butane, whether in port or afloat, that were available for purchase or exchange and that were available for delivery to Wenzhou prior to the arrival of the Sunway. Subsequently, the Court held that there had been no relevant available market for butane at the end of May or in early June. The Court then enquired into the extent to which the reduction in price offered by Glencore in the settlement was referable to Petrochina's claim for delay and whether the settlement was reasonable. The Court held that the amount abated was calculated by reference to, and was solely referable to, Petrochina's claim for lost profit arising from the delay in delivering the butane, although the settlement covered any claim Petrochina might have arising from the failure to deliver propane, including any claim relating to customs duty. In terms of reasonableness, evidence indicated that Petrochina was selling butane as fast as it could import it and as a result, three or four days' sales that would otherwise have been made were lost as a result of the delayed delivery. Because Petrochina would have been able to establish a claim for at least the sum for which it settle before an arbitral tribunal had the dispute gone to arbitration, the Court head that the settlement was reasonable. The proper measure of damages in the absence of an available market was argued to be the difference between the value of the cargo at the time when it should have been delivered and its value at the time of actual delivery by Contichem. The Court found this basis of calculation to be entirely artificial and held that: *"The*

*loss suffered by Petrochina and passed back ultimately to Glencore did not result from any change in the value of butane. It resulted from Petrochina being short of butane and as a result losing profits. The question is whether Glencore can recover damages for having compensated Petrochina for this loss".* The Court answered this question in the affirmative because it was contemplated by the parties that, if delivery was delayed, Glencore would have to compensate a sub-buyer for any loss including loss of profit it suffered as a result of that delay, Glencore did have to compensate the sub-buyer, the compensation was provided by the settlement which was wholly referable to the delay and the settlement was itself reasonable.

**56**

**CO-OPERATIVE CENTRALE
RAIFFEISEN-BOERENLEENBANK
(RABOBANK NEDERLAND) V.
THE SUMITOMO BANK LTD.**
*(The Royan)*
1988, 2 Lloyd's Rep. 250 (C.A.)

Farmers in Holland sold to egyptian buyers a large quantity of natural butter oil to be shipped on four vessels, one of which was named *Royan.* A confirmed irrevocable letter of credit was opened in favour of the sellers. The letter of credit called for payment of the 90% of the price against documents under the credit and the remainder 10% within sixty days after discharge. When the documents of the *Royan* shipment were tendered several discrepancies were found. The sellers' bank arranged with the confirming bank a guarantee covering the latter in case that the documents were rejected by the issuing bank. Under this guarantee, the 90% instalment was paid to the beneficiary under reserve on Oct. 22, 1982. It happened that the issuing bank rejected the documents by sending to the confirming bank a telex saying "please, consider these documents at your disposal until we received our Principal's instructions concerning the discrepancies". The confirming bank decided to claim from the seller's bank reimbursement of the sums paid under reserve, but they did not offer to hold the documents at the seller's bank disposal nor returned them as required by what is now art. 14(e) of the UCP 500 (1993 Rev.). The documents were thereafter rectified by the sellers and re-tendered beyond the expiry date of the credit. On Nov. 30, 1982, the issuing bank telexed the confirming bank advising that the buyers had "lifted" the discrepancies for the first shipment documents and authorized the 90% payment. On Dec 22 1982, payment of the third shipment was also authorised. On Jan. 6 1983, the second and fourth shipments' payment were authorised as well. Regarding the period lapsed between Oct. 22 and Nov. 30, the confirming bank decided to deduct the interests out of the 90% paid from the 10% remaining before paying it to the sellers' bank. The sellers' bank then sued the confirming bank for such deduction.

**Held (for the confirming bank): i)** The issuing bank's telex was not a conditional holding of documents at the presenter's disposal and thus was valid under art. 8(c). The words *"until we received our principal's instructions"* were an expression of hope that the parties might come to some agreement, but not an expression o a condition. **ii)** The sellers, by re-tendering the documents (as amended) beyond the expiry date were indeed asking the buyers to extend the credit and the Buyers by this conduct so accepted it. **iii)** The sellers' bank, insofar issued a guarantee against payment under reserve, were "assuming full responsibility for discrepancies" and, therefore, for the interests arising or resulting from the consequences of such discrepancies.[53] The confirming bank were entitled to recover interest for the period between the first tender of documents in Oct. 22, 1982, and the acceptance of the fresh tender on Nov. 30. **iv)** However, the confirming bank was not allowed to recover interest from the period subsequent to Nov. 30, 1982. The court found that the loss suffered by the confirming bank was due to the unreasonable time spent by the issuing bank in examining and finally accepting the documents rather than to the discrepancies themselves. Therefore, the sellers' bank was not liable under the terms of their guarantee for that delay in accepting the documents after Nov. 30, 1982.

**57**
**CPC Consolidated Pool Carriers GmbH v. CTM Cia. Trasmediterranea S.A.**
*(The CPC Gallia)*
1994, 1 Lloyd's Rep. 68 (Q.B.D.)

The plaintiffs (CPC) were the owners of the vessel *CPC Gallia* and the defendants

---

[53] See *Banque de L'Indochine et de Suez S.A. v. J.H. Rayner (Mincing Lane) Ltd.*

(CTM) a spanish state-owned shipping company operating ferry services between mainland Spain, the Balearics and the Canaries. Negotiations took place between Hamburg brokers (Meridian) acting for CTM and German brokers (Senator) acting on behalf of CPC. They concerned a contract of carriage from Kobe (Kapan) to Las Palmas (Spain) of a high-speed passenger craft which had been manufactured in Japan and sold to CTM. Owing to its size and weight, it was not possible to carry the jet by a standard cargo vessel, and a special vessel like the *CPC Gallia* was needed. In the course of the negotiations, CPC's brokers sent a telex with a long list of terms including a London arbitration clause and the following phrase: *"Conline booking note – subject to details/logical amendments"*. Matters broke down though in a dispute over the form of Conline booking note to be used and the clause 6 of the standard bills of lading headed *"Substitution of Vessel, Transhipment and Forwarding"*, which CTM wanted to be deleted. CPC took the view that a binding agreement had been concluded and that CTM was not allowed to depart from it. CTM contended that the Conline booking note "subject to details/logical amendments" was not meant to be a firm agreement. CPC declared arbitration and CTM challenged the existence of a valid arbitration agreement.

***Held (for CTM):***[54] (Potter, J.) The words "subject to details" meant that a formal contract was to be drawn up on the Conline booking note form, but that there

would be no concluded contract until agreement had been reached on the detailed provisions of the form. Referring to the message sent by CPC's brokers Mr. J. Potter said: *"The text of that telex was at best ambiguous for the purpose relied on, in that it plainly asserted that the deletion sought was a 'detail of the contract' as well as relying on the 'no transhipment' agreement as justifying such deletion. The message most clearly to be derived from looking at the negotiations as a whole is that the parties plainly did not regard them as contractually complete, or consider that the details had been finally agreed at the time Meridian proffered their suggested form of the booking note; after that, it is equally plain that no agreement was reached on the appropriate (amended) form of cl. 6; I therefore refuse the application for a declaration that there was a valid binding contract concluded between the parties and, since the application for appointment of an arbitrator depends upon an arbitration agreement asserted only by reason of such contract, that application must also fail"*.


### 58
### Credit Agricole Indosuez v. Muslim Commercial Bank Ltd.
2000, 1 Lloyd's Rep. 275 (C.A.)

Forbes Reiss Ltd. of Liverpool (sellers) agreed to sell to Ihsan Cotton Products (Pte.) Ltd. of Lahore (buyers) a cargo of Iranian raw cotton for shipment from Jabel Ali Dubai Seaport to Lahore, via Karachi in Pakistan. Payment of the price was to be made by letter of credit. On 5 Sept.. 1997 Muslim Commercial Bank Ltd. of Lahore (MCB) issued their let-

---

[54] The whole decision is referred to *The Junior K.*

ter of credit at the request of buyers. The letter of credit was confirmed by Credit Agricole Indosuez of London (CAI) at the request of MCB. Clause 9 of the letter of credit provided the following: "Original documents along with eight copies each of invoice, packing list, weight and measurement list, Bill of Lading and certificate of origin should be sent to us by courier at the cost of beneficiary". On 6 Oct.1997 sellers sent the confirming bank a letter with a bill of exchange for USD 262,869.39 and a set of documents required by the letter of credit enclosed thereto. CAI accepted the bill of exchange and paid sellers the following day. CAI then forwarded the documents to MCB, who on 13 Oct. replied stating that the documents were defective in a number of respects. More particularly, MCB had not received the weight and measurement list and the certificate of origin, which they argued was necessary. CAI tried to obtain the requested documents, but failed. On 11 Nov. 1997, MCB returned the original documents to CAI. CAI then claimed from MCB the sum of USD 262,869.39 by way of damages and other remedies. Summary judgment was granted to CAI, with damages to be assessed. MCB appealed. The issue before the Court was whether the weight and measurement list and the certificate of origin were essential documents against which negotiation and payment were agreed to be made under the terms of the letter of credit, or whether they were merely documents to be forwarded after negotiation had taken place.

***Held (for CAI):*** Under Article 5 of the UCP 500, letters of credit must state precisely what documents are required

for payment. On examining the letter of credit issued by MCB, there appeared the heading: "Documents required are marked (X) below". Below, there were six boxes, four of which were marked with an "X". However, the weight and measurement list and the certificate of origin did not appear under this heading. There then appeared a section with the heading "Other conditions", followed by a typewritten section filling more than half the letter of credit titled "Special Conditions", which listed eighteen different items which were described as "*a hotchpotch or amalgam of terms that require documents to be provided, terms as to what documents should contain, terms as to performance of the sale contract, terms as to performance of the letter of credit contract and terms which may or may not be one of those things*". Straughton L.J. noted the problem of understanding all eighteen provisions and concluded: "*It seems to me that the letter of credit leaves one in genuine doubt as to whether cl. 9 is stating that the documents which it refers to are stipulated documents, essential to the operation of the credit. It certainly does not, as required by art. 5(b), state precisely that a weight and measurement list, and a certificate of origin, are documents against which payment or negotiation is to be made. I would therefore hold, in agreement with the judge, on the construction of the letter of credit that Credit Agricole were entitled to payment*". In respect to the rule that the ambiguity in a letter of credit is to be construed against the issuing bank and in favour of a beneficiary or a confirming bank, he held: "*But in terms of commerce the confirming bank is the correspondent of the issuing bank, and acts for the issuing bank in order to do what the issuing bank is not present to do for itself. That is in my respectful opinion sufficient to attract the rule that an agent is to be excused for acting on a reasonable, even if ultimately wrong, interpretation of his principal instructions".* Gibson L.J. added: *"[T]he letter of credit must be construed against MCB. The relevant principle was stated by Lord Diplock in Commercial Banking Co. of Sydney v. Jalsard Pty. Ltd., [1972] 2 Lloyd's Rep. 529 at 533; [1973] A.C. 279 at p. 283 in the passage cited by Sir Christopher Staughton. That shows that even though a Court might arrive at a different construction, the banker can safely act upon a reasonable construction of ambiguous or unclear terms. I cannot say that CAI's construction of the letter of credit was unreasonable, nor do I think it should be held liable because it did not make enquiry before payment".*

# 59
## CREMER (PETER) WESTFAELISCHE CENTRAL GENOSSENSCHAFT GMBH AND INTERGRAAN N.V. v. GENERAL CARRIERS S.A.
### (The Dona Mari)
1973, 2 Lloyd's Rep. 366 (Q.B.)

Two parcels of tapioca in bulk were sold c.i.f. Bremen. The sale contract contained the following clause: "Quality. Guarantee…Moisture max. 14%. The buyers have the right to reject the parcel should the analysis show…moisture more than 14%. Shipped quality and analysis to be final as per certificate issued by R. Schaller…Bangkok/Thailand". A certificate was issued by R. Schaller according to which the analysis of the samples showed a moisture level of 12.77% and 13.74%. The parcels were shipped at Bangkok and the vessel proceeded to Bremen (Germany). The mate's receipts were endorsed with the words "not quite dry", but the issued bills of lading were clean and contained the statement "shipped in good order and condition". The sellers indorsed the bills of lading corresponding to one parcel to the buyers, who indeed paid the price of the goods. The bills of lading relating to the other parcel were presented to the carrier in return of two ship's delivery orders incorporating the terms of the bills of lading. When the buyers took delivery of that parcel, they found it moist and claimed damages against the carrier. The carrier contended that (1) any damage was due to the condition of the cargo prior to loading, (2) they were not estopped by the statement of the bills of lading as the buyer was bound to rely on the final certificate only, and (3) the buyers did not have title to sue neither in contract nor in tort since, right before delivery, they were not the owners of any part of the undivided bulk.

***Held (for the buyers):*** (Kerr, J.) **i)** The statement "shipped in good order and condition" is a representation of fact that cannot be reversed by proof of contrary by the carrier. If the bills of lading had stated the true condition of the goods, the buyers would had been entitled to reject the documents under the terms of the contract of sale. To this effect it was irrelevant that the results showed in the final certificate met the sale specifications. **ii)** The buyers were entitled to rely on the estoppel created by the bills of lading as against the carriers. *"A contract incorporating the terms of the bills of lading was to be implied between the plaintiffs and the defendants by reason of the payment of the freight by the plaintiffs and the delivery of the goods by the defendants against the bill of lading; …the plaintiffs in Brandt v. Liverpool, Brazil, River Plate S.N. Co. had also not been the owners at any time (as required by sec. 1, Bills of Lading Act 1855) but they (nevertheless) succeeded in contract".* The fact that the buyer, in the present case, took delivery against a ship's delivery order (instead of a bill of lading) did not prevent him from acquiring the same rights as if he had taken it against a bill of lading. **iii)** The buyers had a good cause of action against the carriers for breach of the contract of carriage. The buyers' right to claim damages for breach of contract was in no way prejudiced by the fact that, prior to delivery, they were not the owners of any part of the undivided bulk. Judgement was for the plaintiffs with interest at 7½ per cent.

**60**

**DAEWOO HEAVY INDUSTRIES LTD. AND ANOTHER V. KLIPRIVER SHIPPING LTD. AND ANOTHER**

(*The Kapitan Petko Voivoda*)
2003, 2 Lloyd's Rep. 1 (C.A.)

A contract of carriage for 3thirty four new excavators from Inchon (Korea) to Istanbul (Turkey), was concluded subject to Conline terms. These contained a General Paramount clause (cl.2) which incorporated the Hague Rules. The excavators were stowed and lashed under-

deck at Inchon for carriage to Istanbul in apparent good order and condition. Six bills of lading were issued in respect to the shipment incorporating the Conline terms, none of which stated that the excavators were stowed on deck. On arrival at Xingang (China), en route to Istanbul, twenty six of the excavators were offloaded and then re-stowed on deck. The vessel departed from Xingang and encountered heavy weather in the Yellow Sea two days later resulting in eight of the excavators being lost overboard and damage to other excavators. The cargo owners sought damages against the shipowners.

***Held (for the charterers):*** Although the owners decision to stow the excavators on deck was found to be in breach of the contract, the Court held that they were entitled to rely on the limitation of liability provided by in Article IV of the Hague Rules. Having established that the problem was one of contract construction, the Court focused on the words "in any event" in Art. IV(5) which have their most natural meaning of "in every case", whether or not the breach of contract is particularly serious, and whether or not the cargo was stowed under deck". Mr. Justice Langley concluded *"A relevant breach of the seaworthiness obligation will cause a* "palpable risk of damage". *A limitation or exclusion from liability for that breach* "seriously undermines the obligation" *yet it is now established by The* Happy Ranger *that art. IV, r.5 applies to such breach. So also, for the same reasons, must it be the case that it applies to the breach of the obligation to stow on deck".*

## 61
### DAVAL ACIERS D'USINOR ET DE SACILOR v. ARMARE S.R.L.
#### *(The Nerano)*
#### 1996, 1 Lloyd's Rep. 1 (C.A.)

A consignment of steel coils was shipped on board the MV *Nerano* at Fos (France) for carriage to Libya. The bill of lading under which the carriage was effected contained an "identity of carrier" clause whereby the contract of carriage evidenced therein was between the shippers and the shipowners only. On the face of the bill there was a clause (the "arbitration" clause) in capital letters saying: *"The conditions as per relevant charter party dated 02.07.1990 are incorporated in this bill of lading and have precedence if there is a conflict. English law and jurisdiction applies"*. A further cls. 1 at the back stipulated that *"All terms and conditions, liberties, exceptions and arbitration clause of the Charter Party, dated as overleaf, are herewith incorporated"*. The charterparty referred to in the bill was a Gencon voyage charter made between Cargill Int. of Antigua as owners and Korf Shipping of Frankfurt as charterers. It authorized the charterer to issue bills of lading on behalf of the master and required these to be issued with the arbitration clause on their face. The charterparty also contained an arbitration clause in these terms: "That should any dispute arise between the owners and the charterers the matter in dispute should be determined in London (England), according to the Arbitration Acts, 1950 to 1979, and any amendments or modifications thereto, and English law to govern". It happened that some coils were damaged by seawa-

ter and rusting during the carriage. The shippers claimed damages and served a writ on the shipowners, who applied for a stay of the action under sec. 1 of the Arbitration Act, 1975. The shipowners' submission was that, by virtue of the "arbitration clause" and clause 1 of the bill of lading, the arbitration agreement contained in the charterparty had been incorporated as between the shippers and themselves.

***Held (for the shipowners):*** **i)** (Saville L.J.) *"[T]he provision on the front of the bill of lading only incorporates the conditions of the charter-party (which it is common ground would not include the arbitration clause in the charter-party) and the reference to English jurisdiction could (in the absence of any reference to arbitration) only be a reference to the english courts. To my mind, however, once this blinkered approach is discarded and the provision is considered together with cl. 1 in the back of the bill of lading, a different meaning emerges. The provision on the face of the bill of lading does not expressly prohibit the incorporation of terms other than conditions from the charterparty, nor is the reference to English jurisdiction couched in language that excludes an English arbitration agreement, which would ex hypothesi be subject to English jurisdiction."* **ii)** *"In the present case the parties have not merely used general words of incorporation.[55] They have expressly identified and specified the charter-party arbitration clause as something to be incorporated into their contract; ...by identifying and specifying the*

---

[55] See *The Miramar*.

*charter-party arbitration clause it seems to me (Saville L.J.) to be clear that the parties to the bill of lading contract did intend and agree to arbitration, so that to give force to that intention and agreement the words in the clause must be read and construed as applying to those parties."* According to the judgment, the stay was granted and the action dismissed.

## 62
### THE DAVID AGMASHENEBELI
### 2002, EWHC 104 (Q.B.)

A cargo of urea was loaded in Kotka (Finland). The master was asked to issue bills of lading containing a description of the cargo. He honestly did not believe that the draft bills accurately reflected the actual condition of the cargo. According to the master, the urea showed abnormal moisture, colour and contamination. The master claused the Statement of Facts, the Mate's receipt and the bills of lading in the following terms: "Cargo discoloured, also foreign materials (e.g.) plastic, rust, rubber, stone, black particles found in cargo". The shippers could not negotiate the claused bills of lading with the buyers and claimed damages against the shipowner.

**Held:** It was found that the master was overcautious in his description of the cargo. Before clausing the bills, he may have obtained assistance from an expert. However, the court held that the master's general obligation to issue a bill of lading is not a contractual guarantee of "absolute accuracy" as to the order and condition of the cargo. In the present case, there was

no basis for the implication of such duty of "absolutely accuracy" in the charterparty or elsewhere. The master is required to exercise his own judgment on the appearance of the cargo being loaded. There is no separate obligation to call in expert help (a surveyor or other expert with specific knowledge on the cargo). On the evidence, the cargo was not actually contaminated and the master was wrong in clausing the bills. Although a small portion of the cargo was discoloured, the master's clausing was too broad and it should have specified the extent (e.g. by percentage) of cargo being discoloured.

## 63
### DAWSON LINE LTD. V.
### AKTIENGESELLSCHAFT "ADLER" FUER
### CHEMISCHE INDUSTRIE
### 1931, 41 Lloyd's Law Rep. 75 (C.A.)

The mv. *Lady Brenda* loaded a cargo of coal at Berdiansk (Ukraine) in the course of a charter with Ghent (Belgium) as port of discharge. The charterparty contained a clause 14 whereby the freight was payable on the bill of lading weight less 2%.[56] The shippers presented bills of lading for signature but the master was not satisfied with the weight stated therein.

---

[56] This type of clause seeks to avoid retaining the ship at port while the cargo is being weighed. Coal being a cargo which by its nature vary in weight between shipment and delivery, owners let charterers pay freight, neither on the bill of lading weight nor on the delivered weight, but on the bill's weight less 2%. There is no weighting in order to let the ship sail off. The 2% freight deduction is a sort of compensation for any variation of weight that the owner give to the charterers in exchange of letting the ship sail quickly.

According to the draught of the steamer, he calculated that a larger quantity had been loaded and issued a letter of protest making the receivers (and charterers) responsible for the freight on the total quantity discharged at Ghent. On that basis, he agreed to sign bills of lading as presented mentioning "Weight, quality and quantity unknown to me" at the bottom. Upon discharge an official weighing was ordered, the outturn being lesser than the quantity showed in the bills of lading. After the weighing, the ship was allowed to sail. The charterers admitted then that the weight stated in the bills of lading was inaccurate. They accepted to pay freight upon the official outturn weight, but deducted therefrom the 2%. The owners challenged the charterers' position and claimed that they were entitled to cash the 2% deduction too.

***Held (for the owners):*** **i)** As a general rule, the shipper is the charterer's agent to supply the cargo and to present the bills of lading. If the shipper presents inaccurate bills, the charterer (as principal) has to indemnify and make good any loss the owner may suffer as a result of the shipper's fault.[57] **ii)** In so far the ship had to remain at Ghent until the result of the official weighing was known, there was not any saving of time for the owners and therefore clause 14 lost its efficacy. According to the judgment, the owners were entitled to recover the 2% deduction.

---

[57] See *The Boukadora*. See also similar decisions of the House of Lords in *Elder, Dempster & Co. v. Dunn & Co.*, 15 Com. Cas. 49 and *Kruger & Co. Ltd. v. Moel Tryvan Ship Co. Ltd.* [1907] A.C. 272 (H.L.).

## 64
### DEICHLAND, THE
1989, 2 Lloyd's Rep. 113 (C.A.)

In Jan. 1986 the plaintiffs' cargo of steel coils was shipped on board the "Deichland" at Glasgow for a carriage to La Spezia. At that time the ship was on demise charter to Deich Navigation S.A. (the "defendants"), a company based in Germany. After discharge at La Spezia, the coils were found wet-stained and rusted. On Jan. 30, 1987, the plaintiffs issued a writ in rem against the ship. On Nov. 23, the writ was served on the vessel but she was not arrested as the ship's P&I Club provided the plaintiffs with a letter of guarantee. Although the Club's security contained no agreement to jurisdiction, the same was accepted by the plaintiffs and the arrest did not take place. The demise charterers acknowledged service of the writ solely for the purpose of contesting jurisdiction. They subsequently gave notice of motion for an order that the Court had no jurisdiction and that, pursuant to art. 2 of the 1968 Convention on Jurisdiction and the Enforcement of Judgments in Civil and Commercial Matters (as enforced in England through the Civil Jurisdiction and Judgments Act, 1982), they were entitled to be sued in their own domicile. The plaintiffs relied on art. 7 of the 1952 Arrest Convention conferring jurisdiction on the merits to the country in which the arrest would be made, as well as on art. 57 of the 1968 Convention. They also contended that the 1968 Convention was not applicable since the action had been commenced in rem only.

***Held (for the defendants):*** The Court decided that the 1968 Convention had to be applied and the English proceedings stayed. Having considered the wording of the 1952 Arrest Convention as a whole, it was decided that jurisdiction could not be extended to cases where security was given to avoid the arrest. (Stuart-Smith, L.J.) *"I conclude…that jurisdiction is not afforded to the English Court by art. 57 of the 1968 Convention or s. 9(1) of the 1982 Act, except in the case of an arrest; In my judgment the 1982 Act and the 1968 Convention provide a comprehensive code. If a defendant is domiciled in a Contracting State he must be sued in that State unless the case falls within the exceptions contained in sections 2-6 of the 1968 Convention or under the provisions of Article 57, which for the purpose of this case means the 1952 Arrest Convention. Articles 1, 2 3 and 57 are clearly intended as it seems to me to apply to actions in rem."*[58]

## 65
## DGM Commodities Corp. v. Sea Metropolitan S.A.
*(The Andra)*
[2012] EWHC 1984 (Comm)

The vessel *Andra* was chartered under a voyage charterparty on the Gencon form for the carriage of a cargo of frozen chicken to St. Petersburg (Russia). During discharge, it was found that the cargo in hold no. 2 was contaminated by gasoil leaking from a bunker tank. Discharging was suspended by an order of the Veterinary Service. The receivers demanded a cash settlement of USD 2 million in relation to the damaged cargo. Owners offered security for the cargo claim in the form of a P and I Club letter of undertaking, or a letter of undertaking from the owners' parent company. Receivers were, however, unwilling to accept security for the claim and insisted on being paid a sum in settlement of the claim. In the meantime, they did not take any further steps to discharge the cargo from hold no. 2. This remained their stance throughout the vessel's stay at St Petersburg until the owners' agreed to pay a cash sum in Oct. 2008. All in all, it ultimately took more than six months to complete discharge in St Petersburg. Thereafter, owners claimed over USD 3 million in demurrage. Charterers argued that the cause of the delay was the order of the Veterinary Service, which prohibited discharge and that, since this was beyond the control of either party, the charter had been frustrated

***Held (for owners):*** The matter was first brought to arbitration and, subsequently, to Court. The award identified the "real reason for the continued failure to discharge the cargo" as being the receivers' conduct in relation to the cargo claim. However, it is clear from the findings made by the arbitrators, taken as a whole, that what was being said was that the Veterinary Service's order prevented discharge throughout the relevant period. This and no other was the

---

[58] As to the applicability of the 1968 Convention to an action in rem while it remains solely in rem, Neill, L.J. said: *"…I find it impossible to conclude that on the proper construction of arts. 2 and 3 of the 1968 Convention, Deich are not being 'sued' in these proceedings. Even though at this stage the proceedings are solely in rem, Deich are liable to be adversely affected by the result of the proceedings and wish to contest the merits of the plaintiffs' claim; I do not consider…that the rules relating to such actions and governing the rights of a plaintiff to levy execution can affect the substance of a matter when the Court is faced with an international Convention designed to regulate the international jurisdiction of national Courts".*

immediate cause of the delay in discharging the cargo because the cargo could not be discharged whilst the order remained in place. However, what the arbitrators found was that the real and effective cause of that order remaining in place, and not being lifted, was the receivers' unwillingness to procure its lifting because of their conduct in relation to the cargo claim. Had the receivers wished to have the order lifted at an earlier stage and to resume discharge so earlier, they would have been able to do so. Thus, the receivers' conduct was ultimately the real reason for the cargo not being discharged. The failure to discharge by the receivers prevented the charterers from relying on what would otherwise be a frustrating event. Such failure was to be treated as self-induced frustration. On this basis, charterers were not relieved from the obligation to pay demurrage.

**66**

**D**UBAI **E**LECTRICITY **C**O. V. **I**SLAMIC **R**EPUBLIC OF **I**RAN **S**HIPPING **L**INES
*(The Iran Vojdan)*
1984, 2 Lloyd's Rep. 380 (Q.B.D.)

In Dec. 1979 a cargo of steel drums of electric cable were loaded on the MV *Iran Vojdan* at Hamburg (Germany) for a carriage to Dubai. A bill of lading was issued providing a clause 2(a) whereby the carrier held an option to declare (i) Iranian law and exclusive jurisdiction of the courts in Teheran, or (ii) German law with exclusive jurisdiction of the courts in Hamburg, or (iii) English law with exclusive jurisdiction of the courts in London. A further clause 2(b) prescribed that, in case that the agreement contained in section 2(a) were not

recognised by the law of the country in which the suit was filed, then the Hague Rules as enacted in that country should apply. During the voyage, the vessel encountered heavy weather and some drums shifted in the holds and were damaged. Once at Dubai, the consignees of the cargo rejected the damaged drums and served a writ on the shipowners claiming damages. The shipowners applied to stay the action on the grounds that there was an exclusive jurisdiction clause under which any dispute was to be tried in the courts of Hamburg and that German law was the applicable one. Alternatively, they contended that english courts, as tried by the consignees, were forum non conveniens. The main issues were to determine the proper law of the contract and the applicable jurisdiction to hear the dispute.

***Held (for the consignees):*** (Bingham, J.)
**i)** Although the law with which the contract had its closest and most real connection was german law, the agreement contained in cl. 2(a) would be treated (by german law) as invalid because the conditions were not decipherable. **ii)** It was accepted then that iranian (and not german) law was the proper law to the contract. On the assumption that iranian law was the same as english law, it was found too that clause 2(a) was invalid as it envisaged what is known as a "floating proper law". As a matter of english law, that clause had no effect.[59] In words of Bingham J.: "*The proper law is something so fundamental to questions relating to the formation, validity, interpre-*

---

[59] See *Armar Shipping Co. Ltd. v. Caisse Algerienne d'Assurance et de Reassurance.*

*tation and performance of a contract that it must…be built into the fabric of the contract from the start and cannot float in an indeterminate way until finally determined at the option of one party"*. **iii)** As to the choice of jurisdiction, Bingham J. said this was so intimately connected with the choice of law that, if the choice of law falls, the choice of jurisdiction should fall too. *"…it is artificial and unreal to give effect to the ancillary provision while rejecting the main provision to which it is, as I* (Bingham, J.) *think, parasitic. Accordingly, I reach the conclusion that this must be treated as a case in which there is no exclusive jurisdiction, applying the principles of English law on the assumption that that is the same as Iranian law"*. **iv)** As far as the shipowners' allegation of "forum non conveniens" is concerned, after reviewing all the factors of the case, Bingham J. found there was no clear balance one way or the other. *"There are some factors tending in one direction and some in the other, but I certainly do not conclude…that the defendants show a forum which is clearly more appropriate than the forum in England. This is, after all, the place in which the defendants then administered their European business and I can see no great inconvenience or expense or difficulty to them in defending their action here."* According to these four points, the application for a stay was dismissed.

**67**

**Eco Swiss China Time Ltd. v. Benetton International NV**
01.06.1999, Case C-126/97
(European Court of Justice)

On July 1, 1986, Benetton in Amsterdam (Neetherlands) concluded a licensing agreement for a period of eight years with Eco Swiss based in Hong Kong, and Bulova Watch Company in New York (USA). Under the agreement, Benetton granted Eco Swiss the right to manufacture watches and clocks bearing the words "Benetton by Bulova", which then would be sold by Eco Swiss and Bulova. The agreement contained a clause whereby all disputes between the parties would be settled by arbitration in accordance with the rules of the Netherlands Institute of Arbitrators and that the applicable law would be Netherlands law. It happened that Benetton gave notice of the termination of the agreement three years before the end of the original period. The parties commenced arbitration proceedings in relation to the termination and Benetton was awarded to pay USD 23.750,000 to Eco Swiss and 2.800,000 to Bulova for damages and loss due to wrongful termination. Benetton applied to the courts of Netherlands for annulment of the award on the ground, inter alia, that it was contrary to public policy within the meaning of art. 1065(1) of the Netherlands Code of Civil Procedure by virtue of the nullity of the licensing agreement under article 81 (ex article 85) of the EC Treaty. Nevertheless, it was admitted that submission had never raised before during the arbitration. The matter reached the Hoge Raad der Nederlanden (i.e. Supreme Court of the Netherlands), which referred to the European Court of Justice five questions for a preliminary ruling on the interpretation of art. 81 (ex art. 85).

***Held (after the opinion of the General Advocate A. Saggio): Question 2:*** Whether a national court to which application is made for annulment of an arbitration award must grant such an application where, in its view, that award is in fact contrary to Article 81 EC (ex Article 85) although, under domestic procedural rules, it may grant such an application only on a limited number of grounds, one of them being inconsistency with public policy. *"According to Article 3(g) of the EC Treaty (now, after amendment, Article 3(1)(g) EC), Article 81 EC (ex Article 85) constitutes a fundamental provision which is essential for the accomplishment of the tasks entrusted to the community and, in particular, for the functioning of the internal market. The importance of such a provision led the framers of the treaty to provide expressly, in Article 81(2) EC (ex Article 85(2)), that any agreements or decisions prohibited pursuant to that article are to be automatically void. It follows that where its domestic rules of procedure require a national court to grant an application for annulment of an arbitration award where such an application is founded on failure to observe national rules of public policy, it must also grant such an application where it is founded on failure to comply with the prohibition laid down in Article 81(1) EC (ex Article 85(1)). That conclusion is not affected by the fact that the New York Convention of 10 June 1958 on the Recognition and Enforcement of Foreign Arbitral Awards, which had been ratified by all the member states, provides that recognition and enforcement of an arbitration award may be refused only on certain specific grounds, namely where the award does not fall within the terms of the submission to arbitration or goes beyond its scope, where the award is not binding on the parties or where recognition or enforcement of the award would be contrary to the public policy of the country where such recognition and enforcement are sought (Article V(1)(c) and (e) and II(b) of the New York Convention). For the reasons stated…above, the provisions of Article 81 EC (ex Article 85) may be regarded as a matter of public policy within the meaning of the New York Convention; The answer to be given to the second question must therefore be that a national court to which application is made for annulment of an arbitration award must grant that application if it considers that the award in question is in fact contrary to Article 81 EC (ex Article 85), where its domestic rules of procedure require it to grant an application for annulment founded on failure to observe national rules of public policy."* **Questions 1 and 3:** *"In view of the reply given to the second question, there is no need to answer the first and third questions."* **Questions 4 and 5:** By these questions the referring court was asking whether community law requires a national court to refrain from applying domestic rules of procedure according to which an interim arbitration award in respect of which no application for annulment has been made within the prescribed time-limit acquires the force of res judicata, and may no longer be called in question by a subsequent arbitration award. *"Community law does not require a national court to refrain from applying domestic rules of procedure according to which an interim arbitration award which is in the nature of a final award and in respect of which no application for annulment has been made within the prescribed time-limit acquires de force of res judicata and may no longer be called in question by a subsequent arbitration award, even if this is necessary in order to examine, in proceedings for an-*

nulment of a subsequent arbitration award, whether an agreement which the interim award held to be valid in law is nevertheless void under Article 81 EC (ex Article 85)."

## 68
### ED & F MAN LTD. V. NIGERIAN SWEETS & CONFECTIONERY CO.
### 1977, 2 Lloyd's Rep. 50 (C.A.)

The plaintiff sellers sold a quantity of sugar to the defendant buyers. Payment was to be made by letter of credit to be opened at a Swiss bank, most shares of which were owned by the nigerian buyers. The credit was an acceptance credit providing for ninety days' drafts on the bank. The sugar was supplied and the nigerian buyers transferred the purchase price to the Swiss bank. Before the bank transferred the funds to the sellers, the money went into a creditors' voluntary winding up. The sellers claimed the price against the buyers.

***Held (for the sellers):*** The credit operates as a conditional payment, unless the seller and the buyer expressly or impliedly stipulate that it should be an absolute payment. In this decision, Ackner, J. said: *"It follows from the finding that the letters of credit were given only as a conditional payment, that if they were not honoured the (buyers') debt has not been discharged. This is because the buyers promised to pay (by letter of credit), not to provide by letter of credit the source of payment which did not pay... The (buyers') liability to the sellers was a primary liability. This liability was suspended during the period available to the issuing bank to honour the drafts*

*and was activated when the issuing bank failed"*. The letter of credit implied condition was discharged by the insolvency of the intermediary. The sellers were entitled to claim the price from the buyers although these had already transferred the money to the bank.

## 69
### ED & F MAN SUGAR LTD. V. UNICARGO TRANSPORTGESELLSCHAFT MBH
### *(The Ladytramp)*
### [2012] EWHC 2879

The MV *Ladytramp* was chartered for a voyage "1-2 safe berths, 1 safe port (intention Santos) but not south of Paranagua". The charterers declared the load port as Paranagua (Brazil), but, shortly afterwards, a fire at the Paranagua terminal rendered inoperable the conveyor belt system which linked the terminal to the warehouse. Following the fire, the port authority rescheduled the loading or discharging of all vessels. While that occurred, the MV *Ladytramp* arrived at Paranagua and tendered NOR. These events forced her to remain off the port for nearly one month until it was agreed that charterers would use a different berth and loading operations took place therein. After completion, the owners claimed demurrage from the expiry of laytime. The charterers denied responsibility for demurrage because, they said, laytime stopped running during that period. They invoked clause 28 of the charterparty, which provided: "In the event that whilst at the or off the loading place... the loading... of the vessel is prevented or delayed by any of the following occurrences: strikes, riots, civil commotion, lock outs of men, accidents and/or breakdowns on railways, stoppages on railway and/or river and/or canal by ice or frost mechanical breakdowns at mechanical loading plants, government interferences, vessel being inoperative or rendered inoperative due to the terms and conditions of appointment of the Officers and crew time so lost shall not count as laytime". The arbitrators held that clause 28 would only be applicable if a specific terminal had been named in the charterparty. As charterers were entitled to nominate an alternative berth, they were not allowed to rely on clause 28. The charterers decided to appeal the award.

**Held:** The clause was applicable irrespectively of the charterers' option to nominate a different berth. If the charterers had been prevented from loading as a result of fire, there was no reason why the force majeure exceptions clause could not have been used to interrupt laytime. Having said that, the court did not allow charterers to rely on the clause simply because the same did not mention "fires", nor was it easy to see how "mechanical breakdowns at mechanical loading plants "could apply in the present case". As a matter of ordinary language and common sense, the destruction of an item is not within the meaning of the term "breakdown", still less within the term "mechanical". Moreover, clause 28 made reference to *"accidents and/or breakdown on railways"* only. The inclusion of the word "accidents" is intended to broaden the scope of that exception to railways, but not to loading plants.

## 70
### E.L. OLDENDORFF & CO. GMBH. V. TRADAX EXPORT S.A.
*(The Johanna Oldendorff)*
1973, 2 Lloyd's Rep. 285 (H.L.)

The MV *Johanna Oldendorff* was chartered on the Baltimore Berth Grain form C for a carriage of grain in bulk from U.S. to "London or Avonmouth or Glasgow or Belfast or Liverpool/Birkenhead or Hull", at charterers' option. The charterparty provided, inter alia, "Time to count from the first working period on the next day following receipt during ordinary office hours of written notice of readiness to discharge whether in berth or not". charterers nominated Liverpool/Birkenhead as port of discharge. At the time the ship reached the port of Liverpool it was congested and no berths were available. She was then ordered to anchor at the Mersey Bar light-vessel, a usual point where grain ships await open berths but some seventeen miles from the nearest berth but still within the administrative limits of the port. Upon reaching Mersey Bar, the owners sent notice of readiness. A dispute arose as to whether the vessel could be considered an "arrived ship" when she was at the Bar anchorage or only after she reached the berth. The owners claimed that laytime commenced when she was anchored awaiting a berth whereas the charterers argued that laytime started sixteen days later, when she reached the berth.

**Held (for the owners):** (Lord Reid) *"On the whole matter I think that it ought to be made clear that the essential factor is that before a ship can be treated as an arrived* *ship she must be within the port and at the immediate and effective disposition of the charterer and that her geographical position is of secondary importance; but for practical purposes it is so much easier to establish that, if the ship is at a usual waiting place within the port, it can generally be presumed that she is there fully at the charterers' disposal."* Lord Reid concluded: *"Before a ship can be said to have arrived at a port she must, if she cannot proceed immediately to a berth, have reached a position within the port where she is at the immediate and effective disposition of the charterer. If she is at a place where waiting ships usually lie, she will be in such a position unless in some extraordinary circumstances proof of which would lie in the charterer; If the ship is waiting at some other place in the port, then it will be for the owner to prove that she is as fully at the disposition of the charterer as she would have been if in the vicinity of the berth for loading or discharge".*[60] (Lord Morris) *"She was at the charterers' disposal and she was as near to any of the places at which she might discharge as the circumstances permitted her to reach. I think that she was an arrived ship."* (Lord Diplock) *"I would…accept as a convenient practical test as to whether a vessel has completed her loading voyage under a port charter so as*

---

[60] Three conditions must thus be met to consider a vessel as "arrived" within the terms of a "port grain charterparty": (1) she must be within the geographical and legal area of the port in the sense commonly understood by its users; (2) most decisive, she must be at the immediate and effective disposition of the Charterers, which means that she is able to reach the berth shortly after informed that one is vacant -it would be on the shipowners the burden to prove compliance with such requisite; and (3) she must be at the usual berth-waiting place within the port.

*to cast upon the charterer the responsibility for subsequent delay in finding a vacant berth at which her cargo can be loaded or discharged, the test as it is formulated by my noble and learned friend, Lord Reid, at the conclusion of his speech."*

## 71
## EDWARD OWEN ENGINEERING LTD. v. BARCLAYS BANK INTERNATIONAL LTD. AND UMMA BANK
### 1978, 1 Lloyd's Rep. 166 (C.A.)

English suppliers entered into a contract to supply and install glasshouses in Libya. The contract was governed by libyan law. Payment was agreed through a confirmed letter of credit to be opened by the libyan customers. It was stipulated that the suppliers should open a performance bond in an english bank "payable on demand without proof or condition". The libyan customers opened the letter of credit but failed to obtain confirmation by the bank. The suppliers subsequently did not accept the letter of credit as opened and repudiated the contract. The customers demanded payment under the performance bond and the suppliers applied for, and obtained an injunction to stop payment under the guarantee. On application of the english bank the injunction was dismissed. The suppliers appealed.

***Held (for the libyan customers):*** (Lord Denning, M.R.) *"[T]he performance guarantee stands on a similar footing to a letter of credit. A bank which gives a performance guarantee must honour that guarantee according to its terms. It is not concerned* *in the least with the relations between the supplier and the customer; nor with the question whether the supplier is in default or not. The bank must pay according to its guarantee, on demand, if so stipulated, without proof or conditions. The only exception is when there is a clear fraud of which the bank has notice; That exception is that where the documents under the credit are presented by the beneficiary himself and the bank knows when the documents are presented that are forged or fraudulent..."* The bank was ordered to honour the performance bond.

## 72
### EFFORT SHIPPING CO. LTD. v. LINDEN MANAGEMENT S.A.
*(The Giannis Nk)*
22/1/98 (H.L.)

The vessel *Giannis NK* loaded a cargo of ground-nut pellets at Dakar. The cargo was fumigated after loading and a SGS certificate was issued. Prior cargoes of wheat pellets had been loaded into other holds at previous ports in the Ivory Coast. The vessel discharged part of the cargo at San Juan (Puerto Rico) and then proceeded to the Dominican Republic to discharge the balance of cargo. When she arrived, the agricultural authorities inspected the cargo and live insects and shed skins were found. The vessel was fumigated twice but it proved ineffective and the vessel was ordered to leave the port with both the ground-nut and wheat cargoes still on board. She sailed back to San Juan, where the agricultural authorities required that the cargo either be returned to its country origin or be dumped at sea twenty five miles from shore. The vessel subsequently had to be fumigated, and there was a delay of 2 ½ months before she was cleared to load the next charter. The shipowners claimed damages against the shippers. They contended that the groundnut cargo was physically dangerous to other cargo, and relied either on art. IV(6) of the Hague-Visby Rules, which were incorporated into the bill of lading, or by virtue of an implied term at common law. The shippers replied that art. IV(6) was subject to art. IV(3) and that they were not al fault since they did not know, and had no means of knowing, that the goods were infested.

***Held (for the shipowners):*** **i)** As to the dangerous nature of the cargo, in the present case, the physical damage to the wheat cargo resulted only from the decision to dump the whole cargo at sea. The groundnut cargo was of a dangerous nature because it was liable to give rise to the loss of the wheat cargo by dumping at sea. In so far as the shipowners would have not consented to the shipment of the groundnut cargo had they been aware of its dangerous nature, the shippers were prima facie liable. **ii)** As to the shipper's liability, the shipper's argument that liability under art. IV(6) was qualified by the shipper's indemnity provisions of art. IV(3) was rejected. Art. IV(6) is a free-standing provision in relation to art. IV(3) and, moreover, the shipper's liability for shipping dangerous goods could not be made to depend on the state of his knowledge. Furthermore, at common law, the liability of a shipper for shipping dangerous goods does not depend on his knowledge or means of knowledge that the goods were dangerous.[61]

---

## 73
### E.G. CORNELIUS & CO. LTD. V. CHRISTOS MARITIME CO. LTD.
*(The Christos)*
1995, 1 Lloyd's Rep. 106 (Q.B.)

By a tanker voyage charterparty the vessel *Christos* was chartered for the carriage of palmoil from Belawan (Indonesia) to Tuapse in the Mediterranean. The charterparty provided, inter alia, the following provisions: "H. Special Provisions: owners have the option to tranship this cargo on a single vessel to the discharge port…", and "27. Substitution: owner shall have the option to substitute another vessel providing she can report within the readiness and cancelling dates and it is suitable for the cargo…" During the voyage the cargo was transhipped at Piraeus onto another vessel called *Mithat Vardal*, which complied with the requirements of cl. 27 and reached the nominated discharge port of Novorossiysk. The owners calculated demurrage at Novorossiysk and claimed

against the charterers the equivalent of twelve onhire days. The charterers argued that the charterparty entitled the owners to demurrage accrued for the *Christos* but not for the *Mithat Vardal*.

***Held (for the owners):*** (Mance, J.) The contractual intention was that the obligations regarding laytime/demurrage, or any other obligation, apply either to the original ship or to the transhipment ship. Although the *Mithat Vardal* was not originally the subject vessel of the charterparty, the substitution made under cl. 27 makes the *Mithat Vardal* "the vessel" for the purposes of many charter-party provisions, including those relating to laytime/ demurrage.

---

## 74
### EGON OLDENDORFF V. LIBERA CORP.
1996, 1 Lloyd's Rep. 380 (Q.B.)

The German plaintiffs ("Egon Oldendorff") claimed damages for breach of an agreement concluded for a 10-year charter of two Panamax bulk carriers. At the time the ships were to be built by the Japanese defendants ("Libera Corp."). Based on the agreement, the defendants were to provide the vessels and to give the plaintiffs an option to purchase each vessel anytime after 30 months from the date of delivery. The agreement was expressed to be subject to the signature of a shipbuilding contract (MOA) and a charterparty (NYPE form) subject to details. The details of the charterparty were finally lifted. The fixture included an arbitration clause providing for arbitration through the London Maritime Arbitrators Associ-

---

[61] Since the shippers were found liable by virtue of art. IV(6), the question of the nature and scope of an implied obligation at common law as to the shipment of dangerous goods was irrelevant. However, regarding the dispute between shippers and carriers on that point, as for more than a century, their lordships have expressed their views in obiter. The conclusion is that the strict liability approach of Lord Campbell in *Brass v. Maitland, 1856, 6 E & B 470* was reaffirmed and is still binding on the same terms today: knowledge on the part of the shipper about the dangerous nature of the cargo is not an necessary requirement for asserting liability on the shipper.

ation. The dollar-yen exchange rate fluctuated to the disadvantage of the defendants, who subsequently faced difficulties in fulfilling the shipbuilding contract. The defendants argued that the condition of the signature had not been fulfilled and that therefore the contract was not binding upon them. The plaintiffs treated such conduct as a repudiatory breach and claimed damages. The preliminary issue was whether english or japanese law applied to the contracts.[62]

***Held:*** (Clarke, J.) **i)** The arbitration clause of the charterparty was a sign that the parties' intention was to choose english law as the applicable law, not only in relation to the charterparty but also to the contract itself. Having agreed english arbitration as a "neutral forum", the reasonable inference was that a "neutral law" (as between german and japanese law) was also intended to apply.[63] **ii)** Former dealings between the parties showed that they were conducting their negotiations by reference to english rather than to japanese or german law. "*So, for example, the expression 'subject to details' has a well settled meaning in English law.*"[64] Accordingly, it was decided that the parties made a tacit choice of english law for both the charterparty and the MOA in the meaning of the art. 3 of the 1980 Rome Convention.

---

[62] The substantial issues were decided later in *Egon Oldendorff v. Libera Corp.*, 1995, 2 *Lloyd's Rep. 64.*
[63] See *The Kominos S.* Contrast with *Compagnie Tunisienne de Navigation S.A. v. Compagnie d'Armement Maritime S.A.*, 1971, AC 572 (H.L.).
[64] For the legal meaning of the words "subject to details", see also *CPC Consolidated Pool Carriers GmbH v. CTM Cia. Transmediterranea S.A.*.

# 75
## EL AMRIA AND EL MINIA
### 1982, Lloyd's Rep. 28 (C.A.)

In 1977 the owners of the *El Amria* and *El Minia* agreed with the Supreme Onion Shipping Committee (SOSC) to carry cargoes of onions aboard their two vessels. The SOSC was an organisation that co-ordinated the onion shipments of egyptian exporters to european ports. The owners agreed with SOSC that the eventual buyers and receivers at destination would pay the freight. The agreement was headed as follows: "Continent Contract covering the F.O.B. shipment of onions from Alexandria to Rotterdam/Hamburg range of the export season 1977". Clause 28 of the contract provided for arbitration at the port of discharge. After loading, bills of loading were issued by the owners containing an exclusive jurisdiction clause for the Egyptian Courts. The cargoes arrived at Rotterdam, some of which were found to be damaged. The receivers brought an action in England against the owners for damages. The owners, in turn, applied for a stay on the grounds (1) that the contracts of carriage evidenced in the bills of lading contained exclusive jurisdiction clauses in favour of the egyptian courts, and (2) that Egypt was the forum conveniens. The preliminary issue for the appeal was whether the contract of carriage between the owners and the receivers was to be found in the Continent Contract, or in the bills of lading conferring jurisdiction upon Egypt. Notwithstanding that, it was agreed by both parties that the dispute should be heard either by the Admiralty Court in England or by the Commercial Court in Egypt depending upon the outcome of the preliminary issue.

***Held (for owners):*** (Donaldson, L.J.)
**i)** *"In deciding whether the receivers were parties to a contract of carriage on the terms contained in the bills of lading, which contained the exclusive jurisdiction clause, or on the relevant terms of the Continent contract, which did not, the law to be applied is that of Egypt. However, it was not suggested that this law differed in any material respect from that of England. Accordingly, the position is that if the receivers were the charterers of the vessel on the terms of the Continent contract, the bills of lading would be bare receipts and not contract of carriage in their hands* (see President of India v. Metcalfe Shipping Co., [1970] 1 Q.B. 289). *It is true that in that case the charter-party required the master to sign bills of lading 'without prejudice to this charterparty' and there is no equivalent clause in the Continent contract, but part of the ratio of the decision was that a master normally has no authority to vary the terms of a charter-party and that to issue a contractual bill of lading to a charterer would have this effect".*
**ii)** *"It would avail the receivers nothing that the sellers in shipping the goods should have made separate contracts of carriage for each parcel on the terms of the continent contract, unless they did so as agents for the buyers. In any other case, the buyers only became parties to any contract of carriage and able to sue on it when the bills of lading were endorsed to them and the only contract of which they could avail themselves is that contained in or evidenced by the bill of lading…Accordingly, all we know is that the sellers arranged for the ship to become available, that the sellers shipped the onions, that*

*the sellers took an order bill of lading and that the sellers endorsed that bill of lading in favour of the receivers and delivered it to the receivers on payment of the price. Using Mr. Justice Devlin's classification, this is a type 2 f.o.b. contract, and the buyer's only rights are under the bill of lading.*[65] *For these reasons we are not satisfied that the contract of carriage to which the buyers were parties was other than that contained in the bill of lading and we would therefore allow the appeal and stay the actions."*


**76**

**ELECTROSTEEL EUROPE S.A. v.
EDIL CENTRO SPA**

Case C-87/10, European Court of Justice

Italian sellers sold goods to french buyers. The contract contained a term providing that delivery was to be 'free from the seller's premises' (in the original: 'Resa: Franco ns. sede') in Italy. The goods were paid for and delivered on to a carrier in Italy and, form there, were transported

---

[65] *"In* Pyrene & Co. v. Scindia Navigation Company [1954] 1 Lloyd's Rep. 321; [1954] 2 Q.B. 402, *at pp. 332 and 424 Mr. Justice Devlin instanced three types of f.o.b. contract. In the first, or classic type, the buyer nominates the ship and the seller puts the goods on board for account of the buyer, procuring a bill of lading. The seller is then a party to the contract of carriage and if he has taken the bill of lading to his order, the only contract of carriage to which the buyer can become a party is that contained in or evidenced by the bill of lading which is endorsed to him by the seller. The second is a variant of the first, in that the seller arranges for the ship to come on the berth, but the legal incidents are the same. The third is where the seller puts the goods on board, takes a mate's receipt and gives this to the buyer or his agent who then takes a bill of lading. In this latter type the buyer is a party to the contract of carriage ab initio."*

to France. The sellers sued the buyers in Italy claiming the price of the goods, but the buyers challenged the jurisdiction of the Italian courts and claimed that the matter should be brought to the French courts. This, in the opinion of the Italian court, might trigger the application of art 5(1)(b) of Council Regulation (EC) No 44/2001 on jurisdiction and the recognition and enforcement of judgments on civil and commercial matters, establishing a jurisdiction additional to the domicile of the defendant. In particular, the ECJ was asked to determine whether "delivery" was affected in the place where the goods were provided to the carrier (Italy) or in the place of the goods' final destination (France).

**Held:** This case concerns the interpretation of Article 5(1) in relation to the place of delivery in a contract for the supply of goods in a distance-selling contract. The ECJ's findings were as follows: "*It is for the national court to determine whether the clause 'Resa: Franco [nostra] sede' in the contract at issue before the referring court corresponds to the Incoterm, 'Ex Works', entailing the application of rules A4 and B4, or to another clause or another usage habitually used in trade or commerce and which is an appropriate means of clearly identifying – without there being any need to refer to the substantive law applicable to the contract – the place of delivery of the goods under that contract. In the light of the foregoing considerations, the answer to the question referred is that the first indent of Article 5(1)(b) of the Regulation must be interpreted as meaning that, in the case of distance selling, the place where the goods were or should have been delivered pursuant to the contract must be determined on the basis of the provisions of that contract. In order to verify whether the place of delivery is determined 'under the contract', the national court seised must take account of all the relevant terms and clauses of that contract which are capable of clearly identifying that place, including terms and clauses which are generally recognised and applied through the usages of international trade or commerce, such as the Incoterms drawn up by the International Chamber of Commerce in the version published in 2000. If it is impossible to determine the place of delivery on that basis, without referring to the substantive law applicable to the contract, the place of delivery is the place where the physical transfer of the goods took place, as a result of which the purchaser obtained, or should have obtained, actual power of disposal over those goods at the final destination of the sales transaction*". In this case, the ECJ saw no need to consider any additional criterion based on the "place of final destination". In this case, the ECJ saw no need to consider any additional criterion based on the "place of final destination". The decisive factor was the physical delivery to the buyer.


77

**ERG PETROLI S.P.A. v. VITOL S.A.**
*(The Ballenita and Bp Energy)*
1992, 2 Lloyd's Rep. 455 (Q.B.)

Some 25,000 tonnes of EEC qualified gasoil was sold c.i.f. Genoa on Sept. 26, 1990. The contract required, inter alia, delivery to be "…M/T 'TBN' or sub. during Oct.11-25, 1990. Vessel nomination to be given latest three London

(England) working days prior to vessel arrival basis Genova. Nominated vessel to be acceptable to buyer such acceptance not to be unreasonable withheld". Clause 4 required the gasoil to conform to italian winter guaranteed specifications. On Oct. 15, 1990, the sellers purchased a cargo of gasoil on board the "BP Energy", samples of which had not yet been drawn and analysed. The same day the sellers nominated the "BP Energy/Sub" to the buyers under the contract of Sept. 26, 1990. The buyers accepted such nomination. When the BP Energy arrived at anchorage at Genoa (Italia), notice of readiness was sent to the buyers. The sellers ordered an inspection and drew samples of the cargo on board which indicated that the gasoil fell outside the required Italian winter specifications. At the time the market price for the gasoil dropped substantially. The sellers, anticipating that the BP Energy gasoil would probably be rejected, nominated another vessel (i.e. the *Ballenita)* in substitution as it had a cargo of gasoil aboard which met the contract specifications. On Oct. 22 the *Ballenita* arrived at Genoa and notice of readiness was tendered. The buyers' reaction was to treat the substitution as a repudiatiory breach of the contract and claimed damages fixed by the difference between the market price and the contract price. The sellers contended that the substitution was permitted by the contract.

***Held (for the sellers):*** (Judge Diamond, Q.C.) **i)** The sellers were not estopped from exercising their right of substitution because (i) the original nomination was for "BP Energy/Sub.", and (ii) they were entitled to nominate three London working days before the date of arrival. The words "TBN or sub." indicated the right of substitution was contemplated in the contract as long as it was exercised before the three-day period had commenced. No term in the contract indicated that the act of tendering a notice of readiness deprived the exercise of such right. *"There was nothing unreasonable in substituting another vessel after discharging instructions had been given in respect of BP Energy; there was no term in the contract which expressly or impliedly indicated that the right to substitute was to lapse once notice of readiness was given and on the evidence the right of substitution was intended to be exercisable at any time until the commencement of discharge".* **ii)** Additionally, the judge found no sufficient evidence supporting the buyers' alleged uncontractual nature of the cargo. The sellers were entitled to the full price (without deductions) for the cargo since it was not successfully proven that the cargo was not "EEC qualified gasoil".

**78**

**ERIDANIA S.P.A. AND OTHERS V. RUDOLF A. OETKER AND OTHERS**
*(The Fjord Wind)*
2000, 2 Lloyd's Rep. 191 (C.A.)

The disponent owners entered into a voyage charter on the *Norgrain* form with the charterers, *Eridania,* for a carriage of a cargo of soya beans from berths or anchorages in the river Plate with completion at one safe port in Brazil to a range of Spanish and Italian ports. The voyage charter party included the following clauses: "1) That the said vessel being tight staunch and strong and in every way fit for the voyage, shall with all convenient speed proceed to [the river Plate]...and there load... 35) Owners shall be bound before and at the beginning of the voyage to exercise due diligence to make the ship seaworthy...". On 30 June, the vessel sailed from Rosario with a cargo of 27,535 tons of soya beans bound for Grande do Sul where she would complete loading and then on to various ports in Europe. The cargo of soya beans was shipped under a single bill of lading, naming Cia. Emiliana de Exportacion S.A. (Emiliana) as shipper, the goods being consigned to order. On 1 July as she was sailing down the river Parana, the main engine experienced difficulties and it was discovered that the No. 6 crankpin bearing had failed and that there was damage to the No. 5 crankpin bearing. Given the fact that the estimated time needed for repairs was ninety five days, the disponent owners gave notice that the voyage had been frustrated to the holders of the bill of lading on 26 July and to the charterers on 27 July. The cargo was subsequently transshipped into a substitute vessel and carried to its destination. Plaintiffs sought to recover the additional costs associated with the transshipment under both the charterparty and the bill of lading. Plaintiffs argued that the disponent owners had given an absolute warranty that the vessel was seaworthy at the beginning of her approach voyage under cl. 1 and, alternatively, that the disponent owners breached their duty to exercise due diligence to ensure that the vessel was seaworthy. Owners responded by arguing that cl. 1 should be read in conjunction with cl. 35 and, so read, the obligation was to exercise due diligence to make the vessel seaworthy so that the nature of the obligation at each stage was the same.

***Held (for the claimants):*** (Clarke, L.J.) i) Regarding the proper reading of clauses 1 and 35, Lord Clarke said: *"If there were no cl. 35 it is likely that it would be held that there was an absolute warranty that the vessel should be seaworthy for both the approach voyage and loading. Yet on any view cl. 35 expressly applies 'before and at the beginning of the voyage", which must include the loading process. Thus under cl. 35 the owners must exercise due diligence to make her seaworthy for the loading process and thereafter they must exercise due diligence to make her seaworthy for the cargo-carrying voyage itself. It follows that cl. 35 directly affects the true construction of cl. 1 and the question arises whether it was intended to affect the whole operation of the clause. In my judgment, it was. The expression "before and at the beginning of the voyage" is apt to include the whole period before the beginning of the voyage."* ii) The court found the vessel was unseaworthy when she departed Rosario because, there was present a defect which meant that it could not operate on an ordinary voyage, since it failed on the voyage down-river, with the consequences ... which were entirely foreseeable. Thus, if the disponent owners had known that such a defect was present the bearing would fail in those circumstances, they would have rectified the defect. Because the vessel was not in a fit condition to withstand an ordinary voyage down the river Prana, she was deemed to be unseaworthy. iii) Had the owners discharged their burden of proving that they had exercised due diligence, thus shielding themselves from liability for useaworthiness? Lord Clarke ruled that the lower court had correctly held that the disponent owners had failed to discharge their burden of showing that had exercised due diligence, through themselves, their servants and agents and independent contractors to make the vessel seaworthy prior to departed from Rosario by sufficiently responding to the earlier bearing failures. This was due to the fact that a thorough investigation was necessary regarding the failure of the bearings and crankshaft which had not been undertaken with the result that owners had not demonstrated what was done regarding the bearings and crankshaft and thus it was impossible to say whether due diligence had been exercised. Subsequently, Lord Clarke held: *"It follows … that the owners have failed to show that due diligence was exercised to make the vessel seaworthy before she sailed from Rosario that, given the further conclusion that the vessel was unseaworthy at that time, the defendants are liable for any loss caused by that unseaworthiness as damages for breach of the charter or the contract of carriage contained in or evidenced by the bill of lading as the case may be"*.

# 79
## EVGRAFOV, THE
### 1987, Lloyd's Rep. 2 (Q.B.)

The MV *Evgrafov* and the MV *Derbenev* carried a consignment of 3,000 tons and 2,329 tons of newsprint, respectively from Canada to England. The cargo was loaded in undamaged condition. The outside temperature was -20 and -15 degrees Celsius on the respective dates of loading and outturned at the destination in a very water-damaged condition. The cargo was carried under a bill of lading incorporating the Canadian Water Carriage of Goods Act and it was agreed that there would be no distinction between this Act and the Hague Rules, or between Canadian and English law. The amount of damage to the cargo was GBP 420,963 and GBP 214,228, respectively. The carrier admitted liability for GBP 7,416 in relation to the MV *Evgrafov* and GBP 1,844 in relation to the MV *Derbenev*. The cargo interests filed a claim against the carriers for the balance.

***Held (for the claimants):*** The claimants alleged that the vessel had been improperly ventilated, resulting in a continuous flow of warm, humid air which, when coming in contact with the cold reels of papers, formed significant amounts of condensation which damaged the cargo. The defendants argued that they were protected from liability under Art. IV(2)(i) act or omission of the shipper, (m) inherent defect, quality or vice of the goods, and (q) any other cause arising without the actual fault or privity of the carrier or without the fault or neglect of the agents or servants of the carrier. The evidence showed that the two vessels had been improperly ventilated in clear breach of Art. III(2). Furthermore, when looking at the history of such shipments of paper cargo from the Canada to England and the corresponding temperature differences, it was deemed possible in the ordinary course to carry newsprint from such loading ports in winter and deliver them undamaged at warmer ports.

# 80
## (1) Far East Chartering Ltd. and
## (2) Binani Cement Limited v. Great Eastern Shipping Co. Ltd.
### (The Jag Ravi)
### 2012, EWCA Civ 180 (C.A.)

PTH sold a cargo of coal to VICAG on FOB terms. VICAG, in turn, on-sold part of the cargo to Binani Cement Ltd. (Binani). It was agreed that, if Binani did not receive the original bills of lading by the time the vessel arrived at the discharge port, the cargo would be discharged against a Letter of Indemnity ("LOI"). The cargo was shipped on board the MV *Jag Ravi*, which had been chartered by FEC, a company associated to VICAG. The voyage charterparty provided that, in the event that the original bills of lading were not available at discharge, the shipowners would allow discharge against the charterers' LOI in the shipowners P&I Club standard terms. A LOI was issued by the receivers, Binani, at the request of the charterers in the International Group of P&I Clubs' standard form. That LOI was addressed to "The owners/disponent owners/charterers of the MV *Jag Ravi*, and extended the indemnity to "you, your servants and agents". The charterers, in turn, issued their own LOI in identical terms, but they addressed it to the shipowners only. The cargo was discharged without production of the original bills of lading against a delivery order issued by the shipowners. A dispute arose between PTH and VICAG under the sale contract, and PTH decided to claim the price of the goods against the shipowners for wrongful delivery. VICAG went into liquidation. As a consequence, its own LOI turned useless.

The shipowners then sought to claim an indemnity from Binani for all the damages they had been found liable of vis-à-vis PTH. The question was whether the shipowners should be allowed to rely on the LOI issued by Binani.

***Held (for the shipowners):*** The Court of Appeal confirmed that the shipowners could rely on the terms of the LOI issued by the receivers, Binani. The fact that such LOI was addressed to the charterers, FEC, and not to the shipowners, did not make a difference in this case. The shipowners were allowed to claim on the LOI because, in the facts, the shipowners had been acting as the charterers' agents in delivering the cargo. Although discharge and delivery were different things, Tomlinson L.J. held that delivery did not mean that the shipowners must themselves hand over the cargo to receivers. What was required was that the shipowners must have actually surrendered possession. Issuing a delivery order and discharging the cargo was, in this case, sufficient to amount to delivery.

# 81
## Farenco Shipping Co. Ltd v. Daebo Shipping Co. Ltd
### (The Bremen Max)
### 2009 1 Lloyd's Rep. 81 (Q.B.)

The MV *Bremen Max* was chartered by Pavey Services Ltd. (owners) to COSCO Bulk Carrier Co Ltd (Cosbulk), which sub-chartered her to Farenco Shipping Co. Ltd (Farenco), and this one, in turn, sub-sub-chartered to Daebo Shopping Co. Ltd. (Daebo). All the charters were back to back. Clause 68 of each of the charters provided the following: "In case original Bills of Lading are not available at discharge port(s), master/owners to allow discharge and release the cargo on board against charterers' single Letter of Indemnity signed by charterers only with wording as per owners' Protection and Indemnity Club recommendation". When the vessel arrived at the port of discharge, the bills of lading were not available. Owners were requested to deliver the cargo without production of the bills against a letter of indemnity ("LOI"). LOIs were provided by each charterer to its disponent owner. Each letter was in the same form and language. The LOI issued by Farenco to Daebo contained a number of undertakings, like putting up bail in case of arrest of the ship or indemnifying owners for any loss or damage caused by delivering the goods without production of the bill of ladings. All such undertakings were signed in consideration for owners delivering the goods to Kremikovtzi AD. At discharge, there was no evidence that the cargo was delivered to Kremikovtzi, but to a different party. The holders of the bills of lading then claimed delivery and arrested the ship. Farenco put up substitute security directly to Semcor and requested Daebo to the same. Daebo declined to do so and Farenco began proceedings against Daebo seeking a mandatory injunction compelling Daebo to provide security in accordance with the LOI. The issues before the court were: (i) whether the obligation in clause 3 of the LOI to provide such bail or other security was no longer a current obligation, the release of the vessel having already been secured; and (ii) whether the undertakings of the LOI were conditional upon delivery to Kremikovtzi.

***Held:*** It was argued by the charterers that the obligation to provide security under the LOI had ceased when owners provided security for release of the vessel. The position taken was that because owners had provided security, it became impossible for any charterer to put up "such bail or other security as may be required to prevent such arrest…or to secure the release of such ship," and that therefore the court should not require specific performance because it cannot order a party to do the impossible. The judge rejected this argument, stating that the intention and commercial purpose of clause 3 of the LOI was to shield the shipowner from arrest of their vessel and that any bail or other security required to prevent such an arrest was the responsibility of the charterer. Teare J. said: *"The action of the owners did not discharge the obligation of the charterers to put up bail or other security. That obligation had accrued. The action taken by the owners to mitigate their loss cannot discharge that obligation or provide the charterers with a defence to the charge that they remained in breach of their obligation to provide bail or other security. Where is to do so the commercial purpose and intention of the clause would be frustrated…"* He added, *"The analysis would or might be different in circumstances where the shipowner, without making a demand of the charterers to provide bail or other security to prevent an arrest or secure a release, himself provided bail for that purpose. No obligation of any charterer to provide bail or other security would have accrued before the vessel was released from arrest".* (ii) The next issue was whether owners were entitled to specific performance without proof that they had delivered to the party named in the LOI. The judge drew the distinction between discharge and delivery, the former being *"the movement of the cargo from the ship 'over the ship's rail' ashore"* and the latter being *"the transfer or possession of the cargo to a person ashore"*. Were the owners obligated to deliver to the party in the LOI? *"The obligation upon the shipowner in clause 68 of the charterparty 'to…release the cargo on board' against the LOI obliges the shipowner to release, in the sense of deliver, the cargo to another against the LOI. The person to whom the cargo is to be released or delivered without production of the bills of lading is to be found in the LOI."* And finally, *"Since the undertaking* [in the LOI] *are given in return for the shipowner complying with the charterer's request that the cargo be delivered to a named receiver without production of the bills of lading and not to anyone else without production of the bills of lading it follows that if the shipowner delivers to anybody else without production of the bills of lading the charterer's undertakings are not engaged"*.

**82**

**FEDERAL COMMERCE AND NAVIGATION
CO. V. MOLENA ALPHA INC.**
*(The Nanfri, Benfri and Lorfri)*
1978, 2 Lloyd's Rep. 132 (C.A.)

The vessels *Nanfri*, *Benfri* and *Lorfri* were chartered under three separate charterparties contained in the Baltime form for a period of six years. The payments of hire became due per calendar month in advance. Clause 6 provided the owners' right of withdrawal of the vessel in default of payment. Clause 9 included an agency or employment proviso upon the master under the orders of the charterers. Clauses 11 and 14 contained the charterers right to deductions of hire for de-

ficiency of speed or disbursements made for the vessel's account, provided that they were supported with vouchers signed by the master. In July and September 1977, the charterers made several deductions of hire for the alleged loss of speed of the vessel. The owners protested and instructed the masters of the three vessels to withdraw all authority to sign bills of lading on their behalf, to refuse to sign or issue bills marked as freight pre-paid and to endorse every bill with a charter incorporation clause (including the lien under cls. 18). After an exchange of messages, the charterers treated the owners' conduct as repudiatory and treated the charter as terminated.

***Held***[66] ***(for the charterers):*** **i)** (Lord Denning) *"The payments due under a time charter are usually now described as 'hire' and those under a voyage charter as 'freight'; 'Freight' is payable for carrying a quantity of cargo from one place to another. 'Hire' is payable for a specified period of time, irrespective of whether the charterer chooses to use it for carrying cargo or lays it up, out of use. Every time charter contains clauses which are quite inappropriate to a voyage charter, such as the off-hire clause and the withdrawal clause. So different are the two concepts that I do not think the law as to 'freight' can be applied indiscriminately to 'hire'. In particular the special rule of English law whereby 'freight' must be paid in full (without deductions for short delivery or cargo damage) cannot be applied automatically to time charter 'hire'. Nor there is any authority which says that it must. It would be a mistake to suppose that the House of Lords had time charter hire and*

---

[66] Cumming-Bruce L.J. dissenting.

*so forth in mind when they decided The Aries, 1977, 1 WLR 185 or the Nova (Jersey) Knit Ltd. v. Kammgarn Spinnerei GmbH, 1977, 1 WLR, 713, or that anything said in those cases can bind this court. Many of us, I know, in the past have assumed that the rule as to 'freight' does apply: and some judges have said so. But now, after full argument, I am satisfied that the 'freight' rule does not apply automatically to 'time charter' hire."* **ii)** Having established that modern distinction, Lord Denning went on to state: *"Likewise if the shipowner has been guilty of some other wrongful conduct which has deprived the charterer of the use of the ship during some days –or prejudiced the charterer in the use of the ship- then the charterer should in fairness be able to recoup himself by making a deduction from the next month's hire. If the charterer quantifies his loss by a reasonable assessment made in good faith –and deducts the sum quantified- then he is not in default. The shipowner cannot withdraw his vessel on account of non-payment of hire nor hold him guilty at that point of any breach of contract. If it consequently turns out that he has deducted too much, the shipowner can of course recover the balance".*[67] Regarding that these

circumstances were met, the charterers were entitled under cls. 11 to deduct "valid claims"[68] from hire without the consent of the owners. **iii)** *"I (Lord Denning) would, as at present advised, limit the right to deduct to cases when the shipowner has wrongly deprived the charterer of the use of the vessel or has prejudiced him in the use of it. I would not extend it to other breaches or default of the shipowner, such as damage to cargo arising from the negligence of the crew…"* **iv)** The owners were found in breach of the charterparty. In particular, they did not comply with cls. 9 as to the agency or employment regime of the master under the charterers' orders. In words of Lord Denning MR, *"it was open to the charterers to accept the repudiation, as they did, and to treat themselves as discharged from any further performance"*.

**83**

**FEDERSPIEL, CARLOS & CO. S.A. v. TWIGG, CHARLES & CO. LTD.**
1957, 1 Lloyd's Rep. 240 (Q.B.)

The plaintiffs were merchants incorporated in San Jose (Costa Rica) and the defendants manufacturers of bicycles and tricycles in Lye (United Kingdom). The plaintiffs agreed to buy a quantity of bicycles from the manufacturers in terms "f.o.b. U.K. port". The insurance and freight were to be charged by the defendants to the plaintiffs as extras. The plaintiffs paid the price and said they were expecting to receive the invoice and the

---

[67] See *The Teno, 1977, 2 Lloyd's Rep. 289, (Q.B.)* where Parker J said: *"…it would be grossly unjust to allow an owner to recover hire in respect of a period during which he had, in breach of contract, failed to provide that for which the hire was payable"*. This new view defeats the traditional approach of Donaldson J in *Seven Seas Transportation v. Atlantic Shipping, 1975, 2 Lloyd's Rep. 188, (Q.B)*, where it was held that there was no general equitable right of set-off for time lost under an off-hire clause. The argument which Donaldson J put forward was that the existence of such right to deduce would involve the risk of the vessel being withdrawn for non-payment of hire, should the claim later prove to be unjustified in whole or in part.

[68] Lord Denning MR at p. 143: "I regard the words 'valid claim' as denoting claims which are made to deduct sums quantified by a reasonable assessment made in good faith".

shipping documents. The manufacturers replied that the goods would be shipped as early as possible. They were packed into cases, marked with the plaintiff buyer's name and registered for shipment in a named ship which was about to call at Liverpool. The goods had not yet been sent to the port of Liverpool when the defendant manufacturers went into bankruptcy and liquidation prior to the bicycles having been shipped. A receiver and manager appointed by the debenture holders of the manufacturers claimed that the bicycles, like all the other assets of the manufacturers, were property interests in favour of the debenture holders. The plaintiffs claimed that the bicycles had been appropriated to the contract and that property of the goods had already passed to them. They sued both the manufacturers and the receivers for conversion. The defendants contended that the property interest was intended to pass on shipment and, as no shipment had yet been effected, the property interest remained with the manufacturers.

***Held (for the defendants): i)*** (Mr. J. Pearson) *"...if and so far as this contract was in its true nature an f.o.b. contract, the natural time at which the property pass would be on shipment. Undoubtedly this contract also contained some c.i.f. features, and there is an express reference to what is called 'approximate c.i.f. charges' in the pro-forma invoice. If and in so far as it was a c.i.f. contract, the effect of the authorities is that the property would pass not earlier than shipment, perhaps later than shipment."* Be as it may, for the purposes of the present case it is sufficient to say that property in the bicycles was intended to pass on shipment or later than shipment, but never before shipment. **ii)** The judge held that there was no appropriation of the goods under the contract since it was proved that: (1) the intention of the parties was that ownership should pass on or after shipment, (2) there was no agreement to a change of ownership before shipment, (3) there was no actual or constructive delivery, (4) there was no suggestion that the goods were at the buyer's risk at any time before shipment, and (5) the last acts of the defendant seller (i.e. to send the goods to Liverpool and having them shipped on board) were not performed.[69] The fact that the goods

_______________

[69] Pearson J. (generally in connection with the appropriation of the goods to a contract): *"I think one can distinguish these principles"* (1) *"the parties must have had, or be reasonably supposed to have had, an intention to attach the contract irrevocably to those goods, so that those goods and no others are the subject of the sale and become property of the buyer"* (rule 5 of sec. 18, Sale of Goods Act); (2) *"it is by agreement of the parties that the appropriation, involving a change of ownership, is made, although in some cases the buyer's assent to an appropriation by the seller is conferred in advance by the contract itself or otherwise";* (3) *"to involve an actual or constructive delivery";* (4) *"one has to remember sect. 20 of the Sale of Goods Act, whereby the ownership and the risk are normally associated";* and, (5) *"usually but not necessarily, the appropriating act is the last act to be performed by the seller. For instance, if delivery is to be taken by the buyer at the seller's premises and the seller has completed his part of the contract and has appropriated the goods when he has made the goods ready and has identified them and placed them in position to be taken by the buyer and so informed the buyer, and if the buyer agrees to come and take them, that is the assent to the appropriation. But if there is a further act, an important and decisive act to be done by the seller, then there is prima facie evidence that probably the property does not pass until the final act is done."*

were packed and marked with the shipping marks is irrelevant and is not to be read as an intended appropriation, but merely a preparation for the shipment. Accordingly, judgement was for the defendants.

**84**
**FICOM S.A. V. SOCIEDAD CADEX LIMITADA**
1980, 2 Lloyd's Rep. 118 (Q.B.)

Sociedad Cadex sold a quantity of bolivian coffee to Ficom f.o.b. Matarani. The sale contract described the quality as "washed Bolivian coffee…as per sample max. 3 black grains in 300 g., no other defects". The contract incorporated the European Coffee Contract, which contained a provision in that a difference in quality did not entitle the buyers to cancel the contract but rather to a penalty if such difference was out of the ordinary. Payment was agreed by irrevocable letter of credit. The letter of credit, as in the form opened by the buyers, requested a quality certificate of SGS which had not been contemplated by the sales contract. That certificate, as per the terms of the credit, should state the quality specifications agreed to under the contract. Further modifications were made regarding the terms of the letter of credit, the more relevant being that the buyers requested (a) an extension of the shipment period, (b) a different port of discharge, and (c) an additional quality certificate showing the lack of other defects in the cargo such as "deteriorated beans, broken beans…". The sellers accepted the amendments (a) and (b), but not (c). Upon tender of documents by the sellers, the bank rejected them because the quality certificate issued by SGS (which was appointed by the buyers) stated that the "goods intended for shipment (were) not contractual". The sellers referred the matter to arbitration before the London Coffee Trade Federation, which decided in their favour. The buyers appealed.

***Held (for the buyers):* i)** The parties to a contract of sale can, by agreeing to terms of the letter of credit which differ from those specified in the contract, vary their original obligations.[70] The same occurs when the sales contract does not define the terms of the letter of credit to be opened, and the letter of credit as opened happens to fill those gaps. This case falls within the second group. The sellers here accepted the original letter of credit which called for an additional quality certificate. The fact that the sellers did not originally agree with the subsequent letter of credit (as amended) is inconsistent with the tender of the quality certificate, which was later rejected by the bank. **ii)** The quality provision of the incorporated European Coffee Contract is not an obstacle to the buyers' right to reject the documents since the letter of credit contemplated that right where the quality certificate was in discrepancy. That inconsistency does not itself detract from the binding effect of the further agreed letter of credit. The buyers were entitled to bring the contract to an end and were entitled to reject the goods.

---

[70] See *Alan (W.J.) & Co. Ltd. v. El Nasr Export & Import Co.*

## 85
### FUTURE EXPRESS, THE
### 1993, 2 Lloyd's Rep. 542 (C.A.)

A sales contract was concluded between a brokerage firm (as sellers) and the Yemen Arab Republic authorities' agents (as buyers) for the supply of 70,000 tonnes of wheat. The contract was on c.& f.. terms and provided for a confirmed irrevocable letter of credit to be opened by the buyers. The credit was in the form of a revolving credit against order bills of lading blank endorsed and payable to the sellers at 180 days from the bills' date. The application of the letter of credit contained a clause authorising the issuing bank to sell the goods in the event that there were insufficient funds in the buyer's account. The issuing bank sent a telex instructing the confirming bank in Switzerland about its duty to notify and add its own confirmation to the credit in favour of the sellers. The cargo was shipped on board two vessels chartered by the sellers. At that time sellers and buyers reached an agreement whereby the bills of lading would be withheld from the bank in case the sellers delayed in presenting the documents under the credit. About a year after the date of shipment, the bank was aware that the goods had already been delivered and dispersed, but the documents (including the bills of lading) were still being negotiated. The sellers, as charterers, had furnished an indemnity to the carriers and/or agents to deliver the goods to the buyers against non-production of the bills of lading. The confirming bank had paid against the documents and debited the sum paid to the issuing bank, which in turn failed to receive cash from the buyers. The issuing bank sued the shipowners and their agents for misdelivery. The issue for decision was whether the bank had any title to sue the defendants.[71]

***Held (for the defendants):*** The transfer of the bill of lading, in principle, gives the transferee a right to possession of the goods sufficient to maintain the latter's claim in tort; alternatively, the application form signed by the buyers to the issuing bank invests the later with a pledge of the goods on receipt of the bill of lading, with a corresponding right to sell them. But these two general propositions are defeated by the circumstances of the present case, where namely (1) sellers and buyers agreed before shipment that property and possession were to pass to the buyers without the bill of lading being tendered to the bank, and indeed so it passed before delivery; and (2) the bill of lading ceased to be document of title since the goods were delivered and dispersed and thus the bill no longer represented the goods (nemo dat quod non habet). Insofar the bill of lading is not as negotiable as a bill of exchange, the bank had no better title to such goods represented under the bill of lading. On these grounds, delivery of the bill of lading was not tantamount to a transfer of the property or of the right

------

[71] Lloyd L.J. said: *"It is to be noticed that the plaintiffs cannot take advantage of the provision of the Bills of Lading Act 1855* (see Sewell v. Burdick, 1884, 10 A.C. 74). *Nor can they rely on the Carriage of Goods by Sea Act 1992, since the Act is not retrospective. So they cannot sue in contract. Their sole cause of action, if any, is in tort for conversion, by reason of the failure of the defendants to deliver on demand (of the bank) in Apr., 1986".*

to possession when it was tendered to the bank.[72] The bank's security depends, not on the contract (or application) between the buyer and his bank, but on the ability of the seller to pledge the documents of title on his behalf, or with his consent. In these circumstances, the sellers were not in a position to give either a pledge of the goods or a document of title. They were in no such position since they frustrated both actions by agreeing with the buyers to facilitate their fraud. The sellers took a risk of being unpaid, but they had no doubt commercial interests for assuming that risk. The court, although noting that the conduct of the buyers had been fraudulent, held that the mere possession of the bills of lading did not suffice to give the plaintiffs a title to sue, even though they were named therein as consignees.

## 86

### FYFFES GROUP LTD. AND CARIBBEAN GOLD LTD. V. REEFER EXPRESS LINES PTY. LTD. AND REEFKRIT SHIPPING INC.

*(The Kriti Rex)*
1996, 2 Lloyd's Rep. 171 (Q.B.)

Importers of bananas entered into a Contract of Affreightment (COA) with an intermediary firm for the carriage of bananas from Central America to the United Kingdom. Upon the COA terms, the latter should provide the former with reefer vessels for such trade. A third firm (the owners) time chartered their vessel *Kriti Rex* to the intermediaries on the Baltime

---

[72] Note the absence of the requirement of section 1 of the Bills of Lading Act 1855.

form charterparty. After the *Kriti Rex* had sailed from Manzanillo (Mexico), several problems were found in her engines. The master eventually anchored at Puerto Cortés (Honduras) and declared general average. The cargo was no longer in a condition to be carried to Europe, and it was subsequently donated since there was no local market at Puerto Cortes. The importers sought recovery from the intermediary firm. Since the COA incorporated the Carriage of Goods by Sea Act 1971, the importers argued that the intermediaries (as contractual carriers under the COA) were in breach of art. III(1) of the Hague-Visby Rules as they failed to exercise due diligence to make the vessel seaworthy, and that they were also in breach of the implied duty to proceed with reasonable despatch.

***Held (for the importers):*** (Moore-Bick J.) **i)** It was proved that the Kriti Rex was unseaworthy before loading at Manzanillo since the lubricating oil of her engines contained an unusual high level of particles. As to the duty of seaworthiness, Moore-Bick said: *"The vessel must be fit in all respects to carry her cargo safely to its destination having regard to the ordinary perils to which such a cargo would be exposed on such a voyage;…having failed to have regular analyses of the lubricating oil carried out, it would be difficult for them (the owners) to argue successfully that they had done all that they could reasonably have done to ensure that the oil was fit for service"*. Therefore the owners failed to exercise due diligence in making the vessel seaworthy and such failure caused or contributed to the casualty. The intermediaries, as contractual carriers, were responsible vis-à-vis the holders of the bill of lading for the owners' failure. **ii)** Unless the parties had stipulated otherwise, the duty to proceed with reasonable despatch generally arises, as an implied term, from the nature of the contract of carriage and it is necessary to give commercial efficacy to such a contract. There was nothing in the COA indicating that the parties had intended to dispense with that duty. Judgment was for the importers.

**87**

**GALAXY ENERGY INTERNATIONAL LTD. V. NOVOROSSIYSK SHIPPING CO.**
*(The Petr Schmidt)*
1998, 2 Lloyd's Rep. 1 (C.A.)

The M/V *Petr Schmidt* was chartered under the Asbatankvoy form for a carriage of gasoil from Tuapse to one or two Mediterranean ports. Clause 30 of the charterparty provided that notice of readiness at the loading and discharging ports was to be generally tendered within 06:00 and 17:00 hours local time. Laytime was to commence six hours following receipt of such notice. The vessel tendered notice of readiness at Tuapse (Russia) on Aug. 10 at 00:40. Loading started at 02:00. The vessel arrived at Trieste (Italy) for the first discharge at 18:00 on Aug. 16, and notice was tendered at that time. She was then ready to discharge. She berthed at 07:50 on Aug. 17 and discharge started 13:45 the same day. The vessel subsequently reached Venice (Italy) at 18:00 on Aug 18 to discharge further cargo remaining on board. Notice of readiness was sent at 18:00 the same day, the vessel being ready to discharge. She berthed at 11:50

on Aug. 19 and discharge commenced at 17:40 that day. In calculating demurrage, the charterers claimed that all notices had been tendered outside the hours specified in clause 30 and, therefore, they were invalid. The owners contended that the vessel was still ready to load and discharge at 06:00 on the relevant day, as according to cls. 30, and no changes in circumstances ever occurred after the tender of each notice.

***Held (for the owners):* i)** *"The telex message was sent out of hours in the knowledge that it would remain on the receiver's machine until the following day when it would be available for office staff to deal with when they began work at or after 06:00. It seems to me that this is a clear case of 'tender' at that time; If the notice was given by a letter hand-delivered the previous evening, to be dealt with the next day, or posted through the office door at some time during the night, or left with a messenger to be handed to the office staff when they arrived at 06:00, then in my view the position would be exactly the same. These were different methods of achieving a 'tender' at 06:00."*[73] **ii)** Charterers contended that, even on that basis, the notices were invalid because the statements contained therein related not to the time of tender but to the earlier time they were sent. In response to that contention their lordships replied: *"I (Evans, LJ) would accept that a notice is invalid if the statements made in the notice are in fact incorrect when the notice is tendered, received or given. But it does not follow that the statements cannot also relate to the time when they were made. In fact,*

---

[73] See *The Mexico I* and *The Tres Flores.*

*the primary requirement is that they should be statements of existing fact*". At this point, their lordships admitted that there was an implied representation that the statements were accurate at the moment when the notice was tendered, but that does not mean that the notice was invalid because the statements (of present readiness) were made at some earlier time. The implied representation was, in such a case, that the statement remained accurate when the notice was tendered. **iii)** Charterers put forward the issue that a notice which was tendered outside the hours permitted in cls. 30 was non-contractual. In respect to this view their lordships stated: *"Notices tendered outside the permitted hours were non-contractual and therefore 'wrong'. I (P. Gibson, LJ) do not see how they can be relied upon as having contractual effect at the time of tender. Whether the defect is 'cured' by the passage of time is a question of fact rather than of law"*.[74] If the circumstances changed so that the ship was in fact not ready at the contractual time of 06:00, the notice would have been invalid in the traditional sense; but that was not the case in so far the vessel was ready when the notice was given and she was also ready at 06:00.

**88**

**GARBIS MARITIME CORP. V. PHILIPPINE NATIONAL OIL CO.**

*(The Garbis)*

1982, 2 Lloyd's Rep. 283 (Q.B.)

On Dec. 15, 1978, the plaintiff owners let the tanker *Garbis* to the defendant charterers under the Exxonvoy Form. The charter was for a carriage of 50,000 tons of fuel oil and 7,000 tons of clean naphtha from Bahrain to the Philippines. Clause 20 of Part II of the charterparty provided as follows: "(a) The master shall, upon request, sign Bills of Lading in the form appearing below for all cargo shipped but without prejudice to the rights of the owner and charterer under the terms of this charter; (b) The carriage of cargo under this Charter Party and under all Bills of Lading issued for the cargo shall be subject to the statutory provisions and other terms…of this clause and such terms shall be incorporated verbatim or be deemed incorporated by the reference in any such bill of lading…" At the end of the charterparty, there was a proforma bill of lading that included a reference to the charterparty with a blank space for the date and parties to the charter. A further clause M.6 stipulated that charterers agreed that some change of colour in the naphtha was acceptable. After loading was completed, the hoses were disconnected and the charterers presented bills of lading to the master for signature. The master refused to sign them as presented and the vessel was detained for four days. The charterers provided the owners with two indemnities and the master thereupon signed the bills of lading. Owners claimed demurrage for the four day detention and their claim was brought to arbitration. Owners alleged that the master was entitled to decline providing his signature because charterers (i) were in breach of cls. 20(a) in that they failed to present bills of lading incorporating verbatim or by reference the proforma bill of lading; (ii) did not permit the master to

---

[74] See *The Agamemnon*.

insert in the bills of lading the date of the charterparty and the names of the parties thereto; and (iii) insisted that clean bills of lading should be issued for the naphtha cargo.

***Held (for the owners):*** (Robert Goff, J.) **i)** Was the general incorporation of the charter in the bills of lading sufficiently effective so as to incorporate the charterparty terms? *"If a bill was presented for signature by the master in a form which did not contain extraordinary terms or terms which were manifestly inconsistent with the charter, then under a charter which required the master to sign bills of lading as presented, he must sign the bills of lading; and if the master did sign such a bill the charterers had to make good any expenses suffered by the owners in consequence."* **ii)** Was the master entitled to insist that the date of the charter and the names of the parties should be inserted in the bills? *"For, under this form of charter, it is not provided that the master should sign bills of lading as presented; he is bound to sign bills of lading 'in the form appearing below', which is the form set out at the end of the charter; In my judgement…it cannot be said that the bill of lading is in such form. The blanks in the form are indications in the form itself that the relevant details should be entered in the blanks which are left for that purpose."*[75] **iii)** Was the master entitled to refuse bills of lading for the naptha cargo as they contained no express reference to cls. M.6? Cls. M.6 was found to be incorporated to the bills of lading by the general words of incorporation

in the bills. Accordingly, the master was bound to sign clean bills for the naptha cargo even though they did not contain any reference to cls. M.6. To sum up, the Judge decided for the owners in that the master was entitled to refuse signing the bills of lading (as presented) on ground (ii) only.

## 89
### GILL & DUFFUS S.A. V. RIONDA FUTURES LTD.
### 1993, 2 Lloyd's Rep. 67 (Q.B.)

The plaintiffs entered into a c.i.f. contract with Cubazucar for the purchase of 11,400 tonnes of sugar on board the ship *Opal Islands*. The contract provided inter alia that demurrage/despatch was to be as per destination terms but with maximum demurrage USD2,000 per day. The plaintiffs, as sellers, then decided to sell the cargo to Paramount Ventures Ltd. (the buyers), and the defendants guaranteed the buyers' performance of the contract terms. The contract of sale provided inter alia "all other terms and conditions as per Sugar Charter Party 1969…despatch and demurrage at discharge to be for buyer's account. Demurrage as per charterparty". The buyers, in turn, sub-sold the cargo to a third party called M. & O. Commodities on similar terms. By the charterparty under which the *Opal Islands* had been let to Cubazucar, demurrage was fixed at USD 5,000 per day and demurrage/despatch was to be settled directly between buyers and sellers. While sailing the vessel had problems with the pumps in the engine room and called at Las Palmas for repairs. The shipowners declared general

---

[75] See *The Ikariada*.

average and agreed to carry on the voyage to the port of discharge, i.e. Misurata. M. & O. Commodities then failed to open the letter of credit and refused to provide general average security. Once at Misurata the ship tendered notice of readiness. As a result of M. & O. Commodities' reluctance to contribute to general average the vessel was on demurrage for 38 days and 11 h. The shipowners exercised a lien on the cargo seeking to recover the contribution for general average and demurrage. The plaintiffs claimed demurrage under the guarantee given by the defendants.

***Held (for the plaintiffs):*** (Clarke, J.) **i)** The expression "as per charterparty" was a genuine commercial arrangement and it did not matter that the charterparty had not been drawn up at the time the contract of sale was made or that the rate of demurrage depended on a standing arrangement between the shipowner and the charterer.[76] Accordingly, the buyers were found liable for demurrage calculated as set out in the sale contract by reference to the charterparty. This being so and under the guarantee so provided to the plaintiffs, the defendants were ordered to pay due to their condition of guarantors. **ii)** The notice of readiness was valid and was not prejudiced by the exercise of the lien on the cargo. By clause 34 of the charterparty the shipowners were allowed to a lien in relation with "demurrage and other charges whatsoever", which included general average. *"Such notice was valid under the contract whether or not the documents were tendered before or after the vessel ar-*

*rived; (it) was valid when tendered on the ground that the vessel was both ready and at the disposal of whoever (the plaintiffs or the buyers) was entitled to possession of the cargo under the bills of lading."* Laytime started running thereby and the buyers were liable to the plaintiffs for demurrage under the terms of the contract of sale. The defendants, as guarantors of the buyers, were called to pay demurrage.

**90**

**GLENCORE GRAIN LTD. V. FLACKER SHIPPING LTD.**
*(The Happy Day)*
2002, Lloyd's Rep. 487 (C.A.)

Flacker Shipping Ltd. (owners) chartered the MV *Happy Day* to Glencore Grain Ltd. (charterers) on a Synacomex form for a carriage of a cargo of wheat from Odessa to Cochin. The charterparty contained the following clauses: "28. If by reason of congestion the vessel is unable to enter the loading/discharging ports, Master…to tender Notice of Readiness ("NOR")…and laytime is to commence as per clause 6, 30 and 31, whether in berth or not, whether in port or not… 30. At first or sole discharging port notice to be given to receivers/agents during normal local office hours and laytime to start counting at 8:00 next working day whether in berth or not, whether in port or not…" When the vessel arrived off the port of Cochin on Friday, 25 Sept. 1998, at 16:30 hours, the NOR was given, but the vessel could not immediately berth because she had missed the tide. The vessel berthed the following day at 13:15 hours and no further NOR was

---

[76] But see *The Heidberg.*

ever given. Discharge commenced on Saturday 26 Sept. and was not completed until 25 Dec., 1998 due to various delays. The owners alleged that laytime had commenced notwithstanding cl. 30 of the charterparty. They argued that charterers were estopped from relying on the fact that no valid NOR had been given because the same was marked "accepted" when tendered, and that, even if the NOR was invalid, laytime commenced no later than when discharge operations began. Charterers in turn argued that, since no valid NOR had ever been given, laytime never commenced pursuant cl. 30 and, therefore, they claimed dispatch. The main question was whether laytime can commence if no valid NOR is ever served, and, if so, when it should commence.

**Held** *(for the owners):* Per Potter, L.J. *"…the court is being asked to spell positive offer and acceptance out of conduct alone in a situation where the parties' obligations were governed by a formal written contract pursuant to which the owners were at all times purporting to act. There was thus no apparent bilateral intention to vary or re-negotiate the express terms of the charter, as opposed to an apparent willingness on the part of the charterer to treat as valid a notice appropriate in form and purportedly served in compliance with the terms of the charter."* Subsequently, the Court of Appeal approached the instant case as a case where waiver operated to cure the imperfect NOR. The Court noted that there are two types of waiver: unilateral waiver and waiver by election. The former *"… arises where X alone has the benefit of a particular clause in a contract and decides unilaterally not to exercise the right or to forgo the benefit conferred by that particular clause".* The latter, in contrast, *"is concerned with the reaction of X when faced with conduct by Y, or a particular factual situation which has arisen, which entitles X to exercise or refrain from exercising a particular right to the prejudice of Y".* In this regard, *"…where two possible remedies or courses of action are to his knowledge open to X and he has communicated his intention to follow one course or remedy in such a manner as to lead Y to believe that his choice has been made, he will not later be permitted to resile from that position".* Turning to the charterers' conduct in the present case, the Court found that *"charterers had waived any reliance on the invalidity of the NOR served upon the receivers or their agents in accordance with the requirements of the charter-party as a means of deferring operation of the laytime regime provided in cl. 30".* This is because the *"receivers' agents themselves accepted instructions to discharge the vessel without any reservation of the charterers' position as to the validity of the NOR they had earlier received. On an objective construction of those matters, although the charterers were not under a contractual duty to indicate rejection of the NOR, by their failure to do so, coupled with their assent to commencement of discharging operations, they intimated, and a reasonable shipowner would have concluded, that the charterers thereby waived reliance upon any invalidity in the NOR and any requirement for further notice".* As to when laytime had commenced, the Court held: *"The unequivocal indication arising from commencement of loading was that the notice previously tendered was at that point ac-*

*cepted as valid, but it was no more than that. On that basis, the detailed provisions as to laytime contained in cl. 30 were apt to apply as from the time of the validation of the notice by acceptance, and neither the conduct of the charterers/receivers, nor the circumstances of the case suggest waiver in that respect".* Subsequently, laytime was held to have commenced at 0800 on Tuesday, 29 Sept.1998.

## 91
### GLENCORE INTERNATIONAL A.G. AND ANOTHER v. BANK OF CHINA
### 1996, 1 Lloyd's Rep. 135 (C.A.)

The plaintiffs sold 1,500 tonnes of aluminium ingots c.i.f. Zhangjiagang to Chinese buyers. The contract provided for an irrevocable letter of credit to be opened by the buyers and payable against the presentation of various documents, including the following: a commercial invoice in three copies, a packing list in three copies, and a set of beneficiary's certificates attached to the courier's receipt. The letter of credit stated "Origin: Any Western Brand". It was expressed to be subject to the UCP 500 (1993 Rev.). After presenting the documents, they were rejected by the defendant reimbursing bank on three grounds: (1) the invoice showed "Any Western Brand-Indonesia (Inalum Brand)" instead of "Any Western Brand", (2) the copies of the packing list did not describe or identify the goods adequately, and (3) the beneficiary's certificates were neither original documents nor (as required by art. 20(b) of the UCP 500) marked as originals. The main question was whether the defendant Bank of China was entitled to reject the documents.

***Held (for the defendants):*** **i)** The origin required by the letter of credit was expressed in a very broad and generic way, and it was an implied meaning that there was more than one "western brand" falling within the genus "Any Western Brand". The court did not accept that the additional words "Indonesia (Inalum Brand)" were such so as to invite litigation. The additional words indicated no more than the precise brand of the goods, and therefore they were not inconsistent with the requirement of the letter of credit. The description of the invoice thus satisfied art. 37(c) UCP 500 (1993 Rev.).[77] **ii)** The letter of credit required the packing list to indicate the quantity and weight of the goods. The alleged discrepancy that it did not contain a description of the goods was rejected. It was found that there was sufficient correspondence and linkage between the packing list and the rest of the documents so tendered without necessity of including a full description of the goods within the packing list. **iii)** (Sir Thomas Bingham, MR) *"There is abundant room to debate what, in the context of modern technology, is an original. A hand-written or typed document plainly is, but other documents can also be plausibly said to be so."* Art. 20(b) UCP (1993 Rev.) though provides a clear rule to apply in such "other documents" produced by re-

---

[77] But see *Rayner (S.H.) & Co. v. Hambros Bank Ltd.*, where the UCP for Documentary Credits was not incorporated and, therefore, strict compliance with the specifications of the credit was required with no exception whatsoever.

prographic, automated or computerized systems. That rule provides that the document must be treated as an original only when it is marked as such.[78] Therefore, in this case, the beneficiary's certificates were rightly rejected since they were produced by such technical means and not marked as originals. The original signature on the document was irrelevant: a signature on a copy does not make it an original, it makes it a mere authenticated copy.

## 92

### GOLDEN STRAIT CORPORATION V. NIPPON YUSEN KUBISHKA KAISHA

*(The Golden Victory)*

2007, 2 Lloyd's Rep. 164 (H.L.)

Nippon Yusen Kubishika Kaisha (NYKK) chartered the MV *Golden Victory* for seven years with one month more or less at NYKK's option on an amended Shelltime 4 form dated 10 July, 1998. The charterparty contained the following war risks clause 33: "If war or hostilities break out between any two or more of the following countries: USA, …UK, …Iraq, both owners and charterers shall have the right to cancel this charter. Either party, however, shall not be entitled to terminate this charter on account of minor and/or local military operation or economic warfare anywhere which will not interfere with the vessel's trade". The charterers redelivered the vessel on 14 Dec. 2001 in repudiatory breach of the charterparty. In a letter dated 17 Dec.,

2001, the owners accepted that breach as terminating the charterparty. At that time, the charterparty was to have expired in just under four years and there was an available charter market for vessels such as the *Golden Victory*. Some fourteen months after the repudiation and some thirty-two months prior to the time the charterparty had originally been negotiated by the parties to expire, the second Gulf War began on 20 Mar., 2003. Disputes subsequently arose concerning the quantum of damages the owners could recover. The owners took the position that the Gulf war was irrelevant to the amount recoverable which should be calculated using the difference between the charterparty rate and the then prevailing market rate at the time of repudiation for the entire remaining period of the charterparty, about four years. The charterers on the other hand argued that because clause 33 would have allowed them to cancel the charterparty when the second Gulf War began, some two years following their repudiation, owners' claim for damages was limited to two years, rather than four years.

***Held (for the charterers):*** Per Lord Scott of Foscote: "*If the charterparty had not been repudiated and had remained on foot, it would have been terminated by the charterers in or shortly after March 2003 when the second Gulf War triggered the clause 33 termination option. But the owners are claiming damages up to 6 Dec. 2005 on the footing, now known to be false, that the charterparty would have continued until then. It is contended that because the charterers' repudiation and its acceptance by the owners preceded*

---

[78] Contrast with *Kreditbank Antwerp v. Midland Bank PLC.*

*the March 2003 event, the rule requiring damages for breach of contract to be assessed at the date of breach requires that event to be ignored. That contention, in my opinion, attributes to the assessment of damages at the date of breach rule an inflexibility which is inconsistent both with principle and with the authorities. The underlying principle is that the victim of a breach of contract is entitled to damages representing the value of the contractual benefit to which he was entitled but of which he has been deprived. He is entitled to be put in the same position, so far as money can do it, as if the contract had been performed. The assessment at the date of breach rule can usually achieve that result. But not always"*. Per Lord Brown of Eaton-Underheywood: *"In my opinion the owners' argument here seeks to extend the effect of the available market rule well beyond its proper scope and to do so, moreover, at the plain expense of Lord Blackburn's fundamental principle: to restore the injured party to the same position he would have been in but for the breach, not substantially to improve upon it. It is one thing to say that the injured party, mitigating his loss as the breach date rule requires him to do, thereby takes any future market movement out of the equation and to that extent crystallizes the measure of his loss; it is quite another to say, as the owners do here, that it requires the arbitrator or court when finally determining the damages to ignore subsequent events (save where the defendants can demonstrate that at the date of breach some suspensive condition would inevitably-and immediately-have operated to cancel the contract). There is no warrant for giving the rule so extended an application"*.

# 93
## GOLODETZ & CO. INC. v. CZARNIKOW-RIONDA CO. INC.
### *(The Galaltia)*
### 1980, 1 Lloyd's Rep. 453 (C.A.)

A contract for the sale of sugar was made on terms c. & f. free out Bandar Shahpour (Iran). The contract provided for payment of cash against documents upon first presentation. The rules of the Refined Sugar Association were incorporated into the contract, which contained, inter alia, the following clauses: "22. Marine insurance shall be effected on Institute Cargo Clauses (All Risks)… Under a c. & f. contract, the buyer's risk shall commence immediately when the sugar is alongside the export vessel. The buyer shall cover Marine and War Risks Insurance and policies shall be for the sellers' protection until payment is made…[79] 23. Payment against full set of signed clean on board bill of lading evidencing freight prepaid, or against ship's clean delivery order". The sellers chartered the vessel *Galaltia* under a charterparty that provided, inter alia, the mate's receipt to be signed by the master for each parcel of sugar once on board. When the vessel was partly loaded at Kandla (i.e. the loading port), a fire broke out and damaged 200 tonnes of sugar. All cargo damaged was discharged and the remainder was later loaded without incident. Two bills of lading were issued, one for the

---

[79] Note that under a c.&f. contract, unlike c.i.f. terms, it is usually for each party to decide to insure his own interest. The risk of the seller ceases on or as from shipment. See art. 32(3) of the Sales of Goods Act 1979 and the Incoterms.

remaining cargo and another for the 200 damaged tonnes. The former was accepted by the buyer, but the latter was rejected on the ground that it was not a clean bill of lading. The two sets of bills of lading (including the one covering the damaged cargo) were on the Congenbill form, which had a printed clause stating "shipment in apparent good order and condition", "weight, measure, quantity, condition, contents and value unknown". The bill of lading in respect to the damaged cargo bore a type-written notation mentioning that the "cargo covered by this bill of lading has been discharged Kandla view damaged by fire and/or water used to extinguish fire for which general average declared".

***Held (for the sellers):*** **i)** A clean bill of lading is one which shows no qualification and according to which the goods were in apparent good order and condition when shipped on board. The crucial time is shipment. The fact that the goods have been lost after shipment or that a liability to contribute in general average or salvage has arisen is no reason for refusing to take up and pay for the documents. Therefore a clause which does not refer to the state of the goods when loaded but refers to the subsequent fate of the goods and to their condition when discharged does not make a bill of lading a claused one. The bill of lading here was therefore clean. **ii)** The bill of lading, although not in a usual form, was merchantable. It called for no enquiry since it showed that the goods were shipped in apparent good order and condition. The rationale behind the case *Hansson v. Hamel* is not applicable here insofar as the bill of lading deprived its holder of protection, which is not the case here. If the buyers wanted a bill of lading not only clean but also "in the usual form", they should have specified that in their contract. **iii)** The estoppel in the bill of lading as to the apparent condition on shipment would remain fully effective so that the presence of the offending clause would not had deprived the buyer of a claim against the carrier for non-delivery. **iv)** The printed clause "weight, measure, quantity, condition, contents and value unknown" does not contain any qualification of the goods, and therefore it is not a valid ground to argue that the bill of lading was not "clean".[80] **v)** The goods were wholly at the risk of the buyers as soon as they passed the board. In the end, the buyers failed to insure the goods, as prescribed by rule 22 of the Refined Sugar Association form, and had to pay the sellers the contract price for the 200 damaged tonnes.

# 94

## GRANIT S.A. V. BENSHIP INTERNATIONAL INC.
### 1994, 1 Lloyd's Rep. 526, (Q.B.)

The plaintiff charterers maintained oral negotiations with the defendant owners regarding the fixture of a vessel to be nominated for a carriage of bulk cargo from France to Bangladesh. The charterers contended that the contract was concluded. The owners alleged that it was

---

[80] But see *The Atlas*.

not insofar as they were not ad idem on certain terms. It was further alleged by the owners that the oral negotiations were specifically made "subject to details" and therefore no binding contract ever existed as between them.

***Held (for the charterers):*** **i)** Evidence showed that the words "subject to details" were never mentioned by the owners during oral negotiations. Hence, the fixture was not "subject to details". **ii)** It was proved that the parties intended to reach a binding agreement. (Waller, J.) *"If they had not intended to do so, they were both clear that the words such as 'subject to details' would have been used. There was nothing of importance left unagreed."*

# 95
## GRANT V. NORWAY
## 1851, 10 CB 665

In 1846 the plaintiffs had done business as merchants in Calcutta (India) under the firm Gladstone & Co. In April of that year, the owners of the ship "Belle" let her on a trip from Calcutta to London for a consignment of silk belonging to the plaintiffs. The master of the ship signed and delivered a bill of lading to the shippers, in the usual form, mentioning that the goods had been shipped in good order and condition. The bill of lading was indorsed to the plaintiffs, but later evidence showed that the goods were actually not shipped on board. The plaintiffs claimed damages against the owners of the ship. The main question was whether the master, who signed a bill of lading for goods that were never loaded, was to be consid-

ered an agent of the owner so as to make the latter liable.

***Held:*** (Jervis, C.J.) *"The very nature of a bill of lading shows that it ought not to be signed until goods are on board; for, it begins by describing them as shipped. It was not contended that such a course is usual. In Lickbarrow v. Mason 2 TR 75, Buller J. says: 'A bill of lading is an acknowledgement by the captain, of having received the goods on board his ship: therefore, it would be a fraud by the captain to sign such a bill of lading, if he had not received the goods on board; and the consignee would be entitled to his action against the captain for the fraud.' It is not contended that the captain had any real authority to sign bills of lading, unless the goods had been shipped: nor can we discover any ground upon which a party taking a bill of lading by indorsement, would be justified in assuming that he had authority to sign such bills, whether the goods were on board or not. If, then, from the usage of trade, and the general practice of ship-masters, it is generally known that the master derives no such authority from his position as master, the case may be considered as if the party taking the bill of lading had notice of an express limitation of the authority; and, in that case, undoubtedly, he could not claim to bind the owner by a bill of lading signed, when the goods therein mentioned were never shipped..."*[81]

---

[81] This decision prompted the enactment of sec. 3 of the Bills of Lading Act 1855 that made the statement of the bill saying that goods had been shipped conclusive evidence of shipment against the master or other person signing the bill (but not necessarily against the owner).

## 96
### GULF VENTURE, THE
1984, 2 Lloyd's Rep. 445 (Q.B.)

The *Gulf Venture* was managed by Gulf Lines Ltd. This firm was appointed by the owners to negotiate all contracts in Europe and Africa. Gulf Lines Ltd., in turn, appointed Gulf Maritime Co. Ltd. as general agents and loading brokers in the U.K. and Europe. The plaintiffs in this action though were the ship agents at Lagos (Nigeria). They had been nominated and authorised by Gulf Maritime Co. The ship agents claimed payment of berthing charges and other expenditures (goods, crew expenses, agency fees...) made for the ships *Gulf Venture* and *Gulf Princess* from 1981 to 1983. They served a writ *in rem* against the *Gulf Venture* in Sharpness seeking reimbursement of their payments. The defendants were the registered owners of the ship, *Gulf Marine* (Cyprus) Ltd. They applied to set aside the writ and for the ship's release on the ground that they could not be liable in an action *in personam*.

***Held (for the plaintiffs):*** (Sheen, J.) **i)** "*In ports all over the world, shipowners or their managers employ shipping agents to make payments in respect of running expenses of a ship. Berthing charges, customs liabilities, the cost of fuel, advances of money to the master and many other expenses have to be met. It must frequently happen that those shipping agents are unaware of the name of the shipowners. But the fact that the principal is not identified does not have the result that he is not liable to reimburse the shipping agent. If it were otherwise, a shipping agent could not safely advance money without being satisfied as to the solvency of the managers. In practice, shipping agents advance money in the belief (sometimes mistaken) that they can look to the value of the ship as security for the debt.*" The defendants' application was dismissed. **ii)** The arrest was maintained but the sum asked for as security was deemed to be higher than that awarded to the plaintiffs. Sheen J. said: "*When plaintiffs are entitled to keep a ship under arrest until her owners provide security for their claim, that security must be for such sum of money as represents their reasonably arguable best case, including interest and their costs of the action....if at the conclusion of the trial it is apparent that the sum demanded by way of security exceeds by a substantial margin the sum recovered, then the plaintiffs will be ordered to pay the cost of providing that part of the security which the Court regards as being unreasonably excessive*".

## 97
### HAIN STEAMSHIP COMPANY LTD. V. TATE & LYLE LTD.
1936, 2 All E.R. 597 (H.L.)

A vessel was chartered to load sugar at two ports in Cuba and one port in Santo Domingo, as ordered by the charterer. The charterparty contained a General Average clause. Orders were given to proceed to the two cuban ports but, owing to a failure of communication of the owner's agent, the master did not receive charterers' instructions concerning the port of Santo Domingo. After loading in Cuba, the vessel sailed straight to

Queenstown (i.e. the port of discharge) for further orders. After noticing the miscommunication, the vessel was ordered back to Santo Domingo to load the cargo remaining. On leaving Santo Domingo she ran aground and part of the cargo was lost. The remaining cargo on board was transhipped onto another vessel bound for the United Kingdom. Shortly before the arrival, a bill of lading was endorsed to Tate & Lyle who took delivery ignoring the deviation. They were asked to sign a Lloyd's average bond to contribute to the general average charges of the lost sugar. After delivery, Tate & Lyle Ltd. claimed back the deposit from the owners arguing that they were not liable to contribute since there had been an unjustified deviation from the agreed route.

***Held (for the owners): i)*** (Lord Wright, M.R.) *"In my opinion deviation is a fault within the principles just stated: the casualty and consequent general average loss must be deemed to have been caused by the deviation since it is impossible to say that the casualty would have occurred if there had been no deviation (…) An unjustified deviation is a fundamental breach of a contract of affreightment. Owing to the peculiar nature of the maritime adventure in which a shipowner and goods owner are jointly concerned, it is a fundamental condition that, in the absence of express liberties, the ship shall proceed by the ordinary and customary route: any deviation changes the adventure (…) It is on similar reasoning that a voyage policy of insurance is avoided from the moment that the vessel actually deviates. This loss of the insurance is sometimes stated as the*

*reason why deviation is treated so drastically under a contract of affreightment."*[82] **ii)** There was, in effect, an unreasonable deviation from the agreed route which constituted a fundamental breach, and so for the charterers were entitled to repudiate the contract. However, they elected to waive their right by ordering the vessel back to Santo Domingo and thereby the contract terms remained in force. Before that, Tate & Lyle Ltd., as indorsees of the bill of lading, were not personally liable to contribute to the general average loss on two grounds: (a) they were not party to the contract of affreightment containing the general average regime, and (b) they ignored the existence of the deviation, i.e. there could be no waiver without knowledge of the breach.[83] However, because general average contributions are chargeable on the goods, and here the owners lifted their lien on the cargo as soon as Tate & Lyle contributed to the general average, it results that Tate & Lyle were legally bound by their bond to make such contribution. **iii)** With regards to the effect of the deviation on the owners' right to recover freight, their lordships found that there was no implied

---

[82] The traditional doctrine of fundamental breach was later overruled by Lord Wilbeforce in *Photo Production v. Securicor Transport,* where it was held that the ordinary law of the contract should apply to the deviation too. Considering old cases like *Hain Steamship Co. v. Tate & Lyle,* their lordship said in *Photo Production v. Securicor Transport* that "it may be preferable that they should be considered as a body of authority sui generis with special rules derived from historical and commercial reasons".

[83] This principle was clearly enunciated in *Leduc & Co. v. Ward.*

obligation to pay the balance freight to the owners, but on a quantum meruit basis only. *"The court would not be slow to infer an obligation, when the goods are received at destination, to pay, not indeed the contract freight, but a reasonable remuneration."*

## 98
### HANSSON V. HAMEL & HORLEY LTD.
### 1922, 2 AC 46 (H.L.)

The present dispute concerns a c.i.f. contract for the sale of goods to be shipped from Braatvag (Norway) to Yokohama (Japan). As there were no available ships sailing directly to Yokohama, the sellers arranged for transhipment at Hamburg (Germany). The goods were shipped from Braatvag to Hamburg with one ship, and from Hamburg to Yokohama with another. In Hamburg, the ship's agent issued a through bill of lading showing that the goods had been transhipped at that port. However, thirteen days had elapsed between the dates of the first bill of lading, which covered the first leg of the voyage, and the bill of lading covering the second leg from Hamburg to Yokohama. When the sellers tendered the documents, the buyers rejected them on the ground that the bill of lading did not provide continuous documentary cover as against the carrier for the whole period of transit from Braatwag to Yokohama. The sellers then sued the buyers for wrongful rejection of the documents.

**Held (for the buyers):** **i)** The tendered bill of lading was not a proper through bill of lading insofar as it gave no continuous documentary cover to the buyers as against the carrier from the original norwegian port. (Lord Sumner) *"When documents are to be taken up the buyer is entitled to documents which substantially confer rights throughout. He is not buying a litigation, as Lord Trevethin says in The General Trading Co.'s Case* [16 Com. Ca. 95, 101], *these documents have to be handled by banks, they have to be taken up or rejected promptly and without any opportunity for prolonged inquiry, they have to be such as can be re-tendered to sub-purchasers, and it is essential that they should so conform to the accustomed shipping documents as to be reasonably and readily fit to pass current in commerce. I am quite sure that, under the circumstances of this case, this ocean bill of lading does not satisfy these conditions. It bears notice of its insufficiency and ambiguity on its face: for, though called a through bill of lading, it is not really so. It is the contract of the subsequent carrier only, without any complementary promises to bind the prior carriers in the through transit; the buyer was left with a considerable lacuna in the documentary cover to which the contract entitled him".* **ii)** In a sale of goods on c.i.f. terms the contract of affreightment must be procured "on shipment", which refers both to time and place. In this respect Lord Sumner said: *"I am quite sure that that a bill of lading only issued thirteen days after the original shipment, at another port in another country many hundreds of miles away, is not duly procured 'on shipment'. Indeed the ocean bill of lading was not procured as part of this c.i.f. shipment at all, and 'on shipment' does not at any rate mean on re-shipment or on transhipment".*

## 99
### Happy Ranger, The
2001, 2 Lloyds Rep. 530

The bill of lading appeared to be a straight bill. In the consignee box, it showed only a named consignee and did not contain the words "to order" or others similar. However, the face of the bill contained, in another body of text, the printed words *"consignee or to his or their assigns"* and these were the only words on the face of the bill indicating negotiability or otherwise. One of the questions was whether the shipowner was could deliver the goods without being presented with the bill of lading.

**Held:** Since those words are accepted to mean *"to order"*, the court decided that they turned the bill a negotiable one.

## 100
### Hellenic Steel Co. v. Svolamar Shipping Co. Ltd.
*(The Komninos S)*
1991, 1 Lloyd's Rep. 370 (C.A.)

A cargo of steel coils was shipped on board the defendant's vessel, *Komninos S*, at Thessaloniki (Greece) for a carriage to Ravenna (Italy). The bills of lading under which the carriage was effected contained exceptions whereby the carrier was, in various circumstances, relieved of liability. The bills included a clause stating "All dispute(s) to be referred to british courts". After discharge, the cargo was found to have been severely damaged by sea water due to inadequately cleaned holds. The cargo-owners issued a writ in the High Court claiming damages for breach of contract, bailment and negligence. The writ was served on the shipowners in their offices in Cyprus. They tried to rely on two exceptions in the bills of lading. Whereas under greek domestic law the exceptions were void and null, under english law they were valid unless the Hague-Visby Rules applied. The main question to be decided was whether greek or english law applied to the contract.[84]

***Held (for the shipowners):*** **i)** (Bingham, L.J.) *"The Hague-Visby Rules were given the force of law* (in England) *by the Carriage of Goods by Sea Act 1971. By virtue of the Act and the Rules themselves the Rules apply:* (sec. 1.3 of the Act) *"…in relation to and in connection with the carriage of goods by sea in ships where the port of shipment is a port in the United Kingdom;* (sec. 1.6.a of the Act)*…in relation to any bill of lading if the contract contained in or evidenced by it expressly provides that the Rules shall govern the contract; and* (art. X of the Rules)*…to every bill of lading relating to the carriage of goods between ports in two different states if (a) the bill of lading is issued in a contracting state, or (b) the carriage is from a port in a contracting state, or (c) the contract contained in or evidenced by the bill of lading provided that these Rules or legislation of any state giving effect to them are to govern the contract, whatever may be the nation-*

---

[84] *"The term 'proper law of a contract' means the system of law by which the parties intended the contract to be governed, or, where their intention is neither expressed nor to be inferred from the circumstances, the system of law with which the transaction has its closest and most real connection."* Dicey and Morris. The Conflict of Laws (11th ed., vol. 2, at p. 116).

*ality of the ship, the carrier, the shipper, the consignee or any other interested person."* Since Greece was not at the time a contracting state, the Rules did not apply by virtue of any of these provisions. **ii)** The next question was whether the parties intended the bills of lading to be governed by the law of the forum that heard the dispute (i.e. England). In that respect, Bingham L.J. concluded: *"…these bills are negotiable instruments which may bind the parties remote from the original contracts. Interpreting X(c) as best I can, I find it impossible to conclude that 'All dispute(s) to be referred to British Courts' amounted to a provision that the legislation of the United Kingdom giving effect to the Rules should govern the contract".*[85] **iii)** *"The consequence of concluding, as I (Bingham, L.J.) do, that the Hague-Visby Rules were not incorporated is that the exemption clauses in the bills of lading protect the shipowners and the cargo-owners are unable to recover; The fact is that the cargo-owners contracted on terms which expressly relieved the shipowners, their master and crew, of responsibility for any act, error, neglect or default in the management, stowage, navigation or preparation of the vessel or otherwise."*

**101**

**HOLLANDIA, THE**
*(The Morviken)*
1983, 1 Lloyd's Rep. 1 (H.L.)

An asphalt road finishing machine was shipped on board Haico Holwerde from Leith (United Kingdom) to Bonaire (Dutch Antilles). A through bill of lading was issued and contained, inter alia, a "Law of application and jurisdiction" clause which stated that the law of the Netherlands (which incorporated the Hague Rules) should apply, as well as that all actions under the present contract of carriage were to be brought before the Court of Amsterdam, with the express exclusion of any other court. The machine was transhipped in Holland from the aforementioned vessel to the *Morviken*, a Norwegian flagged vessel on charter to the original carriers. When the machine was finally discharged at Bonaire, it dropped onto the quay and was severely damaged. The shippers brought an action in rem before the admiralty court against a sister ship, the *Hollandia*, which was owned by the carriers, the Royal Netherlands Steamship Co. The shippers plaintiffs alleged that the Hague-Visby Rules were applicable on the grounds that conditions contained in sec. 1(3) COGSA 1971 and art. X(a and b) were fulfilled. They also argued that the choice of Netherlands law provided, in fact, for lower limits of carriers liability, and thus such clause was to be null and void by virtue of art. II(8) and IV(5.g) of the Hague-Visby Rules.[86] The carriers defendants applied for a stay of proceedings relying on the exclusive jurisdiction clause for the Court of Amsterdam.

---

[85] See also *Egon Oldendorff v. Libera Corp.*

[86] The Netherlands had not in force the Hague-Visby Rules at that time. A Dutch court would have applied the package limit of the Hague Rules, so that the carrier's liability would have been limited to approximately 250 pp. Under the Hague-Visby Rules, the limit would be based on the weight of the goods (9,906 kg), which amounted to about 11,000pp.

***Held (for the shippers):* i)** Concerning the applicable law: *"The Hague-Visby Rules …are to have the force of law in the United Kingdom: they are to be treated as if they were part of directly enacted statute law".*[87] Apart from being applicable by virtue of section 1 (2, 3 and 6) of the Carriage of Goods by Sea Act 1971, the Hague-Visby Rules are also binding to the present case by virtue of article X (a and b) in so far as the bill of lading was issued in a contracting state, as well as applying to a carriage from a contracting state. On these grounds, their lordships found the choice of forum and law clauses in the present bill of lading null and void. The plaintiffs were at liberty to bring the dispute before the UK courts and the carriers' liability was fixed under the Hague-Visby Rules limits.[88] **ii)** Concerning the applicable jurisdiction: (Lord Diplock) *"… a choice of forum clause which selects as the exclusive forum for the resolution of disputes a court which will not apply the Hague-Visby Rules, even after such clause has come into operation, does not necessarily always have the effect of lessening the liability of the carrier in a way that attracts the application of article III, paragraph 8". However, where such clause has the effect of lessening the limits of liability of the carrier, it does attract* the application of art. III(8), and therefore must be rendered "null and void and of no effect". To give effect to such a clause "would leave it open to any shipowner to evade provisions of art. III(8) by the simple device of inserting in his bill of lading issued in, or for carriage from a port in, any contracting state a clause in standard form providing as the exclusive forum for resolution of disputes what might aptly be described as a court of convenience".*

---

**102**

**Hong Guan & Co. Ltd. v. Jumabhoy & Sons Ltd.**
1960, A.C. 684, (P.C.)

Fifty tonnes of Zanzibar cloves were sold. The contract provided that the cloves were to be shipped during Dec. "subject to force majeure and shipment". It resulted though that the sellers were unable to provide enough cargo to perform all the contracts they had formed with other buyers. The cloves the sellers obtained were appropriated to those contracts and no cloves were shipped to the present buyers who subsequently filed a claim for damages. The issue before the court was whether the "subject to force majeure and shipment" clause relieved the sellers of their duty to perform the contract.

***Held (for the buyers):* i)** The clause in the contract did not relieve the sellers of their duty to ship the cloves. The sellers were not entitled to discharge their duties nor excuse their non-performance by reference to their other commitments. *"It must furthermore be borne in mind that the clause now under consideration is not 'sub-*

---

[87] In words of their lordships, *"The Act of 1971 deliberately abandoned what may conveniently be termed the 'clause Paramount' technique employed in section 3 of the Act of 1924…".* (See Vita Food Products Inc. v. Unus Shipping Co. Ltd. and Compagnie Tunisienne de Navigation S.A. v. Compagnie d'Armement Maritime).

[88] Contrast with articles 3(1), 7(2) and 21 of the Rome Convention on the Law Applicable to Contractual Obligations (in force under the Contracts Applicable Law Act 1990 in UK).

*ject to shipment' but 'subject to force majeure and shipment'. It is, therefore, a double-barrelled condition in which there is a juxtaposition of 'force majeure' and of 'shipment'".* Their lordships considered that the clause was (a) conditional on the sellers not being prevented by other circumstances amounting to force majeure from carrying (the contract) out, and (b) conditional on the sellers being able to procure the shipment in Dec. 1950, of cloves to the quantity and of the description referred to in the contract. The protection of the clause "subject to force majeure and shipment" is not available to a seller who has, in fact, received a shipment of the goods sold from his supplier but uses it for the performance of other commitments. **ii)** A "subject to shipment" clause was held to mean that if the seller could prove that it was impossible for him to procure goods for shipment, then he would not be liable. The clause, however, did not mean that the seller could escape liability if he simply decided not to ship. It should not be thought that the phrase "subject to" is a general clause enabling the party in whose favour is directed to withdraw from their duties in any circumstances.

**103**

**HONGKONG FIR SHIPPING CO. LTD. V. KAWASAKI KISEN KAISHA LTD.**

*(The Hongkong Fir)*

1961, 2 Lloyd's Rep. 478 (C.A.)

The vessel *Hongkong Fir* was hired for a period of twenty four consecutive months beginning Feb. 13, 1957. The charterparty contained a heading which stated the vessel was capable of steaming "12 ½ knots in good weather and smooth water". There was also a number of relevant clauses in the charterparty: Clause 1 established that the ship ought to be "in every way fitted for ordinary cargo service". Clause 3 required owners to "maintain her in a thoroughly efficient state in hull and machinery during service". And clause 13 stated "The owners only to be responsible for delay in delivery of the vessel or for delay during the currency of the charter and for loss or damage to goods on board, if such delay or loss has been caused by want of due diligence on the part of the owners or their manager in making the vessel seaworthy and fitted for the voyage..." During the currency of the charter, the freight market dropped. The vessel was off-hire for repeated engine breakdowns amounting to a total repair time of twenty weeks. In view of those delays, the charterers repudiated the contract and elected to treat it as cancelled. The owners claimed damages for wrongful repudiation. The charterers alleged that the owners were in breach in that they failed to deliver and maintain a seaworthy vessel and, alternatively, that the charter became frustrated.

***Held (for the owners):*** **i)** Although the vessel was delivered in a seaworthy state, by reason of her age she needed to be maintained by an experienced and competent engine-room staff. The engine-room staff so provided proved incompetent and insufficient in number. The owners thereby were in breach of clauses 1 and 3 for want of due diligence, negligence of their servants and inability to maintain the vessel's seaworthiness. **ii)** Notwithstanding that, unseaworthiness can either appear by the presence of trivial and easily remediable defects, as well as defects which may result in total loss of the vessel. On the facts of this case, however, the degree of unseaworthiness did not entitle charterers to interpret it as a repudiation and to withdraw from the charter. (Sellers, L.J.) *"Ships have been held to be unseaworthy in a variety of ways and those who have been put to loss by reason thereof (in the absence of any protecting clause in favour of a shipowner) have been able to recover damages as for a breach of warranty. It would be unthinkable that all the relatively trivial matters which have been held to be unseaworthiness could be regarded as conditions…and justify in themselves a cancellation or refusal to perform on the part of the charterer."* Sellers, L.J. added: *"If what is done or not done in breach of the contractual obligation does not make the performance a totally different performance of the contract from that intended by the parties, it is not so fundamental as to undermine the whole contract. Many existing conditions of unseaworthiness can be remedied by attention of repairs, many are intended to be rectified as the voyage proceeds, so that the vessel becomes seaworthy."* **iii)** (Diplock, L.J.) *"There are, however, many contractual undertakings of a more complex character which cannot be categorised as being 'conditions' or 'warranties'… Of such undertakings all that can be predicated is that some breaches will and others will not give rise to an event which will deprive the party not in default of substantially the whole benefit which it was intended that he should obtain from the contract; and the legal consequences of a breach of such an undertaking, unless provided for expressly in the contract, depend upon the nature of the event to which the breach gives rise and do not follow automatically from a prior classification of the undertaking as a 'condition' or a 'warranty'."* With regards the owners' express or implied undertaking to tender a seaworthy ship, Diplock, L.J. said the question was not whether such undertaking was a condition or a warranty: *"It is like so many other contractual terms an undertaking one breach of which may give rise to an event which relieves the charterer of further performance of his undertaking if he so elects and another breach of which may not give rise to such an event, but entitle him to monetary compensation in the form of damages".* **iv)** The delay which arose as a consequence of the incompetence of the engine-room staff was not such as to deprive charterers of the benefit of the use of the ship, and therefore, the charterers were not entitled to repudiate. The delay was considered here to be commercially insufficient to amount to frustration. *"If one party by his conduct frustrates the contract, the law says that the other party may treat the contract as at an end. For breaches of stipulations which fall short of that, the innocent party can only sue for damages."* Accordingly, charterers were entitled only to an action for damages, but not to a repudiation of the contract.

## 104
### HYUNDAI MERCHANT MARINE CO. v. GESURI CHARTERING CO. LTD.
*(The Peonia)*
1991, 1 Lloyd's Rep. 100 (C.A.)

By a charterparty on the New York Produce Exchange form the disponent owners let their vessel to the charterers for a period of (lines 14-15) "…about minimum 10 months maximum 12 months time charter. Exact duration in charterer's option. Charterers have further option to complete last voyage within…trading limits". The vessel was delivered to the charterers on June 11, 1987, and was to be redelivered at the soonest on. April 11, 1988, and at the latest on June 11, 1988. On May 6, 1988, the charterers agreed to a voyage sub-charter with a redelivery date not earlier than July 19. The owners protested and gave June 25 as a latest date on which the vessel was to be redelivered, thereby giving effect to the expression "about" in the charterparty. For each day of hire beyond that date, they asked for an enhanced rate of payment. The charterers declined to accept the terms and the vessel was withdrawn.

***Held (for the owners):*** **i)** Where a charterparty states a final terminal date with no margin of tolerance, the courts imply a reasonable one for the exigencies of the maritime business. Where the charterparty states an express margin or tolerance (e.g. a "more or less" or a "max. min." provision), no such implication is made by the courts. In the present case, the later rule is applied given the express margin and the date of termination comes at the end of the agreed period of leeway. **ii)** Where the charterer gives an order to employ the vessel which cannot reasonably be expected to be performed by the final terminal date, this order is said to be an "illegitimate last voyage" order. Like an order to visit a prohibited port, such an illegitimate order falls outside the charterparty agreement formed with the owner and, in giving it, the charterer commits a repudiatory breach of contract and the owner is not bound to comply with the order. Alternatively, if the owner does comply, he is entitled to payment of hire at the charter rate until the actual redelivery and (provided he does not waive the charterer's breach) to damages (being the difference between the charter rate and the market rate if the later is higher than the former) for the period between the final terminal date and the redelivery date. **iii)** As to the effect of the words "further option" in the charterparty, several charterparty clauses may permit charterers to complete a legitimate last voyage free of liability in damages for late delivery, provided that the unexpected delay is free of fault on the part of the charterers. However, such clauses (just as the ones in the current case) do not confer that right when the last voyage order is illegitimate, unless the clause is so worded as to clearly override the charterer's obligation to redeliver on time.

### 105
### (1) ICL SHIPPING LTD. (2) STEAMSHIP MUTUAL UNDERWRITING ASSOCIATION (BERMUDA) LTD. V. CHIN TAI STEEL ENTERPRISE CO. LTD AND OTHERS
*(The Icl Vikraman)*
2004, 1 Lloyd's Rep. 21 (Q.B.)

China Tai, a Taiwan corporation, were the holders of bills of lading issued by ICL (owners). The bills of lading incorporated a London arbitration clause and acknowledged receipt of 10,078 m of casting billets for a carriage on the vessel *ICL Vikraman* from Poland to Taiwan. On 26 Sept.1997 the vessel collided with

MV *Mount 1* in the Malacca Strait and sank, resulting in the loss of twenty six lives and all of the cargo. Chin Tai arrested a sister ship, the MV *ICL Raja Mahendra*, under proceedings initiated in Singapore. There was disagreement between the parties in relation to the wording of the letter of undertaking (LOU) to be issued by the owners' P&I club in exchange for release of the vessel. Cargo interests wanted the LOU to make express reference to "any sum found to be due to you for damages, interest and costs in a court or tribunal of competent jurisdiction". The matter was referred to the Singapore court, which ruled in the cargo interests' favor in terms of the LOU's wording. The court's determination in this regard was, as a procedural matter, a necessary part of its approval of the release of the sister ship. China Tai's cargo claim was referred to London arbitration and an interim final award was published awarding Chin Tai USD 2,696,127.15 plus interest. The award was based on the fact that owners had failed to exercise due diligence to make the vessel seaworthy at or before commencement of the voyage in breach of the Hague Rules. In the meantime, between the arbitration hearing and the publication of the award, the club and ICL became aware of the fact that any award in cargo's favour would enable Chin Tai to draw on the LOU without regard to the application of the Limitation Convention. There were several other cargo claims in addition to Chin Tai's claim. ICL accordingly issued a limitation claim form and established a limitation fund in England under CPR 61.11(18) and Art. 11 of the 1976 Convention by submitting a payment into court of £1,068,097

on 18 Mar., 2003 (U.S. $1,687,593), an amount significantly less than the amount awarded to Chin Tai. ICL then applied to the Admiralty Court in London for an order releasing the LOU pursuant art. 13.2 of the 1976 Convention, or alternatively, an injunction against the plaintiffs in Singapore from pursuing their in rem action and restraining Chin Tai from presenting the LOU to the club. The court granted the injunction against Chin Tai and allowed the limitation claim form to be served upon Chin Tai in Taiwan. Chin Tai sought to set aside the court's injunction and the granting of service by arguing the court lacked jurisdiction because (i) "legal proceedings" under Art. 11 did not apply to arbitration, (ii) the court lacked jurisdiction to give permission for service out of the jurisdiction of the limitation claim form and to issue an injunction restraining it from making a demand under the LOU, (iii) while the limitation fund had been set up in England, the fund was not 'available' to Chin Tai because the owners had not yet obtained a limitation decree and subsequently they were entitled to enforce the LOU.

***Held:*** (i) The court held that "legal proceedings" in Art. 11 of the Convention do encompass the commencement of arbitration even though the phrase in the ordinary sense refers to proceedings in a court of law. This is because "English Courts have been ready to accord to the convention that meaning wide enough to be consistent with the general practice of the industry" and it is general practice within the industry to include arbitration clauses within bills of lading. In addition, by analogy the word "suit" in art. III, r.

6 of the Hague rules has been widely interpreted to include arbitration. Subsequently, since there were "legal proceedings" in the form of arbitration ongoing, ICL was entitled to constitute a limitation fund under Art. 11 of the Convention. (ii) The injunction restraining Chin Tai from enforcing the arbitration award in its favour by making a demand under the LOU was founded on art. 13.2 of the 1976 Convention. Was this permissible? In that respect, Colman J. said: "*There is, in my judgment, no doubt whatever that the protection provided by art. 13.2 works only by reference to the jurisdiction of the State Party within which a ship or other property has been attached or some other form of security has been given. This provision is directed to the power of a State Party to prevent the utilization as further security for the claim of a vessel or other property within its jurisdiction; further, the Convention cannot be construed so as to create a power in the courts of one State Party to interfere by order with the disposition of property or other security within the jurisdiction of a state that is not a party. The security regime provided by the Convention is clearly confided to State that are party to it*". As the security given by the club lies within the jurisdiction of Singapore in the form of the LOU, which stands in lieu of the vessel, and as Singapore is not a State Party to the 1976 Convention, art. 13.2 of the Convention is not operative and there is subsequently no basis for restraining Chin Tai from making demand of the LOU. (iii) Turning to the availability of the fund, the court held the lack of a limitation decree was not determinative. The limitation fund had been constituted and was thus available within the meaning of

Article 13(3) of the Convention despite the fact that no limitation decree had been made.

## 106
## INDIAN OIL CORPORATION v. VANOL INC.
### 1991, 2 Lloyd's Rep. 634 (Q.B.)

The plaintiff buyers agreed to purchase 25,000 tonnes of kerosene oil c.i.f. Yanbu from the defendant sellers. The contract incorporated the buyers' general terms and conditions for import of oil products, which contained the following provisions: "Article VIII: Any claims regarding…non-delivery…which either party may have against the other party shall be filed with that other party within 150 days from the date of delivery…or the last date on which delivery should have been made…If such a claim is not admitted in full within ninety days of it being filed with the other party, it shall automatically lapse and be forfeited and the other party against whom it is made shall be discharged of all liability with regard thereto, unless arbitration proceedings in respect thereof are commenced and notice thereof is given within 360 days of the delivery date to the party against whom the claim is made; Article XI: Governing Law and Arbitration: (a) The contract shall be governed by the laws of India. (b) In the event of any dispute…arbitration shall take place in India". The contract provided the following further clause: "Law: the validity construction and performance of the agreement shall be governed by English law and all disputes arising thereunder shall be submitted to the jurisdiction of the English courts". The buyers claimed that the sellers were in breach because they failed to deliver 316.402 tonnes. The sellers argued that the buyers' claim was time-barred as it had been filed 150 days after the date of delivery. The question before the court as a preliminary issue was whether the buyers' claim was time barred by virtue of art. VIII of the contract.[89]

***Held (for the sellers):*** (Webster, J.) **i)** *"Where an incorporated document contained provisions which conflicted with provisions of the written document, as did art. XI, and on one construction art. VIII, or part of it which conflicted with the specifically agreed term as to law and jurisdiction, the terms of the written document in the ordinary way prevailed over the terms incorporated by the reference."* **ii)** As far as how art. VIII was to be construed, Mr. J. Webster found that he applicable regime was that: *"(1) if no claim is filed within 150 days of the date of delivery, the claim is barred; (2) if such a claim is filed within 150 days and is not admitted in full within 90 days thereafter it is barred if proceedings are not commenced and notice thereof given within 360 days of the date of delivery; (3) if a claim is filed within 150 days and admitted in full within 90 days there is no time bar except that arising under the relevant English Limitation Act.".* **iii)** *"By having expressly and specifically agreed to submit all disputes to the jurisdiction of the English Courts the parties must be taken to have agreed that the Court's discretionary power to extend time under any Arbitration*

*Act cannot apply."* **iv)** Applying art. VIII in respect with the applicable time-bar, the proceedings were time barred because the buyers failed to produce their claim within 150 days from the delivery date. Accordingly, the answer to the preliminary issue was "yes".

## 107
## INTRACO LTD. V. NOTIS SHIPPING CORP.
### *(The Bhoja Trader)*
### 1959, 2 Lloyd's Rep. 629 (Q.B.)

The MV *Notis* (later renamed *Bhoja Trader*) was sold by a Liberian company, Notis Shipping Corp. (the sellers), to Intraco Ltd. (the buyers). The agreement was concluded under the Norwegian Saleform. This form contained a clause whereby the sellers guaranteed that the vessel, at the time of delivery, was free from all encumbrances and maritime liens or any other debts whatsoever. The clause also provided an indemnity for all consequences of any claim incurred prior to the time of delivery. The price was agreed at USD 810,000. Out of this sum, USD 41,000 had been paid in advance as a deposit, USD 369,000 was paid in cash upon delivery, and the balance of USD 400,000 was payable within ninety days from delivery by means of a guarantee issued at a London Bank. Shortly after delivery, the ship was arrested in Calcutta (India) and the buyers had to furnish a USD 200,000 security to lift the arrest. As a consequence of the arrest, the buyers suffered large losses due to a cancellation of cargo bookings for the ship. The buyers initiated proceedings against the sellers and applied for an ex parte injunction

---

[89] The decision on the merits is found in *Indian Oil Corp. v. Vanol Inc.*, 1992, 2 Lloyd's Rep. 163.

preventing sellers from calling upon the ninety-days guarantee. The ex parte injunction was later dismissed but a Mareva Injunction was indeed granted restraining the sellers from removing their assets from England or otherwise disposing of their assets, in particular of moneys payable under the bank guarantee exceeding USD 50,000.

***Held:*** (Donaldson, L.J.) **i)** The judge refused to interfere with the sellers' right to call on the guarantee since there was no fraud involved. Their decision was argued as follows: "*Irrevocable letters of credit and bank guarantees given in circumstances such that they are the equivalent of an irrevocable letter of credit have been said to be the life blood of commerce. Thrombosis will occur if, unless fraud is involved, the Courts intervene and thereby disturb the mercantile practice of treating rights thereunder as being the equivalent of cash in hand*". **ii)** The sellers were allowed to cash the moneys under the guarantee. However, the Mareva Injunction restraining the removal or disposal of the cash received from the guarantee was maintained. "*Enjoining the beneficiary* (i.e. the seller) *from removing the cash asset from the jurisdiction is not the same as taking action, whether by injunction or an order staying execution, which will prevent him obtaining the cash.*"

### 108
### ISAACS & SONS LTD. V. MCALLUM & CO.
1921 6 Lloyd's Law Rep. 289 (K.B.)

The plaintiff charterers hired a British vessel for four months. When that period was about to expire, they entered into another fixture for twelve months. Shortly after the second charterparty was concluded, the owners sold the vessel to a Greek individual. Under Greek ownership the crew and master were replaced with Greek nationals, the vessel was re-painted and re-named, and most importantly, she was re-lagged with the Greek flag. At the time it was admitted that cargo underwriters required higher premiums for Greek-owned ships and Greek crews than for cargo carried by British-owned ships and crews. Regarding the increase in the cargo-insurance premiums, the charterers claimed damages to the former owners.

***Held (for the charterers):*** (Rowlatt, J.) **i)** "*Lots of changes can be done to a ship, no doubt —painting, and so on, altering the colour, this, that and the other thing; altering the master and all sort of things; but they do not affect the contract.*" However, -Rowlat J., added- "*the law of the flag is of importance and the collateral effects of the law of the flag are also material; I must say that it is a breach to change the flag during the charter-party, and the question is, how much are the damages.*" **ii)** "*I think the plaintiffs are entitled to get a sum to represent the increased difficulty of getting suitable remunerative employment.*"

### 109
### JACKSON V. ROYAL BANK OF SCOTLAND
2005, 1 Lloyd's Rep. 366 (H.L.)

Samson, a business partnership, imported goods from the Far East and sold them to customers in the United Kingdom. Economy Bag, another partnership in the United Kingdom, was Samson's main client. In Sept.1990, Economy Bag placed an order for dog chews from Samson. The Royal Bank of Scotland (the bank), which served as bankers to both partnerships, issued a transferable letter credit to Economy Bag, with Samson named beneficiary and payment upon production by Samson of a commercial invoice, evidence of insurance and a packing list. Samson dealt with import formalities and arranged for carriage from Manchester to Economy Bag's place of business in Preston, with Samson charging 5% of the cif price, exclusive of customs clearance and carriage. Samson kept part of the price paid by Economy Bag as mark up and transferred the remainder of the credit obtained under the letter of credit issued by the Bank to Pet Products, its supplier in Thailand. This pattern of business between Samson and Economy bag continued until March 1993. Samson charged a different mark-up rate on each transaction based on the variety of items sold and it did not disclose the rate of mark-up to Economy Bag. Economy bag was aware of Samson's supplier in Thailand, but it was unaware of the amount of the mark-up. In Jan. 1993 Economy Bag requested a transferable letter of credit in favour of Samson in the amount of USD 50,976 for an order it had placed on 7 Jan. 1993. The letter of credit was issued to Samson on 22 Jan. 1993. Samson instructed the bank to transfer the amount of USD 43,932.50 to Pet Products. The transaction proceeded as usual until 15 Mar. 1993, when a completion statement and other documents including Pet Products' invoice was sent by the bank to Economy Bag instead of to Samson. This resulted in Economy Bag learning about the rate of mark-up by Samson, in this case 19% on the amount payable to Pet Products by Samson, not including the 5% handling charge. Economy Bag subsequently ended the business relationship with Samson and sought a new supplier. As a result, Samson lost most of its business and it was subsequently dissolved. Samson filed a claim against the bank. The court held the bank was in breach of its obligation of confidence and awarded Samson damages for loss of the opportunity to earn profits from its trading relationship with Economy Bag. The court awarded Samson four years' lost profit, with the amount of profit each year being reduced due to uncertainties. The bank appealed and the Appellate Court reduced the damages to one year from the date of breach. Samson appealed, arguing that damages should be extended over a six-year period. The bank countered that there was no foreseeable loss and that any attempt to assess damages was too speculative. The issue was whether the judge was correct in his findings on causation, remoteness and quantum.

***Held (for Samson):*** Although the letter of credit lacked terms that the bank would treat documents received by the beneficiary as confidential, the right of the first beneficiary to substitute his own invoice for that of the second beneficiary, Pet Products, and draw on the credit pursuant its pre-transfer terms was an important feature of the transfer regime, which enabled Samson to keep the amount of its profit confidential. The bank was under a duty to protect such confidentiality despite the fact that Economy Bag knew the name of the supplier in Thailand

and could have discovered the amount of mark-up. As far as damages were concerned, Lord Hope held: *"[T]he loss of repeat orders from Economy Bag was not too remote. As soon as the confidential information was released there was no repeat business. The claimants are entitled to an award of damages to put them in the same place as they would have been if there had been no breach of contract. The question that remains is one of assessment. I would reject [the] …contention that the matter is so speculative that the award should be confined to one of general damages".* Turning to the quantum, Lord Hope pointed out two errors the Appellate Court made in quantifying the damages. The Appellate Court asked what was within the reasonable contemplation of the bank at the time of the breach, but this was in conflict of the relevant date identified in *Hadley v. Baxendale*, which is the date of the making of the contract, not the date of breach. In Lord Hope's words: *"The parties have the opportunity to limit their liability in damages when they are making their contract. They have the opportunity at that state to draw attention to any special circumstances outside the ordinary course of things which they ought to have in contemplation when entering into the contract. If no cut-off point is provided by the contract, there is no arbitrary limit that can set to the amount of damages once the test of remoteness according to one or other of the rules in Hadley v. Baxendale has been satisfied".* The second error follows from the first given the fact that the bank failed to include any provision in the letter of credit limiting its liability for the loss of Samson's repeat business to any particular period which leaves the assess-

ment of the period of liability up to the courts to determine. *"This is when, on the facts, the question whether any loss has been sustained has become too speculative to permit the making of any award. He [Court of First Instance] held that as time passed it was increasing likely that Economy Bag would have acquired the motive and means to squeeze Samson's profit margins and would ultimately have ended their business relationship."* Lord Hope then went on to hold that the award made *"…on a reducing basis extending over a four-year period, is as good an estimate as can now be made of the effect on Samson's profits of the bank's breach of contract".*

<h1 style="text-align:center">110</h1>

JAMES FINLAY & CO. LTD. V. KWIK HOO<br>
TONG HANDEL MAATSCHPPIJ<br>
1929, 1 KB 400 (C.A.)

The plaintiff was a well-known English firm conducting business in India and the defendants sugar merchants in Java. The latter sold to the former a cargo of sugar "c.i.f. Bombay" in three instalments to be made within the months of July, August and Sept. of 1920. The sale contract provided for the opening of a confirmed letter of credit by the buyers through their representatives in London. The last of the three instalments was actually shipped on Oct. 3, but the ship agents back-dated the bill of lading "Sept. 30" stating that the cargo had been "shipped in good order and condition". The documents were accepted by the confirming bank and payment was made effective under the letter of credit. The plaintiffs had made three sub-contracts for the resale, which provided for shipments in July, August and September, and each contract stated that "the bill of lading shall be conclusive evidence of the date of shipment". The market price for sugar had fallen with respect to the price agreed on the date of the contract. The sub-buyers refused the goods alleging that it was not a genuine Sept. shipment. The plaintiffs then sold the sugar by auction and sought damages from the defendants for the difference between the contract price and the market price. The defendants alleged that the bill of lading had been issued according to the custom of the port.

***Held (for the plaintiffs):*** **i)** In shipment contracts the seller owes the buyer not only an obligation to deliver goods according to the contract specifications, but also a separate duty to tender documents conforming with the contract requirements. The buyer is assisted by two separate rights of rejection: one concerning the documents and the other in relation to the goods.[90] In a c.i.f. contract, the contract should be regarded as a sale of documents rather than a sale of goods. It is a condition of the contract not only that the goods should be shipped in Sept., but also that a genuine bill of lading should be tendered showing the correct date of shipment. In that regard, the judge said that generally the effect of misdating the bill is to deprive the buyers of the right to reject the documents by rendering its exercise impossible if they rely on the ac-

curacy of the bill of lading date.[91] **ii)** Regarding the severe market fall, had the bill of lading shown October as the shipment date, the tender would have probably been rejected by the buyers, who could have obtained equivalent goods at the market price. In considering the damages for the plaintiffs, the court held that the plaintiffs were to be put in the same position as they would have been had the bill of lading shown Oct. as the shipment date. As a result, they were entitled to recover the difference between the contract price and the price of the goods realised at auction. **iii)** Contrary to the defendants' submission, the plaintiffs were not bound to enforce the contracts as against the sub-buyers for the purposes of minimising the damages. Doing so, after being aware that the shipment date was incorrect, would have been tantamount to endanger unjustifiably the plaintiffs' commercial reputation.

**111**

**JAYAAR IMPEX LTD. V.
TOAKEN GROUP LTD.**
1996, 2 Lloyd's Rep. 437 (Q.B.)

On 1 Nov. 1994 an agreement for the sale of fourty seven tonnes of Nigerian Arabic gum was reached by phone between Jayaar Impex (as buyers) and Toaken Group (as sellers). A few days later, the sellers mailed the terms of the agreement on their contract form to the buyers. The document provided, inter alia, that

---

[90] See *Bergeco USA v. Vegoil Ltd.* and *Kwei Tek Chao v. Bristish Traders and Shippers Ltd.*

[91] Wright J., at first instance; 1928, 2 KB 604 (K.B.); affirmed at 1929, 1 KB 400 (C.A.)

"IGPA (International General Produce Association Ltd.) Spot terms and conditions to apply". It further stated that "Any dispute arising out of the contract…to be settled by arbitration in accordance with the above rules and conditions". Although the sellers' contract form contained the words "Important - Please sign, date and return this document", the buyers neither signed nor returned it. Among the other provisions, Rule 124 of the incorporated IGPA form provided that no claim in relation to quality, condition or description of the goods would be accepted "after the Prompt Day or after the removal from wharf, warehouse or store if removed prior to the Prompt Day". Upon delivery, the buyers alleged that the goods were of unsatisfactory quality. The sellers, citing Rule 124 applicable to quality claims not promptly received and demanded full payment of the goods. The sellers sought IGPA arbitration, but the buyers alleged they were bound neither by the written contract nor by the IGPA terms. The sellers, through arbitration conducted under the IGPA rules, obtained a favourable award. The buyers sought a declaration that the award was null and void due to the arbitrators' lack of jurisdiction.

***Held (for the buyers):*** **i)** (Rix J.) *"It was unbusinesslike to infer that the buyers intended to accept (by telephone) the terms of the sellers' contract form whatever it should turn out to be."* **ii)** On the evidence before Rix, J., the buyers never accepted the sellers' contract form, which was a variation of the existing oral contract. In addition, there were no precedents or customs between the parties out of which it could be implied that the sellers' contract form

was, by usage, part of the agreement.[92] **iii)** In so far as the IGPA form was not part of the agreement, the IGPA arbitrators lacked jurisdiction and their award was subsequently void and without effect.

**112**

**J.I. MACWILLIAM CO. INC. V.
MEDITERRANEAN SHIPPING CO. S.A.**
*(The Rafaela S)*
2005, 1 Lloyd's Rep. 347 (H.L.)

Mediterranean Shipping Company S.A. (MSC) entered into a contract of carriage with Coniston International Machinery Ltd. (Coniston) to carry a consignment of four containers of printing equipment from Durban (South Africa) to Felixstowe (England) and onward to Boston (USA). A set of three documents, described on their face as bills of lading, were issued with the following words into the "Consignee box": "B/L not negotiable unless 'ORDER OF'". The box contained only the name and address of the respondent-buyers, J. I. MacWilliam Company Inc. (MacWilliams). On its face, the bill of lading was not negotiable; it was a straight bill of lading. The cargo was carried by the MV *Rosemary* from Durban to Felixstowe, where it was unloaded and shipped aboard the MV *Rafaela S* for a carriage to Boston. The consignees alleged that the printing equipment had been damaged beyond repair during the Felixstowe-Boston leg and sought damages. MSC argued that the Hague-Visby Rules were inapplicable in this case be-

---

[92] See *S.I.A.T di dal Ferro v. Tradax Overseas S.A.*

cause a straight (non-negotiable) bill of lading was not a document of title, and, therefore, not a bill of lading within section 1(4) of the Carriage of Goods by Sea Act, 1971. In the appeal to the House of Lords, the sole issue was whether a bill of lading not made out to order or bearer but to a named consignee (a straight bill of lading) is a bill of lading or similar document of title within the meaning of Article I(b) of the Hague-Visby Rules[93] and hence within s. 1(4) of the Carriage of Goods by Sea Act, 1971."

***Held (for the respondents):*** (i) Before adopting the Hague Rules, the practice of issuing straight bills of lading well existed, and such bills were described and treated as bills of lading. Even though that practice existed, the travaux préparatoires of the Hague Rules are not conclusive in determining the intentions of the framers in reference to the issue. However, as Lord Steyn stated, "...*it is a fair inference that the framers of the Hague Rules could not have been unaware of the relatively widespread mercantile use of straight bills of lading at that time. If it had been intended to exclude these bills of lading, special provision to that effect would surely have been made. Instead the gateway to the application of the Hague Rules was expressed in the wide and general terms of the existence of a bill of lading or any similar document of title*". Lord Steyn went on to hold that the words "*any similar document of title*" are words that expand the inclusion of documents, postulating a wider meaning, not words that restrict the types of documents to fall under the rule as the appellants propose. (ii) Regarding the appellants' argument that the function of a straight bill of lading is equal to that of a sea waybill, and thus not a document of title applicable to the Hague Rules, Lord Steyn found the comparison unrealistic, noting that a straight bill of lading in the hands of a named consignee is *his* document of title, while a sea waybill is never a document of title. Further differences include that fact that a straight bill contains the standard terms of the carrier on the reverse side while a sea waybill is blank, and straight bills of lading are invariably issued in sets of three and sea waybills are not. (iii) There is no policy reason why the draftsmen of the Hague Rules would have found it desirable to distinguish between a named consignee who receives an order bill of lading and a named consignee who receives a straight bill of lading. In the words of Lord Steyn, "*There is simply no sensible commercial reason why the draftsmen would have wished to deny the CIF buyer named in a straight bill of lading the minimum standard of protection afforded to the CIF buyer named in an order bill of lading. The importance of this consideration is heightened by the fact that straight bills of lading fulfill a useful role in international trade provided that they are governed by the Hague-Visby Rules, since they are sometimes preferred to order bills of lading on the basis that there is a*

---

[93] Article I(b): "contract of carriage" applies only to contracts of carriage covered by a bill of lading or any similar document of title, in so far as such document relates to the carriage of goods by water, including any bill of lading or any similar document as aforesaid issued under or pursuant to a charter-party from the moment at which such bill of lading or similar document of title regulates the relations between a carrier and a holder of the same.

*lesser risk of falsification of documentation*". Straight bills of lading are treated as sea waybills under the Carriage of Goods by Sea Act, 1992, an assumption made in The Law Commission Report No. 196, Rights of Suit in Respect of Carriage of Goods by Sea, pars. 2.50 and 4.10-4.12. However, this fact has no bearing on the case at hand for two reasons. First, the contract of carriage in the case at hand came into existence three years prior to the enactment of the 1992 Act. Secondly, and more fundamentally, *"s. 5(5) of the 1992 Act specifically provides that it will not affect the Hague-Visby Rules. The terms of the 1992 Act cannot alter the proper construction of art. 1(b) of the Rules"*.

## 113

### JINDAL IRON AND STEEL CO. LTD. AND OTHERS V. ISLAMIC SOLIDARITY SHIPPING CO. JORDAN INC.
### *(The Jordan Ii)*
### 2005, Lloyd's Rep. 57 (H.L.)

A carrier had carried iron coils on FIOST charterparty terms ("free in, out, stowed and trimmed") from Mumbai (India) to Motril. The charter-party had the following provisions: *"3. Freight to be paid (…) FIOST- lashed/secured/dunnaged; 7. Charterers to have full use of all vessel's gear to assist in loading and discharging cargo. Vessel's gear should only be considered as supplementary to the shore gear. Shore winch/cranemen to be used at all time; 17. Shippers/ charterers/ receivers to put cargo on board trim and discharge cargo free of expense to the vessel"*. The bill of lading incorporated the charterparty terms. When the cargo was discharged, it was alleged by the receivers that the cargo had been damaged due to the manner of stowage and the manner of discharge. The terms of the charterparty, which had been incorporated into the bill of lading, when read together, provided that the charterer and shipper would undertake responsibility for stowage, and that responsibility for discharge laid with the charterer and receiver.

***Held (for the shipowners):*** The cargo claimants asked their lordships to depart from earlier established precedent and strike down the contractual clauses under Article III Rule 8 of the Hague Rules.[94] Their lordships declined to do so. Lord Steyn, who gave the leading judgment, stressed the importance of certainty in international trade law. The position established in the earlier case law could only be departed from if it could be demonstrated that it had worked unsatisfactorily in the market place and had produced manifestly unjust results. Their lordships did not find that this high threshold had been reached in this case. None of the arguments advanced by cargo owners to support a literal approach to Article III Rule 2, which would impose a duty on the owners non-transferrable by contract, were accepted. Their lordships found that the approach in the earlier cases was not based on any technical rules of English law, but on "a perspective relevant to the interests of maritime nations generally". Accordingly, the international perspective

---

[94] See *Renton (G.H.) & co. v. Palmyra Trading Corporation (The "Caspiana")*, (H.L.) 1956 2 Lloyd's Rep. 379.

and the need for settled principle supported the owners' position.

## 114
### KALLANG SHIPPING S.A. v. AXA ASSURANCES SENEGAL
*(The Kallang)*
2007, 1 Lloyd's Rep 160 (Q.B.)

There was a substantial shortage while goods were being discharged in Dakar. The cargo insurers, AXA Senegal demanded a provisional guarantee to be replaced by a bank guarantee when the final figures became available upon completion of discharge. This request was repeated in an e-mail dated 10 Mar., 2005, along with the contention that the arbitration clause in the charter-party was not applicable because AXA Senegal was not a party to that contract. In response, the owners' P&I Club refused to provide a guarantee, but instead offered a letter of undertaking under usual club terms as security for the full sum claimed. AXA Senegal declined to accept the club's letter answerable to English law and arbitration, and decided to arrest the vessel in Dakar. Owners then sought and obtained an anti-suit injunction from the English High Courts.

***Held (for the claimant):*** There are at least two categories of cases in which an anti-suit injunction may be ordered: (a) where there is a legal right not to be sued in a foreign court pursuant to a jurisdiction or arbitration clause, or (b) where the is an equitable right not to be sued in a foreign court because the pursuit of foreign proceedings is vexatious and oppressive. *"[T]he conduct of CCMN and*

*Axa Senegal, and their refusal to accept a club letter of undertaking in relation to this cargo claim was effectively frustrating the claimant's contractual entitlement to have that dispute resolved by way of London arbitration."* The English courts could not hinder the arrest of a vessel to obtain security for a claim if no adequate security was forthcoming and, although it is a matter for the arresting court to ultimately decide the terms of the security, an English court is justified in restraining the defendants in the present case through a personal injunction from (a) insisting on a form of security that lifts the arrest which directly or indirectly requires the resolution of the cargo claim in Senegal, (b) submitting before that Dakar court that the only reasonable security which should be accepted was a bank guarantee that required resolution of the cargo dispute in, and subject to, Senegalese jurisdiction, and (c) contending that only a Senegalese bank guarantee was acceptable security where the American Club had offered its letter of undertaking. The judge concluded that, *"In circumstances such as the present, where, given the size of the cargo claim, the American Club letter was clearly adequate and reasonable security, and where there was, on any basis, uncertainty about the willingness of local banks speedily to provide security that responded to determination of the cargo claim by London arbitration, the defendants' conduct in contending for security provisions that directly or indirectly would bring about a situation where the London arbitration clause was frustrated, amounted not only, in my view, to a breach of implied terms of the arbitration clause,…but also oppressive conduct".*

## 115

### Kenya Railways v. Antares Co. Ltd.
*(The Antares, Nos 1 & 2)*
1987, 1 Lloyd's Rep. 424 (C.A.)

The vessel *Antares* was chartered to Mediterranean Shipping Co. S.A. (MSC) under the New York Produce Exchange form. MSC operated a liner service between Europe and East Africa. In Dec. 1983, they loaded some machinery at Antwerp (Belgium) for a carriage to Mombasa (Kenya). The bills of lading were issued on the form of MSC and contained a demise clause which only bound the shipowners. When the cargo was discharged at destination, part of the machinery was damaged as a result of being carried on deck. The holders of the bill of lading sought damages against MSC assuming that MSC were the owners of the vessel when, in fact, MSC were the charterers; they had overlooked the demise clause printed on the back of the bill. A year after the cargo was delivered, the plaintiff discovered that MSC were not the shipowners but the charterer. The plaintiffs set the claim to the true shipowners (called Antares) but the time bar under art. III(6) of the Hague-Visby Rules had already expired. The issues before the C.A. were, inter alia, whether the shipowners' carrying the goods on deck constituted a fundamental breach and if so, whether the shipowners were subsequently precluded from relying on the one-year limitation of the Hague-Visby Rules.

***Held (for the shipowners):* i)** The court found no reason for regarding the unauthorized loading on deck a special case which thereby should be excluded from the modern principles of repudiatory breach. (Lloyd L.J.) "*The doctrine of fundamental breach on which (the plaintiffs) relies, that is to say the doctrine that a breach of contract may be so fundamental as to displace the exception clauses altogether, no longer exists.*"[95] **ii)** The time bar under art. III(6) of the Hague-Visby Rules is entirely applicable irrespective of the nature of the breach. Yet even more insofar as that provision had been given the force of statutory law and was expressed so as to exclude all liability "whatsoever".[96] **iii)** On the other hand, although MSC were authorized as agents by virtue of the terms of the charterparty and were entitled to sign the bill of lading containing such a demise clause, the terms of the charterparty did not give them authority to settle all cargo claims on behalf of the shipowners, but rather only those claims for which MSC was to be liable under the terms of the charterparty.

## 116

### KG Bominflot Bunkergesellschaft für Mineralöle MBH & Co. KG v. Petroplus Marketing AG
*(The Mercini Lady)*
2010 EWCA Civ 1145 (C.A.)

KG Bominflot purchased a cargo of gasoil from Petroplus on FOB Antwerp terms to be shipped on board the MV *Mercini Lady* oir substitute. The contract described

---

[95] Lloyd L.J. (obiter): in answering the question whether deviation cases may have survived the abolition of the doctrine of fundamental breach, L.J. took the view that they "*should now (since Photo Production Ltd. v. Securicor Transport Ltd.) be assimilated into the ordinary law of contract*".

[96] See also *The New York Star.*

various specifications that the gasoil had to meet at the time of shipment, including as to total sediment. It also provided for quality and quantity to be determined basis shore tank by a mutually agreed independent inspector at the loading terminal. In the contract, the inspector's decision was agreed as final and binding on both parties except in case of fraud or manifest error. Clause 18 provided that "there are no guarantees, warranties or representations, express or implied, or merchantability, fitness or suitability of the oil for any particular purpose or otherwise which extend beyond the description of the oil set forth in this agreement". The pre-loading analysis found that the product met the specifications, including the total sediment. However, the buyers alleged that four days later, when the goods arrived at destination, these were off specifications, including as to sediment. It was common ground between the parties that the load port inspection was not invalid as a result of "fraud or manifest error" (both of which would have prevented its finding being final and binding), and no point was taken about the fact that the load port inspectors did not use the contractual test method.

***Held:*** The court found that the implied statutory condition of satisfactory quality contained in Section 14 of the 1979 Act applied only at the time of delivery, but not thereafter. A further term should be applied into the contract at common law to the effect that the goods should "remain on specification for a reasonable time after delivery". As to effect of Clause 18, the court noted that the clause did not specifically exclude "conditions" and, since the implied terms of the Sale of Goods Act are conditions, the clause did not operate so as to exclude the requirements of merchantability, fitness or suitability contained in the Act. However, Rix, L.J. said: *"If...the alleged vice [off-spec quality criteria] is in truth something for which the specification and conclusive determination clauses provide... there may be no room for a separate allegation of breach by reference to the statutory implied term of what is now satisfactory quality or any similar term to be implied at common law".*

**117**

**K**H **E**NTERPRISE (**C**ARGO **O**WNERS) V.
**P**IONEER **C**ONTAINER (**O**WNERS)
*(The Pioneer Container)*
1994, 1 Lloyd's Rep. 593 (P.C.)

The plaintiffs' goods were carried from Taiwan to Hong Kong on board the vessel *KH Enterprise.* The vessel collided with another vessel and sank resulting in a total loss. The plaintiffs claimed damages for the loss of cargo and initiated proceedings in Hong Kong. The defendant shipowners applied for a stay of proceedings in reliance of an exclusive jurisdiction clause inserted in the bills of lading stating that any dispute thereunder shall be governed by Chinese Law and adjudicated before the courts of Taipei. However, not all the plaintiffs were parties to the contracts evidenced in the bills of lading which were issued by the defendants. Whilst some of the plaintiffs contracted directly with the defendants for the carriage of their goods from Taiwan to Hong Kong, others had shipped their goods for lengthier voyages through other vessels. The owners had in turn sub-contracted the feeder service for the Taiwan-Hong Kong leg to the defendants, who therefore acted as sub-bailees. The second group of plaintiffs received bills of lading not from the defendants but from the contractual ocean carriers. Such bills contained a clause entitling the ocean carrier to sub-contract "on any terms" the whole or any part of the carriage. The question to be decided was whether the exclusive jurisdiction clause of the defendants' bills was binding upon the second group of plaintiffs notwithstanding these were not direct parties to such contracts. In words of Lord Goff of Chieveley, "*the question has arisen whether, in an action by the owner against the sub-bailee for loss of the goods, the sub-bailee can rely as against the owner upon one of the terms upon which the goods have been sub-bailed to him by the bailee*".

***Held:* i)** The law of bailment circumvents the principle of privity of contract, under which only a person who is party to a contract may sue upon it. "*Their Lordships …consider that, if the sub-bailment is for reward, the obligations owed by the sub-bailee to the Owners must likewise be that of a bailee for reward notwithstanding that the reward is payable not by the owner but by the bailee.*"[97] **ii)** The plain-

tiffs, when contracted with the ocean carrier (the bailee), expressly consented the sub-bailment "on any terms" for the whole or any part of the carriage.[98] The Board held that "(t)hen to the extent that the terms of the sub-bailment are consented to by the owner, it can properly be said that the owner has authorised the bailee so to regulate the duties of the sub-bailee in respect of the goods entrusted to him, not only towards the bailee but also toward the owner". On this wide construction, it was held that only unusual or unreasonable clauses would be excluded from the ambit of the words "on any terms", and exclusive jurisdiction clauses were neither unusual nor unreasonable. Indeed, being exposed to many claims arising from the same casualty, the incorporation of such clauses by the defendant shipowners was understandable as it allowed "an ordered and sensible resolution of disputes in a single jurisdiction". **iii)** The fact that the defendants' bills of lading contained a Himalaya clause is not sufficient ground for preventing the sub-bailee to take advantage, as against the owner of the goods, of the terms on which the goods have been sub-bailed to him. It is true that the Himalaya clause would give the defendants another regime of indemnity to invoke, which can be regarded as alternative to that of the sub-bailment, but both regimes are not inconsistent with each other.[99]

---

[97] In *Morris v. C.W. Martin & Son (1965, 2 Lloyd's Rep. 63; 1966, Q.B. 716)*, Lord Denning said that: "*the owner (bailor) is bound by the conditions (contained in the contract between the bailee and the sub-bailee) if he has expressly or impliedly consented to the bailee making a sub-bailment containing those conditions, but not otherwise*". The first question to look at was whether the sub-bailment was authorised by the owner, and, if so, whether the terms of the sub-bailment were indeed authorised and binding upon the relationship between the owner and the sub-bailee.

---

[98] For the implied consent of sub-bailment see *Singer (UK) Ltd. v. Tees & Hartlepool Port Authority.*
[99] But see *The Mahkutai.*

## 118
### KLEINJAN & HOLST NV ROTTERDAM V. BREMER HANDELSGESELLSCHAFT MBH HAMBURG
#### 1972, 1 Lloyd's Rep. 11 (Q.B.)

The plaintiff buyers agreed to purchase a quantity of sugar-beets c.i.f. Rotterdam. Shipment was to be made in Feb. or Mar., 1971. The contract incorporated the Cattle Food Trade Association standard form no. 100, which provided, inter alia, the following clauses: cl.10(d) "Every such Notice of Appropriation shall be open to correction of any errors occurring in transmission, provided that the sender is not responsible for such errors…"; cl.10(g) "When a valid Notice of Appropriation has been received by buyers, it shall not be withdrawn except with their consent". The sellers sent notice of appropriation erroneously naming the vessel as "Mahout" whilst her actual name was "Mahsud". Three days later, they sent a further notice amending the mistake with the correct name typed. The buyers then refused to accept the amended notice and insisted that the sellers should tender shipping documents mentioning the ship as in the original message i.e. "Mahout". The buyers eventually accepted the bill of lading mentioning the goods were on board the steamship "Mahsud". They paid the contract price but claimed damages thereafter.

***Held (for the buyers):*** **i)** It was the sellers' duty to tender shipping documents in accordance with the original notice of appropriation and their failure put them in breach of a condition of the contract. A mistake in a notice of appropriation under the CFTA 100 form can be amended only if such mistake was one "occurring in transmission". Any other amendment will not have valid effect in itself. **ii)** Since the buyers had accepted the shipping documents referring to the steamship Mahsud, the breach of condition was reduced to a breach of warranty. Section 11 of the Sale of Goods Act 1893 shall be applicable here insofar the buyers elected to treat the sellers' failure as a breach of warranty and not as a ground for repudiation of the contract.[100] **iii)** The true measure of damages for breach of a warranty in this case was the difference between the contract price and the market price at the date of the breach.

## 119
### KNUTSFORD LTD. SS. V. TILLMANNS & CO.
#### 1908, AC 406 (H.L.)

A cargo of coal was shipped on board a vessel for a voyage from Middlesbrough (England) to Japan, and thereafter to Vladivostock (Russia) to discharge the remaining cargo. The voyage was under the validity of a time charter. Forty miles from Vladivostock, the master decided not to carry on the voyage for fear that the ice could damage the propeller. Three bills of lading had been issued and a fourth had been signed by the time charterers instead of the master. In cl. 4 of the charterparty they provided that the

---

[100] But see *Panchaud Freres SA v. Establissements General Grain Co.* and *Vargas Pena y Cía. SAIC v. Peter Cremer GMBH.*

ship was to discharge at some other safe port "should the entry and discharge at a port be deemed by the master unsafe or inaccessible in consequence of war, disturbance or any other cause". By clause 2 the owners were to be exempted from liability because of "error in judgement of the master…whether in navigating the ship or otherwise". For three days the master tried in vain to navigate through the ice and then returned to Nagasaki and discharged the cargo there. The day after her turning back the ice cleared and the port became safe to access. The charterers claimed and obtained judgement as against the owners before the Court of Appeal. The owners appealed.

***Held (for the charterers):*** **i)** (Lord Dunedin) *"Here the practical inaccessibility lasted but three days, and though the captain may have been right, in view of the danger of his anchorage under the lee of Askold Island, to give up the attempt to enter Vladivostock when he did, I see no reason why he should not have renewed his attempt when the weather conditions changed as they did on the very next day."* Their lordships held that the proper conduct of the master was to proceed to Vladivostock once he had learned that the port became accessible. **ii)** The words in clause 4 of the bills of lading did not entitle the master to refuse that port as unsafe for reasons other than war or disturbance. The last words of the clause (i.e. "or any other cause") must be read as being ejusdem generis with war or disturbance; they are not applicable to ice. The words in clause 2 are also of no benefit to the owners since the non-delivery at Vladivostock was not due to an error in navigation. **iii)** As to whether the owners were bound in respect of the fourth bill of lading signed by the charterers themselves, their lordships responded affirmatively since the charterers indicated on the bill that they were signing on behalf of the master and the owners. The time charterer has a general right to sign bills of lading under the general employment and agency clause under the charterparty. Lord Dunedin, however, added: *"Had the bill of lading contained stipulations of such an extraordinary character that the master might have refused to sign, then that defence would have been equally open upon the question whether the signature of the charterers bound the owners".*

**120**

**K**ODROS **S**HIPPING **C**ORP. OF **M**ONROVIA
**v. E**MPRESA **C**UBANA DE **F**LETES[101]
*(The Evia, No.2)*
1982, 2 Lloyd's Rep. 307 (H.L.)

On Nov. 12, 1979, the vessel *Evia* was chartered on a Baltime form for eighteen months, two months more or less at the charterers' option. The vessel was expressly agreed (in cls. 2) to be employed "only between good and safe ports". In March 1980, she was ordered to load a cargo of building materials in Cuba for Basrah in Iraq. At that time, there was no reason to believe that Basrah was unsafe or was likely to become so in a foreseeable future. The vessel berthed in Basrah on Aug. 20, 1980. Just by the time the discharge had been completed, the Iran-Iraq war broke out, the result being that all navigation

---

[101] The *Chatt-al-Arab* cases.

in the area ceased resulting in the *Evia* being indefinitely trapped. The umpire held that the charterparty was frustrated and rejected the shipowner's claim that the charterers were in breach of the safe port clause. The Court of Appeal reversed the decision, but the House of Lords ultimately dismissed the shipowner's appeal.

***Held (for the charterers):* i)** The safe port warranty does not amount to a continuing guarantee but refers only to the prospective safety of the port at the time it was nominated. (Lord Diplock) *"It is with the prospective safety of the port at the time when the vessel will be there for the loading or unloading operation that the contractual promise is concerned, and the contractual promise itself is given at the time when the charterer gives the order to the master or other agent of the shipowner to proceed to the loading or unloading port."* The charterer was not liable for such "unexpected and abnormal" events (i.e. the hostilities); he was supposed to do all that he could effectively do to protect the vessel at the time of nomination. To suggest the opposite, in the words of Lord Roskill *"would make the charterer the insurer of such unexpected and abnormal risks which in my view should properly fall upon the ship's insurers under the policies of insurance the effecting of which is the owner's responsibility under clause 3 unless, of course, the owner chooses to be his own insurer in these respects"*. The "continuous guarantee" approach was therefore rejected. **ii)** What if the port becomes actually or prospectively unsafe to the knowledge of the charterer while the vessel is sailing towards it? Then their lordships view is to impose a "secondary obligation" to the charterer,

which consists of cancelling the original nomination and order the ship to go to a second (safe) port. Where the vessel is already in the actual unsafe port (as in the reference), the "secondary obligation" will only arise where it is still possible for the vessel to leave. (Lord Roskill) *"…the question whether clause 2, on its true construction, imposes a further and secondary obligation on the time charterer will depend on whether, having regard to the nature and consequences of the new danger in the port which has arisen, it is possible for the ship to avoid such danger by leaving the port. If, on the one hand, it is not possible for the ship so to leave, then no further and secondary obligation is imposed on the time charterer"*.


# 121
## KOLBIN & SONS AND OTHERS V. KINNEAR CO. LTD. AND OTHERS
### *(The Altai)*
1931, 40 Lloyd's Law Rep. 241 (H.L.)

A firm of Russian merchants (Kolbin & Sons) shipped a cargo of bales of flax and tow on board *Altai* for a carriage to Dundee (Scotland). After loading, they were given a bill of lading which remained in their possession until it was destroyed in a fire. The bill of lading had been issued to the order of the War Office "for account of Kolbin & Co. or their assigns". Meanwhile, the ship *Altai* reached Dundee and the cargo was discharged there. As the bill of lading was not presented, the ship agents Kinnear & Co. warehoused the goods in Dundee. A so-called Mr. Renny approached the ship agents and asked for delivery in his alleged capacity as agent for the Russian merchants. It happened that the War Office authorised delivery to Mr. Renny. The ship agents then delivered the cargo to Mr. Renny without production of the bill of lading, but requested a letter of indemnity signed by Mr. Renny and the Royal Bank of Scotland in return. On the evidence, the War Office had paid Mr. Renny for the goods, but the latter did not transfer the money to the Russian merchants. The Russian merchants alleged that Mr. Renny had never acted as their agent and that the ship agents had wrongfully delivered the goods. According to this, they filed an action against the ship agents for conversion and claimed the price of the goods plus interests as damages.

***Held (for Kolbin & Sons):*** It was not proved that Mr. Renny had ever acted as agents of the Russian merchants. The ship agents were in breach of the contract of carriage evidenced on the bill of lading and were negligent in delivering the goods to Mr. Renny without production of the bill of lading. The Russian merchants were awarded the price of the goods although without interest.

**122**

**KREDITBANK ANTWERP V. MIDLAND BANK PLC.**

1999, 2 Lloyd's Rep. (C.A.)

A letter of credit was opened at Midland Bank PLC (the issuing bank), which, in turn, opened an equivalent credit in Kreditbank Antwerp (the confirming bank). After loading the goods, the sellers presented the documents to the confirming bank and were re-forwarded by the latter to the issuing bank. The confirming bank paid the proceeds to an assignee of the beneficiary of the credit. The issuing bank nevertheless rejected the documents on the following grounds: (i) the insurance policy was "to order" and was not marked as an "original", contrary to what was required by art. 20(b) of the UCP 500; and (ii) the draft survey report and certificate of quality were not issued by "Griffith Inspectorate" but by "Daniel C. Griffith BV". The parties entered into discussions as to the validity of both certificates, and the confirming bank brought an action against the issuing bank for undue rejection of documents.

***Held (for the confirming bank):*** The C.A. decided that the documents conformed to the terms of the credit and that they ought not to have been refused. The grounds for the decision were basically as follows: **i)** A document is an original as long as it is not a copy of some other document and does not appear to be a copy (e.g. a photocopy or a carbon copy). According to this construction, the insurance policy was found to be an original as it had been produced by word processor and laser printer, even without bearing the words "original".[102] **ii)** The policy was not invalidated merely because it was made "to order" and did not mention the assured's name: a policy endorsed in blank was valid under the credit. **iii)** The draft survey report and the certificate of quality issued by a firm which was a member of the Griffith group (such as Daniel C.

---

[102] See *Glencore Int. AG v. Bank of China* and *Rayner (S.H.) & Co. v. Hambros Bank Ltd.*

Griffith BV) met the requirement that the document was to be issued by "Griffith Inspectorate".

## 123
### KROHN & CO. v. THEGRA N.V.
### 1975, 1 Lloyd's Rep. 146 (Q.B.)

A cargo of Thailand manioc chips was sold c.i.f. Rotterdam on the GAFTA 100 form. The contract provided for arbitration in London and required payment to be "net cash against documents". Clause 13(2) stated that documents required were, inter alia, a full set of "on board bill(s) of lading and/or ship's deliver order(s)". Shipment was to be made monthly by instalments of about 300 tonnes each. A vessel was time chartered by an associated company of the sellers on the Baltime 1939 form to carry full cargo of manioc chips. Under the charterparty, the charterers were authorised to sign bills of lading on behalf of the master and to issue delivery orders. For the first monthly shipment, bills of lading were issued to order of the shippers for the full cargo of the vessel. The sellers sent the buyers notice of appropriation for their correspondent part of the cargo shipped in bulk. They "split" the bills and instructed that delivery orders be issued by the charterers. The delivery orders were, on their face, addressed to the charterers' agents at Rotterdam and signed by the charterers "for and on behalf of the owners/master". They were endorsed in blank by the sellers and tendered, with other relevant documents, to the buyers through a Rotterdam bank. The buyers returned the delivery orders to the bank

and refused payment on the ground that they were not ship's delivery orders as required by clause 13(2) of the GAFTA 100 contract form. They required the delivery orders should be certified directly by the shipowners or a first-class bank, and not merely signed by the charterers though on behalf of the owners/master. The sellers sold the cargo to a different buyer at the market price, which was inferior to the original contract price. The sellers sought a claim against the buyers for the balance lost and the dispute was referred to arbitration. The arbitrator held the buyers were not liable.[103]

***Held (for the buyers):*** The court held that the arbitrators' findings on the meaning of a ship's delivery order were not binding. The arbitrators' definition lacked certainty and reliability. The delivery orders were, in the present case, defective since (1) they were addressed to persons who were not in possession of the goods, and (2) they contained no undertaking of the shipowners that the goods would be delivered to the buyers, but merely an instruction to the charterers (the addressee) to deliver them to the order of the sellers. Ship's delivery orders *"[M]ust…be documents issued by or on behalf the shipowners while the goods are in their possession or*

---

[103] Finding no. (v) of the GAFTA Board of Appeal: *"The term 'ship's delivery order' in the context of GAFTA Contract Form No. 100 does have a special meaning, in relation to any goods of the kinds normally sold on the terms of this contract form, and means a document issued by the owner or master of the carrying vessel or their agents at a time when the goods are on board a ship by the terms of which the owner or master expressly undertakes to deliver the goods to the holder or his order".*

*at least under their control and containing some form of undertaking that they will be delivered to the buyers (or perhaps to the bearer) on presentation of the documents. If they contain such an undertaking, then it appears to me to be irrelevant whether the documents were originally issued by shipowners or their agents, or whether they began their life by being addressed to the shipowners or their agents with instructions to deliver to the buyers followed by a re-issue of the documents by the shipowners or their agents incorporating such an undertaking. In either event, such documents will attain, as far as possible, the object of a c.i.f. contract performable by means of ship's delivery orders by placing the buyers as nearly as possible in the same position as if they had been given bills of lading;...it then inevitably follows in my judgment that the delivery orders tendered in the present case fall far short of what was required; First, they are addressed to persons who are not in possession of the goods. If the goods never reached the addressees, then these documents were obviously worthless as the basis of any claim against the addressees. Secondly, they contain no undertaking by anyone that the goods will be delivered to the buyers, but merely an instruction to the addressees to deliver them to the order of the sellers".*

**124**

**KRONOS WORLDWIDE LIMITED V.
SEMPRA OIL TRADING S.A.R.L.**
2004, 1 Lloyd's Rep. 260 (C.A.)

Kronos contracted to supply oil to Sempra on 24 Apr., 2001. The contract called for Kronos to supply a maximum of 14 cargoes of oil of 25,000 m plus or minus 5% f.o.b. Constantza. Additionally, the contract stipulated that Kronos would "declare cargo availability, namely one cargo or two cargoes each month..." with a 15 day loading range for each cargo which was "to be mutually narrowed to three days loading range..." by the 15th day of the month. In addition, the contract provided that payment was to be secured by an irrevocable letter of credit to be opened promptly. There was also a laytime provision is the contract which read, "As per charter party and to be divided by two plus 6 hours NOR SHINC... unless sooner berthed, both SHINC, otherwise calculated as per charter party terms, conditions and exceptions". A demurrage provision was also contained in the contract which read in relevant part, "Demurrage, if any, will be calculated in accordance with the charter party rate... Valid claim(s) shall be payable as against buyer's claim. Duly supported by the NOR statement, charter-party, timesheet or statement of facts, demurrage calculation and invoice provided same is received within 90 days from B/L date, otherwise claim will be null and void..." Notice of readiness was to be served after the vessel had arrived in Constantza at the customary anchorage, berth or no berth, and for the running of laytime to commence six hours after such service or from when the vessel was ready to load, whichever occurred first. As per the terms of the contract, Kronos declared it would two shipments for June 2001 on 8 May 2001, with June 5-15 and June 20-30 being the loading ranges of the respective shipments. Kronos subsequently requested that the second shipment be postponed until 1-5 July on 15 June due to refinery schedule difficulties. On 18 June Sempra nominated MT *Spear I* to receive the second shipment of oil, which arrived at Constantza on 28 June, 2001 and tendered notice of readiness. Although a berth was then available, the vessel did not proceed to the berth because no cargo was available. On 5 or 6 of July, 2001 Kronos requested a letter of credit from Sempra for the second shipment of oil, which was issued immediately. The vessel then berthed on 9 July, 2001. Sempra claimed demurrage in the amount of USD 167,857.62 under the contract which it was awarded. Kronos appealed. The preliminary issue before the court was "whether (subject to waiver) laytime did not run under this contract until after a letter of credit had been opened."

***Held (for Kronos):*** Kronos was obligated to organize all aspects of the loading operation which included berthing, connection of hoses, and the actual shipment of goods on board within the maximum period of fifty four hours. Furthermore, because the contract called for prompt opening of a letter of credit, that letter of credit should have been opened before 28 June 2001. Delay of issuance of the letter of credit effectively delayed Krono's obligation to berth. In the words of Lord Justice Mance, *"I have no doubt that the provision of a letter of credit should be regarded as a condition precedent to any obligation on the part of the seller to perform any aspect of the loading operation which is the sellers' responsibility. So, if the contract had been one under which notice of readiness could only be given in berth and the vessel had berthed, the seller could not have been obliged, for example, to connect the*

*hoses, before refusing to pump gasoil through them"*. Thus, until the appropriate letter of credit is to hand, a seller is not obliged to perform any part of the loading operation. Subsequently, laytime began to run under this contract after the letter of credit had been opened, in this case 5 or 6 July, 2001.

**125**

**KURT A. BECHER V. VOEST ALPINE
INTERTRADING**
*(The Rio Apa)*
1992, 2 Lloyd's Rep. 586 (Q.B.D.)

The defendants as sellers and the plaintiffs as buyers entered into an f.o.b. contract of sale for soya bean extracted toasted pellets. Delivery period was July 1988, shipment to be from San Martin (Argentina) at buyers' call with twelve days notice. The contract incorporated GAFTA Form No. 119 and the Centro terms. Extension of delivery and carrying charges were as per Centro Terms, which provided the following clauses: "Carrying Charges: Should buyers not load within the delivery period…buyers are to pay sellers carrying charges…Should the goods for reasons not imputable to sellers not have been loaded within 60 days from the last day of the delivery period…buyers shall be automatically at default. In such event buyers shall pay immediately to sellers (1) Default damages if any (2) Carrying charges…"; "Extension of Delivery: Should buyers not tender vessel(s) in readiness to load within the specified period for delivery he shall be in default unless he gives notice to the seller…that an extension is claimed". The buyers tendered the MV "Rio Apa" and gave notice of readiness on July 18, 1988. Owing to congestion, the vessel was unable to berth until July 31. The buyers did not claim extension of the delivery period. The vessel completed loading on Aug. 4. The sellers claimed carrying charges of USD17, 850 for the period Aug. 1-4.

***Held (for the buyers):*** (Hirst, J.) **i)** *"… once one side or the other has failed to conform with his obligation by the end of the contractual delivery period on July 31, that constitutes a final default and the contract is at an end as a result of that breach, unless there is either a subsequent variation or the buyers claim extension of delivery".* **ii)** *"… if no notice of extension of delivery is given, the contract expires at midnight on July 31, and the sellers then have the option under cl. 25 of GAFTA 119 either to sell against the buyer or not to sell…; If on the other hand the buyer extends, but then fails to take delivery throughout the ensuing 60 days, it is fair and just that he should pay both damages for default, and also carrying charges…"* **iii)** *"The carrying charges clause and the extension of delivery clause are inextricably interconnected, since…the only way in which carrying charges can become payable under this contract is where an extension of time is required; As a result, I have concluded that on the proper construction of this contract, carrying charges are the price which the buyer pays for his option to claim an extension, and that in the present circumstances, where no extension was claimed, no carrying charges were due."* In sum, the buyers fulfilled their obligations by tendering valid notice of readiness to load on July 31. No carrying charges were due.

# 126
## KUWAIT PETROLEUM CORP. V. I & D OIL CARRIERS LTD.
### *(The Houda)*
1994, 2 Lloyd's Rep. 541 (C.A.)

The tanker *Houda* was chartered on the Shelltime 4 form to a state-owned oil corporation domiciled in Kuwait. The charterparty contained, inter alia, an off-hire clause for breach of orders or neglect by her master or the crew, an employment clause putting the master under the charterer's orders, and a further clause stating: "Charterers hereby indemnify owners against all consequences or liabilities that may arise from…delivery of cargo without presentation of bill of lading…Letter of indemnity to owners' P & I Club wording to be incorporated in this charterparty". While the cargo of oil was being loaded at Mina Al Ahmadi, Iraq invaded Kuwait and the vessel departed immediately, but only partly loaded. Before her departure, blank bills of lading had been issued and signed by the master, and were to be completed by the charterers when the amount of cargo was known. The bills were consigned to the order of the charterers, who appeared to be the shippers. After the ship's departure, the bills were left behind in Kuwait and subsequently disappeared in the confusion of the invasion. After the event, the head office of the charterers moved to London and from that point the charterers gave the subsequent orders in respect of the voyage. The shipowners refused to accept subsequent orders until they had taken legal advice as to who had authority to give orders on behalf of the charterers. After twelve days of impasse, the shipowners agreed to proceed with the voyage under the orders of the charterers' London branch. Upon arrival, there was a further delay of 23 days as a result of the shipowners' refusal to discharge the cargo without production of the bills of lading. An agreement without prejudice was entered as between the charterers and the shipowners and the cargo was finally discharged without the bills being surrendered. The charterers claimed that the shipowners were in breach of the charterparty since they had refused to obey the charterer's orders with reasonable dispatch, depriving them of the use of the vessel for about thirty six days, which they argued fell within the off-hire clause before the court.

***Held (for the shipowners):*** **i)** Compliance with the charterers' orders: Where a vessel is under a time charter the owners are obliged to comply with the orders of the charterers as quickly as is practicable,. Three exceptions to this rule have been established by precedent: (1) where compliance is linked to serious risk of danger to the vessel, its cargo or crew, (2) where the order is ambiguous or requires further clarification, and (3) when certain information, not available to the charterers, affects the orders. However, the court held that this was not an exhaustive or closed list of only three items. (Neill L.J.) *"I consider that it is necessary to take a broad and comprehensive view of the duties and responsibilities of the owners and master and to ask… 'how would a man of reasonable prudence have acted in such circumstances?"* Millet, L.J. also took the view that *"(t)here is no rule of law that an agent*

*is forbidden to question the authenticity of his instructions or acts at his peril if he does so. He is to act reasonably, no more and no less"*. Regarding the fact that the present circumstances were so unusual, it was impossible to conclude that they were incapable as a matter of law of constituting reasonable grounds for delay on the part of the master. Therefore, the failure to comply immediately with the orders and the 12-days delay in proceeding with the voyage does not fall within any period of off-hire. **ii)** Delivery without production of bills of lading:[104] On its true construction, the indemnity clause did not impose any express obligation on the shipowners to discharge the cargo without production of the bills of lading; it merely provided for a letter of indemnity if such discharge took place. (L.J. Neill) *"I can see no good reason to depart from the general rule that the owners do not fulfil their contractual obligations if the cargo is delivered to a person who cannot produce the bill of lading; it was of course open to a shipowner to decide that he was adequately protected by a letter of indemnity and to deliver in the absence of a bill of lading, but the right of a time charterer to give orders did not entitle him to insist that cargo should be discharged without production of the bill of lading."* A shipowner who delivers the goods without production of a bill of lading does so at his own peril; this is a general principle which in no way can be overruled by the contractual right of a time charterer to direct orders to the shipowners with regard to the vessel.

---

[104] See *Barclays Bank Ltd. v. Commissioners of Customs and Excise.*

## 127
### KWEI TEK CHAO V. BRITISH TRADERS AND SHIPPERS LTD.
### 1954, 2 Lloyd's Rep. 459 (Q.B.)

London exporters sold to Hong Kong merchants a quantity of chemicals under a c.i.f. contract. Shipment was to take place not later than Oct. 31, 1951. Payment was agreed through letter of credit to be payable upon production of "shipped" bills of lading at the buyer's bank. The goods were received on the quay by Oct. 31, but they were not shipped until Nov. 3. The bill of lading was issued saying: "received for shipment and since shipped Oct., 31". Without knowledge of the sellers, the sellers' forwarding agents deleted the leading five words of that phrase and the bills of lading were thereafter presented to the bank. The bank ordered payment against the documents. Owing to the late shipment, the buyers lost their contract for resale and were unable to sell the goods owing to a fall in the market price. Although they knew beforehand that the goods had been shipped late, they nevertheless took them from the ship and stored them in a go-down. The buyers sued the sellers and claimed damages for breach of contract.

***Held:*** (Per Curiam): *"Under a c.i.f. contract, if the property passes when the documents are transferred, that property is subject to the condition that the goods should revert in the seller if on examination by the buyer he finds them not to be in accordance with the contract. No dealing by the buyer is an act inconsistent with the seller's ownership, within the meaning of section 35 of the Sale of Goods Act, 1893, so that the buyer loses his right to reject the goods, unless he deals with something more than his conditional property, as by dispatch of the goods to a third party, but not a mere transfer of documents under a string contract or a pledge of the goods".*[105]
**i)** (Devlin J.) *"The right to reject the documents arises when the documents are tendered, and the right to reject the goods arises when they are landed and when after examination they are not found to be in conformity with the contract;*[106] *having a right to reject the documents separately from a right to reject the goods, it is obvious that as a matter of business very different considerations will govern the buyer's mind as he applies himself to one or other of those questions."* However, since the defect in the documents was undiscoverable at tender, the buyers' acceptance does not preclude them from recovering damages for having been deprived of the right to reject the documents at the time they were tendered. **ii)** The true measure of damages was the difference between the sale contract price and the value of the goods when the buyers discovered the breach of the sellers' obligations. The sellers' knowledge that the buyer was buying generally for resale did not exclude the ordinary measure of damages based on the market price. It was only where, in case of non-delivery,

---

[105] See *Empresa Exportadora de Azucar v. Industria Azucarera Nacional S.A. (The Playa Larga and Marble Islands)*, also known as *Cubazucar v. Iansa*, 1983, 2 Lloyd's Rep. 171, at p. 179; see also *Gill & Duffus S.A. v. Berger & Co. Inc.*, 1984, 2 WLR 95, at p. 103.
[106] See *Bergeco U.S.A. v. Vegoil Ltd.* and also *James Finlay v. Kwik Hoo Tong Handel Maatschppij.*

the buyer were not able to replace the goods by a purchase on the market that the sub-sale could be relevant, and thus the Buyer would be entitled to the loss of profit recoup. **iii)** So far as the sellers did not know about the fraud of their forwarding agents, they were not liable. They were the ones against whom the fraud was practised in the first instance. But even if fraud were proved to be with knowledge of the sellers, the buyers had not rejected the goods until the issue of the writ, and the lapse of time was so great as to be conclusive that an election has been made to affirm the contract.

**128**

**L.D. SEALS N.V. v. MITSUI OSK LINES LTD.**
*(The Darya Tara)*
1997, 1 Lloyd's Rep. 42 (Q.B.)

The disponent owners (Mitsui Osk Lines) let their vessel *Darya Tara* to the charterers (L.D. Seals) for a time charter concluded under the New York Produce Exchange Form. The relevant clauses of the charterparty were as follows: line 25. "Charterers to have the option to load a full deck cargo…at their own risk and expense…", cl. 8 "The captain (although appointed by the owners) shall be under the orders and directions of the charterers as regards employment and agency; and charterers are to load, stow, trim and discharge the cargo at their expense under the supervision of the captain", and cl. 57(3) "Charterers' option deck cargo: OK---but vessel has no lashing materials on board and cargo to be loaded always at charterers' risk and expense…" There was also a clause (cl. 15) whereby, in the event of deficiency or breakdown of the vessel, the payment of hire should cease and the extra fuel and expenses should be for the owners' account. Pursuant to the charter, the ship loaded on deck and holds a whole cargo of steel beams, plant and crane material at Teesport (UK) for a carriage to Hong Kong. She encountered heavy weather and some deck cargo shifted and was lost. In order to restow the cargo on board, she called at Brixham and remained there about four days before resuming the voyage. There was a dispute as to whether the vessel was off-hire during the time spent in Brixham. The disponent owners claimed (1) the 4-day hire lost while the vessel remained at Brixham, (2) an indemnity for all liabilities to the head owners in respect of the costs of repairing the vessel and the disbursements made at Brixham, and (3) the costs of surveys carried out to assess the extent of the damages. The main question was whether line 25 and cl. 57 of the charterparty were sufficient so as to create a full indemnity to the disponent owners in respect of whatsoever loss resulting from the deck cargo.

***Held:*** (Mance, J.) **i)** Contrary to the disponent owners' submission, cl. 8 in itself did not entitle them to recover since, by permitting the carriage of cargo on deck, they were impliedly accepting the risk associated therewith.[107] Once said, the judge generally considered that the "risk and expense" accepted by the charterers

---

[107] See *The Island Archon.*

in line 25 and cl. 57 in respect of deck cargo did relieve the disponent owners of liability for the loading, stowing, trimming, discharge, and -most important- for the carriage of deck cargo. Quoting Mr. J. Mance: *"It was deck cargo which was at charterers' risk and expense. 'Risk' in this context appears to me to focus on responsibility for the safety and condition of the cargo loaded on deck, while 'expense' focuses on expenditure involved in the loading and…carriage of such cargo on deck. So too under the present line 25 and cl. 57, it is the deck cargo which is to be loaded at charterers' '(own) risk and expense'. The word 'own' in line 25 emphasises that it is the deck cargo loaded by charterers which is at charterers' risk and expense. For owners to recover from charterers under this clause…owners must establish some expense relating specifically to the deck cargo"*. On these grounds, however, Mr. J. Mance found that the claim for hire lost and bunkers was not within the scope of line 25 and cl. 57 as they did not relate *specifically* to the deck cargo or to restowing, but *"to the need to restow"*. **ii)** Concerning the disbursements made at Brixham, the owners were entitled to an indemnity to the extent that they related specifically to the restowage and on-carriage of the deck cargo only. Concerning the disponent owners' claim for repair costs to the vessel, the learned judge said: *"Repairs to the vessel fall outside the scope of expenses relating specifically to the loading, carriage and discharge of the vessel in each case. They are not recoverable under line 25 or cl. 57"*. Following the same criteria, the cargo survey fees were found to be recoverable depending on the nature and purpose of each survey.

## 129
### LAEMTHONG INTERNATIONAL LINES CO. LTD. V. ARTIS AND OTHERS
*(The Laemthong Glory No. 2)*
2005 1 Lloyd's Rep. 688 (C.A.)

The MV *Laemthong Glory* was voyage-chartered for a carriage of bagged sugar from a port in Brazil to Hodeidah or Aden in Yemen at charterers' option. Clause 42 of the charterparty provided the following: "In the event of the original bills of lading are not being available at discharge port on vessel's arrival, if so required by charterers, owners/master to release the cargo to receivers on receipt of faxed letter of indemnity ("LOI"). Such letter of indemnity to be issued on charterers head paper, wording in accordance with the usual P&I Club wording, and signed by charterers only always without a bank counter-signature." It became apparent to the receivers that the vessel would arrive in f Aden prior to the availability of the bills of lading. They requested that charterers issue a LOI to owners for discharge and delivery of the cargo without the original bills of lading. Charterers then requested that receivers issue to charterers a LOI as "some backup" for any LOI that the charterers issue to the owners. Following discharge of the cargo, the vessel was arrested by the Yemen Bank, in which the letters of credit had been opened. The bank held all the original bills of lading and filed a claim for the value of the cargo. Owners sought to enforce the terms of the LOI against both the charterers and receivers by pursuing an order that charterers and receivers should provide bail or other security to secure the release of the vessel. The receivers argued that their LOI had been addressed only to the charterers and that they had not entered into any direct contractual commitment towards the owners. The owners' case was that they had a right to enforce the LOI pursuant the terms of the Contracts (Rights of Third Parties) Act 1999.[108]

***Held (for the owners):*** (i) Whether owners, as agents of charterers, were allowed to enforce a third party claim under the 1999 Act. The Court held, *"The charterers needed the assistance of the owners because the only way they could procure the delivery of the cargo to the receivers was through the owners or, to put it another way and in ordinary language, through the agency of the owners. The owners were accordingly the agents of the charterers for the purpose of complying with the receivers' request in the receivers' LOI, namely to deliver the cargo to them under the receivers' LOI, and were thus properly to be regarded as falling within the category of "agents" whom the receivers promised to indemnify in cl. 1 of the LOI".* (ii) The receivers' second argument was that the "you" in the receivers'

LOI meant the charterers only, and even if the owners were within the expression "agents", any loss suffered by the owners is not loss to which the LOI extends. The Court disagreed. It held that the receivers' interpretation *"…cannot be accepted if the words used are construed in the context of the LOI as a whole and if the LOI is in turn viewed against its surrounding circumstances or factual matrix. ".* It subsequently followed that the owners were entitled to enforce the LOI in their own name. There was *"nothing in the LOI to lead to the conclusion that the parties did not intend cll. 1 and 3 to be enforceable by the owners. The whole purpose of the receivers' LOI was on the one hand to ensure that the receivers received the cargo from the ship without production of the original bills of lading and on the other hand to ensure that the owners were fully protected from the consequences of arrest or other action which might be taken by the holders of the original bills of lading".*

### 130
## LAGE V. SIEMENS BROTHERS & CO. LTD.
### 1932, 42 Lloyd's Law Rep. 252 (K.B.D.)

Siemens Brothers were manufacturers and layers of submarine telegraphic cables. They owned a special fitted cable-laying ship called the *Faraday*. They made a contract with an Italian company whereby they undertook to lay cable from some point in the mid-Atlantic across to Brazil. Pursuant to the contract, the *Faraday* sailed with some 1800 miles of cable in her holds. As it was to be laid in the ocean and not imported into Brazil, Siemens did not enter the 1800 miles of cable on her manifest. After laying most of the subma-

---

[108] Section 1 of the Contracts (Rights of Third Parties) Act 1999: *"Right of third party to enforce contractual term 1(1) Subject to the provisions of this Act, a person who is not a party to a contract (a "third party") may in his own right enforce a term of a contract if (a) the contract expressly provides that he may; or (b) subject to subsection (2), the term purports to confer a benefit on him. (2) Subsection 1(b) does not apply if on a proper construction of the contract it appears that the parties did no intend the term to be enforceable by the third party. (3) The third party must be expressly identified in the contract by name, as a member of a class or as answering a particular description but need not be in existence when the contact is entered into".*

rine cable, the ship buoyed the end of the cable at three miles outside Rio Janeiro because she could not sail further owing to the draught near the shore. She then proceeded into the harbour with fourty one tons of cable on board which corresponded to the three miles remaining. The cable on board was then discharged into a lighter which was to carry on the work to the dry land. Once the two ends of cable were joined the *Faraday* sailed back to Europe. Eleven months later the customs authorities called the ship agents, Lage, to justify the difference of ourty one tons which had not been landed at the Customs House. The ship agents did not reply to that intimation. They could not reply with a reasonable explanation as they were not aware of the whereabouts and of the fate of the fourty one tons of cable and failed to inform Siemens Brothers about the apparent discrepancy. Fines were subsequently imposed for non-declaration of the fourty one tons of cable which apparently had entered Brazil. The fines were paid by the ship agents, who then sought recovery from the owners, Siemens Brothers.

***Held (for Siemens Brothers):*** *"[A]fter the fine was imposed, if the plaintiffs* (i.e. the ship agents, Lage) *had exercised reasonable diligence and intelligence in obtaining from the defendants* (i.e. the owners, Siemens Brothers) *promptly an account of what they had done with this fourty one tons, in so far as they did not know it already, and the necessary documents to support that, they would have been able to get a remission of the fine from the Customs authorities."* According to this, the plaintiffs' case fails and the judgement was for the defendants.

## 131
## LAURITZENCOOL A.B. v. LADY NAVIGATION INC. AND ANOTHER
## 2005, 2 Lloyd's Rep. 63 (C.A.)

The respondents time-chartered the MV *Lady Racisce* and the MV *Lady Korcula* from a Liberian company (the owners) on Coaltime 95 terms for a period of ten years. These two vessels were part of a "pool" of reefer vessels, a number of ships owned by other Lauritzen related companies and external owners who agreed to charter their vessels to Lauritzen for it to manage on a fleet basis. The owners received hire from Lauritzen based on a formula based on the total revenue of the fleet, which was then apportioned to the owners of the pool vessels in shares based on various factors related to each vessel. In 2003 there was a change in the ownership of the company that owned the two *Lady* vessels. Owners sought clarification about the operation of the pool and the revenues owed therefrom. They wrote Lauritzen stating that the pool was an illegal capacity cartel, which did not qualify for exemption under the available block exemptions or under the provisions of article 81 of the EC Treaty. Lauritzen commenced arbitration proceedings on 15 Sept., 2004 and sought an interim injunction against the owners pursuant to section 44(2)(e) of the Arbitration Act 1996. The issue on appeal was whether an injunctive relief could be granted restraining an owner from withdrawing a vessel from her time charter employment if the practical effect of such an injunction was to compel performance of the time charter.

***Held (for respondents):*** While the courts have held that contracts for personal services cannot be the subject of an order for specific performance and the only remedy available for such cases are claims for damages for breach of contract, time charter parties are different from contracts for personal services. The present case concerned *"commercial arrangements made between independent companies involving the employment of no named individuals, where the services are not 'personal' in nature, notwithstanding the fiduciary obligations owed by one commercial entity to another".* Subsequently, *"…neither the fact that the contracts involved were for services in the form of a time charter nor the existence under such contracts of a fiduciary relationship of mutual trust and confidence represents in law any necessary or general objection in principle to the grant of injunctive relief precluding the appellants from employing their vessels outside the pool pending the outcome of the current arbitration. Nor does it afford any such objection to the grand of such relief that the only realistic commercial course which it left the appellants was, as I am prepared to assume, to do what they have done, namely to continue to provide the vessels to the pool and to perform the charters".*

**132**

**LEDUC & CO. v. WARD AND OTHERS**

1888, 20 QBD 475 (C.A.)

The plaintiffs purchased goods to be shipped from Fiume (Croatia) to Dunkirk (France). The price was payable in exchange for shipping documents. The bill of lading showed Dunkirk as port of discharge and contained a liberty clause "to call at any ports in any order", as well as a usual clause excepting perils of the sea. The vessel, instead of proceeding directly to Dunkirk, sailed for Glasgow (Scotland) and was lost by perils of the sea. The plaintiffs, as indorsees of the bill of lading, claimed against the shipowners for non-delivery and contended that the goods were lost when the defendants deviated from the agreed route. The defendants alleged that the non-delivery of the goods was due to perils of the sea and that the shippers of the goods, who acted as agents for the plaintiffs at loading, accepted that the vessel was intended to proceed to Dunkirk via Glasgow.

***Held (for the plaintiffs):* i)** (Lord Esher) *"It is true that, where there is a charterparty, as between the shipowner and the charterer the bill of lading may be merely in the nature of a receipt for the goods, because all the other terms of the contract of carriage between them are contained in the charterparty; and the bill of lading is merely given as between them to enable the charterer to deal with the goods while in the course of transit; but, where the bill of lading is indorsed over, as between the shipowner and the indorsee, the bill of lading must be considered to contain the contract, because the former has given it for the purpose of enabling the charterer to pass it on as the contract of carriage in respect of the goods. Where there is no charterparty, as between the grantee of the bill of lading and the shipowner, the bill of lading is no doubt a receipt for the goods and as such, like any other receipt, it is not conclusive, for it may be controverted by evidence showing that the goods were not received; the question whether it will be more than a receipt as between the shipper and the shipowner depends on* *whether the captain has received the goods, for he has no opportunity to make a contract of carriage to bind the shipowner, except in respect of goods received by him."* **ii)** (Lord Esher) *"If the goods have not been received, the bill of lading cannot contain the terms of a contract of carriage with respect to them as against the shipowner.*[109] *But, if the goods have been received by the captain, it is the evidence in writing of what the contract of carriage between the parties is; it may be true that the contract of carriage is made before it is given, because it would generally be made before the goods are sent down to the ship;*[110] *but when the goods are put on board the captain has authority to reduce that contract into writing: and then the general doctrine of law is applicable, by which, where the contract has been reduced into a writing which is intended to constitute the contract, parol evidence to alter or qualify the effect of such writing is not admissible, and the writing is the only evidence of the contract, except where there is some usage so well established and generally known that it must be taken to be incorporated with the contract."*[111] So far as the present bill of lading is concerned, the indorsee and the shipowner are not bound by terms other than those contained in the bill of lading. On these grounds, the plaintiff receivers

are not bound by any agreement between the shipper and the shipowner other than that contained in or evidenced by the bill of lading. **iii)** The question that remains is whether the power of the liberty clause entitles the carrier to go to Glasgow, which appears to be about 1.200 miles out of the ordinary course of the voyage from Fiume to Dunkirk. It is commonplace that where the bill of lading describes the voyage as from one port to another, any departure from the ordinary sea track between both ports should, in the absence of necessity, be considered a deviation. By virtue of such usual clause, the ship is allowed only to call, for any purpose (loading, bunkering,…), at any port within the usual route of the agreed voyage, but not to any port in the world. Again in words of Lord Esher, this clause *"has always been interpreted to mean that the ship may call at such ports as would naturally and usually be ports of call on the voyage named. If the stipulation were only that she might call at any ports, the invariable construction has been that she would only be entitled to call at such ports in the geographical order; and therefore the words 'in any order' are frequently added; but in any case it appears to me that the ports must be ports substantially on the course of the voyage".*

---

[109] But see the more recent Carriage of Goods by Sea Act 1992, sections 1(2) and 4.

[110] See also *Pyrene Co. Ltd. v. Scindia Navigation Co. Ltd.* and *The Ardennes.*

[111] Fry L.J. added, in this case, that the nature of the proviso contained in sec. 1 of the Bills of Lading Act 1855, *"was inconsistent with the idea that anything which took place between the shipper and the shipowner and not embodied in the bill of lading could affect the contract".* Contrast this point with the decision in *The Ardennes.*

## 133

### LEIGH AND SILLIVAN LTD. V. ALIAKMON SHIPPING CO. LTD.

*(The Aliakmon)*

1986, 2 Lloyd's Rep. 1 (H.L.)

The plaintiff buyers agreed to buy a quantity of steel coins c.&f. free out Immingham (England). The price was payable by a 180 day bill of exchange to be endorsed by the buyers' bank in return for the bill of lading corresponding to the goods. The buyers, who were traders in steel rather than end users of it, made a contract for resale of the coins to a third party with a view to finance the main transaction. The goods were loaded on board the *Aliakmon* and proceeded to Immingham. However, the buyers' contract for the resale of the goods failed. Subsequently, the buyers' bank refused to endorse the bill of exchange by which payment of the goods was to be made. Sellers were informed of that fact, and some meetings took place between themselves and the buyers. The sellers then agreed to send the bill of lading to the buyers subject to their agreement to the following provisions: (1) the sellers reserved for themselves the right of disposal of the goods, (2) the buyers were to take delivery of the goods, not as principals on their own interest, but merely as agents for the sellers, and (3) after discharge the goods were to be warehoused to the order of the sellers. On discharge, the goods proved to be damaged due to improper stowage in the ship. The buyers paid the price of the goods to the sellers and claimed damages from the shipowners on contract, and alternatively, on tort. The shipowners contended that the buyers had no title to sue.

***Held (for the shipowners):*** **i)** (Lord Brandon) *"[U]nder the usual kind of c.i.f. or c.&f. contract of sale, the risk in the goods passes from the seller to the buyer on shipment, as is exemplified by the obligation of the buyer to take up and pay for the shipping documents even though the goods may already have suf-fered damage or loss during their carriage by sea. The property in the goods, however, does not pass until the buyer takes up and pays for the shipping documents. Those include a bill of lading relating to the goods which has been endorsed by the seller in favour of the buyer. By acquiring the bill of lading so endorsed the buyer becomes a person to whom the property in the goods has passed upon or by reason of such endorsement, and so, by virtue of s. 1 of the Bills of Lading Act, 1855, has vested in him all the rights of suit, and is subject to the same liabilities in respect of the goods, as if the contract contained in the bill of lading had been made with him."* **ii)** *"In the events which occurred, however, what had originally been a usual kind of c.&f. contract of sale had been varied so as to become, in effect, a contract of sale ex warehouse at Imming-ham."* Although Lord Brandon found that the risk had passed on shipment, *"the buyers, however, did not acquire any rights of suit under the bill of lading by virtue of s. 1 of the Bills of Lading Act, 1855. This was because, owing to the sellers' reservation of the right of disposal of the goods, the property in the goods did not pass to the buyers upon or by reason of the endorsement of the bill of lading, but only upon payment of the purchase price by the buyers to the sellers after the goods had been discharged and warehoused at Immingham. Hence the attempt of the buyers to establish a separate claim against the shipowners founded in the tort of negligence"*.[112] **iii)** As far as the claim in tort was concerned, the general law is that the legal ownership or possessory title to the property is necessary to

---

[112] Look though at the more recent Carriage of Goods by Sea Act, 1992, where the endorsement of the bill of lading is contemplated as not necessarily linked to the transfer of property.

enable a person to claim in negligence for reason of loss or damage to that property. Hence, since the buyers were neither the legal owners of the goods nor had a possessory title to them at the time the damage occurred, their lordships took the view that they were not even entitled to sue on tort.

## 134
### LEWIS EMMANUEL & SON LTD. V. SAMMUT
1959, 2 Lloyd's Rep. 629 (Q.B.)

A contract for sale of Maltese potatoes was agreed on Apr. 14, 1958 between the plaintiff buyers and the defendant sellers. It was agreed on terms c.i.f. "shipment on or before 24th Apr. 1958 to London". The sellers were unable to obtain space on the only vessel that called at Malta between Apr., 14 and 24. The sellers contended that the contract was frustrated since finding space in a vessel was a fundamental condition to the contract, which thereby became impossible to fulfil. Alternatively, the buyers argued that there was no frustration since the sellers might have bought the goods afloat.

***Held (for the buyers):* i)** It was not within the true construction of the contract that, where the sellers were unable to find space, the contract ought to be cancelled due to frustration. This was an absolute (not conditional) contract in that respect, and the duties of the sellers towards the carriage are not relevant towards the sale. The sellers might have ensured that there was space available before committing himself to an absolute contract. (Mr. J. Pearson) *"Under a contract of this kind the seller has an ob-ligation of finding or providing cargo, shipping space and insurance; If he is not sure of being able to provide (these three things) he can guard himself by some provisions in the contract, that it is subject to shipping space being available, to such potatoes being available and to a contract of insurance being procurable".* **ii)** The doctrine of frustration can still be applied to a c.i.f. contract relating to unascertained goods, but in view of the nature of such contract and the possibility of buying goods afloat, it is more difficult to find a frustrating event in c.i.f. contracts than in other types of contracts.

## 135
### LICKBARROW V. MASON
1794, 1 Smith's Leading Cases 703

Merchants at Middlebourg (Netherlands), shipped a cargo of corn on board the ship *Endeavour* for Liverpool (England). The master signed four bills of lading "unto order or assigns". There was a rubric saying: "in witness the master hath affirmed to four bills of lading, all of this tenor and date". Two of the bills were indorsed in blank and sent together with the commercial invoice to the intended buyers; a third one was retained by the sellers; and the remaining fourth was kept by the master. The intended buyers entered bankruptcy at a time the sellers had not yet been paid for the goods. The sellers then decided to endorse the third bill of lading to a third party which came to be the defendants. They sent this bill with another invoice and authorized the defendants to take delivery on account of the sellers only. Upon the arrival of the vessel at Liverpool, the defendants took possession of the goods by producing the indorsed bill of lading to the master and sold them out on account of the sellers. The plaintiffs, creditors of the intended buyers, tendered the freight and charges to the defendants, and claimed the goods on the ground that they were in possession of three bills of exchange which had been drawn (and unpaid) by the intended buyers.

***Held (for the plaintiffs):*** **i)** (Ashurst, J.) *"[W]herever one of two innocent persons must suffer by the acts of a third, he who has enabled such third person to occasion the loss must sustain it; when a man sells goods, he sells them on the credit of the buyer: if he delivers the goods, the property is altered, and he cannot recover them back again, though the vendee immediately become bankrupt. But where the delivery is to be at a distant place, as between the vendor and vendee, the contract is ambulatory till delivery; and therefore, in case of the insolvency of the vendee in the meantime, the vendor may stop the goods in transitu. But, as between the vendor and third persons, the delivery of a bill of lading is a delivery of the goods themselves; if not, it would enable the consignee to make the bill of lading an instrument of fraud."*[113] **ii)** (Buller, J.) *"Whether a bill of lading is by law a transfer of the property: …for, if the bill of lading transfer the property, an action of trover against the captain for non-delivery, or against any other person who seizes the goods, is a proper form of action. If an action be brought by a vendor against a vendee, between whom a bill of lading has passed, the proper action is for goods sold and delivered (…) As the plaintiff in this case has paid a valuable consideration for the goods, and there is no colour for imputing fraud or notice to him, I am of the opinion that he is entitled to the judgment of the court."*

---

### 136
#### LIBAU WOOD CO. V. SMITH & SONS LTD.
1930, 37 Lloyd's Law Rep. 296 (K.B.)

A contract was entered into by Libau Wood Co. (as sellers) and Smith & Sons Ltd. (as buyers). It provided for the sale of about 700 to 800 fathoms of wood goods on c.i.f. terms. The contract stated that the goods were to be accepted according to measurements taken at Libau beach, which was agreed to be the port of loading. Payment was to be made upon presentation of the invoice, the certificate of measurement, the charterparty, the bill of lading and the insurance policy. Pursuant to the terms of the contract, the sellers chartered a vessel for the goods, the charterparty being made out on the "Scanfin" printed form. The charterparty provided, inter alia, that the bill of lading was to be issued as per the charterparty; that the shipowners were not responsible for any loss or damage on the cargo while lying alongside the vessel in lighters waiting shipment; that the buyers were to act as stevedores at the port of discharge; and also, that the shipowner would have a lien

---

[113] "The vendee of goods may, by assignment of the bills of lading to a bona fide transferee, defeat the vendor's right to stop them in transitu in case of the vendee's insolvency. The consignor may stop the goods in transitu before they get into the hands of the consignee, in case of the insolvency of the consignee; but, if the consignee assign the bills of lading to a third person for a valuable consideration, the right of the consignor, as against such assignee, is divested."

upon cargo for all freight, dead freight, demurrage, … While loading some 854 fathoms from rafts onto the vessel, a strong breeze sprang up and some cargo was washed away and lost. . The measurement certificate stated that unascertained cargo had been lost. The master signed the bill of lading mentioning therein that an unknown part of the cargo had been lost, and extended protest at Libau beach. The buyers refused the presented documents, alleging that they were not in order. The main issues before the court were whether the buyers were entitled to reject the documents as (i) the bill of lading, although stated 854 fathoms shipped, had the master's indorsement according to which part of the cargo was lost during loading by rafting, and whether (ii) the buyers had already started to discharge and dump the cargo at the destination port.

***Held (for the buyers):*** (Mr. J. Macnaghten) **i)** The statement contained in the bill of lading according to which the 854 fathoms had been shipped was plainly not in accordance with the facts. It was nothing more than an acknowledgement of the shipment of an unknown quantity of the goods on board. This being so, it was held that the bill of lading was not a proper bill of lading which a buyer under a c.i.f. contract is bound to accept. *"A bill of lading which the buyer is bound to accept must be a document acknowledging the shipment of a quantity of goods according with the quantity specified in the invoice and for which the seller demands payment. And if there is an invoice for a specified quantity and the bill of lading is for either an unknown quantity of goods or a quantity of good substantially different from that in the invoice, the bill of lading would not be a proper bill of lading which the buyer would be compelled to accept."* **ii)** The sale contract provided that the sellers were under the duty to furnish a sworn certificate that all the props measured had been duly shipped. In this regard, the sellers were unable to provide the certificate of measurement according to the sale contract, and the breach of such condition constituted another valid ground for rejecting the goods. **iii)** *"The buyers, having said they were the receivers, were engaged as stevedores to discharge the cargo, and they acted as agents of the ship, and in no other capacity at all; I am really unable to appreciate by what process of reasoning it can be said that can amount to an acceptance of the goods, because, being under a duty to take the props out of the wagons and stack them, the buyers stacked them in a convenient way."* On this ground, the judge held that the buyers' effective role in the discharge of the timber cannot be regarded as a waiver or acceptance of the goods.

## 137
### LONDON EXPLORER, THE
1971, 1 Lloyd's Rep. 523 (H.L.)

A charterparty was agreed for "12 months, 15 days more or less in charterers' option". Clause 4 of the charterparty provided the charter to continue until the hour of the day of the vessel's redelivery. Since delivery was effected on Dec. 29, 1967, the charter period ended Dec. 29, 1968 or, at latest, on Jan. 13, 1969. In Oct., the charterers sent the vessel on what was intended to be the last voyage, no reason to suppose that the vessel would not be redelivered before the final terminal date. But, as a result of strikes at two discharge ports, the vessel was not redelivered until Apr. 24, 1969. As the market rate was lower than the charter rate, the owners claimed the charter rate of payment for the extra-period. The charterers contended that the market rate was the only measure of damages.

***Held (for the charterers):*** **i)** *"A definite date for the termination of a time charter should be regarded as an approximate date only."* Jan. 13, 1969 was not to be regarded as the final terminal date under the charterparty and a reasonable extension of time was to be allowed for redelivery. If a charterer failed to redeliver within the period of such reasonable extension he might be in breach of contract and so liable to apply damages (the difference between the charter rate and the market rate if the latter were higher) for the period from the final terminal date to the time of actual redelivery. **ii)** There was no finding of breach against the charterers, and no finding whereby the date of redelivery was in the circumstances not a reasonable one and the last voyage was one on which the vessel was reasonably sent. The owners were not entitled to claim a market rate as damages since the vessel was sent on a *legitimate* last voyage.

**138**

**Louis Dreyfus Trading Ltd. v.
Reliance Trading Ltd.**

2004, 2 Lloyd's Rep. 243 (Q.B.)

A company associated with Reliance Trading Limited (Reliance) agreed to sell 5,000 tons of sugar to Boule & Co. (Boule) in Banjul (Gambia). The MV *Bahia*, which was carrying the cargo of white crystal sugar, was delayed. Reliance learned that Louis Dreyfus Trading Limited (LD) had on board the MV *Dawn* a 7,000 tons parcel of sugar similar to that which it had agreed to sell Boule. LD insisted that Reliance buy the entire parcel of 7,000 tons even though Reliance needed only 5,000 to cover its sale to Boule. Boule agreed to purchase the extra 2,000 tons from Reliance or its associated company at a discount of USD 253 per ton, and accepted the cargo from the MV *Dawn* in lieu of that of the MV *Bahia*. Subsequently, LD agreed to sell further cargo of sugar to Reliance on terms C&F FO Banjul. The latter cargo could not be discharged and delivered in full to Reliance in Banjul due to an exclusivity agreement LD had reached with another party for sugar to be discharged locally. When it became available, the market had dropped and Reliance refused it. LD put Reliance in default for that cargo and offered the same at a reduced price. The dispute between LD and Reliance was referred to arbitration, where it was held that LD was in breach of the warranty of quiet possession implied into the contract for sale under sec. 12(2)(b) of the Sale of Goods Act, 1979 (the Act). The tribunal considered this breach analogous to a breach of warranty of quality, and damages were calculated by reference to the difference between the reduced value of the sugar when it became available to Reliance and the contract price. LD appealed to the High Court on the issue of damages, arguing that the arbitrators had wrongly ignored the sub-sale to Boule, proper regard of which would displace the measure set out in s. 53(3) of the Act.[114]

***Held:*** *(Justice Smith): "Profit or loss made by a buyer on a sub-sale is generally irrelevant to the assessment of his damages for breach by a seller of a warranty of quality or a failure to deliver (except, it may be, as evidence of market price). This is an application of general principles governing remoteness of damage, and not an exception to them (…) However, if the parties to a sale contract had within their contemplation when making their contract a particular sub-sale, different considerations can arise. In these circumstance, the buyer might be entitled to have the sub-sale brought into account to increase his damages. Equally, the seller might be entitled to have it brought into account in order to reduce the award against him (…) I consider that in a case such as the present, where the parties had in their contemplation when making their contract that the buyer was committed to deliver the same goods to a sub-buyer under a specific contract, principles of remoteness do not require that the sub-sale be disregarded in assessing the buyer's damages. It is to be taken to have been within the parties' reasonable contemplation, as a serious possibility or consequence not unlikely to result from LD being in breach of their obligations, that the loss suffered by Reliance*

*might depend upon the impact of the sub-sale to Boule".* Having said that, Smith J. found that it did not necessarily follow that the calculation of damages made by the arbitrators was incorrect. It was LD's burden to demonstrate that the sub-sale made the *prima facie* measure of damages, which otherwise should be the difference between the value of the goods at the time of delivery and the value of the goods had the contract been observed. As the arbitrators failed to consider whether or not LD had rebutted the presumption that the *prima facie* measure of damages should be applied, the case was remitted to arbitration for a reconsideration of the quantum of damages.

## 139

### M.B. Pyramid Sound N.V. v. Briese Schiffarts G.M.B.H. and Co.
### *(The Ines)*
### 1995, 2 Lloyd's Rep. 144 (Q.B.)

The vessel *Ines* was chartered under a Baltime charterparty for a liner service during a period of three months 15 days more or less in charterers' option. The charterparty contained, inter alia, clause 9 by which the charterers agreed to indemnify the shipowners against any liability arising from the master, the crew or the ship's agents signing bills of lading complying the charterers' orders. A consignment of telephones was to be shipped on containers on board the vessel for a carriage to St. Petersburg. "Received for shipment" bills of lading were issued. They were signed by the charterers' agents "as agents for the carrier", but contained the following clause 19: "Responsibility

---

[114] Section 53 of the Sale of Goods Act, 1979: *"(2) The measure of damages for breach of warranty is the estimated loss directly and naturally resulting, in the ordinary course of events, from the breach of warranty. (3) In the case of breach of warranty of quality such loss is prima facie the difference between the value of the goods at the time of delivery to the buyer and the value they would have had if they had fulfilled the warranty".*

when joint service: the contract evidenced in this bill of lading is between the shipper and the owner of the ocean vessel named herein…and it is therefore agreed that the said shipowner only shall be liable for any loss, damage…". There was also a "cesser clause" providing a period of responsibility for the carriers which was stated to cease after discharge, and further, that the goods were stated to be carried at the owner's sole risk; and a "reception clause" by which the receiver might be ready to take delivery as soon as the vessel was ready to discharge. The sellers were not paid by the buyers and decided to retain the original bills of lading. At the arrival of the vessel, the containers were discharged and stored, and subsequently delivered without requiring production of the bills of lading to the actual receivers. The sellers, as shippers, claimed damages for misdelivery against both the charterers and the shipowners.

***Held (for the shippers):* i)** The evidence of the bills of lading shows that the contract of carriage was made by the charterers' agents on behalf of the shipowners. Under clause 9 of the charterparty, the charterers had implied authority to sign bills of lading on behalf the shipowners. The parties to the contract of carriage were the shippers on the one side and the shipowners at the other. The meaning of clause 19 of the bills ratified this assertion. **ii)** The misdelivery occurred after the goods were stored in the docks by the stevedores. None of the terms of the bills of lading seem to justify misdelivery of the goods; not even the "cesser clause" which, although intended to allocate the risks after discharge to the owner, appears

to be a clause concerned with loss, damage or theft of the goods, rather than with misdelivery of them. Moreover, although the plaintiffs might be in breach of the "reception clause" in that they were not ready to take delivery, such breach was not causative of the loss. The shipowners were not protected by any of the clauses of the bills of lading. They were found liable for conversion.[115] **iii)** Under the sale contract, both the seller and the buyer agreed that the documents would be delivered against payment, so that property in the goods was not intended to pass until payment. Since the evidence showed that payment was not completed, the property in the goods remained with the sellers, who therefore retained a cause of action against the shipowners.

**140**
**Maciej Rataj, The**[116]
06.12.1994, Case C-406/92
(European Court of Justice)

A cargo of soyabean oil was loaded on board the vessel *Tatry* in Brazil for a carriage to Rotterdam (Netherlands) and Hamburg (Germany). Upon delivery, all of the receivers claimed that their cargo was contaminated with diesel oil. Before any other proceedings had commenced, the

---

[115] Clause 5 of the NYPE form also permits withdrawal "on any breach of this charter". However, the precise effect of such words have been limited by the courts. For instance, in *The Antaios (No.2), 1984, 2 Lloyd's Rep. 235*, Lord Diplock took the view that this clause only applied to repudiatory breaches. See also *The Tropwind* and *The Athos*.

[116] Sub nom. *The Tatry*.

shipowners brought an action in Rotterdam against the receivers of the cargo delivered in Rotterdam and Hamburg seeking a declaration that they were not liable for the contamination. They also initiated proceedings seeking to limit their liability under the International Convention of 10 Oct., 1957, relating to Limitation of Liability of Owners of Sea-going Ships. Some time later, the receivers in Hamburg issued a writ in rem against the *Tatry* and another vessel within the same ownership called *Maciej Rataj*. The *Maciej Rataj* was arrested in England and the Admiralty Court based its jurisdiction on the Arrest Convention of 1952. The shipowners asked the court to decline jurisdiction in favour of the courts of Rotterdam. They contended that the courts of Rotterdam were already seized of the proceedings involving the same cause of action and between the same parties, and alternatively, that those courts were the appropriate forum to hear the dispute. As a precautionary measure in the event that the English Courts declined jurisdiction, the receivers commenced actions in the Netherlands. The Court of Appeal referred to the European Court of Justice a number of questions on the interpretation of articles 21, 22 and 57 of the Convention of 27 Sept., 1968, regarding Jurisdiction and the Enforcement of Judgments in Civil and Commercial Matters (the Convention).[117]

***Held:*** (after the opinion of the General Advocate Mr. G. Tesauro): **1.** *"On a proper*

------

[117] As amended by the Convention of 9 Oct. 1978 on the Accession of Denmark, Ireland and the United Kingdom.

*construction, art. 57 of the Brussels Convention of Sept. 27, 1968 on Jurisdiction and the Enforcement of Judgments in Civil and Commercial Matters…means that, where a Contracting State is also a contracting party to another convention on a specific matter containing rules of jurisdiction, that specialized convention precludes the application of the provisions of the Brussels Convention only in cases governed by the specialized convention and not in those to which it does not apply."* **2.** *"On a proper construction of art. 21 of the Convention, where two actions involve the same cause of action and some but not all the parties to the second action are the same as the parties to the action commenced earlier in another Contracting State, the second Court seized is required to decline jurisdiction only to the extent to which the parties to the proceedings before it are also parties to the action previously commenced; it does not prevent the proceedings from continuing between the other parties."* **3.** *"On a proper construction of art. 21 of the Convention, an action seeking to have the defendant held liable for causing loss and ordered to pay damages has the same cause of action and the same object as earlier proceedings brought by that defendant seeking a declaration that he is not liable for that loss."* **4.** *"A subsequent action does not cease to have the same cause of action and the same object and to be between the same parties as a previous action where the latter, brought by the owner of a ship before a Court of a Contracting State, is an action in personam for a declaration that that owner is not liable for alleged damage to cargo transported by his ship, whereas the subsequent action has been brought by the owner of the cargo before a Court of another Contracting State by way of an action in rem concerning an arrested ship, and has subsequently continued both in rem*

*and in personam, or solely in personam, according to the distinctions drawn by the national law of that other Contracting State."*
**5.** *"On a proper construction of art. 22 of the Convention, it is sufficient, in order to establish the necessary relationship between, on the one hand, an action brought in a Contracting State by one group of cargo-owners against a shipowner seeking damages for harm caused to part of the cargo carried in bulk under separate but identical contracts, and, on the other, an action in damages brought in another Contracting State against the same shipowners by the owners of another part of the cargo shipped under the same conditions and under contract which are separate from but identical to those between the first group and the shipowner, that separate trial and judgment would involve the risk of conflicting decisions, without necessarily involving the risk of giving rise to mutually exclusive legal consequences."*

**141**

**Mahkutai, The**

**1996, 2 Lloyd's Rep. 1 (P.C.)**

The vessel *Mahkutai* was time-chartered to an Indonesian company and sub-chartered to a third company for a carriage of plywood from Jakarta (Indonesia) to China. The sub-charterers acted as shippers. A bill of lading was issued by the time charterers incorporating a Himalaya clause, which extended to any sub-contractor the benefit of all defences, exceptions and immunities which were available to the carrier under the bill of lading. There was also an exclusive jurisdiction clause providing that the contract was governed by the law of Indonesia and that

the Indonesian courts had exclusive jurisdiction for all disputes arising therefrom. Damages caused by sea water were found after the discharge in China. The cargo owners arrested the vessel in Hong Kong and issued a writ against the shipowners in that jurisdiction. The shipowners, who were not a party to the contract of carriage evidenced in the bill of lading, tried to rely on the jurisdiction clause by virtue of the Himalaya clause contained in the bill. They issued a summons seeking a stay of proceedings in Hong Kong in reliance on the exclusive jurisdiction clause. The Hong Kong Court of Appeal reversed the decision of the trial judge, ruling that the shipowners were not entitled to rely on the jurisdiction clause in so far as they were not parties to the bill of lading, and there had not been bailment on terms.

***Held (for the plaintiffs):*** **i)** The effect of the Himalaya clause is generally to protect a sub-contractor against claims in tort by providing a bilateral contract between the sub-contractor and the cargo owner.[118] The Himalaya clause does not operate in relation to provisions benefitting both parties, but rather only in relation to those conferring a one-sided benefit upon the carrier. **ii)** In the present case, however, the exclusive jurisdiction clause does not fall within the scope of the Himalaya clause. It embodies a mutual agreement under which the parties reach an agreement as to the appropriate jurisdiction for the resolution of disputes. The Privy Council took the view that the

---

[118] See *The Eurymedon* and *The New York Star.*

present jurisdiction and law clause did not confer any unilateral benefit for the defendant sub-contractors, but created mutual rights and obligations for both parties. **iii)** Lord Goff of Chieveley distinguished the present case from that of The Pioneer Container[119] in these terms: *"The present case is however concerned not with a question of enforceability of a term in a sub-bailment by the sub-bailee against the head bailor, but with the question whether a sub-contractor is entitled to take the benefit of a term in the head contract. The former (The Pioneer Container) depends on the scope of the authority of the intermediate bailor to act on behalf of the head bailor in agreeing on his behalf to the relevant term in the sub-bailment; whereas the latter (The Mahkutai) depends on the scope of the agreement between the head contractor and the sub-contractor, entered into by the intermediate contractor as agent for the sub-contractor, under which the benefit of a term in the head contract may be made available by the head contractor to the sub-contractor".* **iv)** Their lordships also rejected the defendants' submission that they had took possession of the goods as bailees and on the same terms as those contained in the original bills of lading, including the exclusive jurisdiction clause. In their opinion, any such implication might be rejected as inconsistent with the express terms of the bill of lading. Accordingly, the shipowners were not entitled to in-

---

[119] In *The Pioneer Container*, it was held that a jurisdiction clause contained in a feeder bill of lading was enforceable by the sub-contracted (feeder) carrier as against the cargo claimant by virtue of a sub-bailment "on any terms" clause contained in the head (ocean) bill of lading.

voke the Himalaya clause to give effect to the jurisdiction agreement contained in the bill of lading. The appeal was dismissed.

## 142
### MALLOZZI V. CARAPELLI SPA
*(The Italmotor)*
[1976] 1 Lloyd's Rep. 407 (C.A.)

On May 20, 1970, Carapelli sold c.i.f. Genoa to Mallozzi 5,000 m of oats to be shipped between May 20 and June 20, 1970. A second contract was entered into between the parties for 5,000 m of maize. Both contracts called for an average rate of discharge of 3,000 m per 24 hours provided that the ship could discharge at such rate, and demurrage/half despatch to be at the rates indicated in the charterparty. On Apr. 30 Carapelli chartered the MV *Italmotor* under a time charterparty for two round voyages to carry cereals to the United Kingdom. The charterparty contained no provisions as to demurrage. The bills of lading for the oats were falsely dated in order to make them conform the contract. On July 17 the vessel was ordered to Naples, and there she exceeded the permitted laytime by 14 days 21 hours and 31 minutes. Carapelli claimed demurrage from Mallozzi and Mallozzi, in turn, counterclaimed (a) damages for breach of contract for ordering vessel to Naples rather than Genoa, (b) repayment of the demurrage paid, (c) damages in respect of the falsely dated bills of lading. The matter was referred to arbitration.

***Held (for Mallozzi):*** Mallozzi could not recover the demurrage because Carapelli was under no obligation to pay demurrage under the time charterparty; Per Megaw LJ: "*…having regard to the fact that the sellers had chosen —no doubt for their own good purposes- to enter into a contract with shipowners, namely the time charterparty, which did not involve any provision for demurrage, no indicate any rates for demurrage, there was nothing to be paid*". (2) Mallozzi was under no legal obligation to negotiate as to whether Naples or Genoa should be the port of discharge, and, subsequently, there was no breach for failing to do so.

**143**

**M**ARBIENES **C**OMPAÑÍA **N**AVIERA **S.A.** v.
**F**ERROSTAAL **A.G.**

*(The Democritos)*
1976, 2 Lloyd's Rep. 149 (C.A.)

The vessel *Democritos* was time chartered on the New York Produce Exchange form. Although it was a time charterparty, it stated that "The owners agree to let and the charterers agree to hire the said vessel from the time of delivery for a trip via port or ports via the Pacific, duration about 4 to 6 months". The charterers were to pay hire at the rate of U.S. $1450 per day or pro rata until redelivery at an authorised port. The vessel was delivered on Dec. 18, 1969, so that the six months expired on June 18, 1970. At the time of delivery, the twin deck in n° 2 hold was found to be collapsed but the master guaranteed she was capable to load the interested cargo in the rest of her holds. The vessel was redelivered on July 23, 1970; that is, thirty five days later than the six months period. On that date the market rate had doubled

the charter rate. The owners complained and sought damages.

***Held (for the owners):*** **i)** It is not accepted in the charterers submission that they were entitled to damages since the vessel was in an unfit condition. As the charterers did not exercise the cancellation clause, they waived any right to reject the vessel. Alternatively, the damages would be for loss incurred by her not being able to carry a full cargo. **ii)** Neither was accepted the charterers' submission that the vessel was not delivered on time. Where no delivery date is provided in the charterparty, the sole obligation of the owners is to tender it with reasonable dispatch and due diligence. The burden to proof the opposite is on the charterers. **iii)** Although the charterparty specified a particular route or within certain trade limits, it must be considered a time charter; the words "duration about 4 to 6 months" are typical time charter periods which prevail in significance. Therefore, in time charters, the charterer is always allowed a little latitude as to the time of redelivery, much more in this case, where the words "about" before the charter period were taken as an express incorporation of the implied reasonable allowance. Such allowance was fixed in five days (23 June). However, since actual redelivery was not until July 23, and the last voyage being illegitimate, the charter rate was payable until June 23 and the market rate thereafter.[120]

---

[120] See also *The Gregos*, where the order was also rightly given at first, but by the time set sail on the final voyage it was evident that the voyage was not to be completed in time, and so became illegitimate.

## 144
### Marc Rich & Co. AG v. Bishop Rock Marine Co. Ltd.
*(The Nicholas H)*
1995, 3 All. E.R. 307 (H.L.)

The *Nicholas H* was on a voyage from South America to Italy when a crack appeared in the hull. The vessel anchored at San Juan (Puerto Rico) where further cracks were discovered. A surveyor acting for the vessel's classification society (NKK) recommended permanent repairs and dry-docking at San Juan. However, the owners did not want to discharge the cargo and re-load it again, so that they decided to effect temporary repairs carried out to the shell plating. The surveyor authorized the temporary repairs and pronounced the vessel ready to sail. After commencement of the voyage, the temporary repairs cracked and the ship sank. The owners of the cargo sued the shipowners as carriers, the charterers and the classification society which employed the surveyor. The proceedings against the charterers were not pursued and those against the shipowners were settled for the amount of the vessel's tonnage limitation. The plaintiffs proceeded against the classification society for the balance of the loss in tort. They alleged negligence which caused physical damage to the plaintiffs' property; that they had failed to exercise their duty of care because the damage was reasonably foreseeable. The class society contended that the existence of a contractual claim derived from the Hague Rules by the cargo owners against the shipowners for breach of a non-delegable duty to use due diligence to ensure the seaworthiness of the vessel meant that it would not be fair, just or reasonable to impose a tortuous duty of care on the class society in respect of their surveyor's alleged negligence.

***Held (for the class society):***[121] **i)** It is settled law that the concepts of foreseeability and proximity, as well as considerations of fairness, justice or reasonableness, applies to all cases of negligence whatever the nature of the harm sustained. In this regard, there is no distinction between cases of direct physical damage and (such in the present case) indirect physical damage or economic loss. There was, on the facts, sufficient degree of proximity between the damage done and the class society's acts for the existence of a duty of care. **ii)** However, imposing such a duty would not be just, fair and reasonable regarding the special role of class societies in the international trade. They are independent and non-profit-making entities created for the sole purpose of promoting the collective welfare, namely the safety of lives and ships at sea. Furthermore, class societies do not have the benefit of the Hague Visby Rules and tonnage limits of liability, so that, if a duty of care was held to exist, the cost of insuring potential claims would make more difficult their non-lucrative activity.

## 145
### March Rich & Co. AG v. Societa Italiana Impianti PA
*(The Atlantic Emperor)*
1992, 1 Lloyd's Rep. 342
(European Court of Justice)

On Jan. 23, 1987, March Rich & Co. (the plaintiffs) made an offer to purchase a

---

[121] Lord Lloyd dissenting.

quantity of Iranian crude oil from Società Italiana Impianti (the defendants). On Jan. 25, the defendants accepted the plaintiffs' order subject to certain additional conditions. The plaintiffs, in turn, sent another message on Jan. 26 accepting those additional conditions. A further message was sent by the plaintiffs on Jan. 28 setting out the terms of the contract, which included the following clause: 'Law and Arbitration: construction validity and performance of this contract shall be construed in accordance with English law. Should any dispute arise between buyer and seller the matter in dispute shall be referred to three persons in London. One to be appointed by each of the parties hereto and the third by the two so chosen, their decision or that of any two of them should be final and binding on both parties'. There was no reply to that message. After the cargo was loaded onto the ship nominated by the plaintiffs, the plaintiffs complained that the cargo was seriously contaminated and claimed damages. On Feb. 29, 1988, the defendants issued a writ in Italy declaring they were not liable to the plaintiffs. On Oct. 4 the plaintiffs served defence and counterclaimed relying on the arbitration clause and asserting that the Italian courts had no jurisdiction. Also on Feb. 29 the plaintiffs commenced arbitration proceedings in London, in which the defendants refused to take part. Upon the plaintiffs' request, the English High Court granted leave to serve summons on the defendants in Italy for the appointment of an arbitrator. The defendants sought to set aside the order contending that the dispute should be heard in Italy as it fell within the scope of art. 1(4) of the Convention of 27 Sept. 1968 on Jurisdiction and the Enforcement of Judgments in Civil and

Commercial Matters. The first paragraph of art. 1 provides that the Convention applies in civil and commercial matters whatever the nature of the court or tribunal. According to the second paragraph of that article, the Convention shall not apply to "…4. Arbitration". On appeal, the Court of Appeal of England referred a number of questions to the European Court of Justice for a preliminary ruling.

***Held (after the opinion of the General Advocate Mr. M. Darmon): Question 1 (first part)*** Whether art. 1(4) of the Convention must be interpreted in such a manner that the exclusion provided for therein extends to proceedings pending before a national Court concerning the appointment of an arbitrator. *"The purpose of the Convention, according to the preamble thereto, is to implement the provisions of art. 220 of the EEC Treaty concerning the reciprocal recognition and enforcement of judgments of Courts or tribunals. Pursuant to the fourth paragraph of art. 220, the Member States shall, so far as is necessary, enter into negotiations with each other with a view to securing for the benefit of their nationals the simplification of formalities governing the reciprocal recognition and enforcement of judgments of Courts or tribunals and of arbitration awards; The international agreements, and in particular the…New York Convention on the recognition and enforcement of foreign arbitral awards…lay down rules which must be respected not by the arbitrators themselves but by the Courts of the Contracting States. Those rules relate, for example, to agreements whereby parties refer a dispute to arbitration and to the recognition and enforcement of arbitral awards. It follows that, by excluding arbitration from the scope* *of the Convention on the ground that it was already covered by international conventions, the Contracting Parties intended to exclude arbitration in its entirety, including proceedings brought before national Courts. More particularly, it must be pointed out that the appointment of an arbitrator by a national Court is a measure adopted by the State as part of the process of setting arbitration proceedings in motion. Such a measure therefore comes within the sphere of arbitration and is thus covered by the exclusion contained in art. 1(4) of the Convention."* **ii) Question 1 (second part)** Whether the exclusion of art. 1(4) also applies where in those proceedings concerning the appointment of an arbitrator a preliminary issue is raised as to whether an arbitration agreement exists or is valid. *"In order to determine whether a dispute falls within the scope of the Convention, reference must be made solely to the subject-matter of the dispute. If, by virtue of its subject-matter, such as the appointment of an arbitrator, a dispute falls outside the scope of the Convention, the existence of a preliminary issue which the court must resolve in order to determine the dispute cannot, whatever that issue may be, justify application of the Convention (…) It follows that, in the case before the court, the fact that a preliminary issue relates to the existence or validity of the arbitration agreement does not affect the exclusion from the scope of the Convention of a dispute concerning the appointment of an arbitrator. Consequently, the reply must be that art. 1(4) of the Convention must be interpreted as meaning that the exclusion provided for therein extends to litigation pending before a National Court concerning the appointment of an arbitrator, even if the existence or validity of an arbitration agreement is a preliminary issue in that litigation."*

# 146
## MARDOF PEACH & CO. LTD. v. ATTICA SEA CARRIERS CORP. OF LIBERIA
### (The Laconia)
### 1977, A.C. 850 (H.L.)

The vessel *Laconia* was chartered in Jan. 1970 for 3 months 15 days more or less at charterers' option. The charterparty, on the New York Produce Exchange form, provided in clause 5[122] that hire was to be paid in cash USD currency semi-monthly in advance to the owners and with terms expressly stated that, should the charterers fail to punctually and regularly submit hire payments, the owners would be at liberty to withdraw the vessel. The seventh and final instalment became due on Sunday. Since this was a non-banking day, payment by the charterers was made on Monday. The charterers' bankers delivered by hand to the shipowners' bank at 15:00. the following day a payment order for the appropriate sum under the London Currency Settlement Scheme. The shipowners' bank took delivery and informed its customer, who immediately refused the money and instructed the bank to return it to the charterers' bank. The same Monday the shipowners withdrew the vessel. The charterers, inter alia, submitted that the original acceptance by the shipowners' bank might be treated as a waiver of the default.

---

[122] Clause 5 of the NYPE form also permits withdrawal "on any breach of this charter". However, the precise effect of such words have been limited by the courts. For instance, in *The Antaios (No.2), 1984, 2 Lloyd's Rep. 235*, Lord Diplock took the view that this clause only applied to repudiatory breaches. See also *The Tropwind* and *The Athos.*

***Held (for the shipowners):*** **i)** About the meaning of the withdrawal clause: *"My Lords, I* (Lord Wilbeforce) *cannot find any difficulty or ambiguity in this clause. It must mean that once punctual payment of any instalment has not been made, a right of withdrawal accrues to the owners. Conversely, it is incapable of meaning that a charterer who has failed to make punctual payment, can (unless the owners have waived the default) avoid the consequences of his failure by later tendering an unpunctual payment. He would still have failed to make punctual payment, and it is on this failure and by reason of it that the owners get the right to withdraw".* The immediate consequence of this quotation is that, in cases (like the present one) where the date of payment falls on a non-banking day, payment to be "punctual" must be effected on the preceding business day.[123]
**ii)** Concerning waiver of the default: (Lord Salmon) *"Certainly it was not within the banker's express or implied authority to make commercial decisions on behalf of their customers by accepting or rejecting late payments of hire without taking instructions. They did take instructions and were told to reject the payment. They did so and returned it to the charterers on the following day which in any view must have been within a reasonable time".* iii) (Lord Wilbeforce) *"The result of my conclusions on these two points leaves the*

*matter as follows: (1) Under the withdrawal clause, as under similar clauses, including the Baltime clause properly interpreted, a right of withdrawal arises as soon as default is made in punctual payment of an instalment of hire. Whether or not this rule is subject to qualification in a case of punctual but insufficient payment as some authorities appear to hold, is not an issue which now arises and I* (Lord Wilberforce) *express no opinion upon it. (2) The owners must within a reasonable time after the default give notice of withdrawal to the charterer. What is a reasonable time —essentially a matter for arbitrators to find- depends on the circumstances. In some, indeed many cases, it will be a short time —viz. the shortest time reasonably necessary to enable the shipowner to hear of the default and issue instructions. If, of course, the charterparty contains an express provision regarding notice to the charterers, that provision must be applied. (3) The owners may be held to have waived the default, inter alia, if when a late payment is tendered, they choose to accept it as if it were timeous, or if they do not within a reasonable time give notice that they have rejected it."*

147

MAREDELANTO COMPAÑÍA NAVIERA **S.A.**
V. BERGBAU-HANDEL **G.M.B.H.**
*(The Mihalis Angelos)*
1970, 2 Lloyd's Rep. 43 (C.A.)

On May 25, 1965, the owners of the *Mihalis Angelos* let her to the charterers for a voyage from Haiphong (North Vietnam) to Hamburg (Germany) the cargo to be carried being apatite in bulk. The fixture expressing that the vessel was "expected ready to load under this Charter about 1 July 1965" and contained a cancelling

---

[123] As a consequence of the strict and harsh interpretation by the courts of such clauses, a number of "anti-technicality clauses" were inserted in modern time charterparty. These clauses tempered the strictness by providing that, in the event of default in payment of hire, the shipowner must give specific notice of withdrawal and the charterer is given a 48-hour "breathing space" to pay up (see NYPE '93, clause 11: 'Grace period').

clause for the charterers in case the vessel was not ready to load on or before July 20, 1965. It was proved that when the fixture was made the owners had no reasonable grounds for expecting the vessel to be ready to load on July, 1. The vessel had, in fact, previous engagements that made readiness by that date improbable. On 17 July while the vessel was still engaged in a previous voyage at Hong Kong, the charterers elected to cancel the charterparty. They alleged force majeure on the ground that no apatite was available at Haiphong due to the hostilities with the United States. The owners immediately treated this conduct as a repudiation of the charter and claimed damages for the loss of profit.

***Held (for the charterers):*** i) The charterers were entitled to cancel on the ground that the owners had broken the "expected ready to load" clause.[124] If an owner states such a clause in a charterparty, he should

make a representation as to his own state of mind and is bound by the term to its truth. (Lord Denning, M.R.) *"If he or his agent breaks that term by making the statement without any honest belief in its truth or without any reasonable grounds for it, he must take the consequences. It is, at lowest, a misrepresentation which entitles the other party to rescind; and, at highest, a breach of contract which goes to the root of the matter. It may, therefore, properly be described as a 'condition'; I hold, therefore, that on July 17, 1965, the charterers were entitled to cancel the contract on the ground that the owners had broken the 'expected ready to load' clause."* ii) (Edmund Davies, L.J.) *"That the owners were in breach of (the "expected ready to (load" clause) is common ground. It is equally undisputed that if, as I think, the circumstances entitled the charterers to repudiate on July 17, the fact that they did so by reliance on an untenable plea of force majeure does not invalidate their act of cancellation."*

---

<sup>124</sup> In *Evera S.A. Commercial v. North Shipping Co. Ltd.* [1956] 2 Lloyd's Rep. 367, at p. 370, Devlin J. described the ratio behind the "expected ready to load" clause as follows: *"A charterer manifestly wants, if he can get it, a fixed date for the arrival of the ship at the port of loading. He has to make arrangements to bring down the cargo and to have it ready to load when the ship arrives and he wants to know as near as he can what that date is going to be. On the other hand, it is to the interest of the shipowner, if he can have it, to have the date as flexible as possible because of the inevitable delays due to bad weather or other circumstances that there might be in the course of the voyage. He can never be sure that he can arrive at a port on a fixed and certain day. Therefore, in order to accommodate these two views as far as possible it has been the general practice for a long time past to have a clause under which the shipowner, without pledging himself to a fixed day, gives a date in the charterparty of expected readiness, that is the date when he expects that he will be ready to load".*

## 148

### MARIMPEX MINERALÖL MBH v. LOUIS DREYFUS ET CIE. GMBH
### 1995, 1 Lloyd's Rep. 167 (Q.B.)

The plaintiffs sold c.i.f. Paktank (Hamburg) some 18,000 tonnes of "normal Russian gasoil" to the defendants. Risk and property were to pass at the port of loading. When the contract was made the gasoil had already been shipped on board the vessel *Zaks Diklo*. It was an express or implied term of the contract that the gasoil should be of merchantable quality. The contract was governed by English law. Upon the vessel arriving at destination the sellers took delivery, but deducted a part of the original price from the invoice. The reason for the deduction was that the sellers found the cargo not complying with the description of "normal Russian gasoil", and that it was not of merchantable quality. They contended that the gasoil had been contaminated by bacteria to such an extent that it was no longer merchantable. The sellers sought reimbursement for the deduction.

***Held (for the buyers):* i)** Although contamination sometimes occurs while the cargo is in the ship's tanks, in this case the court found no evidence that the cargo had been contaminated on board or at any time other than prior to loading. **ii)** In the absence of a particular specification in the contract, there was no internationally accepted criteria as to what degree of contamination was required to render the gas-oil in breach of contract. To bridge this gap, the learned judge found that *"the market rightly or wrongly regarded this gasoil as being worth significantly less than the market value of uncontaminated Russian gasoil".* It was found that the gasoil neither met the description of "normal Russian gasoil" nor was of merchantable quality[125] In addition to that, since the gasoil was not fit for its original use without treatment, it did not observe the requirements of merchantability.[126] Hence the plaintiffs were in breach of the condition of merchantability of the goods which is implied in any contract of sale. **iii)** The defendants took all reasonable steps to minimise the

loss by intending to re-sell the gasoil for ultimate use for heating or as diesel oil; it was not marketable as uncontaminated oil. The contamination was such that it was not merchantable without treatment or a significant price discount.

**149**
**MASH & MURRELL LTD. V. EMANUEL (JOSEPH I.) LTD.**
1961, 2 Lloyd's Rep. 326 (C.A.)

The defendants sold to the plaintiffs a cargo afloat of Cypriot potatoes c. & f. Liverpool. The vessel had loaded the consignment of potatoes in Limassol (Cyprus) and later called to an intermediate port before reaching Liverpool (England). The evidence showed that from Limassol to the intermediate port the hatches of the holds were left open. For that reason the thermo-tank ventilation system of the ship was unable to work during that period. On the ship's arrival, the potatoes were found rotten. They had to be re-sold as pig feed by the buyers, who then sought damages against the sellers on the following grounds: (a) the cargo was not fit to travel, (b) the sellers were in breach of the implied condition of sec. 14(2) and 15(2.c) of the Sale of Goods Act 1893, in so far the goods were not fit for their purpose and were not merchantable, and (c) the sellers' were in breach of the implied warranty of c. & f. contracts in that the goods should be fit to stand a normal voyage.

***Held (for the sellers):* i)** The implied term of fitness and merchantability of the goods, regarding their perishable na-

---

[125] See section 13 of the Sale of Goods Act 1979.
[126] See also section 14 of the Sale of Goods Act 1979.

ture must be observed not only when the goods are loaded but also upon arrival after a normal voyage. (Harman, L.J.) *"It is the extraordinary deterioration of the goods due to abnormal conditions experienced during transit for which the buyer takes the risk. A necessary and inevitable deterioration during (a normal) transit, which will render the goods unmerchantable on arrival, is normally one for which the seller is liable."* **ii)** There is no evidence showing that the potatoes were not fit to travel when loaded. It was proved that the deterioration of cargo was produced by the high temperature during the period between Limassol and the intermediate port. Furthermore, the fact that the issued bill of lading was clean and not "claused" is prima facie evidence that the cargo was shipped in apparent good order and condition. **iii)** On the evidence the deterioration of the cargo was produced after shipment and due to the abnormal circumstances of the voyage. Therefore, there being no breach on the part of the sellers, the risk passed to the buyers on shipment, as it is normally the case under c. & f. terms.

**150**

**MAURITIUS OIL REFINERIES LTD. V. STOLT-NIELSEN NEDERLANDS B.V.**

*(The Stolt Sydness)*

1997, 1 Lloyd's Rep. 273 (Q.B.)

Under a voyage charterparty dated Jan 31, 1992, the defendants as disponent owners let the vessel *Stolt Sydness* to the plaintiff charterers for a carriage of vegetable oil from the River Plate (Argentina) to Port Louis (Mauritius). The charterparty con-

tained a London arbitration clause and a jurisdiction clause for English law, but incorporated the USA clause Paramount "subject to the Carriage of Goods by Sea Act of the United States, 1936".[127] The charter stated "ETA Up River Feb. 22, 1992" as the present position the ship and the cancelling date was Feb. 29, 1992. The vessel was seriously delayed before and after loading because of engine troubles. That failure did not damaged the cargo on board physically but made it less valuable. The charterers then had to buy a substitute cargo afloat for Mauritius to mitigate their loss. The one-year limit of art. III(6) Hague Rules elapsed on Apr. 7, 1993. On Nov. 1, 1995 the charterers appointed an arbitrator and on June 13, 1996, and claimed damages arguing that art. III(6) was not applicable since their claim was in reference to substitute cargo carried aboard a different vessel. Alternatively, they applied for an extension of time for the commencement of arbitration under sec. 27 of the Arbitration Act 1950.

***Held (for the defendants):*** (Rix, J.) **i)** As to the object of the claim: The charterers' submission was rejected that their claim was not for "loss or damage" in respect of "the goods" carried on the Stolt Sydness but in respect of the condition of the vessel and/or substitute cargo, and therefore their claim fell outside the art. III(6) time-bar. The judge took the view that the claim was in respect of the cargo carried on board of the Stolt Sydness. He admitted: *"The delay*

---

[127] The U.S. Carriage of Goods by Sea Act 1936 incorporates the Hague Rules; sec. 3(6) of the former is equivalent to art. III (6) of the latter.

*is ascribed to the owners' failure to exercise due diligence to provide a seaworthy vessel. There may be many difficulties in principle or in fact in the path of that claim, but it seems to me that it is a claim in respect of the cargo carried; therefore this first attempt to escape the effect of sec. 3(6) fails".*[128] **ii)** As to the proper applicable law: *"In the present case the unusual feature is that English and U.S. law have thrown up conflicting decisions on the meaning of art. III(6). Whatever might have been the position if the U.S. decision has stood alone, it can hardly be said, in the light of The Merak, that the parties, in choosing English law and the incorporation of U.S. COGSA, must have intended to give precedence to the U.S. decision in Son v. DeFosse".*[129] Rix J. added: *"The parties have deliberately chosen not only English law, but also London arbitration. If one asks, therefore, whether the parties must have intended that failure to arbitrate within the year was a bar within sec. 3(6) or not, it seems to me that there can be only one possible answer: such a failure was intended to bar the claim, and the approach in The Merak was to prevail".*[130] **iii)** As to the extension of time under sec. 27 of the Arbitration Act 1950: The delay in commencing the arbitration was about two and a half years and it was due to the own charterers' fault, and not beyond their control. Rix J. expressed that in the circumstances of this case undue hardship was not caused if time were not extended, and therefore, the extension under sec. 27 was not granted.

---

[128] See *The Marinor.*

[129] *Son Shipping Co. v. DeFosse & Tanghe*, 199 F. 2d. 687 (2d. Cir. 1952).

[130] See also *Vita Food Products Inc. v. Unus Shipping Co. Ltd.*

## 151

## MAXINE FOOTWEAR CO. V. CANADIAN GOVERNMENT MERCHANT MARINE LTD.

### 1959, 2 All E.R. 740 (P.C.)

After loading had begun, the defendants' ship caught fire and was destroyed before she sailed out on her voyage. The fire had been caused by negligence when some frozen pipes were being thawed out with an acetylene torch by an employee of an independent contractor on the authority of the master. As a result of the casualty, the cargo became a total loss. A bill of lading had been issued incorporating the Hague Rules. The plaintiff shippers claimed to recover damages for non-delivery of the goods on the ground that the ship was not seaworthy. The shipowners invoked the fire exception of art. IV of the Hague Rules and further contended that they had exercised due diligence to make the ship seaworthy as prescribed by art. III(1), i.e. "before and at the beginning of the voyage". They said that the ship was seaworthy at the time of loading, and that the moment of the "beginning of the voyage" was never reached.

***Held (for the plaintiffs):*** The shipowners were found in breach of art. III(1) of the Hague Rules as the duty to provide a seaworthy ship "before and at the beginning of the voyage" is a continuous and overriding warranty the breach of which does not entitle the shipowner to invoke any of the immunities of art. IV. (Lord Sommervell of Harrow) *"In their lordships' opinion 'before and at the beginning of the voyage' means the period from at least the beginning of the loading until the vessel starts on her voyage. The word 'before' cannot, in their opinion, be* *read as meaning 'at the commencement of the loading'. If this had been intended, it would have been said. The question when precisely the period begins does not arise in this case, hence the insertion above of the words 'at least'. On that view the obligation to exercise due diligence to make the ship seaworthy continued over the whole of the period from the beginning of loading until the ship sank. There was a failure to exercise due diligence during that period. As a result the ship became unseaworthy and this unseaworthiness caused the damage to, and loss of, the [shippers' goods]…It is also unnecessary to consider the earlier cases as to 'stages' under the Common Law.[131] The doctrine of stages had its anomalies, and some important matters were never elucidated by authority. When the warranty was absolute, it seems at any rate intelligible to restrict it to certain points of time. It would be surprising if a duty to exercise due diligence ceased as soon as loading began only to reappear later shortly before the beginning of the voyage."*

**152**

**MEDITERRANEAN FREIGHT SERVICES LTD. v. BP OIL INTERNATIONAL LTD.**
*(The Fiona)*
1994, 2 Lloyd's Rep. 506 (C.A.)

The tanker *Fiona* was chartered to carry fuel oil from a range of loading ports including Rotterdam (Netherlands) to a range of discharging ports including New York (USA). The charterers required the shipowners to have the tanks free of any condensate sediments before loading fuel oil. The tanks were washed and the shippers performed the loading. The vessel arrived at an off-shore platform at Northport, New York. While a surveyor was taking samples from the vessel's tanks an explosion occurred and the surveyor was thrown over the side of the vessel and died. The shipowners sought to recover the loss suffered by the vessel from the shippers for shipping a dangerous cargo or, alternatively, the indemnity clause of art. IV(6) of the Hague-Visby Rules. They contended that the fuel oil was dangerous because it had a propensity to produce hydrocarbon vapours which gave rise to the explosive gas in the vessel's tanks, such facts being known to the shippers and to other oil companies generally but not to the shipowners. They submitted that they would not have consented to the cargo's shipment had they known of its nature and character. The shippers alleged that the flammable gas mixture was due not to the cargo itself but to the contamination created as a result of residues from the previous condensate cargoes, and further, from a static electrical discharge caused by steam from leaking heating coils. They said that, even if the cargo was dangerous, the explosion was caused by the failure of the shipowners to exercise due diligence in making the vessel seaworthy. The shippers counter-claimed against the shipowners after the elapse of the one-year period from the date of discharge.

***Held:*** i) Both parties, shippers and shipowners, were in breach of their correspondent duties under the Hague-Visby Rules. The question was whether the party indemnified was entitled to rely on his indemnity notwithstanding his own fault. Art. IV(6) proceeds on the assumption that

---

[131] See *The Vortigen*, [1895-99] All E.R. 387.

dangerous goods were shipped without the shipowners' consent and, as it seems, the nature and character of the particular cargo fell clearly outside the scope of the intended contract. **ii)** But a shipper is not liable under art. IV(6) where the cause of damages incurred by the carrier was either a breach of his obligations under art. III(1 and 2). The failure of the shipowners to remove condensate residues from the vessel before loading began constituted a breach of art. III (1 and 2). (Hirst, L.J.) *"It would be wholly contrary to the scheme of the rules and likewise inconsistent with equity and commercial common sense that a carrier should be entitled to destroy dangerous goods without compensation and without liability, except to general average, if the cause of the goods having to be destroyed was a breach by the carrier of his obligations as to seaworthiness"*. Thus the exceptions of art. IV(6) are subject to the performance of the obligations set out in art. III(1 and 2). For the same reasons, the one-year time bar provision does not prevent the shippers from raising as a defence that the relevant damages and expenses were caused by the owner's breach of art. III. In conclusion, regarding that the shipowners were negligent in that they did not exercise due diligence to make the vessel seaworthy, they were not entitled to invoke the indemnities of the rules.[132]

---

[132] In *Maxine Footwear Co. Ltd. v. Canadian Government Merchant Marine, 1959, A.C. 589*, the Privy Council held that the implied undertaking as to seaworthiness in art. III(1) constituted an overriding obligation the breach of which deprived the carrier of the protection of the exceptions contained in art. IV. The carrier was not entitled to invoke the fire exception since the fire was caused from a breach of such undertaking.

## 153

### MEREDITH JONES (A) & CO. LTD. V. VANGEMAR SHIPPING CO. LTD.

*(The Apostolis)*
1997, 2 Lloyd's Rep. 241 (C.A.)

The bulker *Apostolis* called at Piraeus while she was in route to Varna (Bulgaria) carrying a cargo of sugar. In Piraeus she loaded a 100 steel plates which were to be used to repair the hatch covers of the vessel. Once in Varna, the sugar was discharged and the vessel dry-docked to repair the hatch covers. The vessel left Varna under a fixture providing for a carriage of raw cotton in bales to Salonika (Greece). The bills of lading were issued incorporating the Hague-Visby Rules. During the loading operations, a fire was discovered in holds 4 and 5 containing the cargo and it was severely damaged by the heat and the water used to extinguish the fire. The charterers claimed damages based on the fact that the shipowners were in breach of art. III of the Hague-Visby Rules. They argued that the fire was caused by the welding operations carried out on deck while the cargo was being loaded. The owners contended that the cause of the fire was due to a discarded cigarette which fell under the responsibility of the charterers, and counterclaimed for loss on the vessel.

***Held:*** **i)** There was no reliable evidence that the fire was caused by the welding. The onus probandi was on the charterers and they failed to prove that welding was the most probable cause of fire. The owners, for their part, failed to prove that the most probable cause was a discarded cigarette for which the charterers would have been liable. **ii)** (Leggatt L.J.) *"To show breach of art. III(1), A.M.J. (i.e. the plaintiffs) had to show that the owners failed to make the ship seaworthy and that their loss or damage was caused by the breach i.e. the fire was caused by unseaworthiness; nothing about the state of the ship rendered her unseaworthy."* The mere fact that the welding could have exposed the cargo to an ephemeral risk of ignition did not put the owners in breach of art. III(1) of the Hague-Visby Rules.

**154**

**METVALE LTD. AND ANOTHER V. MONSANTO INTERNATIONAL SARL AND OTHERS**

*(The Msc Napoli)*
2009, 1 Lloyd's Rep. 246 (Q.B.)

Hapag-Lloyd AG (HPL) were slot charterers of the container vessel *MSC Napoli* under a slot charter agreement with Mediterranean Shipping Co (MSC). HPL issued its own bills of lading or seaway bills which provided for German law and jurisdiction in respect to 172 laden containers. H. Stinnes Linien GmbH (Stinnes) was also under a slot charter agreement with MSC. Stinnes had issued twenty four bills of lading, which provided for German law and jurisdiction. In the course of the voyage, the vessel suffered damage in heavy weather and grounded on the South coast of England. The casualty resulted in claims against the shipowners of the MSC Napoli in excess of 100 million Pounds. A limitation fund (the fund) was constituted by the shipowners under the convention on Limitation of Liability for Maritime Claims 1976 (the Convention)

in the amount of £ 14,710,000. Holders of the bills of lading issued by HPL and Stinnes lodged claims against them. HPL and Stinnes subsequently sought claims against the fund in respect of their claims for an indemnity for cargo claims brought against them, the loss and damage of their own containers, general average and salvage claims and certain transshipment claims. The preliminary issues before the court were: (i) Whether HPL and Stinnes were shipowners for the purposes of article 1 of the Convention and were entitled to limit their liability under the Convention and under the Merchant Shipping Act 1995, (ii) Whether if the answer to (i) is yes, the limitation fund constituted in this action is deemed to be constituted by HPL under and for the purpose of the Convention and under the Merchant Shipping Act 1995.

***Held:*** (i) There was no reason why the word "charterer" in Article 1(2) of the Convention should not also encompass slot charterers given the fact that slot charterers are considered charterers given the ordinary use of the term as evidenced by such use in standard textbooks in addition to considerations of the purpose of the Convention which is to encourage trade by limiting liabilities on any distinct occasion. Were slot charterers excluded from the Convention, an efficient way of organizing the carriage of goods could fall into disuse, serving to discourage trade, which is antithetical to the purpose of the Convention. (ii) Concerning the second issue, the Court held, *"Pursuant to article 11(3) of the Convention a fund constituted by one of the persons mention in article 9 or his insurer shall be deemed constituted by all persons* *mentioned in article 9. The fund was constituted by the claimant. The claimant is the owner of a seagoing ship, MSC Napoli, and is therefore a person mention in article 1(2) and accordingly a person mention in article 9. HPL and Stinnes, being the charterers of MSC Napoli are persons mentioned in article 1(2) and accordingly persons mentioned in article 9 It follows that the fund is deemed to be constituted by HPL and Stinnes".*

## 155
### MIDLAND SILICONES LTD. V. SCRUTTONS LTD.
1961, 2 Lloyd's Rep. 365 (H.L.)

The owners of the steamer *American Reporter* engaged a firm of stevedores to discharge their vessels at London (England) and to act as their agents in delivering the goods to the consignees. The stevedoring contract provided that the stevedores were to be responsible for any damage caused by their negligence, but contained the following fragment: "…The stevedores to have such protection as is afforded by the terms, conditions and exceptions of the Bills of Lading Westbound and Eastbound". Owing to the stevedores' negligence, a drum of chemicals was damaged while it was being discharged from the *American Reporter*. The consignees of the drum claimed damages from the stevedores, who replied that they were entitled to the limitation of liability contained in the bill of lading governing the relations between the consignees and the "carrier". Clause 3 of the bill of lading stipulated that "…the word 'carrier' shall include the ship…her owner, operator and demise charterer, and also any time charter-

er or person to the extent bound by this bill of lading, whether acting as carrier or bailee…" The U.S. Carriage of Goods by Sea Act, 1936, as incorporated to the bill of lading, provided that the term "carrier" included the owners or the charterer who entered into the contract of carriage with the shipper. The main question for the appeal was whether the term "carrier" covered the stevedores' acts and these were entitled to the limitation of liability contained in the bill of lading.

***Held (for the consignees):***[133] **i)** The term "carrier" either in the bill of lading and in the U.S. COGSA 1936 cannot include the stevedores in this case. **ii)** The contractual role of the stevedores vis-à-vis the owners was that of independent contractors only. It could not be implied from any clause of the bill of lading that the owners were contracting as agents of the stevedores. **iii)** The consignees were unaware of the relations between the owners and the stevedores and there was no ground for implying a contract between the consignees and the stevedores. **iv)** It is an established principle of English law that only a party to a contract can sue or rely on the defences contained in it. On this basis, the stevedores were not entitled to rely on the protection of the contract evidenced by the bill of lading as they were not a party to it. Notwithstand-

---

[133] Lord Denning dissenting: "*It was negligence in the very course of performing the contract –done it is true by the sub-contractor and not by the principal-, but if you permit the owner of the goods to sue the sub-contractor in tort for what is in truth a breach of the contract of carriage, then at least you should give him the protection of the contract. Were it otherwise, there would be an easy way round the conditions of the contract of carriage*".

ing that, Lord Reid left open the case where one of the parties contracts as an agent of the third party (i.e. the stevedores). He stated the four conditions for the validity of such an agency contract: "*I (Lord Reid) can see a possibility of success of the argument if (first) the bill of lading makes it clear that the stevedore is intended to be protected by the provisions in it which limit liability, (secondly) the bill of lading makes it clear that the carrier, in addition to contracting for these provisions on his own behalf, is also contracting as agent for the stevedore that these provisions should apply to the stevedore, (thirdly) the carrier has authority from the stevedore to do that, or perhaps later ratification by the stevedore would suffice, and (fourthly) that any difficulties about consideration moving from the stevedore were overcome. And then to affect the consignee it would be necessary to show that the provisions of the Bills of Lading Act 1855 apply*".[134]

## 156
### MIRAMAR MARITIME CORP. V. HOLBORN OIL TRADING LTD.
#### (*The Miramar*)
#### 1984, 1 AC 676 (H.L.)

The tanker *Miramar* was voyage-chartered on the Exxonvoy 1969 form[135] to a Singaporean company. Clause 8 of the charter-party provided, inter alia, that the "Charterer shall pay demurrage" at a specified rate. After loading oil at one port, the shipowners issued a bill of lading on the Exxonvoy bill of lading standard form, which contained a clause incorporating the terms of the charterparty clause with the words "all terms whatsoever of the charter except the rate and payment of freight…apply to and govern the rights of the parties concerned in this shipment". When the vessel arrived, the Singaporean charterers failed to pay demurrage, which they were owing at the port of Trincomalee, and they were found insolvent. The shipowners sought to recover demurrage due under the charterparty from the holders of the bill of lading. They alleged that the consignees were liable to pay such credit by virtue of the charterparty incorporation clause of the bill of lading. The question was whether the holder of the bill of lading, not being the charterer, was personally liable to the shipowners for the full amount of demurrage payable under the charterparty.

***Held (for the consignees)*: i) Regarding** the incorporation clause of the bill of lading: The words "all terms whatsoever of the charter" have the effect of incorporating the terms of the charter verbatim into the bill of lading. As a matter of construction, such words are sufficiently broadly drafted in the present case so as to incorporate the charterparty demurrage provisions verbatim into the bill of lading. **ii)** Regarding the demurrage clause in the charterparty: Although the incorporation clause was fully effective, the words "charterer shall pay demurrage" in the charterparty indicated clearly that such obliga-

---

[134] Since the enactment of the UK Carriage of Goods by Sea Act 1992, however, the binding effect of the "Himalaya" clause in relation to the consignee or the indorsee of the bills of lading is no longer subject to the compliance of the requisites of Section 1 of the 1855 Act. See later cases as *The Eurymedon* and *The Mahkutai*.

[135] This is now known as Asbatankvoy form.

tion were to be undertaken by no one other than the charterer. (Lord Diplock) "In the instant case,…every reference to the 'charterer' by that designation in Exxonvoy 1969, although it would not necessarily affect directly legal obligations as between the owner and the consignee, would nevertheless make perfectly good sense, when incorporating verbatim in the Exxonvoy bill of lading, if it mean the person designated as 'the charterer' in the charterparty and no-one else."[136]

### 157
### Motis exports Ltd. v. Dampskibsselskabet AF 1912 Aktieselskab and Aktieselskabet Dampskibsselskabet Svendborg
1999, 1 Lloyd's Rep. 837 (Q.B.)

Motis Exports Ltd., (Motis) shipped goods at ports in China and Hong Kong in July and Aug. 1996, and Jan. 1997 under various Maersk Line bills of lading issued "to order" for a carriage to Cotonou (Benin) and Abidjan (Ivory Coast). The liner ser-vice was operated by the two defendants. In the bills of lading there was the follow-ing clause: "Carrier's Responsibility: 3 Carriage to and from Countries other than the USA… (b) Where the carriage called for commences at the port of loading and/or finishes at the port of discharge, the car-rier shall have no liability whatsoever for any loss or damage to the goods while in its actual or constructive possession before loading or after discharge over ships rail, or if applicable, on the ships ramp, however caused". The carrier delivered the goods against production of forged bills of lad-ing. Motis claimed damages for conversion and the defendants denied liability under the clause.

***Held (for the claimants):*** The nature of the bill of lading is such that "*a shipown-er is both entitled and bound to deliver the goods against production of an original bill of lading, provided he has no notice of any other claim or better title to the goods,*" and "*it is no defence to a shipowner or to the defendants in this case, innocently to be deceived by production of a forged bill of lading into release of a cargo*". For reasons of policy, such a defense cannot stand be-cause it would, "*…undermine the integri-ty of the bill as the key to a floating ware-house… Moreover, as between shipowner and true goods' owner it is the shipowner who controls the form, signature and issue of his bills, even if as a matter of practice he may delegate much of that to his time char-terers or their agents. If one of two innocent people must suffer for the fraud of a third, it is better that the loss falls on the shipowner, whose responsibility it is both to look to the integrity of his bills and to care for the car-go in his possession and to deliver it aright,*

---

[136] Lord Diplock found that the maxim of construc-tion "falsa demonstratio non nocet cum de corpore constat", which was applied validly in *The Adamastos (Adamastos Shipping Co. Ltd. v. Anglo-Saxon Petroleum Co. Ltd., 1959, AC 133)*, by treating the words "This bill of lading" as if they were "This charterparty", was unjustified in the present case so as to treat the words "the charterer" as if they were expressing "consignee". Furthermore, regarding the potential liability which could accrue to every consignee in accepting a bill of lading with a charterparty incorporation clause, Lord Diplock strictly suggested that there was no reason for indulging such a verbal manipulation of the actu-al words used in the charterparty so as to give them effect into the bill of lading.

*rather than on the true goods' owner, who holds a valid bill and expects to receive his goods in return for it"*. The clause was not comprehensive enough as to release the shipowners from liability for conversion.

## 158
## MOTOR OIL HELLAS (CORINTH) REFINERIES S.A. V. SHIPPING CORP. OF INDIA
### (The Kanchenjunga)
### 1990, 1 Lloyd's Rep. 391 (H.L.)

The *Kanchengunga* was a 272,000 ton. crude tanker. She was chartered for four consecutive voyages with an option to extend the charter four more voyages, which was in fact exercised. The charterparty was on the Exxonvoy form and the fixture limited the loading ports as 1/2 safe ports Arabian Gulf. The vessel was sub-sub-chartered for a single voyage to a company called Petronor on the Asbatankvoy form. Clause 20 (War Risks) of the charter provided the charterers had the right to nominate "any other safe port" if owing to war the entry into the original port was considered dangerous by the master or the owners "in his or their discretion". Petronor nominated Kharg Island as the loading port for a cargo of crude oil. The owners gave orders to proceed to Kharg Island on Nov. 20, 1978. When the vessel arrived, the master gave notice of readiness to load asserting that laytime was running against the charterers on Nov. 23. While the vessel was still waiting for berth, Iraq bombed the island. The master weighed anchor and immediately proceeded twenty five miles out to sea seeking a safe point. The owners required further instructions from the

charterers to nominate a further safe port. The charterers insisted upon loading in Kharg Island and instructed the master to do so. The master refused to follow such instructions and the charterers filed a claim against the owners for damages. The owners appealed the decision of the trial judge and the charterers cross-appealed.

***Held:*** **i)** (Lord Goff) *"…the situation in which the owners found themselves was one in which they could either reject the charterers' nomination of Kharg Island as uncontractual, or could nevertheless elect to accept the order and load at Kharg Island, thereby waiving or abandoning their right to reject the nomination but retaining their right to claim damages from the charterers for breach of contract."* **ii)** A shipowner can refuse a nomination if he is aware that the port is unsafe.[137,138] But if he ignores the obvious danger and agrees with the nomination (i.e. by giving notice of readiness), his conduct may be treated as a waiver of his right to object to the nomination, or even a novus actus interveniens which creates a new contractual state preventing him from recovering damages occurring thereafter. By serving notice of readiness, Lord Goff took the view that *"the owners were asserting that the vessel was available to load; they were also calling upon the charterers to arrange priority berthing, and referring to the fact that lay-*

---

[137] For the concept of "safe port" see *The Khian Sea*. For the time at which the port must be safe see *The Evia (No.2)*.

[138] The existence (implied or express) of a safe port warranty *"does not mean that a master can enter ports that are obviously unsafe and then charge the Charterers with damage done"*. Devlin J., in *The Stork*, 1995, 2 Q.B., at p. 77.

*time was running. In these circumstances, the owners were asserting a right inconsistent with their right to reject the charterers' orders".* Having waived their right to object to the nomination of Kharg Island, the owners put themselves in breach by refusing to load at Kharg Island. The owners' cross-appeal was dismissed. **iii)** As to the charterers' appeal, the owners successfully relied on the clause 20 (War Risks) to exclude their liability for damages. (Lord Goff) *"The clause expressly refers to the discretion which the owners and the master are entitled to exercise in a situation of danger and must, in my opinion, impliedly recognize that in the exercise of that discretion they may decline to load or discharge at the relevant port."* The charterers' submission that -by waiving their right to reject the port nomination- the owners also waived their right to rely on clause 20 was not accepted by their lordships on these grounds: *"The owners, presented by the charterers with an uncontractual nomination, had in the end to decide whether or not to reject it, and they elected not to do so. I cannot see that this election had any effect upon cl. 20…".* The charterers' appeal was also dismissed.

**159**

**MSC M**EDITERRANEAN **S**HIPPING **C**O. V.
**P**OLISH **O**CEAN **L**INES
*(The Tychy)*
1999, 31 May LMLN 510 (C.A.)

On May 17, 1993, the plaintiffs (as shipowners) and the defendants (as charterers) entered into an agreement whereby the plaintiffs were to "charter" container slots to the defendants on vessels operating on its North Atlantic service. The defendants then ran into financial difficulties and became debtors of the plaintiffs. The plaintiffs issued a writ claiming the sums due and arrested the *Tychy* (a vessel owned by the defendants at the time), relying on sections 20(2)(h) and 21(4)(ii) of the Supreme Court Act 1981. Under sections 20(1) and 20(2)(h) of the Act, the Admiralty Court had power to hear and determine "any claim arising out of any agreement relating to the carriage of goods in a ship or to the use or hire of a ship". Further, section 21(4) provided that: "In the case of any such claim as mentioned in section 20(2)(e) to (r), where – the claim arises in connection with a ship; and the person who would be liable on the claim in an action in personam ('the relevant person') was, when the cause of the action arose, the…charterer of…the ship, an action in rem may…be brought in the High Court against: - (ii) any other ship of which, at the time when the action is brought, the relevant person is the beneficial owner as respects all the shares in it." The defendants applied to the Admiralty Court to set aside the arrest alleging lack of jurisdiction since they were not the "charterers" of the ship in the meaning of section 20.

***Held (for the plaintiffs):*** **i)** What was the meaning of the term "charterer" in sec. 21(4)? The purpose of section 21(4) was to ensure that, prior to the arrest of a sister ship to secure a maritime claim, the relevant person had some connection with the ship. Section 21(4) was not confined to a demise charterer.[139] In principle, there is no reason why a time or voyage charterer

---

[139] See *The Span Terza* [1982] 1 Lloyd's Rep. 225.

should not be included. The only condition is that the ship had to be wholly beneficially owned by the person who would be liable on a claim in personam. **ii)** Did "charterer" include a part charterer in the meaning of sec. 21(4)? It made no sense to hold that a sister ship could only be arrested if the charterer hired a whole ship and not just a few tanks or holds. Provided that the requirements in sections 20(2) and 21(4) were fulfilled, the ships of a part charterer were not immune from arrest. **iii)** Could a slot charterer be described as a "charterer"? Just as a ship can have two registered owners, it can also have two or more charterers. The meaning of "charterer" was so extended to slot charterers and there was no good reason for them not to be considered as such. Accordingly, the arrest by the plaintiffs of the charterer's ship (the *Tychy*) was maintained.

**160**

**N.V. Bunge v. Compagnie Noga d'Importation et d'Exportation S.A.**
*(The Bow Cedar)*
1980, 2 Lloyd's Rep. 601 (Q.B.)

Five hundred tonnes of Brazilian crude groundnut oil was sold on f.o.b. terms. The contract was contained in a "confirmation of sale" document. The acidity of the oil was required to have a basis 2% max. 3% and a moisture content of max. 0.5%. In addition, "Weight and quality final at loading as per certificate of independent surveyor nominated by sellers…" was also stipulated. FOSFA Form No. 53 form was incorporated providing, inter alia, the following clauses: (1) Quality: the oil shall be of good merchantable quality at time

of shipment…(3) Sampling and Analysis: analysis final at time of shipment…". The goods were shipped in Paranagua (Brazil) in the vessel *Bow Cedar* for a carriage to Rotterdam (Netherlands). Some 250 tonnes of crude groundnut oil and 250 tonnes of soyabean oil were loaded on the *Bow Cedar*. Due to the admixture, the goods appropriated for the contract could not properly be described as groundnut oil. The certificate showed 0,98% acidity and 0,18% moisture. The buyers claimed damages based on the difference of value between sound groundnut oil and the oil so delivered. The sellers denied liability and relied on the final and conclusive effect of the certificate. The Board of Appeal of FOSFA awarded in favour of the buyers. The sellers appealed to the court.

***Held (for the buyers):*** (Lloyd, J.) **i)** It was agreed that what was subject to certificate was the moisture and acidity of the goods, but not the type of commodity itself. Accordingly, the surveyors were only certifying the result of their chemical analysis but not whether the goods were Brazilian crude groundnut oil or not. Even if the certificate did certify the commodity as well as the chemical analysis, such certification was to be final as to moisture and acidity but not as to the commodity itself. The contract provided for the certificate to be conclusive and final only as to the result of the analysis. **ii)** The presence of soyabean oil did not affect the quality of the oil which was excellent in terms of moisture and acidity. Although the goods were not the contracted for goods, there was nothing in the present case which made the certificates final also as to the description of the goods. The goods appropriated to the contract did not comply with the contract description of the goods sold and the certificates, even if final as to quality, do not protect sellers from a claim for damages.

## 161
## NEW ZEALAND SHIPPING CO. LTD. V. A.M. SATERTHWAITE & CO. LTD.
### *(The Eurymedon)*
### 1975, A.C. 154 (P.C.)

A drilling machine was shipped on board the vessel *Eurymedon* at Liverpool (England) for a carriage to Wellington (New Zealand). The bill of lading, as issued, incorporated the Hague Rules in the Schedule to the Carriage of Goods by Sea 1924. It also contained a (Himalaya) clause extending the benefit of rights, defences, exceptions and immunities conferred thereunder upon the carrier as against the cargo owners to the servants, agents and/or independent contractors to whom the carrier might contract.[140]

For the purposes of such extension, the clause itself conferred to the carriers the condition of agents contracting on behalf of those subcontracted parties. As a result of the stevedore's negligence, the drill was damaged while being discharged. After the lapse of one year, the consignees brought an action against the stevedores for damages. The stevedores admitted liability but pleaded the one-year time bar of the art. III(6) of the Hague Rules. The main issue before the P.C. was whether the stevedore could take advantage of the time limitation provision.

***Held (for the stevedores):***[141] **i)** The contract contained in the bill of lading satisfied all the requirements for a valid agency contract.[142] **ii)** (Lord Wilbeforce)

---

[140] The so called Himalaya clause was created by a skilled draftman seeking to elude the implications in *Adler v. Dickson (The Himalaya)*. In that case a member of the ship's crew was sued in negligence for causing injury to a passenger and it was held he could not rely on the exception clause in the contract of carriage concluded between the passenger and the shipowners. Similarly, in *Scruttons v. Midland Silicones* a firm of stevedores was not entitled to invoke the protection of the Hague Rules limitation of liability provisions when sued for negligence on discharging the goods. In neither cases could the party being sued be regarded as a party to the contract of carriage. Where the Hague-Visby Rules (art. IV bis 2) apply, the Himalaya clause is no longer needed to protect servants or agents of the carrier, but it is still necessary for independent contractors. See also *The Eurymedon* and *The Mahkutai*.

[141] Viscount Dilhorne and Lord Simon of Glaisdale, dissenting.

[142] Regarding the conception of agency contracts, Lord Reid's words in *Midland Silicones Ltd. v. Scruttons Ltd., 1962, A.C., 446*, were quoted as follows: "*I can see a possibility of success of the argument if (first) the bill of lading makes it clear that the stevedore is intended to be protected by the provisions in it which limit liability, (secondly) the bill of lading makes it clear that the carrier, in addition to contracting for these provisions on his own behalf, is also contracting as agent for the stevedore that these provisions should apply to the stevedore, (thirdly) the carrier has authority from the stevedore to do that, or perhaps later ratification by the stevedore would suffice, and (fourthly) that any difficulties about consideration moving from the stevedore were overcome. And then to affect the consignee it would be necessary to show that the provisions of the Bills of Lading Act 1855 apply*". Since the enactment of the Carriage of Goods by Sea Act 1992, however, the binding effect of the Himalaya clause as in relation to the consignee or indorsee of the bill of lading, is no longer subject to the compliance of the requirements of section 1 of the 1855 Act.

*"By the (Himalaya) clause 1 of the bill of lading the shipper agrees to exempt from liability the carrier, his servants and independent contractors in respect of the performance of this contract of carriage. Thus, if the carriage, including the discharge, is wholly carried out by the carrier, he is exempt. If part is carried out by him, and part by his servants, he and they are exempt. If part is carried out by him and part by an independent contractor, he and the independent contractor are exempt. The exemption is designed to cover the whole carriage from loading to discharge, by whomsoever is performed: the performance attracts the exemption or immunity in favour of whoever the performer turns out to be."* **iii)** (Lord Wilbeforce) *"...their Lordship would accept that the bill of lading brought into existence a bargain initially unilateral but capable of becoming mutual, between the shipper and the appellant (the stevedore), made through the carrier as agent. This became a full contract when the appellant performed services by discharging the goods. The performance of these services for the benefit of the shipper was the consideration for the agreement by the shipper that the appellant should have the benefit of the exemptions and limitations contained in the bill of lading."* **iv)** Furthermore, as it is established under common law, *"the consignee is entitled to the benefit of, and is bound by, the stipulations in the bill of lading by his acceptance of it and request for delivery of the goods thereunder".*[143]

---

[143] See *Brandt v. Liverpool and River Plate Navigation Co., 1923, 17 Lloyd's Rep. 142; 1924, 1 K.B. 575.*

## 162

### NGO CHEW HONG EDIBLE OIL PTE. LTD. v. SCINDIA STEAM NAVIGATION CO. LTD.

### *(The Jalamohan)*
### 1988, 1 Lloyd's Rep. 443 (Q.B.)

The disponent owners of the vessel *Jalamohan* let her on the New York Produce Exchange form to the charterers. She was delivered at Singapore for a time charter trip to West Africa. She was subsequently sub-chartered on back-to-back terms to a liner company operating between the Far East and West Africa. A fixture was concluded between the subcharterers' agents at Singapore and another company, acting as shippers of vegetable oil in drums for a carriage on FIOS terms from Singapore to Lagos, "other terms as per carrier's bill of lading". Freight prepaid bills of lading were issued and signed by the subcharterers' agents including a demise clause stating: "Contracting parties: (A) The contract contained in or evidenced by this bill of lading is between the owner or demise charterer of the ship...and the merchant. (B) If the ship is not owned or chartered by demise to the company ...by whom this bill of lading is issued, ...this bill of lading shall take effect only as a contract with the owner or demise charterer ...as principal made through the agency of the said company...who act as agents only and shall be under no personal liability whatsoever in respect thereof". The bills were subsequently altered replacing the name of the subcharterer's agents by that of the subcharterers. The charterers failed to pay the hire and the vessel was withdrawn by the owners who then completed the voyage themselves. The owners claimed the freight to the shippers contending that the true contract was not evidenced by the bill of lading but contained in the fixture, in which there appeared not to be any demise clause. The shippers alleged that the bills of lading were the evidence of the contract and the terms of the demise clause bound directly the owner.

***Held (for the shippers):*** (Hirst, J.) **i)** The words "other terms as per carrier's bill of lading" in the fixture anticipate that the terms of the issued bills of lading (including the demise clause) were to govern the contract. The fixture was thus overruled in such other terms not contained in the issued bills of lading, which did bind the owners by virtue of the demise clause. The fixture was held to be the contract and validly incorporated the demise clause in the bills of lading. **ii)** The charterers or their agents were authorised by the terms of the head charterparty to issue and sign bills of lading. Moreover, the subcharterers were authorised in the same way, and finally, the sub-charterers' agents were equally authorised by virtue of a written agency agreement. Hirst J. held that an unbroken chain of authority from the owners down to the subcharterers' agents.

**163**

**NICKOLL & KNIGHT V. ASHTON EDRIDGE & CO.**

1901, 2 KB 126 (C.A.)

The defendants sold to the plaintiffs a quantity of Egyptian cotton-seed. The contract stated that the cargo was to be shipped to the United Kingdom at an Egyptian port during the month of Jan., 1900. The words "ship or ships" had been removed and printed "per steamship *Orlando*". There was a further clause providing that "In case of prohibition of export, blockade, or hostilities preventing shipment, this contract or any unfulfilled part thereof is to be cancelled". In Dec. 1899, the vessel *Orlando* was stranded by perils of the sea and so badly damaged as to make loading during the contract period impossible. The charterers informed the plaintiffs of that fact on Dec. 20. The market price of cotton-seeds rose above the contract price from Dec. 1899 to the end of Jan. 1900. On Dec. 28, the defendants communicated to the plaintiffs that performance was impossible and treated the contract as cancelled. The plaintiffs claimed damages for the difference between the contract price and the market price calculated on Jan. 31.

***Held:***[144] (A.L. Smith MR) *"It is perfectly plain upon the face of the signed contract that the parties deliberately agreed that the shipment of the seed should not be in any ship or ships, but in one particular named ship… From the beginning, the parties must have known that the performance of the contract would become impossible unless the particular thing specified, that is, the steamship* Orlando, *continued to exist as a cargo-carrying ship down to and during the month of January, 1900."* The contract was found subject to the implied condition that, if the vessel ceased (without default on the defendants) to be available at the port of loading in Jan., the contract would then be frustrated and could be treated as cancelled.

---

[144] Vaughan Williams L.J. dissenting.

## 164
### NOBLE RESOURCES LTD. v. CAVALIER SHIPPING CORP.
*(The Atlas)*
1996, 1 Lloyd's Rep. 642 (Q.B.)

1.380 bundles comprising a total of 12.038 tonnes of Russian steel were loaded at Nakhodka in eastern Russia for a carriage to Kaohsiung in Taiwan. The ship *Atlas* had been subchartered for that voyage by the f.o.b. buyers, a Swiss firm called Noble. Once the goods were loaded, the disponent owners issued three "freight prepaid" bills of lading on the shipowners' behalf. The bills were made out to the order of the Russian sellers and named the buyers as "Notify" party. They recorded in print that the goods were "shipped in apparent good order and condition", and continued: "All particulars (weight, measure, marks, numbers, quantity, contents, value…) thereof as stated by Merchant but unknown to the Carrier". The buyers on-sold the goods to three Taiwanese receivers in terms c.i.f. Kaohsiung, but wished to keep the Russian suppliers' identity unknown. To that end, they had agreed a clause in the voyage charterparty under which the disponent owner agreed to issue a second set of freight prepaid bills of lading (the "switch bills") against a letter of indemnity and full payment of freight.[145]

As there was no similar clause in the head charter, the disponent owner issued the switch bills with no authorization from the head shipowners. The "switch bills" contained the same cargo details, including the clauses "Shipper's description of goods" and "Weight…quality…unknown". The sellers tendered the switch bills to the Taiwanese receivers who took delivery of the goods at Kaohsiung. After discharge, the receivers noticed shortages and claimed against the shipowners for the shortfall of cargo. They contended: (i) that the bills of lading were prima facie evidence of the quantity so shipped and the clause "quantity/weight unknown" was contrary to the art. III(3) and (8) of the Hague Rules; (ii) that the rail tally (ex rail wagon to quay) and the cargo tally (ex quay onto vessel) revealed a weight difference with regards to the quantity discharged at Kaohsiung; (iii) that they had gained title to sue against the shipowner by virtue of the contract evidenced by the switch bills, in tort and in bailment.

***Held (for the shipowners):*** (Longmore, J.) **i)** *"If the bill of lading provides that the weight is unknown, it cannot be an assertion or representation of the weight in fact shipped… and, if the Russian bills are construed as a whole, they must be held to mean that the shipowners are not committing themselves, one way or the other, as to the weight of cargo shipped; Do the Russian bills show the number of packages or weight (as furnished in writing by the shipper)? In one sense it can be said they do, because the bills have figures which were in fact provided by the shipper in writing. But if the bills provide 'Weight… number…quantity unknown' it cannot be said that the bills 'show' that number or weight. They 'show' nothing at all because*

---

[145] *"No doubt this provision for a second set of bills of lading to come into existence was agreed for not unreasonable commercial motives but is a practice fraught with danger; not only does it give rise to obvious opportunities for fraud (which is not suggested in this case) but also, if it is intended that the bills of lading should constitute contracts of carriage with the actual owner of the ship (as opposed to any disponent owner), the greatest care has to be taken to ensure that the practice has the shipowners' authority."* (Longmore, J.)

*the shipowner is not prepared to say what the number or weight is. He can, of course, be required to show it under art. III(3) but, unless and until he does so, the provisions of art. III(4) as to prima facie evidence cannot come into effect; I therefore conclude that neither the Russian bills nor the switch bills constitute prima facie evidence of the number of bundles or quantity shipped and I must look at the underlying facts of shipment without the assistance of any evidentiary presumption."* **ii)** It was proved that the number of bundles recorded on the bills of lading were, in fact, loaded onto the *Atlas*. The (rail and cargo) tally sheets were admissible evidence on this point. The plaintiffs, however, failed to purport that any particular weight was discharged from the ship, and failed to prove as well that a lesser quantity than that shipped was indeed landed on the quay. **iii)** *"(1) Contract: I cannot see how it can be said that the defendant shipowners are bound by the terms of the switch bills. They were issued by the charterers pursuant to a specific clause in the voyage charter. There is no similar specific clause in the head charter between the shipowners and Navix Line Ltd...; (2) Tort: On my finding that the plaintiffs became the owners of the steel billets on shipment, they can sue in negligence. Of course they have the onus of showing negligence. They have not sought to discharge it...; (3) Bailment: In fact, the plaintiffs could not sue in tort without regard to the terms on which the ship owners received the goods viz. the terms of the Russian bills. One of these terms was that the shipowners would deliver the cargo shipped at Kaohsiung. This bailment, to my mind, gives the plaintiffs their title to sue, even if they have not specifically pleaded the terms on which the bailment was made. They failed, however, on the facts not on their title to sue."*

## 165
### NORANDA INC. V. BARTON (TIME CHARTER) LTD.
*(The Marinor)*
1996, 1 Lloyd's Rep. 301 (Q.B.)

The defendant owners let their newly constructed vessel, called the *Marinor*, for a period of ten years with a five years' extension option for the carriage of sulphuric acid from Quebec (Canada) to US East Coast ports. The time charterparty included a rider headed as "Canadian clause Paramount" which read: "This Bill of Lading…shall have effect subject to the provisions of the Carriage of Goods by Water Act". At the time the Act incorporated the Hague-Visby Rules into the Canadian national law. On her voyage no. 32, the plaintiff charterers alleged that the cargo had repeatedly been contaminated by chrome resulting from the vessel. They continued with their regular shipments of sulphuric acid but through substitute vessels and sought damages from the owners. The charterers argued that the Hague-Visby Rules were not validly incorporated into the charterparty and that the vessel was unseaworthy. The owners grounded their defence on art. III(6) of the Hague-Visby Rules pleading that the claim was time-barred.

***Held:*** (Colman, J.) **i)** The incorporation of the Hague-Visby Rules into a charterparty is usually motivated by a desire that the owner's rights and duties vis-à-vis the charterer be coextensive with their rights and duties vis-à-vis the holders of the bill of lading. *"If the effect of the incorporation is to enable the owners to rely on the protection of art. IV, there is no reason why the protection of art. III(6) should not apply"* to a broad spectrum of claims in relation to the goods. Hence, the liability "in respect of the goods" of art. III(6) is, in the context of a time charterparty, not only directly referred to damaged or lost cargo, but also to the financial loss sustained in relation to the cargo being either shipped or intended to be shipped. What really matters is that the cargo which was to be shipped was within the contemplation of the parties when concluding the charterparty. **ii)** The Canadian Paramount clause formed part of the charterparty and operated as a general incorporation of the Hague-Visby Rules. The time-bar provision of the Rules were not deprived of its genuine effect by its incorporation into the charterparty through the Canadian national law, let alone by its inclusion as a rider and not as a clause in the standard form.

## 166
### Nordglimt, The
1987, 2 Lloyd's Rep. 470 (Q.B.)

In Dec. 1983 the MV *Nordkap* loaded at Antwerp (Belgium) some 115,506 bags of barley for a carriage to Jeddah (Saudi Arabia). Two bills of lading were issued incorporating the Hague-Visby Rules: there was a genuine bill of lading stating the correct quantity of bags shipped, and another purported falsely to have been issued on behalf of the shipowners mis-stating the number of bags. When the goods were delivered at Jeddah they were found damaged and short. The receivers and their insurers brought an action in Belgium against the shipowners and the charterers. While proceedings took place at Belgium, an action in rem was issued by the receivers and the shippers in England against the MV *Nordglimt*, which was a vessel in the same ownership as the MV *Nordkap*. For the proceedings in rem, the false bills of lading were produced as evidence to the court. However, the court accepted that mis-statement came about as the result of an oversight and that it had not been deliberate. The same day as the writ was issued, a warrant of arrest was also issued for the MV *Nordglimt* and security was given to release the ship. The shipowners asked for relief arguing, inter alia, that: (1) the plaintiffs failed to make full and frank disclosure of the facts by presenting a false bill of lading; (2) that the plaintiffs' claim was extinguished by virtue of the 1-year limit contained in art. III(6) of the Hague-Visby Rules; and (3) that, although the 1952 Arrest Convention generally confers jurisdiction to the courts of the country in which the arrest was made, the court had no jurisdiction under the Civil Jurisdiction and Judgments Act 1982[146] and thus should decline jurisdiction because of the lis pendens in the Belgium Court.

---

[146] Section 2 of the 1982 Act provides that certain conventions (one of which is the Convention on Jurisdiction and the Enforcement of Judgments in Civil and Commercial Matters of 1968) *"shall have the force of law in the United Kingdom and judicial notice shall be taken of them".* Article 21 of the 1968 Convention provides: *"Where proceedings involving the same cause of action and between the same parties are brought in the courts of different contracting states, any court other than the court first seized shall of its own motion decline jurisdiction in favour of that court".* Art. 57 though prescribes: *"This convention shall no affect any conventions to which the contracting states are or will be parties and which, in relation to particular matters, govern jurisdiction…".*

*Held (for plaintiffs):* (Hobhouse, J.) **i)** The inaccuracy contained in the bill of lading so produced to the court was not deliberate, and could not be taken as a reason sufficient to set aside the warrant of arrest. **ii)** In connection with the time-bar issue, the judge said: *"[T]he proceedings in personam in Belgium, having been started in Belgium within time and it being accepted that both the parties and the court were competent, the defendants' liability has not been discharged under art. III(6) and this ground of objection to the arrest of Nordglimt in the present proceedings must fail. It will also be appreciated that because the Belgian proceedings are still pending there can be as yet no issue estoppel or other determination of the parties' rights which shows that the plaintiffs' claim in the present action is unfounded".* **iii)** Finally, the issue of jurisdiction was ruled as follows *"[I]t is contemplated by the 1968 Convention, so construed, that it is permissible and proper that there should be an arrest of a vessel in one jurisdiction in support of a determination of the merits of a dispute by a court of competent jurisdiction in a another contracting state and to provide security for the satisfaction of the judgment given by that court; …on the correct interpretation of art. 21 an Admiralty action in rem is not at the time of its inception an action between the same parties as an action in personam. It will only become an action between the same parties when and if a shipowner, liable in personam, chooses to appear in the action and defend it(…) It is of the character of proceedings in rem that they are not alternative to proceedings in personam; they are cumulative. The cause of action in rem does not merge with a judgment in personam given in respect of a cause of action in per-*

*sonam arising from the same facts".*[147] According to these points, the court accepted jurisdiction and the arrest was maintained.


**167**

**Novologistics Sarl v. Five Ocean Corporation**
*(The Merida)*
2009, EWHC 3046 (Q.B.)

The MV *Merida* was chartered to carry steel plates from China to Spain. The charterparty provided for loading at "one good and safe charterers' berth", but it also said that the Notice of Readiness could be given at the anchorage and time spent shifting to the berth should count as laytime. The vessel sent Notice of Readiness at the anchorage point of the loading port, but she had to wait twenty days until a berth became available. For all that period, the owners claimed demurrage.

*Held (for charterers):* The charterparty defined the agreed destination as "charterers' berth". This provision was not overridden by any other terms of the charter. Per Gross, J.: *"The opening term [of the charter] concisely defines the contractual destinations – both as to place of loading and place/s of discharge. The opening term does so in a manner which, if it stood alone, makes it plain that this is a berth charterparty".* It was necessary to identify what was the "specified destination" under the charter (**The "Johanna Oldendorff"** [1974] AC 497) and whether that destination was the port or was a berth within the port (**The**

---

[147] See *The Maciej Rataj (ECJ).*

**"Radnor" [1955] 2 LLR 668, The "Finix" [1975] 2 LLR 415 and The "Puerto Rocca" [1978] 1 LLR 252).** Following review of the authorities, Gross J. considered that the charter was in fact a berth charter. The provision for shifting time to count as laytime did not change the nature of the charter at all. On this basis, owners were not entitled to demurrage and time did not start counting any time before the vessel reached the berth.

**168**

OCEAN MARINE NAVIGATION LIMITED V.
KOCH CARBON INC.
*(The Dynamic)*
2003, 2 Lloyd's Rep. 693 (Q.B.)

The claimants time-trip-chartered the MV *Dynamic* to the respondents for a carriage of cement and clinker in bulk from Dalian, in the People's Republic of China, to Myrtle Grove, in the Mississippi River (USA). Clause 60 of the charterparty provided the following: "Should the vessel be arrested during the currency of this Charter party at the suit of any persons having, or purporting to have, a claim against or any interest in the vessel, hire under this Charter party shall not be payable in respect of any period whilst the vessel remaining under arrest or remains unemployed as the result of such arrest. However if the arrest is the consequence of an act or omission by charterers and/or their agents and /or their servants hire to continue". The vessel was delivered under the charter at 23:06 hours on 28 Apr. 1999. On 28 July 1999 the vessel arrived at Myrtle Grove and completed discharge around midday on 3 Aug. However, on 2 Aug. the charterers decided to arrest the ves-

sel in order to obtain security for an under-performance claim against the owners. The vessel was ordered to shift to a new anchorage, where she remained under arrest until 17 Aug. 1999. The owners argued that the vessel remained on hire from 3 Aug. until 17 Aug.but the charterers took the position that she had been actually re-delivered at 12:20 hours on 3 Aug., when discharge was completed. One of the questions was whether, on the proper construction of cl. 60 of the charter-party, the vessel was off hire while she was under arrest.

***Held (for the owners):*** It is settled law that hire is *prima facie* payable continuously and that the charterers bear the burden of proving that they fall within the off-hire clause. In the case at hand, the judge agreed with the arbitrator's finding that the charterers were liable for hire under cl. 60 if there was an arrest during the currency of the charterparty and the arrest was the consequence of a deliberate act or omission by the charterers or their agents. In the judge's words: *"[T]his clause was never intended to deal with an arrest by the charterer during the currency of the charter-party. If the charterers wished to avoid paying hire when they had themselves arrested the vessel during the currency of the charter-party, then very much clearer words would have been required"*.

**169**

OK PETROLEUM A.B. v.
VITOL ENERGY S.A.
1995, 2 Lloyd's Rep. 160 (Q.B.)

By two contracts the plaintiffs, OK Petroleum sold quantities of gasoline to the defendants, Vitol Energy. Under the first contract dated 25 Nov. 1991, the plaintiffs sold 20,000-25,000 tonnes c.i.f. Genoa. The contract provided that demurrage was "as per charterparty" and laytime was "36 hours + 6 hours SHINC". Under the second contract of 24 Jan. 1992, the plaintiffs sold 10,000 tonnes c.i.f. Dunkirk and Rouen. Demurrage was "as per charterparty" and laytime was "12 hours SHINC + 6 hours NOR (for each port)". For each contract, the plaintiff sellers chartered two different vessels, the *Chemical Venture* and the *Jade*, respectively. The charterparties were both on the Asbatankvoy form and provided, inter alia, the following clause 10: "Time bar: Charterers shall not be liable for demurrage incurred and/or other costs and/or charges incurred under the charterparty and pertaining to charterers use of the vessel unless charterers within 90 days... [from the date of the disconnection of the hoses] have received notification of the claim...". It happened that the buyers took longer than the laytime allowed to discharge the cargo under both contracts of sale. The sellers naturally claimed demurrage under the two contracts. The buyers then objected that the sellers' claim was time-barred because, in view of cl. 10 of the charterparty, they had failed to give notification of their claim within 90 days from the date of disconnection of the hoses. The main questions was whether the time-bar provisions of the charterparties had been incorporated into the respective sales contracts.

***Held (for the plaintiffs):*** (Colman, J.)
**i)** *"[T]he established approach to construction is that general words of incorporation will not normally be construed as wide enough to incorporate any provision from the other contract unless that provision is part of the subject-matter of that contract and not merely ancillary to it, such, for example, as an arbitration clause or a jurisdiction clause. Such ancillary provisions will not generally be treated as relevant or germane to the rights and obligations of the parties under the incorporating contract."* **ii)** The words of incorporation in the sale contracts of the reference do not suffice to incorporate the time-bar clauses of the charterparties. *"[A]t the very least, the sale contracts incorporated the provisions in the charter-parties specifying the rate of demurrage and those clauses going to the calculation of laytime, such as the notice of readiness clause from...the standard Asbatankvoy form; In the present case cl. 10 – the time bar provision- although excessively applicable to claims for demurrage under the charter-party, is essentially ancillary to the substantive or subject-matter provisions of that contract relating to demurrage. Its ancillary nature is conclusively demonstrated by the fact that its contractual function is confined to the enforcement of already-accrued contractual rights. It is exclusively concerned with recovery of such demurrage as has already fallen due. The words of incorporation in the sale contracts, being in general terms, do not, in my judgment, clearly express a mutual intention to incorporate into those contracts any provision of the charter-party which is not part of the demurrage subject-matter of that contract but is merely ancillary to it."*[148]

---

[148] See *Gill Duffus S.A. v. Rionda Futures Ltd.* Contrast with *The Heidberg.*

## 170
### ORINOCO NAVIGATION LTD. V. ECOTRADE S.A.
*(The Ikariada)*
1999, 2 Lloyd's Rep. 365 (Q.B.)

Orinoco Navigation Ltd., the owners, let their vessel *Ikariada* to the charterers Ecotrade S.A. for a carriage of furnace slag from Taranto (Italy) to Elefsis (Greece). The charter was on an amended Gencon form dated Feb. 19, 1997. The charter provided, inter alia, the following provisions: "9. The Captain to sign Bills of Lading at such rate of freight as presented without prejudice to this charterparty... 35. ... Any act, neglect, default or error of judgement whatsoever...in the management and/or navigation of the vessel...always excepted". After loading, the charterers required the master to sign bills of lading on the Congenbill form. Clause 1 of the bills prescribed that "All terms and conditions, liberties and exceptions of the charterparty, dated as overleaf, are herewith incorporated". However, the blank space left for the date of the charter was not filled in. Besides, the box "Freight payable at" was completed with the words "as per C/P". Once in Elefsis, the vessel was negligently navigated causing damage to the consignees' discharging crane. The consignees filed a claim for damages on tort before the courts in Piraeus against the owners. The owners then sought an indemnity from the charterers on the grounds of cls. 35 of the charter, as incorporated into the bills of lading. The charterers, in turn, contended that the charterparty was not effectively incorporated into the bill of lading and therefore cl. 35 was not applicable.

***Held:*** (Cresswell, J.) **i)** "*In my judgment the defendants were not in breach of any express and/or implied terms of the charter-party in failing to fill in the blank on the face of the bill of lading, in particular in failing specifically to identify the governing charter-party by date or otherwise. Nor in my judgment are the defendants under an obligation to indemnify the claimants against the consequences of requiring the master to sign the bill of lading in that form.*" **ii)** "*It is necessary to distinguish between charters which require the master to sign bills of lading 'as presented' and charters which provide that the master shall sign bills of lading in a specified form.*[149] *This case falls into the former category... The bill of lading as presented was in a form which did not contain extraordinary terms or terms which were manifestly inconsistent with the charter. It did not impose more onerous terms than the charter.*" Accordingly, the judge found that the failure to fill the blank of the charterparty date did not prevent its incorporation into the bill of lading.

## 171
### OVERSEAS TRANSPORTATION CO. V. MINERALIMPORTEXPORT
*(The Sinoe)*
1972, 1 Lloyd's Rep. 201 (C.A.)

This case concerns a claim by shipowners against charterers for demurrage. In performance of the charter, the MV Sinoe carried 10,000 tons of bagged cement be-

---

[149] Cresswell J. found that the position here was not comparable to that in *The Garbis*. As opposed to the present case, *The Garbis* concerned a charterparty that required the master to sign bills of lading in a specified form.

longing to the charterers to Chittagong (Bangladesh). Upon arrival, there was a gross delay in discharging the vessel. Stevedores were appointed by the receivers on behalf of the charterers. It was found that the stevedores were somewhat inexperienced, unequipped and too few in number. The bags got cut and cement escaped in large quantities into the holds. As a result, a substantial delay resulted and the shipowners claimed demurrage thereupon. The charterers replied that they were relieved of liability on the grounds of a cesser clause, and that, in any event, charterers were not at fault as the stevedores were the servants of the shipowners. The following were the relevant clauses of the charterparty: 23. "Stevedores to be employed by charterers in loading and by shippers in discharging who shall be considered as owners servants and subject to the orders and direction of the master. Charterers not to be responsible for any negligence default or error in judgement of stevedores employed..."; 27. "Charterers' liability shall cease as soon as the cargo is on board owners having an absolute lien on the cargo for freight, deadfreight, demurrage and average".

***Held (for the owners):*** **i)** In connection with cls. 23... (Lord Denning, M.R.) "There is no provision which is sufficiently clear to make the stevedores the servants of the owners. The result is that the charterers cannot say that the delay was the fault of the shipowners. So the charterers must pay demurrage as it was their obligation to unload in the stated time; It was their duty to appoint stevedores who were competent to do the discharging. The stevedores here turned out to be ut-

terly incompetent. I do not think the bad conduct of the stevedores can be the fault of the owners, when the real cause of it was the fault of the charterers in appointing stevedores who were incompetent."
**ii)** As regards cls. 27 (the "cesser clause"), Lord Denning said "[I]t is sensible to require that the lien should be an effective lien. It is no use for the shipowner to be given a right of lien unless he can exercise it so as to get the money due to him; Holding therefore that the lien must be an effective lien, it was not effective because the Government of Bangladesh would not permit it to be exercised. Not being effective, it means that the charterers are not relieved by this cesser clause of their liability for demurrage".

## 172
### PACOL LTD. AND OTHERS V. TRADE LINES LTD. AND R/I SIF IV
*(The Henrik Sif)*
1982, 1 Lloyd's Rep. 457 (Q.B.)

The vessel *Henrik Sif* was chartered for a period of twelve months. The charterparty provided that the charterers were to be liable, inter alia, for all cargo claims except for those attributable to unseaworthiness of the vessel or to personal fault of the owner. Under the charterparty, three consignments of cocoa butter were shipped at Apapa (Nigeria) for a carriage to sharpness. Three bills of lading were issued by the charterers including a demise clause stating: "If the ship is not owned by or chartered by demise to the company... by whom this bill of lading is issued... this bill of lading shall take effect only as a contract with the owner or demise charterer as the case may be as principal made through the agency of the said company…who act as agents only and shall be under no personal liability whatsoever in respect thereof". After delivery was performed at sharpness, the cargo owners alleged that the cargo was contaminated and in part short-delivered. They brought their claim against the charterers through their general agents at sharpness. Acting upon the assumption that the charterers were the proper party to sue, the cargo owners obtained several time extensions from the charterers until the one-year period of the Hague Rules had elapsed. After such period, the cargo owners started proceedings against both, the charterers and the shipowners. The charterers replied that they were neither bailees nor carriers and no duty of care was upon them; the shipowners relied of the time bar of the Hague Rules.

***Held (for the plaintiffs):*** **i)** It was proved that the charterer's general agents at sharpness, as on behalf of their principals, knew about the terms of the bills of lading (including the demise clause) and were aware that the plaintiffs were mistakenly under an assumption that their principals were the proper party to sue under contract. An "equitable estoppel" by silence or acquiescence had arisen from the charterer's conduct. They had a duty to speak as an honest and reasonable person would have done and they did not. **ii)** The charterer's agents not only did not alert the plaintiffs to the true facts but also encouraged them to keep up their claims against their principals by granting them several extensions of time as if they were apparently liable. The correspond-

ence between both parties was such that the judge held a legal relationship existed between them. As long as the charterer's agents acted in the way that they did, the charterers were prevented from further denying the claim. The charterer's conduct pushed the plaintiffs to believe and rely on the assumption that the charterers would not enforce their rights as against them. The judge found that the plaintiffs had established a "promissory estoppel" as against the charterers.

## 173
### Pagnan SpA v. Tradax Ocean Transportation S.A.
### 1987, 2 Lloyd's Rep. 342 (C.A.)

Some 35,000 tonnes of Thailand tapioca pellets were sold "f.o.b. stowed/trimmed Sriracha" for shipment in Feb., Apr. and May 1983 to Europe. GAFTA Form 119 was incorporated into the contract cl. 19 of which provided that in the case of prohibition of export, the contract, or any unfulfilled part of it, would be cancelled. The heading "special conditions", contained the following stipulation: "Sellers to provide for export certificate enabling buyers to obtain import license into EEC…". The contract also contained a hierarchy clause stating "the special terms and conditions shall prevail in so far as they may be inconsistent with the printed clauses". At the time the contract was entered into by the parties there was a quota system restricting the export of Thailand tapioca to the ECC. The quantity permitted for export for the first quarter of 1983 was exceeded and the Thai authorities then prohibited further tapioca exports to the EEC. As the defendants could not obtain the April and May export certificates, only the February instalment was indeed fulfilled. In view that the April and May shipments were not effected, the buyers declared sellers in default and claimed damages based on the difference of the goods between the contract price and the market price.

***Held (for the sellers):*** **i)** The clause providing for the sellers to obtain the export licence imposed an absolute obligation on the sellers, not merely a duty of best endeavours or due diligence, so that the sellers' pleading that the contract was frustrated was not accepted by the court. As the clause was not drafted as a conditional one (i.e. "subject to export certificate") the obligation was absolute on the sellers. **ii)** However, the two relevant clauses were not inconsistent with each other. The natural construction of the contract was that the sellers were to provide the export licence but, in the case of an executive prohibition, the unfulfilled part of the contract was to be cancelled. That construction did not deprive the "special condition" of its intended effect. The obligation to provide the export certificate remained on the sellers. It was simply that the "special condition" did not override clause 19 of the GAFTA Form as there was no inconsistency between both clauses. The contract was thereby cancelled as the sellers, although in breach of their absolute obligation, were excused of performance by virtue of cls. 19. (Woolf, L.J.) *"In any contract in which there are standard terms and special terms, it is desirable to have a provision to avoid conflict between the standard and the special terms".* The special terms would have otherwise prevailed only insofar as they were inconsistent with the incorporated standard terms.

## 174
### PANCHAUD FRÉRES S.A. v. ESTABLISSEMENTS GENERAL GRAIN CO.
1970, 1 Lloyd's Rep. 53 (C.A.)

A consignment of Brazilian maize was sold c.i.f. Antwerp. Shipment was agreed to take place in June/July, 1965. In reality, the cargo happened to be shipped on Aug. 10-12, but the bill of lading was backdated to July 31. A certificate of quality at loading was required to be attached to the usual documents for tender. The buyer accepted the documents, including the bill of lading dated July 31 and the certificate of quality, without noticing that the certificate stated that the samples had been drawn on Aug. 10-12. On the arrival of the goods, the buyers rejected the goods on the ground of the forgery and breach of contract for the non-contractual shipment date. The sellers argued that this breach had already been accepted previously by the buyers with their taking up the documents, who were thereby prevented from rejecting the goods on those grounds.

***Held (for the sellers):*** **i)** (Lord Denning) *"The present case is not a case of 'waiver' strictly so called. It is a case of estoppel by conduct; if a man, who is entitled to reject goods on a certain ground, so conduct himself as to lead the other to believe that he is not relying on that ground, then he cannot afterwards set it up as a ground of rejection, when it would be unfair or unjust to allow him to do so. By taking up the documents and paying for them, they (the buyers) are precluded* *afterwards from complaining of the late shipment or of a defect in the bill of lading."* The principle of estoppel is based, in words of Winn L.J., on *"a requirement of fair conduct... negativing any liberty to blow hot and cold in commercial conduc".* **ii)** (Winn L.J.) *"Where there is a condition that a bill of lading in accordance with the contract terms, and a genuine correct bill of lading, should be tendered, breach of that obligation is a breach of condition relating to the tender of such a document, whereas failure to deliver goods which were in fact timeously within the contract period is a breach of different condition: that is so in one sense of language-in another sense, much more realistic, when one is talking of commercial matters, they are both really breaches of the same condition, that is to say of shipment within the contract period."* The doctrine of equitable estoppel is based on what is fair conduct between the parties. It is considered a relaxation of the strict performance of contract, an exception to the general rule that there are two independent rights as to rejection of goods and documents.[150]

<br>

## 175
### Papera Traders Co. Ltd. and Others v. Hyundai Merchant Marine Co. Ltd. and Another
*(The Eurasian Dream)*
[2002] 1 Lloyd's Rep. 719 (Q.B.)

By a time charter on the NYPE 46 form, Hyundai Merchant Marine Co. Ltd. chartered the pure car carrier *Eurasian*

---

[150] See *Gill Duffus S.A. v. Rionda Futures Ltd.* Contrast with *The Heidberg.*

*Dream* on 25 Mar., 1994. The vessel's technical manager was Univan Ship Management of Hong Kong (Univan). Pure car carriers employ a $CO_2$ system as the primary means of suppressing fires by which compartments are sealed and $CO_2$ expelled to suppress fires. On 23 July, 1998 while the vessel was at Sharjah (United Arab Emirates), a fire started on deck four of the vessel and eventually led to damage and destruction of the vessel's cargo of new and used automobiles, and to a constructive total loss of the vessel. There was evidence that the fire began as a consequence of stevedores having simultaneously refueled and jump-started automobiles. Cargo interests brought a claim against the carriers based on the fact that the vessel was unseaworthy and the failure of Univan to exercise due diligence because the crew was not supplied with enough walki-talkies, the fire extinguishers were defective, and the main valve for the $CO_2$ system was corroded. They also argued that the master and the crew were incompetent and inefficient due to the fact that they were neither aware of the particular hazards of car carriage nor of the characteristics and equipments of the vessel, that was improperly or inadequately trained in fire fighting techniques, and that failed to supervise the stevedores as they offloaded automobiles.

***Held (for the claimants):*** Nearly all the claimants' contentions were admitted. The defendants were unsuccessful in proving that they had exercised due diligence to make the ship seaworthy in all relevant aspects and thus could not rely on the fire exception in Art. IV of the Hague Rules. The court said: *"The defendants as bill of* *lading carriers are liable for the want of due diligence by the owners/managers and for the want of due diligence of the master in so far as the first defendants or the owners or managers delegated to him their duties as to seaworthiness. The exercise of due diligence is equivalent of the exercise of reasonable care and skill. Lack of due diligence is negligence and in this case there were numerous failures and errors of judgment that amounted to professional negligence...*"

## 176

PARSONS CORPORATION AND OTHER
v. C.V. SCHEEPVAARTONDERNEMING
"HAPPY RANGER" AND OTHERS
*(The Happy Ranger)*
2002, Lloyd's Rep. 357 (C.A.)

The claimants entered into a contract with the owners of the MV *Happy Ranger* for a carriage of three reactors from Porto Marghera (Italy) to Jubail (Saudi Arabia). On 11 Mar. 1998, one of the vessel's cranes was loading a reactor when the crane's hooks broke, causing the reactor to fall to the ground and resulting in a USD 2.4 million damage. The contract of carriage consisted of three documents: the signed printed front page, a six-page printed rider with 18 clauses and an attached specimen form of bill of lading. The printed front page was titled "Contract of Carriage". There were a number of clauses on the back of the specimen bill of lading. Clause 3 titled "General Paramount clause" stated "The Hague Rules...dated Brussels 25 Aug.1924, as enacted in the country of shipment shall apply to this contract. When no such enactment is in force in the coun-

try of shipment, Articles I to VIII of the Hague Rules shall apply. In such case the liability of the Carrier shall be limited to 100.-sterling per package. In the second paragraph of Clause 3 under "Trades where Hague-Visby Rules apply" it was stated: "In trades where the International Brussels Convention 1924 as amended by the Protocol signed at Brussels on 23 Feb. 1968 – the Hague-Visby Rules – apply compulsorily, the provisions of the respective legislation shall be considered incorporated in this Bill of Lading. Clause 5 of the contract stated, "The carrier's regular form of Bill of Lading as per specimen attached, is applicable and shall form part of this Contract. In the event of a conflict between the Bill of Lading and this Contract, the terms, conditions and exception of this Contract shall prevail to the extent of such conflict. Clause 15 provided that, "Any dispute arising under this Contract of Carriage and Bill of Lading" was to be settled under English law in London. The question before the court was (i) whether the Hague-Visby Rules were applicable, and, if they were not, (ii) whether the carriers' liability was limited to GBP 100 per package.

***Held:*** (i) the Hague-Visby Rules were applicable to the contract of carriage. It was important to consider the intention of the parties. The words "apply compulsorily" in the second paragraph of Clause 3 could not be ignored. Since Article 1(b) determined when the Hague-Visby Rules apply compulsorily, it was necessary to conduct an analysis of Article 1(b) in relation to the contract of carriage. Article 1(b) required the contract of carriage to be "covered by a bill of lading". The contract of carriage was indeed covered by a bill of lading making the Hague-Visby Rules compulsory and thus part of the contract of carriage under the second paragraph of Clause 3. The court held that "...*the rules are [not] concerned with whether the bill of lading contains terms which have been previously agreed or not. It is the fact that it is issues or that its issue is contemplated matters*". (ii) The claim was subject to the limitation of liability imposed by art. IV(5). The words "in any event" of art. IV(5) "mean what they say" and are "unlimited in scope." "A limitation of liability is different in character from an exception. The words "in any event" do not appear in any of the other art. IV exemptions including r. 6 and as a matter of construction ...were intended to refer only to those events which give rise to the exemptions of art. IV.

<br>

### 177

**Partenreederei M/S "Heidberg" v. Vega Reederei Friedrich Dauber v. Grosvenor Grain and Feed Co. Ltd.**
*(The Heidberg)*
1994, 2 Lloyd's Rep. 287 (Q.B.)

On July 23, 1990, a contract of affreightment was concluded between UNCAC and Peter Dohle on the Synacomex form, which provided for arbitration in Paris. The contract provided for tonnage nominated by the latter to perform a minimum of six and a maximum of twelve voyages, each of which was to carry 2,500 tons of bulk maize. That contract was in pursuance of a sale contract between UNCAC (as sellers) and Grosvenor (as buyers). On Mar. 7 Peter Dohle had no vessel capable

of meeting the cancelling date of Mar. 8, and negotiated by telephone a fixture of the vessel *Heidberg* with English brokers. They concluded the main terms of a voyage charter by telephone and agreed that the terms of a previous fixture used would apply, which was on the Synacomex 90 amended form and provided for arbitration in London. After the agreement, the English brokers sent a "recap telex" referring erroneously to the Synacomex form instead of to the Synacomex 90 form. When the cargo was loaded, a bill of lading was issued incorporating the terms of a non-identified charterparty. At the time of issuance, there was only the head charterparty on the Synacomex form (Paris) and an oral agreement for the Synacomex 90 form. The MV *Heidberg* collided on transit and suffered fire damage. The sound cargo was transhipped onto another vessel and the rest was lost. Grosvenor, as holders of the bill of lading, claimed shortages and was paid by the underwriters. Various actions were brought in both England and France. In France, the Tribunal de Commerce held that the bill of lading did not incorporate de London arbitration clause. In England, the shipowners of the MV *Heidberg* claimed the freight stated in the contract of affreightment and issued a writ in English courts against the UNCAC, Grosvenor and the underwriters. The defendants contended that the claim was barred by res judicata by reason of the judgement before the Tribunal de Commerce.

***Held:*** (Judge Diamond, Q.C.) **i)** Art. 25 of the Brussels Convention does not exclude judgements on preliminary issues nor distinguishes these from the final judgements on the merits. No objection was found to the recognition of the judgement of the French courts since the parties under the two proceedings were not the same. **ii)** *"It was beyond doubt that that the judgement of a foreign contracting State on the substance of a dispute, even if given in breach of a valid arbitration agreement, must be recognised by this court under art. 26; The judgement of the Tribunal de Commerce did not fall within exception 4° (of art. 1) relating to 'arbitration' and this court was bound to recognise it."* **iii)** *"It would be commercially unsound to hold that on the proper construction of the bill of lading, it was capable of incorporating the terms of an oral contract."* Where a bill of lading seeks to incorporate the terms from a charterparty which, although already fixed, is not yet reduced to writing, the incorporation of the terms of the oral fixture is not valid.[151] The "recap telex" did not qualify otherwise. Therefore, the charterparty agreed by telephone did not succeed in incorporating the London arbitration clause of the Synacomex 90 form. **iv)** *"The words set out in the bill of lading were more apt to refer to an instrument in writing than to an oral contract evidenced by a recap telex and the parties were more likely to have intended the freight referred to in the bill of lading to be that defined in the (head) charter… than that defined in the voyage charter. The terms of the contract of affreightment of July 23 were incorporated in the bill of lading and those of the voyage charter of Mar. 7 were not."*

---

[151] But see *OK Petroleum v. Vitol Energy* and *Gill Duffus S.A. v. Rionda Futures Ltd.*

## 178
## PARTENREEDEREI M/S TILLY RUSS AND ANOTHER V. HAVEN & VERVOEBEDRIFJ NOVA N.V. AND ANOTHER
## 19.06.1984, Case 71/83
## (European Court of Justice)

A Belgian firm purchased a quantity of timber from an American company. The German shipowner Partenreederei MS. *Tilly Russ* (the carrier) was commissioned to carry the goods by sea from Toronto (Canada) to Antwerp (Belgium). When loading was completed, bills of lading were issued to the "order of shipper" by the agents of the carriers in Toronto. The bills of lading were in pre-printed form and contained the following clause on the back of each: "4(e): Any dispute arising under this bill of lading shall be decided by the Hamburg courts". When the timber was discharged, some of it was found damaged and the Belgian holders of the bills of lading (to whom the bills had been assigned by the shipper) brought an action against the carrier in the Commercial Court of Antwerp. The carrier contended that the courts of Antwerp had no jurisdiction in accordance with art. 17 of the Brussels Convention 1968 and applied for a stay of proceedings. On the appeal, the Hof van Cassatie stayed the proceedings in Belgium and referred the following question to the European Court of Justice for a preliminary ruling: "Can the bill of lading issued by the carrier to the shipper be considered, having regard to the relevant generally accepted practices, to be an 'agreement in writing' or an 'agreement evidenced by writing' between the parties within the meaning of article 17 of the Convention of 27 Sept. 1968 on Jurisdiction and the Enforcement of Judgments in Civil and Commercial Matters and, if so, does that also apply in relation to a third party holding the bill of lading?".

***Held:*** (after the opinion of the General Advocate Sir Gordon Slynn) *"(1) If under the applicable national law a bill of lading constitutes an agreement between the carrier and the shipper, which expressly states or clearly incorporates by reference a choice of jurisdiction clause, the bill of lading can be an agreement in writing for the purpose of article 17 of the Brussels Convention 1968. A bill of lading may constitute evidence in writing of an oral agreement as to a choice of jurisdiction for the purpose of article 17 if the oral agreement expressly incorporates the conditions in the bill including the choice of jurisdiction clause, and the clause is known to the shipper (or could with reasonable diligence have been ascertained by him prior to the making of the contract), or if such a clause has been adopted in a course of dealing between the parties. (2) A holder of such a bill may be bound by a choice of jurisdiction clause if he has expressly agreed to be bound by it in writing, or in a written statement evidencing an oral agreement to be bound by it, or if, under the law applicable to the transfer of the bill, the holder succeeds to all the rights and obligations of the shipper under the bill which, as between shipper and carrier, constituted an agreement in writing, or written evidence of an oral contract for the purposes of article 17, and in either case so long as the dispute between the carrier and the holder of the bill is one falling within the scope of the choice of jurisdiction clause."* According-ing to this opinion, the court ruled that the jurisdiction clause printed in a bill of lading constituted a valid agreement for

the purposes of art. 17[152] if (i) the agreement to the bill had been expressed in writing, or (ii) if the jurisdiction clause had been orally agreed before its incorporation in the bill, or (iii) if the bill was part of a continuing business relationship between the parties which was governed by the general conditions including the jurisdiction clause. On these grounds, if the jurisdiction clause was effective between the carrier and the shipper, it was also effective as between the carrier and the holder of the bill of lading provided that, under the relevant national law, the holder of the bill of lading acquired the shipper's rights and duties under it.


# 179

## Pavia & Co. Spa v. Thurmann-Nielsen
### 1952, 1 All ER, 492 (C.A.)

The parties entered in a contract of sale for 3.000 tonnes of Brazilian groundnuts on c.i.f. terms. Delivery was to be made by instalments in February, March, April and May 1949. A confirmed letter of credit was agreed to be opened in favour of the sellers. However, the credit was not available to the sellers until 22 Apr. 1949. The sellers contended that the credit should be opened at the latest in Jan..

---

[152] Note that art. 17 was later amended by the Convention of Accession to the Brussels Convention by Denmark, Ireland and United Kingdom of 9 Oct. 1978 (Official Journal 1978, L. 304, p. 1) in that the agreement conferring jurisdiction must *"be either in writing or evidenced in writing or, in international trade or commerce, in a form which accords with practices in that trade or commerce of which the parties are or ought to have been aware"*.

They claimed damages against the buyers for breach of the contract of sale.

***Held (for the sellers):*** Where the availability of the letter of credit is a condition precedent to the performance of the contract, and a certain period for shipment is stipulated in the sale contract, in the absence of a stipulation to the contrary, the buyer has to give the seller the benefit of the whole shipment period. This is so because the seller is entitled to be assured, before he ships, that on shipment he will get paid. In words of Somervell, L.J. *"When a seller is given a right to ship over a period and there is machinery for payment, that machinery must be available over the whole of that period. If the buyer is anxious, as he might be if the period of shipment is a long one, not to have to put the credit machinery in motion until shortly before the seller is likely to want to ship, then he must insert some provision in the contract by which the credit shall be provided, e.g. fourteen days after a cable received from the seller".* In other cases, where the sale contract is silent as to the period, the letter of credit will have to be opened within a "reasonable time" calculated back from the first date of shipment, not calculated forward to the conclusion of the contract. These rules apply always to c.i.f. contracts and f.o.b. contracts.

**180**

**PETROLEO BRASILIERO S.A. V. KRITI AKTI SHIPPING CO. S.A.**
*(The Kriti Akti)*
2004, 1 Lloyd's Rep. 712 (C.A.)

The MV *Kriti Akti* was chartered on the Shelltime 3 form for two consecutive periods of 11 months, 15 days more or less at charterers' option. The charterparty provided, inter alia, the following clause 18: "Notwithstanding the provisions of clause 3 thereof, should the vessel be upon a voyage at the expiry of the period of this charter, charterers shall have the use of the vessel at he same rate and conditions for such extended time as may be necessary for the completion of the round voyage on which she is engaged and her return to a port of redelivery as provided by this charter...". There was a further clause 50, which read: "Any loss of time during which the vessel is off hire shall count as part of the charter period and may be used by charterers at their option as an extension of the aforesaid charter period". The eleven-month period expired on 24 Apr. 2001. During the charter the vessel was off-hire at various times for thirty six days. On 13 Mar. 2001 the charterers informed the owners of their intention to extend the final date of the charter to June 14 by exercising their options under clause 50 and adding fifteen days and 36 off-hire days respectively. On 1 June 2001 the charterers issued instructions for a voyage from Saó Sebastiaó, where the vessel was discharging, to Santos, and then to New York. Owners considered the charter to have already expired and demanded an increased rate of hire to follow the charterers' instructions, which the charterers rejected. Owners then took back the vessel at Santos. Charterers claimed against the owners for damages resulting from the owners' failure to comply with their legitimate voyage instructions.

***Held (for the charterers):*** (Mance, L.J.) First, the court held that that *"the period of this charter"* included any period which the charterers elected to take as an extension of the basic period in cl. 50. Furthermore, there was *"no reason for restricting charterers' freedom to give voyage directions by reference to any date, except the final terminal date"*. This meant that the time allotted in cl. 50 read meant the charterers had the vessel *"for all practical purposes for any period they wish between 11 months plus and 11 months minus 15 days"*. Subsequently, *"…a voyage within cl. 18 may be commenced at any time during that period, up to its terminal date of 11 months plus 15 days (or here, 11 months plus off-hire days plus 15 days). Cl. 18 had the effect of exposing the owners "to a final round voyage of no fixed length, which it is clear form the outset will extend very considerably beyond the final terminal date. But this is not a problem which derives from including any margin period of 'days more in charterers' option' in the charter period during which cl. 18 may be operated"*.

### 181

### PETROTRADE INC. V. STINNES HANDEL GMBH

1995, 1 Lloyd's Rep. 142 (Q.B.)

In 1992 the plaintiff sellers sold to the defendant buyers 10,000 tonnes of premium 0.15 leaded gasoline. The quality was described as "lead 0.15g/l maximum scavenger free" and "BRC Refining Antwerp running production". Quantity and quality of the cargo was to be established at the loading port by independent surveyor appointed mutually, to be final and binding on both parties. The contract included f.o.b. Antwerp terms, and delivery was to be made during July 1-15

by barges, or July 12-17 by coaster. The buyers elected to lift the cargo by coaster and nominated the vessel *Rava*. The cargo was inspected before loading and it was found that that it did not comply with the contract requirement "scavenger free". In the meantime, on July 18 the vessel was still anchoraged off Antwerp awaiting a berth. The buyers then telexed a message whereby they required a new product in compliance with the requirements of quality, and fixed July 20 as the latest date for delivery. The sellers then offered 10,000 tonnes of another cargo of gasoline free of scavenger for delivery f.o.b. Flushing. Flushing is a port located on the way from the outer anchorage to Antwerp. The buyers refused the new offer alleging that it was in breach of contract on various grounds. Three months later the sellers resold the cargo to different buyers and claimed damages for wrongful rejection and sought compensation based on the difference between the resale price and the contract price.

***Held (for the buyers):*** (Colman, J.) **i)** The first tender in Antwerp was not a valid tender so far as the quality of the cargo was concerned. It was open to the buyers to treat the sellers' conduct as a repudiatory breach terminating the contract thereby. However, the buyers waived their right to terminate and preferred to extend the delivery date up to July 20. **ii)** The subsequent tender in Flushing was still defective. *"In a f.o.b. contract where the buyer has to nominate the ship the precise identification of the delivery point is vital to the buyer; The fact is that in f.o.b. contracts when the buyer has to nominate the ship the need for the precise matching of the contract of affreight-*

*ment with the contract of affreightment with the contract of sale, both as to timing and as to place of shipment, is essential and obvious in all cases."* The place of shipment can be considered here as part of the description of the goods and therefore a condition the breach of which entitles the buyer to treat the contract as terminated.[153] The sellers' submission that Flushing was on the way from the outer anchorage to Antwerp, lying closer to the position of the vessel was irrelevant. Moreover, it was never established that the refinery in Flushing was within the legal limits of the port of Antwerp. Accordingly, delivery at Flushing was uncontractual. **iii)** Since "BRC Refining Antwerp running production" was also expressed to be within the quality clause, that provision was equally part of the description of the goods. Therefore, a parcel to be delivered f.o.b. Flushing did not correspond with that description and thus is non-contractual. **iv)** *"Once it is accepted that the entire parcel could have been sold in approximately two weeks, there can be no basis for adopting as the basis for the calculation of damages the resale prices achieved over the ensuing three months. The seller's genuine belief that by holding the parcel for a much longer period he would be able to recover a larger return on resale does not justify departing from the market price obtainable at and immediately*

*after the buyer's non-acceptance. Accordingly, if the plaintiffs, Petrotrade, had been entitled to damages for non-acceptance of the gasoline by Stinnes, the correct measure of damages would…have been the difference between the contract price and the average of barge sale market price…ex Antwerp over the period of two weeks from July 20, 1992."* For all the above the sellers' claim was dismissed.

<hr>

### 182
### PHOTO PRODUCTION LTD. V. SECURICOR TRANSPORT LTD.
### 1980, 1 Lloyd's Rep. 545 (H.L.)

The respondents (Securicor Transport) undertook to provide a night patrol service for the appellant's (Photo Production) factory. The contract provided, inter alia, that Securicor would not be responsible for any "injurious act or default by any employee of the company unless such act or default could have been foreseen and avoided by the exercise of due diligence on the part of the company…" A fire broke out in the factory resulting in a total loss. The cause was attributed to one employee of Securicor, who lit a fire in the factory while on patrol.

***Held (for the respondents):*** Since the exclusion clause of the contract covered deliberate and negligent acts of the employees, the defendants were not responsible of the loss. In considering whether the breach was "fundamental" (as according to the so called "rule of law") and, if so, whether the party in breach would be deprived of the benefit of the exemption clause, Lord Wilbeforce considered: **i)** *"The doctrine of fundamental breach served a useful purpose*

---

[153] See *Benjamin's Sale of Goods* at pars. 18-116: *"It has been settled ever since the decision of the House of Lords in Bowes v Shand (1877) 2 App Cas 455 that stipulations as to the time of shipment form part of the description of the goods, and that breach of such stipulations entitles the buyer to reject…Stipulations as to the place of shipment and as to the time at which the goods are to be ready for shipment are similarly part of the description of the goods".*

*in the past, but since then the Parliament has taken a hand, it has passed the Unfair Contract Terms Act 1977. This Act applies to consumer contracts and those based on standard terms and enables exemption clauses to be applied with regard to what is just and reasonable. It is significant that the Parliament refrained from legislating over the whole field of contract. After this Act, in commercial matters generally, when the parties are not of unequal bargaining power, and when risks are normally borne by insurance, not only is the case for judicial intervention undemonstrated, but there is everything to be said, and this seems to have been Parliament's intention, for leaving the parties free to apportion the risks as they think fit and for respecting their decisions."* **ii)** *"…I must add to this, by way of exception to the decision not to 'gloss' the Suisse Atlantique, 1967, 1 AC 361 a brief observation on the deviation cases, since some reliance has been placed upon the, particularly upon the decision of this House in Hain Steamship Co. Ltd. v. Tate and Lyle Ltd., 1936, LT 177 (so earlier than the Suisse Atlantique) in the support of the Harbutt doctrine.*[154] *I suggested in the Suisse Atlantique that these cases can be regarded as proceeding upon normal principles applicable to the law of contract generally viz., that it is a matter of the parties' intentions whether and to what extent clauses in shipping contracts can be applied after a deviation, i.e. a departure from the contractually agreed voyage or adventure. It may be preferable that they should be considered as a body of authority sui generis with special rules derived from historical and commercial reasons. What on either view they*

cannot do is to lay down different rules as to contracts generally from those later stated by this House in Heyman v. Darwins Ltd., 1942, AC 356."*[155] **iii)** (Lord Diplock) The expression "breach of condition" should be reserved for situations *"where the contracting parties have agreed, whether by express words or by implication of law, that any failure by one party to perform a primary obligation, irrespective of the gravity of the event that has in fact resulted from the breach, shall entitle the other party to elect to put an end to all primary obligations of both parties remaining unperformed…".*[156]

**183**

**PRESIDENT OF INDIA V. METCALFE SHIPPING CO. LTD.**

1970, 1 QB 289 (C.A.)

The Government of India (hereinafter, "the charterers") bought on f.o.b. terms a quantity of fertiliser from sellers in Italy. The contract of sale provided that the risk on the goods was not to pass until the bill of lading was given to the charterers in India. The charterers hired a vessel to carry the cargo from Ancona (Italy) to Madras (India). The charterparty provided, inter alia, that the master should "sign bill of lading…without prejudice" to the terms of the charterparty. There was also a clause providing for London arbitration.

---

[154] *Harbutt's Plasticine Ltd. v. Wayne Tank and Pump Co. Ltd.,* 1970, 1 All E.R. 225.

[155] See *Kenya Railways v. Antares Co. Ltd ("The Antares"),* for the application of this doctrine on unauthorised deck carriage.

[156] But see *Schuler (L.) A.G. v. Wickman Machine Tool Sales Ltd.* where the H.L. found an exception to that rule where an unreasonable result would be produced thereupon.

As agreed, the sellers loaded the cargo and were issued a bill of lading consigned "to order". The bill of lading contained the terms "Freight payable by the charterers as per charterparty" and "All conditions and exceptions as per charterparty", but did not incorporate expressly the London arbitration clause. The sellers endorsed the bill of lading in blank and tendered it to the charterers. Payment was made effective upon receipt of the full set of bills of lading in India. When the cargo was discharged at Madras, the charterers claimed against the shipowners for short delivery. They sought arbitration in London according to the arbitration clause of the charterparty. The shipowners refused the arbitration since -they said- the carriage was governed by the terms of the bill of lading rather than by the charterparty, and the bill of lading did not expressly contain the arbitration clause. The main question was whether the relevant terms were to be found in the bill of lading or in the charterparty.

***Held (for the charterers):*** **i)** (Lord Denning M.R.) *"It seems to me that whenever an issue arises between the charterer and the shipowner, prima facie their relations are governed by the charterparty. The charterparty is not merely a contract for the hire of the use of the ship. It is a contract by which the shipowners agree to carry goods and to deliver them. If the shipowners fail to carry the goods safely, that is a breach of the contract contained in the charterparty; and the charterers can claim for the breach accordingly, unless that contract has been modified or varied by some subsequent agreement between the parties. The signature by the master of a*

*bill of lading is not a modification or variation of it. The master has no authority to modify or vary it. His authority is only to sign bills of lading 'without prejudice to the terms of the charterparty.'"*[157] **ii)** (Lord Denning M.R.) *"After full consideration, I am prepared to hold that in a case such as this the relations between shipowner and charterer are governed by the charterparty. Even though the charterer is not the shipper and takes as indorsee of a bill of lading, nevertheless their relations are governed by the charter, at any rate when the master is only authorised to sign bills of lading without prejudice to the charter."* The indorsement of the bill of lading to the charterer had no impact upon the terms of the charterparty, the arbitration clause of which was still binding as between the shipowner and the charterer. **iii)** Per curiam: *"There is no authority for the general proposition in leading commercial textbooks since 1910 that where a bill of lading, different in terms from the charter, is issued to a shipper who is not the charterer, or his agent, and is subsequently indorsed to the charterer, the bill of lading necessarily supersedes the charterparty and governs the relations between charterers and shipowners".*[158]

---

[157] Cited: The "without prejudice" clause is for the benefit of both shipowners and charterers. In *Turner v. Haji Goolam Mahomed Azam, 1904, AC 826*, Lord Lindley, giving the judgment of the Privy Council said at p. 837: *"The words 'without prejudice to this charter' mean that the rights of the shipowners against the time Charterers, and viceversa, are to be preserved. In this case, therefore, the bill of lading did not modify or vary the charter. And there is nothing else. So the charter governs".*

[158] See also *Calcutta S.S. Co. Ltd. v. Andrew Weir & Co.* and *Rodocanachi v. Milburn Bros.*

## 184
### PRINSENGRACHT, THE
### 1993, 1 Lloyd's Rep. 41 (Q.B.D.)

The plaintiffs claimed damages against the defendant Dutch shipowners for alleged cargo damage. In Apr. 1991 they issued a writ but, as the shipowners' vessel (the *Prinsengracht*) did not come within the jurisdiction, the writ could not be served until some months later.[159] In Jan. 1992 it was anticipated that the ship would enter an English port and the plaintiffs' solicitors wrote to the shipowners' solicitors requesting security. They enclosed a draft letter of undertaking providing, inter alia, for the exclusive submission to the English High Courts. The defendants' solicitors then informed that a bail bond would be issued in the usual form. They acknowledged the issue of the writ and filed the bond at the Admiralty and Commercial Registry providing submission to the jurisdiction of the court. Immediately thereafter, the plaintiffs' solicitors filed papers for the arrest notwithstanding the fact that they had been informed that the bail bond had been filed. The arrest was effectively made. The defendants argued that the bail bond deprived the plaintiffs of the right to arrest the ship, and that jurisdiction was not established subsequent to the arrest which they regarded as wrongful.

***Held (for the plaintiffs):*** (Sheen, J.)
**i)** *"The defendants took the voluntary step*

of acknowledging the issue of the writ. They thereby became a party to the action, which, from that moment, became in personam as well as in rem. By acknowledging the issue of the writ the defendants voluntarily submitted to the jurisdiction of the court because they 'desired to take part in the proceedings'; To my mind the voluntary act of the defendants in acknowledging the issue of the writ at a time when no action by them was called for, because the writ had not been served, was the clearest submission to the jurisdiction."* **ii)** *"Contractual security may be given without submitting, or agreeing to submit, to the jurisdiction of this court (as in* The Deichland*), but bail cannot be given without submitting to the jurisdiction."* **iii)** *"In the instant case there has been only one arrest, which lasted less than a day. It was not vexatious or oppressive. Indeed the ship was arrested solely because the defendants declined to agree expressly to submit to the jurisdiction of this court and because it was thought that the decision in* The Deichland *might have made it necessary to arrest the ship, even though bail had been given; If the arrest of the ship is necessary to preserve the jurisdiction of this court it cannot be wrongful to arrest the ship."*

## 185
### PROCTER & GAMBLE PHILIPPINE MANUFACTURING CORP. V. KURT A. BECHER GMBH & CO. KG.
### 1988, 2 Lloyd's Rep. 21 (C.A.)

The plaintiffs sold goods in bulk c.i.f. Rotterdam, to be shipped by 29 Feb. 1984 at the latest. The sale contract incorporated GAFTA Form No. 100. Clause 6 of the

---

[159] It was known that the plaintiffs' claim was time-barred in the Netherlands, so that if jurisdiction in England could not be established the defendant could probably have resisted the claim.

contract provided the following: "Period of shipment…as per bill(s) of lading dated or to be dated; the bills of lading to be dated when the goods are actually on board; date of the bill(s) shall be accepted as a proof of date of shipment in the absence of evidence to the contrary". The sellers tendered a bill of lading dated Jan. 31, 1984. Upon the tender of documents the buyers raised doubts about the true shipping date, but agreed to pay 98% of the price under reserve. Once the vessel reached Rotterdam, the buyers telexed the sellers asserting that the goods had been actually loaded on Feb. 6-10. The buyers communicated their intention to reject the cargo as the ship reached Rotterdam and claimed reimbursement of the price. The dispute was referred to arbitration as per GAFTA and the Board of Appeal held that the buyers had correctly reserved their rights and that the sellers were in breach of the contract terms. The buyers appealed.

***Held:* i)** In c.i.f sales, breach of the sellers' duties as specified in the shipping documents entitle the buyers to reject the goods.[160] The shipment period stipulated in the sale contract forms part of the description of the goods,[161] and therefore, late shipment involves a breach of both documentary and physical duties. (Kerr, L.J.) *"There is usually no difference whatever between goods loaded at the end of January instead of the beginning of February. The goods are the same. But this is not a trade in goods but in contracts for the*

*shipment of goods. A January contract may be far more valuable than one for shipment in February. More important, on a plunging market the inability to present a bill of lading evidencing shipment within the contract period can have very serious financial consequences."* **ii)** When dealing with contracts of future performance, a misrepresentation in the documents (e.g. the bill of lading) may give rise to disputes although there is no difference in the nature of the goods itself. (Kerr, L.J.) *"A falsely dated bill of lading becomes effectively unmerchantable…once its true date is known. Its presentation by the seller was a breach of contract even if the goods were in fact shipped during the contractual shipment period, as in the present case. In such circumstances it may well be possible for the buyers to show that they suffered loss as the result of this breach. Thus, they may have found themselves "locked in" on a falling market by holding a non-transferable bill of lading, when they might otherwise have been able to show that if the bill of lading had been correctly dated they could have used it to fulfil a previously concluded sub-sale covered by a notice of appropriation with which they were now unable to comply."* **iii)** In the present case, although the shipment date was incorrectly stated in the bill of lading, the shipment still took place in the early part of the contractual period so that the documentary breach involved not a physical breach itself. The court found that the misrepresentation entitled the buyers to the right of rejection of the goods, even though the sellers actually shipped the goods within the contractual period. Although clause 6 was not observed by the sellers, the buyers accepted the doc-

---

[160] See *The Hansa Nord.*
[161] See *Bowes E. and others v. Shand C. and others.*

uments when tendered since they did not know of the existence of the breach at that time. The buyers, then, lost the remedy of rejecting the documents. **iv)** Finally, the buyers were still assisted by the right of recovering damages. However, in estimating the amount of damages, the court found that the buyers were not entitled to damages since it was not proved that the breach caused any loss or damage. The buyers received goods conforming to the contract.

# 186
## Pyrene Co. Ltd. v. Scindia Steam Navigation
### 1954, 2 Q.B. 402 (Q.B.)

The plaintiffs shippers sold fire tenders f.o.b London to the government of India. They delivered the goods to the dock for loading on to the defendants' ship. As one of the tenders was being lifted by the ship's tackle and before it had crossed the ship's rail, it dropped on to the quayside and was damaged. When the bill of lading was issued, the damaged tender was not included in the goods covered by the bill of lading. The shippers sued the owner of the ship seeking to recover the cost of repairing the tender (i.e. GBP 966). The owners admitted liability but relied on the 1924 Hague Rules to limit their liability to GBP 200 only. The shippers contended that (1) as the damaged fire tender had not yet crossed the ship's rail, it had not been "loaded on" to the ship and, therefore, the accident occurred outside the period specified in art. I(e), and the Rules did not apply; (2) that at the time the tender was damaged the contract was not yet "covered by" a bill of lading as required by art. 1(b), and therefore the Rules did not apply; (3) that even if the Rules were to apply at the moment of loading, they had no application as between themselves (the f.o.b. shippers) and the owners because they were not a party to the contract of affreightment.

***Held:*** **i)** The application of the Hague Rules does not attach to a period of time but to a contract or part of a contract. However narrow the literal meaning of art. I(e) may seem, the loading of the goods is actually within its scope as long as the operation of loading "relates to the carriage of goods by sea". The reference "loaded on" in art. I(e) does no more than to define the first of the operations in a series which constitutes the carriage of goods by sea, but it does not restrict the scope of the Rules. Thus the object of the Rules is not to define the scope of the contract, but rather the terms on which that service is to be performed. Furthermore, the word "loading" in art. II is not confined to that stage of loading occurring after the goods have crossed the ship's rail, but does cover also the whole operation of loading. It cannot be said that the Rules apply only to the 2nd stage of the loading (i.e. once ship's rail is crossed), as the loading must be seen as a whole joint operation. **ii)** Whenever a contract of carriage is concluded which contemplates that a bill of lading will be issued, the contract is "covered" from its creation by the bill of lading. The use of the word "covered" in art. I(b) recognises the fact that the contract of carriage is always concluded before the bill of lading is issued.[162] The bill of lading is only evidence of the terms of the contract previously agreed. If it were otherwise, the bill of lading would mean a variation of the contract, which would lead to the absurdity that the terms of the contract are to be changed once the bill of lading is issued. **iii)** The f.o.b. contract has become a flexible instrument. In the "classic type", the seller's duties are to put the goods on board for account of the buyer and procure a bill of lading. Sometimes (in a variation called f.o.b with additional services), the seller is requested to make some other arrangements such as to contract the insurance or to nominate the ship in his own name; in those cases, they obtain payment against the transfer of the bill of lading, as in a c.i.f. contract. Finally, there are other cases (called straight f.o.b.) in which the buyer engages his own forwarding agent at the port of loading to book space and to procure the bill of lading; if freight has to be paid in advance, this method may be the most convenient. In such a case, the seller discharges his duty by putting the goods on board, getting the mate's receipt and handing it to the forwarding agent to enable him to obtain the bill of lading. The present case belongs to this third type

and no doubt there is still a contractual relationship between the carrier and the seller as shipper. If no contract existed, the seller would not be entitled to sue the carrier if the latter put the former in breach of his sale contract by sailing the ship off without having loaded the goods. (Devlin J.) *"By delivering the goods alongside, the seller impliedly invited the shipowner to load them, and the shipowner, by lifting the goods impliedly accepted that invitation. The implied contract so created must incorporate the shipowner's usual terms; none other could have been contemplated; the shipowner would not contract for the loading of the goods on terms different from those which he offered for the voyage as a whole."*[163]

**187**

**RAYNER (J.H.) & CO. LTD. V. HAMBRO'S BANK LTD.**

1943, 1 K.B. 37 (C.A.)

The defendant bank received instructions from a customer to open a confirmed irrevocable letter of credit in favour of the plaintiffs covering a cargo of "Coromandel groundnuts". The bank opened the credit and notified the plaintiffs that it was available against invoice and bill of lading for "Coromandel groundnuts". The plaintiffs though presented a bill of lading describing the goods as "machine-shelled groundnut kernels" and having in its margin the letters "C.R.S.", which were

---

[162] Devlin L.J. based this argument on the original French text of the Convention of 1924, which literally stated in its art. I(b) that *"Contrat de transport (…) s'applique uniquement au contrat du transport constaté par un connaissement"*. As the term "constaté" means "confirmed", it is thereby understood that a contract does already exist before the bill of lading is issued. However, it may be arguable whether this interpretation of the French text of art. I(b) is consistent with the shipper's right to demand a bill of lading under art. III(7).

[163] As regards the doctrine of the "implied contract of carriage", see also the following cases: *Brandt v. Liverpool, Brazil and Riverplate S.N. Co.*, *The Captain Gregos* and *The Dona Mari*.

an abbreviation of "Coromandel groundnuts", and also presented an invoice for "Coromandel groundnuts". The bank refused payment and the plaintiffs sued for breach of the bank's undertaking under the letter of credit. Evidence was accepted by the learned judge that "machine-shelled groundnut kernels" were universally understood in that particular trade to be the identical with "Coromandel groundnuts". The defendants appealed and the Court of Appeal reversed the judge's decision.

**Held**[164] **(for the defendants): i)** The bank is not supposed to be aware of the terms and customs of the particular trade of its customers. (Mackinnon, L.J.) *"It is quite impossible to suggest that a banker is to be affected with knowledge of the customs and customary terms of every one of the thousands of trades for whose dealings he may issue letters of credit; It would be quite impossible for business to be carried on, and for bankers to be in any way protected in such matters, if it were said that they must be affected by a knowledge of all the details of the way in which particular traders carry on their businesses."* **ii)** (Mackinnon, L.J.) *"It is elementary to say that a person who ships in reliance of a letter of credit must do so in exact compliance with its terms. It is also elementary to say that a bank is not bound or indeed entitled to honour drafts presented to it under a letter of credit unless*

*those drafts with the accompanying documents are in strict accord with the credit as opened."* The bank were entitled to refuse the drafts since the bill of lading tendered did not comply strictly with the terms of the letter of credit. **iii)** It is irrelevant that what was really shipped under such bill of lading was nothing different than "Coromandel groundnuts". That fact is immaterial because the bank had to pay not against goods but against documents. The bank knows nothing about the terms of the carriage or about the conditions of the transaction entered into by the parties.

<br>

**188**

**REARDON SMITH LINE LTD. V. BLACK SEA & BALTIC EXCHANGE INSURANCE CO.**
1939, AC 562 (H.L.)

A vessel was chartered to carry a cargo of ore from a port in the eastern Black Sea to Baltimore (USA). After leaving the port of loading she headed for Constantza on the west of the Black Sea, where cheap fuel oil was available. While entering Constantza she ran aground and part of the cargo had to be jettisoned. After temporary repairs, the remaining cargo was discharged, by agreement, at Rotterdam. The plaintiff shipowners claimed a general average contribution plus the unpaid freight. They brought the present action on a bond agreed with the charterers as security in order to obtain delivery of the cargo. The charterers relied on the fact that Constantza was 200 miles to the direct geographical route to Baltimore; they contended that such deviation deprived the shipowners of their right to claim the general average contribution.

---

[164] Note that in this case the UCP for Documentary Credits was not incorporated by the parties into the letter of credit. In a case involving disputes under the UCP for Documentary Credits the outcome of the decision could have been different. Contrast this case with art. 37(c) of the UCP 500 (1993 Rev.) and with *Glencore Int. v. Bank of China.*

***Held (for the shipowners):*** Although there is a presumption that the proper route is the direct geographical route between the ports of loading and discharge, this presumption can be rebutted by evidence of the customary route in the trade, unless a specific route is prescribed by the charterparty or the bill of lading. (Lord Porter) *"It is the duty of a ship, at any rate when sailing upon an ocean voyage from one port to another, to take the usual route between these two ports. If no evidence be given, that route is presumed to be the direct geographical route but it may be modified in many cases, for navigational or other reasons, and evidence may always be given to show what the usual route is, unless a specific route be prescribed by the charterparty or bill of lading."* In the present case, it was successfully proved that vessels engaged in the ore trade always called on Constantza for bunkers and that 25% of ocean-going, oil-burning vessels passing the Bosphorus followed a similar practice. The H.L. held that there was no unjustifiable deviation and the shipowners were entitled to recover the sums from the charterers.


**189**
**REARDON SMITH LINE LTD. V.
HANSEN-TANGEN**
*(The Diana Prosperity)*
1976, 2 Lloyd's Rep. 621 (H.L.)

A shipbuilder firm formed a time charter agreement using the shelltime 3 form with a company called Hansen-Tangen. The charterparty stipulated the vessel "… to be built by Osaka Shipbuilding Co. Ltd. and known as Hull nº 354 until named and shall have a deadweight of about 87,600 tons". Hansen sub-chartered the vessel on similar terms to a firm called Reardon Smith. As the Osaka yard could not build ships over 45,000 tons, the ship was built 300 miles away at Oshima. Once the vessel was built (and named as *Diana Prosperity*), the ship market fell drastically. The sub-charterers contended that the vessel had been build at a different yard and with a different hull number. They rejected the tender on the ground that she did not meet the contractual specifications and sued Hansen-Tangen for the return of the sums paid.

***Held (for the appellants):*** **i)** Both the yard and the hull number served no other purpose other than to identify the vessel and to show where it could be located. The defendants' argument that both features were an essential part of the description of the ship was rejected by the court. *"Even if (according to the Sale of Goods Act) a strict and technical view must be taken as regards of unascertained future goods as to which each detail of the description must be assumed to be vital (we should ask) whether a particular item in a description constitutes a substantial ingredient of the identity of the thing sold, and only if it does, to treat it as a condition".* **ii)** But here, the use of both items was merely for the "identification" of the goods. *"It is one thing to say of given words that their purpose is to state an essential part of the description of the goods (i.e. identity), and it is another different thing to say that they provide one party with a specific indication (i.e. identification) of the goods so that he can find them and, if he wishes, sub-dispose of them."* In the first sense, the fulfilment of both items (the vessel to be built at Osaka and to bear yard n° 354) would have been an essential term of the description, but this was not the case. Both items, the hull and yard numbers, were in fact just "labelling" or identifying the ship rather than creating obligations themselves.[165]

## 190
### REP. OF INDIA AND ANOTHER V. INDIA STEAMSHIP CO. LTD.
*(The Indian Grace)*
1997, 3 WLR 818 (H.L.)

Munitions were loaded on board the defendant's ship *Indian Grace* for a carriage to Cochin (India) and delivery to the plaintiffs, the Indian Ministry of Defence. In the course of the voyage a fire occurred in hold no. 3. Although the cargo was extinguished with water, some of the goods were jettisoned and the rest were repacked under the supervision of the cargo manufacturers. Two separate claims were sought by the plaintiffs: one being for the total loss of the cargo in no. 3 hold due to damage, and the other being in respect of the cargo jettisoned. The plaintiffs proceeded with their in personam claim for the 51 artillery shells jettisoned before the Cochin Subordinate Courts and obtained judgement in their favour for the equivalent of GBP 7,200. The appeal against that judgement was at that time pending. Meanwhile the same plaintiffs also brought an in rem action in England for GBP 2.6 million for alleged damage to the entire cargo of 12,000 shells, which were became valueless as a result of radiant heat from the fire. The writ in rem was served on a sister ship of the mv. *Indian Grace*. The parties subsequently agreed to the application of English law and the defendants submitted to the Admiralty Court in England. The defendant shipowners challenged the action in rem relying upon sec. 34 of the Civil Jurisdiction and Judgement Act 1982 which provides that: "*No proceedings may be brought by a person in England and Wales…on a cause of action in respect of which a judgement has been given in his favour in proceedings between the same parties…in the courts of an overseas country*".

**Held (for defendants): i)** An action in rem is, in reality, an action against the owner of the ship. (Lord Steyn) "*The role of fictions in the development of the law has been likened to the use of scaffolding in the construction of a building. The scaffolding is necessary but after the building has been erected scaffolding serves only to obscure the building. Fortunately, the scaffolding can usually be removed with ease… The idea that a ship can be a defendant in legal proceedings was always a fiction; It is now possible to say that for the purposes of section 34 an action in rem is an action against the owners from the moment that the Admiralty Court is invoked by the service of a writ, or, where a writ is deemed to be served, as a result of the acknowledgement of the issue of the writ by the defendant before service: The Banco [1971] P. 137. From that moment the owners are parties to the proceedings in rem.*" As a consequence of this construction, sec. 34 becomes a bar

---

[165] In attending to the nature and gravity of a breach or departure of a contractual specification, the general law of contract has turned less rigid. See *Hongkong Fir Shipping Co. Ltd. v. Kawasaki Kisen Kaisha Ltd., 1961, 2 Lloyd's Rep. 478.*

to the action in rem. Under that section, the plaintiffs were not allowed to proceed in rem since the foreign judgment in personam was being held "between the same parties or their privies" on the same cause of action.[166] **ii)** The defendants were not estopped by convention or acquiescence from relying on the bar created by sec. 34.

**191**

**RÈUNION EUROPÈENNE SA v.
SPLIETHOFFS BEVRACHTINGSTKANTOOR
BV AND THE MASTER OF THE VESSEL
ALBALSGRACHT V002**

27.10.1988, Case C-51/97
(European Court of Justice)

In May 1992 a cargo of peaches in refrigerated containers was carried from Melbourne (Australia) to Rotterdam (Netherlands) on board the vessel *Albalsgracht V002* under a bearer bill of lading issued and headed by Refrigerated Container Carriers Pty. Ltd. (hereinafter "RCC") whose registered office was in Sydney. Despite not being mentioned in the bill of lading, the goods were actually carried by Spliethoffs Bevrachtingstkantoor BV (hereinafter, SB), which was established in Amsterdam (Netherlands). Once in Rotterdam, the cargo was carried by road to Rungis (France) under an international consignment note. On delivery, Brambi (hereinafter the consignee) based in Rungis, found that the peaches had been damaged owing to a breakdown in the cooling system. After compensating the consignee for the damage suffered, the in-

surers (whose lead insurer acted as plaintiffs) subrogated and brought proceedings in Rungis to recoup their loss against RCC, SB, and the master (resident in Holland) as representative of the owners and charterers. The Tribunal de Commerce of Rungis declared jurisdiction against RCC, but declined jurisdiction as regards SB and the master under art. 5(1) of the Convention of 27 Sept. 1968 on Jurisdiction and the Enforcement of Judgments in Civil and Commercial Matters[167] (the "Brussels Conventions"), which prescribes: "[A] person domiciled in a Contracting State may, in another Contracting State, be sued (1) in matters relating to a contract, in the courts for the place of performance of the obligation in question...". The Tribunal de Commerce took the view that the operation did not constitute a through transport from Melbourne to Rungis since an international consignment note had been drawn up for the inland carriage from Rotterdam to Rungis, and therefore declined jurisdiction in favour of the courts of Rotterdam, this being the place of performance of the obligation within the terms of art. 5(1), or those of Amsterdam or Sydney pursuant to article 6(1) according to which a person who is one of a number of defendants may be sued before the courts of the place where any one of them is domiciled. The Cour d'Appel of Paris confirmed the judgment and the plaintiff

---

[166] See also *The Maciej Rataj.*

[167] As amended by the Convention of 9 Oct. 1978 on the Accession of Denmark, Ireland and the United Kingdom, by the Convention of 25 Oct.1982 on the Accession of the Hellenic Republic, and by the Convention of 26 May 1989 on the Accession of Spain and Portugal.

insurers brought the matter to the Cour de Cassation. They claimed that it had not been established that the insured consignees had concluded an agreement with SB and the master, so that art. 5(1) could not be applied to them, and that art. 5(3), relating to tort,[168] should have been applied. The Cour de Cassation then stayed proceedings pending a preliminary ruling from the European Court of Justice on a number of questions concerning the interpretation of the Brussels Convention.

***Held:*** (After the opinion of the General Advocate Mr. G. Cosmas): **Questions 1 and 2:** *"In this case, it is clear from the findings of the national courts at first instance and on appeal that the bearer bill of lading issued by RCC covers the carriage of the goods by sea to Rotterdam, the port of discharge and delivery, that it specifies Brambi as the person to whom the arrival of the goods must be notified and that it indicates that the goods are to be carried aboard the* Alblasgracht V002. *It must therefore be held that that bill of lading discloses no contractual relationship freely entered into between Brambi on the one hand and, on the other,* Spliethoffs Bevrachtingskantoor BV *and the* Master of the Alblasgracht V002, *who, according to the insurers, were the actual maritime carriers of the goods. In those circumstances, the action brought against the latter by the insurers cannot be a matter relating to a contract within the meaning of Article 5(1) of the Convention. [I]t must be held*

*that such an action is a matter relating to tort, delict or quasi-delict within the meaning of Article 5(3) of the Convention and that, therefore, the general principle that the courts of the State in which the defendant is domiciled are to have jurisdiction, laid down in the first paragraph of Article 2 of the Convention, is inapplicable. The jurisdiction in matters relating to tort, delict or quasi-delict of the courts for the place where the harmful event occurred is one of the special jurisdictions listed in Articles 5 and 6 of the Convention, which constitute exceptions to the general principle laid down in the first paragraph of Article 2. The answer to the first two questions must therefore be that an action by which the consignee of goods found to be damaged on completion of a transport operation by sea and then by land, or by which his insurer who has been subrogated to his rights after compensating him, seeks redress for the damage suffered, relying on the bill of lading covering the maritime transport, not against the person who issued that document on his headed paper but against the person whom the plaintiff considered to be the actual maritime carrier, falls within the scope not of matters relating to a contract within the meaning of Article 5(1) of the Convention but of matters relating to tort, delict or quasi-delict within the meaning of Article 5 (3) of the Convention."* **Question 3:** *"[T]he place where the damage arose in the case of an international transport operation of the kind at issue in the main proceedings can only be the place where the actual maritime carrier was to deliver the goods. That place meets the requirements of foreseeability and certainty imposed by the Convention and displays a particularly close connecting*

---

[168] *"A person domiciled in a Contracting State may, in another Contracting State, be sued …(3) in matters relating to tort, delict or quasi-delict, in the courts for the place where the harmful event occurred".*

*factor with the dispute in the main proceedings, so that attribution of jurisdiction to the courts for that place is justified by reasons relating to the sound administration of justice and the efficacious conduct of proceedings. The answer to be given to the third question must therefore be that the place where the consignee of the goods, on completion of a transport operation by sea and then by land, merely discovered the existence of the damage to the goods delivered to him cannot serve to determine the 'place where the harmful event occurred' within the meaning of Article 5(3) of the Convention of 28 Sept. 1968, as interpreted by the court."* **Question 4:** *"[T]wo claims in one action for compensation, directed against different defendants and based in one instance on contractual liability and in the other on liability in tort or delict cannot be regarded as connected. Finally, as the court held in paragraph 20 of* Kalfelis,[169] *whilst it is true that disadvantages arise from different aspects of the same dispute being adjudicated upon by different courts, it must be pointed out, on the one hand, that a plaintiff is always entitled to bring his action in its entirety before the courts for the domicile of the defendant and, on the other, that Article 22 of the Convention allows the first court seised, in certain circumstances, to hear the case in its entirety provided that there is a connection between the actions brought before the different courts. The answer to the fourth question must therefore be that Article 6(1)[170] of*

*the Convention of 27 Sept. 1968 must be interpreted as meaning that a defendant domiciled in a Contracting State cannot be sued in another Contracting State before a court seised of an action against a co-defendant not domiciled in a Contracting State on the ground that the dispute is indivisible rather than merely displaying a connection."*

**192**

**REWIA, THE**

1991, 2 Lloyd's Rep. 325 (C.A.)

In July 1988, a cargo of nutmegs and mace was loaded in six containers on board the *Rewia* for a carriage from St. George's (Grenada) to Rotterdam (Netherlands). She had been chartered on a NYPE form, which expressly authorised the charterers or their agents to sign bills of lading on behalf of the master provided that they were in accordance with the Mate's Receipts. A complete set of bills of lading were issued on the sub-charterers' standard form, and signed by the charterers' agents "for the master". The bills included the following clause: "3. Jurisdiction: Any dispute arising under this bill of lading shall be decided in the country where the carrier has its principal place of business and the law of such country shall apply...". During the voyage the six containers were lost overboard. The plaintiff cargo-owners claimed damages against the sub-charterers and the owners under the contract of carriage evidenced by the bills of lading, and alternatively, for breach of their duties as bailees. The owners sought reliance on clause 3 and invoked art. 17 of the Brussels Conven-

---

[169] *Kalfelis v. Schröder, Case 189/87 [1988] ECR 5565.*

[170] Article 6(1) of the Convention provides that where a person domiciled to be sued is one of a number of defendants, he may also be sued in the courts for the place where any one of them is domiciled.

tion 1968 for declining jurisdiction of the English Courts, as they were based on Hamburg, West Germany.[171] The questions for the appeal were, inter alia, (1) whether the owners were actual parties to the bills of lading, and (2), assuming that the owners' principal place of business was Hamburg, whether cl. 3 is valid to set aside jurisdiction of the court under art. 17 of the Convention.

**Held: i)** (Legatt, L.J.) *"The master was in fact the servant of the shipowners; …a bill of lading signed for the master cannot be a charterers' bill unless the contract was made with the charterers' alone, and the person signing has authority to sign, and does sign, on behalf of the charterers and not the owners. Accordingly, the bills of lading in this case were owners' bills. The plaintiffs have no claim against the first defendants (i.e. the sub-charterers)."* **ii)** *"I (Legatt, L.J.) do not consider that the reference to the 'principal place' of the third defendants' business (i.e. the owners') requires the identification of a particular building. For purposes of cl. 3 of the bills of lading it is sufficient that the principal business of the third defendants should have been conducted from West Germany."* Accordingly, the owners could not be brought before the English Court by virtue of art. 6 of the Brussels Convention of 1968.

---

[171] Article 17 of the Brussels Convention, 1968, provides that where parties, one or more of whom is domiciled in a Contracting State, have agreed that the Courts of a Contracting State are to have jurisdiction to settle particular disputes, those Courts shall have exclusive jurisdiction, and that such an agreement must be in writing or in accordance with international trade practices.

## 193
### RIVER GURARA, THE
1998, 1 Lloyd's Rep. 225 (C.A.)

The vessel *River Gurara* suffered an engine breakdown on her way from West Africa to Europe. Consequently, she broke up and sank off the Portuguese coast resulting in a total loss of cargo. Much of the lost cargo had been originally shipped in containers. These were covered by bills of lading on the UK.-West Africa Line Form under which the Hague Rules applied. Art. IV(5) of the Rules provides that "Neither the carrier nor the ship shall in any event be or become liable for any loss…to…goods in an amount exceeding GBP 100 per package or unit… unless the nature and value of such goods have been declared by the shipper before shipment and inserted in the bill of lading…" The bills of lading stated that the containers "said to contain" a given number of separate items such as pallets, crates, cartons or bags, and included the following general clause 9 on the reverse side: "If a container has not been packed or filled by or on behalf of the carrier… (b) notwithstanding any provision of law to the contrary the container shall be considered a package or unit even though it has been used to consolidate the goods, the number of packages or units constituting which have been enumerated on the face hereof as having been packed therein by…the merchant, and the liability of the carrier…shall be calculated accordingly". Against this backdrop, the cargo-owners commenced proceedings in the UK Admiralty Court. The defendant shipowners sought to limit their liability to "GBP 100 per package or unit" under art. IV(5) arguing that the container itself should be treated as a sole package by virtue of cls. 9 of the bills. In reply, the cargo-owners submitted that the said clause was void and null by reason of art. III(8) of the Rules.

***Held (for the cargo-owners):*** **i)** Their lordships agreed that, in this case, the container itself does not fall within the scope of the term "package" under art. IV(5). (Phillips, LJ) "*...where the Hague Rules limit falls to be computed in relation to parcels of cargo which are loaded in containers, it is the parcels, and not the containers, which constitute the relevant packages; ...the shipowners' limit of liability should be calculated on the basis of the number of packages carried in the containers rather than the number of containers, unless the manner in which the cargo has been described in the bills of lading requires a contrary approach.*" Echoing the reasons set out by Beeks, J. in *The Aegis Spirit* [1997] 1 Lloyd's Rep. 93. Phillips, LJ. continued, "*The Hague Rules limitation provisions were designed to prevent shipowners imposing on shippers unrealistically low limits of liability. If the parties are permitted to agree on their own definition of 'packages', shipowners will, by applying that definition to containers, succeed in evading the minimum limit of liability that the Hague Rules aimed to secure. The American Courts repeatedly held that the so-called 'boilerplate' clauses in bills of lading, stating that containers were to be deemed to be 'packages', were ineffective as being in conflict with the COGSA limit*". **ii)** In connection with the language "said to contain" qualifying the description of the goods in the bills of lading, their lordships held that such a qualification does

not constitute an agreement between the parties as to an unknown quantity of the cargo. That qualification has no effect on the evidential status of the bills of lading. "*...it seems to me (Phillips, LJ) at least arguable that the words 'said to contain' do not do more than make plain that the carrier is, as required by art. III(3), stating on the bill the 'number of packages...as furnished in writing by the shipper' without dissenting from the description, so that the description can be relied upon as providing prima facie evidence as to what was within the containers.*"

## 194
## RIVERSTONE MEAT CO. PTY. LTD. v. LANCASHIRE SHIPPING CO. LTD.
### *(The Muncaster Castle)*
### 1961, 1 Lloyd's Rep. 57 (H.L.)

Several cases of tinned food were shipped at Sydney (Australia) under a bill of lading subject to the Sea Carriage of Goods Act 1924 of Australia.[172] During the voyage the goods were damaged by water entering the holds via the inspection covers on the storm valves. Prior to that voyage, a load line survey of the vessel had been undertaken by a firm of ship-repairers. During that survey the storm valves were inspected under the supervision of a Lloyd's surveyor. When the survey was concluded, a fitter was employed by the repairers to close each cover and secure them with nuts. It was further discovered that the water entered into the holds as a

---

[172] The Sea Carriage of Goods Act 1924 incorporated the Hague Rules into the Australian law.

result of the negligence of the fitter, who failed to secure the nuts sufficiently. After noticing the damages, the cargo-owners sued the carriers.

***Held (for the cargo owners):*** **i)** The carrier failed to discharge the burden of proving that he had exercised due diligence in making the ship seaworthy, as required under art. IV(1) of the Hague Rules. The obligation to use due diligence in the cases stated in articles III(1) and III(2) was not limited to the carrier's personal diligence, but also to his servants, agents and even his independent contractors. *"The carriers must answer for anything that has been done in the work (of keeping or making the vessel seaworthy). It is the work itself that delimits the area of the obligation, just as it is the period 'before or at the beginning of the voyage' that delimits the time."* Therefore, the carrier was in breach of his duty of due diligence despite the fact that there had been no negligence on his part in delegating such technical work to a reputable firm. The carrier may employ some other person to exercise due diligence, but, if the delegate is not diligent, then the carrier shall be responsible therefor. **ii)** *"I (Lord Radcliffe) should regard it as unsatisfactory, where a cargo owner has found his goods damaged through a defect in the seaworthiness of the vessel that his rights of recovering from the carrier should depend upon particular circumstances in the carrier's situation and arrangements with which the cargo owner has nothing to do; as, for instance, that liability should depend on the measure of control that the carrier had exercised over persons engaged on surveying or repairing the ship, or on such questions as whether the carrier had or could have done whatever was needed by the hands of his own servants or had been sensible or prudent in getting done by other hands, carriers will find themselves liable or not liable according to circumstances quite extraneous to the sea carriage itself."* **iii)** However, those considerations do not apply when the carrier puts his vessel into the hands of third parties for repair, or when the vessel is built for him or newly comes into his hands by purchase. The carrier would hardly be held responsible for the negligence or fault of the shipbuilders or their employees in so far as these are not acting as his servants or agents, and the fault arising thereby would come out of his control and at a time before he takes over the ship.

# 195
## RODOCANACHI, SONS & CO. V. MILBURN BROTHERS
### 1886, 18 QBD 67 (C.A.)

The plaintiffs chartered a vessel for a carriage of cottonseed from Alexandria (Egupt) to the United Kingdom. The charterparty provided, inter alia, that the master was to sign bill of lading "at any rate of freight and as customary at port of loading". The bill of lading issued to the charterers (Rodocanachi, Sons & Co.) contained a clause exempting the shipowners (Milburn Brothers) from liability for any act, neglect or default of the master. The charterparty had no such clause. During the voyage, the cargo was lost by the negligence of the master. The charterers claimed damages for non-delivery to the shipowners. The shipowners relied on the efficacy of the exemption clause in the bill of lading, which was alleged to be customary in Alexandria. The charterers contended that the clause was not enforceable as against them because the same was not contained in the charter.

***Held (for the charterers):*** (Lopes L.J.) *"The main question in this case is whether the charterparty or the bill of lading is to govern the liability of the defendants. There is an exception in the later which is not contained in the former, the bill of lading exempting the shipowners from loss occasioned by the negligence of their servants. It is urged that the charterparty must be read as incorporating the terms of the bill of lading; and the defendants rely on a supposed custom at Alexandria to insert such an exception in the bill of lading, though not contained in the charterparty. According to my construction of the charterparty, no such contention can be made on the terms of the 10th clause. I (Lopes L.J.) am inclined to believe that all that is meant by 'as customary at the port of loading' is 'as usual', and that the clause must be construed as subject to the condition that the bill of lading is to be signed without prejudice to the stipulation as to freight and other terms of the charterparty. But I will assume that more was intended, and that it was intended that the master should sign the bill of lading in the form in which this bill of lading was signed. Even then I am clear that, unless there is a distinct expression of intention to the contrary, in such a case the charter must prevail. I believe the law to be that, when there is a charterparty, as between charterers and shipowners, the bill of lading operates prima facie as a mere receipt for the goods, and a document of title which may be negotiated, and by which the property is transferred, but does not operate as a new contract, or alter the contract contained in the charterparty."*

<h1 style="text-align:center">196</h1>

SA Sucre Export v. Northern River Shipping Ltd.<br>
(The Sormovskiy 3068)<br>
1994, 2 Lloyd's Rep. 266 (Q.B.)

The vessel *Sormovski 3068* was time chartered for a carriage of sugar. The charter was on the Sugar Charter-Party form 1969, which provided the discharge was to be done on FIOST terms. The charter was expressly governed under English law. The charterparty contained a clause numbered 46 authorising the shipowners to discharge the cargo against production of a bank guarantee if the original bills were not at the place of discharge on time. The plaintiffs, as charterers, agreed to purchase 3,000 tons of sugar from the shippers on f.o.b. Antwerp terms, payment to be cash against documents, title not to pass until payment. The plaintiffs subsequently sold the cargo to a third company, who, in turn, sold it to the final purchasers. The cargo had been shipped on board the vessel and order bills of lading were issued naming the original sellers as shippers and the final purchaser's address as to notify address. The bills incorporated "all the terms and conditions as per charterparty". When the vessel arrived at Vyborg (Russia), the stevedores engaged by the final purchasers were allowed to discharge and load the cargo onto railway wagons without requiring the production of the bills. The unpaid plaintiffs, being the current holders of the bills and still vested with title on the goods, gave immediate orders to suspend the discharge operation. Nevertheless, some 2,070 tonnes had already discharged and removed before the orders had been executed. The plaintiffs sought to recover from the shipowner the loss of cargo. They brought an action for damages for breach of contract or, alternatively, for conversion. The defendants contended that (1) they delivered in accordance with the practice and custom of the law of Vyborg, and that (2) the plaintiffs were estopped from their claim since they had conferred ostensible authority to the final purchasers to appoint a stevedore company as their agents for the purposes of discharging the cargo.

***Held (for the cargo owners):* i)** It is a common law rule that the shipowner is obliged to deliver the goods to the person who is entitled to possession under the bill of lading.[173] Since, in the present case, the bills of lading were consigned "to order", the person entitled to take delivery was no other than the plaintiffs as they were the current holders of the blank-endorsed bills. **ii)** (obiter) The presentation rule admits, however, several exceptions in certain situations, at least, when the law of the port of discharge requires delivery without presentation of the bills of lading; or, when there is a binding custom at that port with the same requirement; or when the bills of lading might have been lost or stolen and a further arrangement is needed.[174] However, none of these three situations arose in the present case. **iii)** In

respect of the agency estoppel, the plaintiffs at no time appointed the stevedore company as their agents for the discharge. The mere fact that the final purchasers were named as notify party in the bills of lading, or that the copies of the bills and invoice were sent with the ship, did not amount to a representation that they were entitled to receive the cargo or to appoint the stevedores as agents for the plaintiffs. **iv)** The incorporation clause of the bills of lading was wide enough to incorporate clause 46 of the charterparty. However, the purpose of that clause was to ensure that the defendants would discharge the cargo even if the bills of lading were not available for presentation, but always on terms that they would be protected by a letter of indemnity; thus, clause 46 did not exempt the shipowners from liability to the holder of the bills of lading, but provided for an option to discharge against an indemnity. The shipowners were liable for breach of contract and for conversion.

**197**

**SALMOND AND SPRAGGON (AUSTRALIA) PTY. LTD. V. PORT JACKSON STEVEDORING PTY. LTD.**
*(The New York Star)*
1980, 2 Lloyd's Rep. 317 (P.C.)

The plaintiffs were the consignees of 37 razor blades shipped on the vessel *New York Star* in New Brunswick (Canada), for delivery at Sydney (Australia). A bill of lading was issued in Quebec (Canada) on the Blue Star Line, and contained, inter alia, these provisions: (cls.2) a Himalaya clause extending the benefit of de-

---

[173] See *Barclays Bank Ltd. v. Commissioners of Customs and Excise, 1963, 1 Lloyd's Rep. 81.*
[174] Clarke J: *"The precise nature of the exceptions will no doubt require further consideration in the future."*

fences and immunities conferred by the bill of lading upon the carrier to independent contractors; (cls.5) the carrier's responsibility as carrier should terminate as soon as the goods left the ship's tackle and thereafter would continue as an ordinary bailee; (cls.8) delivery of the goods was deemed to be taken by the consignees from the vessel's rail; and (cls.17) a one-year time bar provision for claimants to bring her suit. The first defendants were engaged by the shipowners as their agents at the port of discharge; the second defendants were appointed as stevedores by the first defendants. When the goods were discharged at Sydney they were put in a separate warehouse to provide greater security. A thief approached the watchman of the warehouse and said he had come for the razor blades. The watchman told him to go to the delivery office and he did. He saw him speak to one of the tally clerks and thought he was authorised to take delivery. The thief loaded part of the goods onto his truck and left at a high speed without having presented a sole document. After twelve months from the time the goods were supposed to be delivered, the lawful consignee of the bill of lading claimed damages from the shipowners' agents and the stevedores.

***Held (for the both defendants):* i)** The shipowners' agents had never been in possession of the goods. Subsequently, the plaintiffs' action seeking damages from the shipowners' agents as alleged bailees of the cargo failed. **ii)** In relation to the action as against the stevedores, their lordships gave effect to clause 2 of the bill of lading. *"The Himalaya clause is capable of conferring upon a third person falling with the description (of cls.2) defences and immunities conferred upon the carrier as if such persons were parties to the contract contained or evidenced by the bill of lading".* The stevedores, as independent contractors, fell within the meaning of clause 2, and so, were conferred the benefit of cls. 17 of the bill of lading-the time bar clause.[175] **iii)** *"Thirdly, as to fundamental breach, the proposition that exemption clauses may be held inapplicable to certain breaches of contract as a matter of construction of the contract (…) was not disputed. The 'fundamental nature of the breach' (as the plaintiffs referred to the stevedore's act of negligence) did not deprive the stevedores of the contractual benefit of clause 17."*[176]

## 198
### SCANDINAVIAN TRADING TANKER CO. V. FLOTA PETROLERA ECUATORIANA
*(The scaptrade)*
1983, 2 Lloyd's Rep. 253 (H.L.)

The tanker *Scaptrade* was originally chartered for 12 months 30 days on the Shelltime 3 form. The charter had become, by extension, a three-year charter. It included, in clause 8 of the charterparty, a withdrawal proviso for default in payment, which was to be made monthly in advance. In July 1979, one year before the expiration of the charterparty, the freight market was rising steeply over the charter rate. At that time, the charterers failed to pay on the date due.. Four days later, the owners gave notice of withdrawal to

---

[175] See also *The Eurymedon* and *The Mahkutai*.
[176] See *Photoproduction Ltd. v. Securicor Transport Ltd.*

the charterers. Tender of the overdue hire was made on the following day, but the owners refused to accept it. After some negotiations, the vessel was re-chartered by the owners to the same charterers on a "without prejudice" agreement. The question about the rate of hire to be applied to the subsequent charter (i.e. the prior charter rate or at the market rate) was left for litigation.

**Held (for the owners):** (Lord Diplock) **i)** *"A time charter, unless it is a charter by demise,…transfers to the charterer no interest in or right to possession of the vessel; it is a contract for services to be rendered to the charterer by the shipowner through the use of the vessel by the shipowner's own servants, the master and the crew, acting in accordance with such directions as to the cargoes to be loaded and the voyages to be undertaken as by the terms of the charter-party the charterer is entitled to give to them. Being a contract for services it is thus the very prototype of a contract of which before the fusion of law and equity a court would never grant specific performance."* On the basis of this argument[177] their lordships held that *"if the withdrawal clause so provides, the shipowner is entitled to withdraw the services of the vessel from the charterer if the latter fails to pay an instalment of hire in precise compliance with the provisions of the charter. So the shipowner commits no breach of contract if he does so; and the charterer has no remedy in damages against him".*[178] **ii)** (Lord Diplock) *"To grant an injunction restraining the shipowner from exercising his right*

*of withdrawal of the vessel from the service of the charterer, though negative in form, is pregnant with an affirmative order to the shipowner to perform the contract; juristically it is indistinguishable from a decree for specific performance of a contract to render services; and in respect of that category of contracts, even in the event of a breach, this is a remedy that English Courts have always disclaimed any jurisdiction to grant."*

**199**
**SCHELDE DELTA SHIPPING B.V. V. ASTARTE SHIPPING LTD.**
*(The Pamela)*
1995, 2 Lloyd's Rep. 249 (Q.B.)

The owners of the vessel *Pamela* let her for a period delivery of 3/3/3/3 months in charterers' option fifteen days more or less at charterers' option. Payment became due every fifteen days in advance. The charter provided, inter alia, the following clauses: "7…In default of payment the owners to have the right of withdrawing the vessel from the service of the charterers without noting any protest and without interference by any court or any other formality whatsoever. See clause 27". If hire is due and not received, the owners before exercising the option of withdrawing the vessel will give charterers forty-eight (48) hours notice, Saturday, Sunday and Holidays excluded, and will not withdraw the vessel if the hire is paid within these 48 hours." The vessel was delivered to the charterers on Aug. 19, 1994. On Friday, Dec. 2, 1994, the eighth instalment was not punctually paid and the owners gave notice in accordance with cl. 27 of the charter. The notice was

---

[177] See *The Chikuma.*
[178] See *The Laconia* and *The Afovos.*

received by the charterers at 23:41 hours that night, a time at which the office had already closed for the weekend. The vessel was withdrawn on Dec. 7 on the ground of non-payment. There were two issues to be resolved: (i) whether the notice was considered to be 'received' at the moment it was recorded by the charterers' telex machine or at the opening of their business on the following Monday; and (ii) whether the notice so sent complied with the requirements under the anti-technicality clause. The matter was brought to the arbitrators who found for the charterers. Owners appealed.

***Held (for the charterers):*** (Gatehouse, J.)
**i)** *"What matters is not when the notice is given/sent/despatched/issued by the owners but when its content reaches the mind of the charterer. If the telex is sent in ordinary business hours, the time of receipt is the same as the time of despatch because it is not open to the charterer to contend that it did not in fact then come to his attention; a notice which arrives at 23.41 on a Friday night is not to be expected to be read before opening hours on the following Monday, and that was a conclusion of fact arrived at by the arbitrators as a matter of commercial common sense."* The tribunal was right in finding that the notice sent under the anti-technicality clause (cl.27) was not, in fact, received by the charterers until the start of the business day on Dec. 5, and it was not premature or invalid.
**ii)** In relation to the requirements of the notice, Gatehouse, J. added: *"In addition to the notification that hire is overdue, the notice itself must clearly tell the charterers that the Owners require them to remedy their default within 48 hours or risk los-*

*ing the vessel; the bare message 'please notify charterers of withdrawal of the vessel' is not sufficient".* On that ground, the notice was found ambiguous and not valid under cls. 27 of the charter.[179]

<br>

**200**
## SCHULER (L.) A.G. v. WICKMAN MACHINE TOOL SALES LTD.
### 1973, 2 Lloyd's Rep. 53 (H.L.)

In 1963 the respondent (Wickman) entered into a "distributorship agreement" with the appellant (Schuler). The former was a selling organisation and the latter a manufacturer of panel presses used by motor manufacturers. Under the "distributorship agreement", Schuler granted to Wickman the right to sell Schuler products in the United Kingdom. For that purpose, Wickman were to act as agents for Schuler. Wickman's obligations with regards to the promotion of sales were contained, inter alia, in clause 7: headed "Promotion by Sales": "...(b) it shall be a condition of this Agreement that (i) Sales shall send its representatives to visit the six firms (the largest manufacturers of cars in U.K.) at least once in every week for the purpose of soliciting orders for panel presses (ii) the same representative shall visit each firm on each occasion unless there are unavoidable reasons preventing the visit being made by that representative in which case the visit shall be made by an alternate representative and sales will ensure that such a visit is always made by the same alternate representative." Clause 11

---

[179] See *The Rio Sun* and *The Afovos*.

stated that the contract would last until the end of 1967 provided, inter alia, that Wickman had communicated (by notice in writing) any material breach committed and have failed to remedy it within 60 days of being required in writing to do so. Regarding the contract, Wickman was required to make 1.400 visits during the period of the agreement. It happened that Wickman failed in their duties to perform the stipulated number of visits. In 1964 Schuler terminated the contract by treating that failure as a repudiatory breach. The main question on appeal was whether a clause headed to be a condition should necessarily be regarded as such, entitling the innocent party to terminate the contract because of its breach by the other party.

**Held**[180] **(for wickman):** The failure to comply with clause 7 is not a breach of a condition although the clause was described as such. Since each firm had to be visited more than 200 times, it seems unreasonable that just one missing visit is enough to entitle the appellant to discharge the contract. Lord Reid: *"This is so unreasonable that it must make me search for some other possible meaning of the contract. The word 'condition' would make a breach of clause 7(b), however excusable, a material breach. That would then entitle Schuler to give notice under clause 11 requiring the breach to be remedied. There would be no point in giving such a notice if Wickman were clearly not in fault but, if it were given, Wickman would have no difficulty in showing that the breach had been* remedied. *If Wickman were at fault then on receiving such a notice, they would have to amend their system so that they could show that the breach had been remedied. If they did not do that within the period of the notice, then Schuler would be entitled to rescind. In my view, that is a possible and reasonable construction of the contract…".* Lord Morris: *"It was not the intention of the parties to give to the word 'condition' in clause 7(b) the meaning contended for by the appellants, viz. "a stipulation such that any breach of it however slight would give the promisee a right to be quit of his future obligations and sue for damages".* Lord Simon of Glaisdale: *"To read 'condition' in clause 7(b) in what I regard as its primary sense as a term of art produces…such absurd results that this cannot be the meaning to be ascribed to it, provided that it is reasonably capable of some other meaning. I agree with (Lord Reid) that, in the light of the rest of the contract, it means a contractual term breach of which if unremedied (i.e. unrectified for the future, if capable of rectification) gives Schuler the right to terminate the contract in accordance with clause 11".*

---

## 201
### Seaconsar Far East Ltd. v. Bank Markazi Jomhouri Islami Iran
1997, 2 Lloyd's Rep. 89 (Q.B.)

The defendant was the bank appointed by the buyers to issue a letter of credit in favour of the claimant sellers. The cargo was to be shipped in partial shipments as agreed under the sale contract. The credit allowed the sellers to present documents to the bank in sequences corresponding to each shipment. On Jan. 16, 1987, the

---

[180] Lord Wilberforce dissenting.

paying bank and the sellers were both advised that the credit was opened. After the first shipment, the relevant documents were presented to the paying bank, which found seven discrepancies. Four of these discrepancies were remedied by the sellers' representative at a meeting with the paying bank's clerk on Oct. 5, but three remained. The paying bank subsequently refused payment based on the discrepancies and retained the documents at the sellers' order. Sellers argued that they were unaware that the documents had been rejected. After the second shipment, four discrepancies were found by the paying bank in the relevant documents tendered. The paying bank rejected the documents again and retained them at the sellers' order sending a telex with the message "please instruct, meanwhile documents held at your risk and disposal". The sellers subsequently sued the issuing bank, and the court considered the following questions: (i) Could the documents relating to the first shipment be rejected orally under art. 16(d) UCP 400: Rev. 1983? (ii) Were the documents relating to the second shipment rejected within the time constraints of art. 16(c)?

***Held (for the issuing bank):*** **i)** For the purposes of art. 16(d), which is equivalent to art. 14(d)i. of the UCP 500 (Rev.1993), it is enough that the bank's notice (1) conveys that the documents have been rejected, (2) points to the discrepancies found, and (3) returns the documents or provides notification that they remain at the disposal of the sellers. In the present case, it was proved that the sellers' representative was informed of these three issues at the meeting with the bank's clerk on Oct. 5.

The wording of art. 16 requires the bank to give notice of rejection "by telecommunication or, if that is not possible, by other expeditious means…to the beneficiary…". Tuckey J. took the view that provided that a "face to face" meeting is possible just immediately after the bank has decided to refuse the documents, an oral rejection will be valid because a rejection could not have been telecommunicated without delay. On the evidence, the most "expeditious means" of informing the sellers was in attendance of their representative at the bank. **ii)** As to the documents corresponding to the second shipment, the question differed in that the issue was whether the paying bank made notice of rejection within a "reasonable time", as required by article 16(c).[181] Tuckey J. considered that the longer a bank takes to decide whether or not the documents are to be rejected the less time it has to notify the presenter of the documents of the decision. In the present case, the documents were received by the bank on Dec. 3 and the decision to reject was taken Dec. 4, but the telex to the sellers was not sent until Dec. 8. It was impossible for the judge to set rigid rules attending to the different sizes and procedures of banks and transactions. In this case, however, he took the view that no undue delays were produced as in relation to the notice of rejection. Since the notice was given at the beginning of the fourth working day after the receipt of the documents, the bank's decision was communicated within a "reasonable time".

---

[181] Note that the equivalent art. 14(d)i of the UCP 500 (Rev. 1993) provides a maximum of 7 banking days following the day of receipt the documents. See *Bayerische Vereinsbank v. National Bank of Pakistan.*

## 202
### SEA SUCCESS MARITIME INC. V. AFRICAN MARITIME CARRIERS LTD.
*(The Sea Success)*
2005, EWHC 1542 (Q.B.)

Sea Success Maritime Inc. time-chartered its vessel to African Maritime Carriers on the New York Produce Exchange Form. The vessel was further sub-time-chartered on similar terms. During the trip, the master twice refused to accept cargoes of steel pipes and coils because they were damaged. The master justified his refusal to load based on the final sentence of clause 52 of the time charter, which stated that he had 'the right and must reject any cargo that are subject to clausing of the bills of lading'. 'Clausing' is trade usage for any modification to a bill of lading by a master to denote that the goods or their packaging were received in a defective condition. There was no dispute as to the actual condition of the steel cargo in question. The parties agreed that the steel coils were rusty and had dents and buckles. The charterers claimed that the master had no good reason for refusing to load because they were willing to accurately declare the damaged condition of the goods in the bill of lading. The vessel's owner argued that it was impractical to expect a master to have discussions with shippers or charterers at a loading port on how to describe the cargo that is being or is about to be loaded.

***Held (for the owners):*** The ship-owner agreed to allow its vessel to be employed by charterers to carry different types of cargo, as defined in the charterparty. It is for the time charterers to decide how the vessel should be employed. Subject to any restrictions in the charterparty, the charterers are entitled to order the vessel to carry any lawful merchandise. In a time charter, the master is obliged to sign bills of lading "as presented" by charterers, but there is no requirement that the bills should describe the cargo as being in "good condition". If the bill of lading fairly describes the cargo and the master signs a bill that says that the goods are in "apparent good order and condition" all he would be doing is to confirm that the description of the goods in the bill of lading is "proper". However, if the master has to make a notation on the bill to reconcile the goods' description with the statement that they are in "apparent good order and condition", then the cargo would have been subject to clausing of the bill of lading.

## 203
### SEATRADE GRONINGEN BV V. GEEST INDUSTRIES LTD.
*(The Frost Express)*
1996, 2 Lloyd's Rep. 375 (C.A.)

Seatrade Groning BV were the managers of a pool of reefer ships under an agreement (the pooling agreement) made with various shipowners. Under the pooling agreement the shipowners authorised Seatrade (the managers) to enter into contracts for the employment of the shipowners' vessels on their behalf. Pursuant to this agreement, the managers entered into a contract for the chartering of some vessels (the "chartering contract") with Geest Industries Ltd. (the charterers). Under the chartering contract the managers and the charterers entered into a charterparty for a particular vessel called *Frost Express*. In Box 3 calling Owners/Place of business of the charterparty, the name of the managers appeared "as agents to owners or as disponent owners". In the box headed "Signature (owners)" at the bottom, the signature of the director of the managers appeared without any qualification. It was alleged by the charterers that the cargo on board the *Frost Express* had been improperly refrigerated and suffered damages. The managers then sought a declaration that they were not a party to the contract as they contracted as agents for the disponent owners, Lawin Maritime Co.

***Held (for the charterers):*** **i)** Although the charterers knew that the managers were authorized by the shipowners to enter into contracts on their behalf, they could not be presumed to be aware of the terms of the pooling agreement or of the precise extent of the authority given to the managers. **ii)** In the charter, the party who undertook the obligations of the shipowners were the managers "as agents to owners or as disponent owners". It would be absurd to hold that the director of the managers undertook his personal and individual liability by the mere fact that his signature was stamped with no qualification. **iii)** (Evans, L.J.) *"...the description of Seatrade 'as agents' in the body of the charter does not necessarily preclude their liability as principals, and even though (the director's) signature can be read in conjunction with Box 3, it does not follow...that his signature should be regarded as qualified by the words 'as agent' which refer to Seatrade in Box 3. The signature itself is unqualified and the fact that it was not expressly made on behalf of Seatrade does not affect the nature of Seatrade's obligations which are derived*

*from the whole of the charter-party terms. Finally, if Seatrade undertakes personal liability... there is no disparity between the two situations envisaged in Box 3. It is immaterial to charterers whether Seatrade was disponent owner or agent to owners in the particular case, if in both cases Seatrade is personally liable. If on the other hand Seatrade is personally liable in one case but not the other, then the charterers do not know to which party they should look for performance of the charter-party without going outside the charter-party itself."*

**204**

**SENG, SOON HUA V. GLENCORE GRAIN LTD.**

1996, 1 Lloyd's Rep. 398 (Q.B.)

The claimants entered into two contracts for the sale of Thai rice in bulk to the defendants. The contract called for the goods to be shipped "c.& f. liner-terms Rotterdam... full out-turn weight at port of destination". Quality, condition and fumigation was "final at time of shipment as per certificate independent surveyors...". Payment was to be effected upon arrival of the vessel but not later than fourty five days after bill of lading date. While the vessel was in transit she ran aground, resulting in a total loss. Within the above-mentioned fourty five-day period, the documents were twice rejected by the buyers on different grounds, like, for example, that the bill of lading had been issued FIOT (i.e. free in out trimmed), and not liner terms as agreed in the contract. The sellers sued the buyers claiming damages. The sellers contended that the contracts did not contain any requirement that the bill of lading contain liner terms, and alternatively, that any such requirement was an innominate term which did not entitle buyers to reject. In the respondents' notice, the buyers argued that no price ever became due since there was never any outturn.

***Held (for the buyers):*** (Mance, J.) **i)** "Liner terms" indicate that discharge is at the carrier's responsibility. That refers to a right of indemnity and continuous documentary cover, which buyers must be generally given as against the carrier until the goods have been effectively discharged. However, a FIOT contract of carriage imposes a number of charges, obligations and responsibilities on the buyers that conflicts with the contract's terms. *"Sellers were bound under each contract to make a 'proper' contract of affreightment and to procure a 'proper' bill of lading. In the context of the present contracts, a proper contract and bill of lading means a contract and bill not merely covering carriage to destination, but also providing for discharge at destination on liner terms."* **ii)** *"On the basis that the carriage contracts and bills of lading should have stipulated for discharge on liner terms, the next question is whether their failure to do so justified the buyers' rejection of the documents; In principle, I consider that presence in the bills of lading of provision for discharge on liner terms was a condition precedent to buyers' obligation to take up the documents. It is of the nature of documentary requirements that they should be strictly complied with. This is so whether or not a third party such as a bank is involved in the transaction."*[182] On these grounds, by tendering a bill of lading FIOT the sellers

were in breach of a condition of the contract. Hence, buyers were entitled to reject the documents. **iii)** The words "full outturn weight at port of destination" mean that, when the goods arrive and outturn, they are to be weighed and the price to be invoiced thereupon will be adjusted by reference to the outturn weight. This clause is intended only for the determination of the price, but does not affect itself the true nature of a c. & f. contract whereby risk on the goods pass on or as from shipment. *"[T]he contracts must be viewed as essentially c. & f. in their nature, with the simple proviso that, if and when the goods do arrive and outturn, they will be weighed and the price will in that event be adjusted by reference to the outturn weight. If the goods covered by the shipping documents and invoice are lost in transit and do not arrive at all, the risk of loss remains on the buyers and no question of any adjustment to the payment due against the commercial invoice can arise."*

<hr>

[182] See *SIAT di dal Ferro v. Tradax Overseas S.A.*

## 205

**SERENA NAVIGATION LTD. AND ANOTHER v. DERA COMMERCIAL ESTABLISHMENT AND ANOTHER**
*(The Limnos)*
2008, 2 Lloyd's Rep. 166 (Q.B.)

A cargo of 43, 998, 66 m of US corn was carried from Louisiana (USA) to Aqaba (Jordan) on the carrier's vessel *Limnos*. The Hague-Visby Rules were incorporated into the bill of lading. In Aqaba, it was discovered that a small amount of wetting damage had occurred apparently by leaky hatch covers. The damaged cargo, of about 12 m, was separated from the remainder and disposed of. In addition, up to 250 m of the cargo was also damaged because it had to be offloaded with bulldozers, resulting in an increased number of broken kernels. The total amount of cargo physically damaged, roughly 262 m, was referred to as "the conceded tonnage". There was no issue that the conceded cargo would fall within the definition of "goods lost or damaged" contained in Article IV Rule 5(a) of the Hague-Visby Rules. Unexpectedly, the whole cargo discharged in Aqaba acquired a reputation in the market as a distressed cargo. As a consequence, its sound arrived market price decreased substantially. The question was if the decrease of value of the sound cargo matched the meaning of the words "goods lost or damaged" in Article IV Rule 5(a) of the Hague-Visby Rules.[183]

***Held (for the carrier):*** Per Burton, J.: "*I am not persuaded by … [the] submission that lost or damaged goods are necessarily to be construed in the same way as loss or damage. Loss and damage is a familiar expression in the field of tort and contract. It normally, though not necessarily, suggests that loss is economic and damages is physical, though there seems to be no etymological reason why that should be so. The words are very frequently found together to cover all kinds of loss in the sense of loss incurred. However, in my judgment the expression lost or damaged goods is referring to two categories of goods, goods that are lost in the sense of vanished, gone, disappeared, destroyed, and goods that are damaged, in the sense of not being lost, but surviving in damaged form. The two expressions, in my judgment, in this context do not carry the same meaning, and so … [the] attempt to construe the latter by reference to the former fails. It was neither possible nor sensible to describe the undamaged cargo as "economically damaged." The cargo's value may have been affected, its price decreased or its value depreciated, but it was not sensible to classify the undamaged cargo in such a way so that it may fall under Article IV Rule 5(a).*

## 206
### S.I.A.T. DI DAL FERRO V. TRADAX OVERSEAS S.A.
1980, 1 Lloyd's Rep. 53 (C.A.)

The plaintiffs bought a quantity of soyabean meal c.i.f. free out Venice (Italy) from the seller-defendants. The sellers forwarded an additional memorandum of the contract which included an additional memorandum whereby the buyers were obliged to accept documents, even if defective or incomplete, provided that the sellers wire a performance bond. The buyers neither react to nor answered the memorandum and decided to merely file it. When the documents were tendered, they were rejected by the buyer's bank on the grounds that (i) one bill of lading stated "destination as per charterparty" and no charterparty had been in fact attached, and (ii) the other bill of lading stated "Ancona/Ravenna". The sellers then assured the buyers that the destination appearing in the charterparty was Venice and offered to hold the buyers harmless from any consequence or liability arising out of this fact. The bills of lading

---

[183] Article IV Rule 5(a): "…neither the carrier nor the ship shall in any event be or become liable for any loss or damage to or in connection with the goods in an amount exceeding 666.67 units of account per package or unit or 2 units of account per kilogramme of gross weight of the goods lost or damaged, whichever is the higher.

were altered by crossing out "destination as per charterparty" and "Ancona/Ravenna" and, instead, inserting in both bills the word "Venice". They were presented again to the bank but they were again rejected.

***Held (for the buyers):*** **i)** Contrary to the buyers' submission, the additional memorandum did form part of the contract. Since in previous transactions between the buyers and the sellers, the former had expressly accepted the latter's additional memorandum, the failure to sign and return the confirmation this time was due to a mere oversight.[184] The buyers ought to have done something positive to express their rejection. **ii)** As no performance guarantee stricto sensu was received by the buyers, these were entitled to reject the "Ancona/Ravenna" bill of lading showing destinations other than Venice. They were also entitled to reject the bill of lading showing "destination as per charterparty", even if the charterparty were attached to the documents, in so far as Venice was only one of the two ports appearing in the charterparty to which the charterer could order the vessel to go.[185] **iii)** Alterations on the bill of lading did not cure the pre-existing defects so as to oblige the buyers to treat them as acceptable. Under c.i.f. terms, buyers are entitled to reject any document which is not "reasonable and ready to pass current in commerce". Accordingly, the buyers were also entitled to reject the bills of lading with the crossed words "destination as per charterparty" and "Anconna/Ravena" and adding "Venice".

---

[184] See *Jayaar Impex v Toaken Group Ltd.*
[185] See *The Northern Progress.*

## 207
### SIBOTI K/S v. BP FRANCE S.A.
### 2003, Lloyd's Rep 364

The claimant chartered its vessel *Siboti* on the Asbatankvoy form dated 16 Oct. 2001 to Enron International Corporation (EIC) through Enron Europe Finance and Trading Ltd. (EEFT) for a carriage of petroleum products from India to France via Malta. The voyage charterparty contained the following clause: 49. Governing Law/Dispute Resolution …the parties hereby agree as follows: (a) This Charter Party shall be construed and interpreted in accordance with, and governed by, the laws of England. (b) … any dispute of whatsoever nature arising under this Charter-Party shall be determined by the English [Court] … and the parties hereby expressly submit to the exclusive jurisdiction of the English … Courts … (c) All bills of lading under this Charter Party shall incorporate this exclusive dispute resolution clause … Acknowledgment of shipment of the cargo in apparent good order and condition by Enron Capital and Trade Resources International Corporation (ECTRIC) through EEFT for carriage to and delivery at Sete, France was made by the claimant under a bill of lading dated Malta 19 Nov., 2001. The bill of lading included the following: "This shipment is carried under and pursuant to the terms of the charter dated between … and all the terms whatsoever of the said charter apply to and govern the rights of the parties concerned in this shipment". The cargo was discharged at Sete; however, EIC failed to pay both the freight and the loadport demurrage allegedly due under the charterparty. Claimants subsequently sought to recover freight and demurrage due from the defendant, arguing that the defendant, as an indorsee of the bill of lading and lawful holder thereof, was bound by the exclusive English jurisdiction clause (EJC) which gave the English court jurisdiction pursuant art. 23 of Council Regulation (EC) 44/2001 (the Regulation). The defendant argued that the English court lacked jurisdiction and that jurisdiction lay with the courts in France, its country of domicile pursuant art. 2 of the Regulation. The principal issue before the court was whether the ECJ was incorporated into the bill of lading.

***Held:*** The ECJ was not incorporated into the bill of lading for the following reasons. First, the words "… all the terms whatsoever of the said charter…" of the bill of lading were too general and failed to explicitly refer to the ECJ. Furthermore, based on case law, general wording such as "all terms," in the words of the judge, is *"insufficient to incorporate an ancillary[186] charter-party arbitration clause into a bill of lading: Thomas v. Portsea: The Federal Bulker. The same result must follow with regard to charter-party jurisdiction clauses. Does the addition of the word "whatsoever" make all the difference? I do not think it does or should"*. A distinction must be made between general words of incorporation and explicit reference to ancillary clauses in the charterparty. With or without the word "whatsoever", the incorporation wording

in the bill of lading was general wording. Subsequently, if the wording "all the terms whatsoever" is insufficient to incorporate the EJC (cl. 49 (b) of the charter-party), then the wording is insufficient too to bring cl. 49 (e) of the charter-party into the bill of lading in any manner; plainly, cl. 49 (e) is every bit as ancillary to the subject-matter of the bill of lading as the EJC itself. How might the EJC have been successfully incorporated into the bill of lading? *"Had the original parties to the bill of lading intended to do so, they could very simply have put the matter beyond argument, by doing no more than adding to the language of incorporation in the bill of lading the words 'including the dispute resolution clause'"*.

**208**

**Soproma Spa v. Marine & Animal By-Products Corp.**
1966, 1 Lloyd's Rep. 367 (Q.B.)

Italian buyers entered into a purchase contract of "fish full meal" from US sellers in terms c. & f. Savona. An irrevocable confirmed letter of credit was opened stipulating the presentation of the following documents: (1) full set of clean shipped bills of lading issued to order, blank endorsed and marked with the words "freight prepaid"; and (2) an analysis certificate stating that the goods had a minimum of 70% protein content. The sellers presented to the advising bank a set of bills of lading marked "freight collect" and they were not issued "to order". They also presented an analysis certificate showing a protein content of only 67%. The bills of lading described the goods as "Fishmeal" whilst the invoice referred to

---

[186] A distinction must be made between ancillary provisions contained a bill of lading in reference to a charterparty, such as arbitration clauses and provisions which are directly germane to the shipment, carriage and delivery of the goods. General wording is sufficient to incorporate the latter, but not the former.

them as "Fish Full Meal". The documents were rejected by the bank. The period of validity of the credit having expired, sellers made a second tender directly to the buyers adding a freight receipt and an analysis showing a 70% protein content. That out-of-credit second tender was also rejected. The sellers sued the buyers for wrongful rejection of the goods.

***Held (for the buyers):*** (McNair, J.) **i)** The first tender of documents to the bank was defective in so far as the documents showed a number of discrepancies, namely that: (a) The bills of lading were marked "freight collect". Even if accompanied with a freight receipt, they would not fit the stipulation of the credit since they were supposed to be marked. (b) The bills of lading were straight bills consigned to Marine Midland Trust Co. and not issued to the order as stipulated in the letter of credit. McNair J. found that *"The bills of lading in this condition would not have been a good tender under a c.i.f. contract or c. & f. contract at common law since the essential characteristic of these forms of contract is that by the shipping documents the buyer to whom the property passes under bills of lading is given contractual rights which he can by endorsement transfer to a subsequent purchaser"*; and (c) The analysis certificate showed a deficiency in the minimum protein content. **ii)** Nevertheless, the description of the bill of lading in general terms ("Fishmeal") was found to be in accordance with the terms of the credit. The goods were correctly described in the commercial invoice according to art. 33 UCP: 1951 (equivalent to art. 37.c UCP: Rev. 1993), and no inconsistency was noted in the bill of lading

description as in relation to the other documents.[187] **iii)** The second direct tender was irrelevant. Bypassing the letter of credit was not justified and thus was ineffective. The judge said: *"It seems to me to be quite inconsistent with the express terms of a contract such as this to hold that the Sellers have an alternative right to obtain payment from the buyers by presenting the documents directly to the buyers".*[188]

**209**

**SPILIADA MARITIME CORP. V. CANSULEX LTD.**
*(The Spiliada)*
1987, 1 Lloyd's Rep. 1 (H.L.)

The owners chartered their ship *Spiliada* to an Indian firm called Minerals & Metals Trading Corporation of India (hereinafter M.M.T.C.) for a carriage of sulphur from Vancouver to Indian ports. The owners were registered in Liberia and the ship flew the Liberian flag, but the managers were based in Greece and some part of their business was conducted from England. The charterparty provided for London arbitration. The cargo of sulphur was loaded by order of Cansulex, an export firm based in British Columbia which sold it on f.o.b. terms to M.M.T.C. Cansulex, as shippers, took delivery and accepted bills of lading

---

[187] In contrast with *Rayner (J.H.) & Co. Ltd. v Hambro's Bank Ltd.*, where the doctrine of strict compliance was strongly applied. The Soproma case distinguished from the Rayner in that the former was decided on the basis of the UCP (as included in the letter of credit) but the latter was not.

[188] Contrast with *Alan (W.J.) & Co. Ltd. v El Nasr Export & Import. Co.*

that were expressly construed and governed by English law. The owners alleged that the cargo of sulphur was wet when loaded and caused severe corrosion to the holds and tank tops of the vessel. They claimed damages against Cansulex, as shippers, under the contract of carriage evidenced by the bills of lading on the ground of art. 4(6) of the Hague Rules incorporated in the bills, and on a warranty implied by English law that dangerous cargo could not be shipped without notice to the owners. Leave was obtained to issue and serve the writ upon Cansulex outside the jurisdiction. Cansulex then applied for an order to set aside such leave and all subsequent proceedings on the ground that English courts were "forum non conveniens".

***Held (for the owners):*** (Lord Goff)[189] "…
*it is to be observed that the owners' cause of action against Cansulex in the present case must have been accrued in November, 1980 (when the loading of the cargo on board Spiliada in Vancouver was completed) and so was prima facie time barred in British Columbia by November, 1982,…In my judgment, had the point arisen, I would have been minded to hold that, in all the circumstances of the case, the owners had acted reasonably in commencing proceedings in this country, and that they had not acted unreasonably in failing to commence proceedings in British Columbia before the expiry of the limitation period there. In these circumstances, had I agreed with the Court of Appeal that the judge erred in the exercise of his discretion, I would nevertheless only have set aside the proceedings, to enable proceedings to be brought in British Columbia, on the condition that Cansulex should waive its right to rely on the time bar in British Columbia."*

---

[189] See the principles set out in the following authorities quoted by Lord Goff in their judgment: (Lord Kinnear) *Sim v. Robinson* [1892] 19 R. 665, p. 668: *"…the plea can never be sustained unless the court is satisfied that there is some other tribunal, having competent jurisdiction, in which the case may be tried more suitably for the interests of all the parties and for the ends of justice.";* *Clements v. Macaulay* [1866] 4 M. 583, p. 594: (Lord Cowan) *"The object, under the words 'forum non conveniens' is to find that forum which is the more suitable for the ends of justice, and is preferable because pursuit of the litigation in that forum is more likely to secure those ends.";* *MacShannon v. Rockware Glass Ltd.* [1978] A.C. 795, p. 812: (Lord Diplock) *"In order to justify a stay two conditions must be satisfied, one positive and the other negative: (a) the defendant must satisfy he court that there is another forum to whose jurisdiction he is amenable in which justice can be done between the parties at substantially less inconvenience and expense, and (b) the stay must not deprive the plaintiff of a legitimate personal or juridical advantage which would be available to him if he invoked the jurisdiction of the English court".*

## 210
### SPURLING LTD. V. BRADSHAW
1956, 1 Lloyd's Rep. 392 (C.A.)

A merchant bought eight casks of orange juice and deposited them into a warehouse. The warehousemen sent a receipt which on its face said: "The Company's conditions as printed on the back hereof cover the goods held in accordance with this notice". On the receipt's back there were the so-called "Contract Conditions" in small print. These included the following disclaimer: "We will not in any circumstances…be liable for any loss, damage or detention howsoever, whensoever, or wheresoever occasioned in respect of any goods entrusted to or carried or handled by us in the course of our business, even when such loss, damage or detention may have been occasioned by the negligence, wrongful act or default of ourselves or our servants or agents or others for whose acts we would otherwise be responsible". There was a dispute over the rent due and the warehouseman brought a claim against the merchant for the unpaid balance. The merchant then counter-claimed alleging that some of the goods had been damaged while stored owing to the warehouseman's negligence.

***Held (for the warehouseman):*** (Denning, L.J.) **i)** *"The essence of the contract by a warehouseman is that he will store the goods in the contractual place and deliver them on demand to the bailor or his order. If he stores them in a different place, or if he consumes or destroys them instead of storing them, or if he sells them, or delivers them without excuse to somebody else, he is guilty of a breach which goes to the root of the contract and he cannot rely on the exempting clause. But if he should happen to damage them by some momentary piece of inadvertence, then he is able to rely on the exempting clause: because negligence by itself, without more, is not a breach which goes to the root of the contract."* **ii)** *"Another thing to remember about these exempting clauses is that in the ordinary way the burden is on the bailee to bring himself within the exception. A bailor, by pleading and presenting his case properly, can always put on the bailee the burden of proof. In the case of non-delivery, for instance, all he need to plead is the contract and a failure to deliver on demand…Likewise with goods that are returned by the bailee in a damaged condition, the burden is on him to show that the damage was done without his fault; or that, if fault there was, it was excused by the exempting clause."* **iii)** *"This brings me to the question whether this clause was part of the contract; I* (Denning, L.J.) *quite agree that the more unreasonable a clause is, the greater the notice which must be given of it. Some clauses I have seen would need to be printed in red ink on the face of the document with a red hand pointing to it before the notice could be held to be sufficient. The clause in this case…does not call for such exceptional treatment, especially when it is construed, as it should be, subject to the proviso that it only applies when the warehouseman is carrying out his contract and not when he is deviating from it or breaking it in a radical respect."*[190] The result was that, although the warehouseman was found negligent, the conditions on the back were part of the contract of bailment and did exempt him from liability.[191]


## 211
### SOUFFLET NEGOCE v. BUNGE S.A.
[2010] EWCA Civ 1102 (C.A.)

Goods were sold on f.o.b. terms for delivery "between 9th - 22nd Oct. 2006 at Buyers' call both dates included (no extension)". Weight, quality and condition

---

[190] For the "red hand" rule see also *Phoenix Insurance Company of Hartford v. De Monchy, 1929, 45 T.L.R. 543; MacLeod Ross & Co. Ltd. v. Compagnie d'Assurances Générales L'Helvetia of St. Gall, 1952, W.N. 56; Interfoto Picture Library Ltd. v. Stiletto Visual Programmes Ltd., 1988, 2 W.L.R. 615.*

[191] Some points of the judgment could perhaps now be revisited under the light of the *Unfair Terms in Consumer Contracts Regulations 1999.*

were agreed final at load port as per surveyor's certificates at "sellers' option and costs". The contract incorporated GAFTA Form No. 49. Clause 6 of GAFTA 49 provides that "the sellers shall have the goods ready to be delivered to the buyers at any time within the contract period of delivery... provided the vessel is presented at the loading port in readiness to load within the delivery period, sellers shall if necessary complete loading after the delivery period...". The sale contract also contained "shipping terms", which included laytime and demurrage provisions and required a valid tender of a notice of readiness (NOR) and referred "all other terms and conditions as per relevant c/p". On 22 Oct. 2006, the ship tendered NOR at the loadport, but the sellers' surveyor issued a certificate on that same day saying the vessel's holds were not fit to receive and carry the cargo due to coal residue. The next morning, the master advised the vessel's holds were ready for re-inspection. By that time, the sellers had already declared the buyers in default of the sale contract on the grounds that the vessel had not been presented ready to load within the delivery period. The buyers sued the sellers for damages for non-delivery of the goods.

***Held (for the buyers):*** Whether or not the cargo holds were clean and fit to receive the cargo was irrelevant from the sellers' point of view because they were not at risk if the goods were damaged in the ship's holds. Sellers were bound to commence loading when the vessel was capable to load the goods. The Court of Appeal distinguished the reference to a NOR in a charter party from the words "readiness to load" in an FOB sale contract. "Readiness to load" did not mean that a valid NOR must have been given or must have been capable of being given by the shipowners, because that was not what GAFTA 49 said. Rather, the reference in the shipping terms of the sale contract to a NOR being given was only relevant in relation to the commencement of laytime.

**212**

**Stag Line Ltd. v. Foscolo, Mango & Co. Ltd.**

1932, AC 328 (H.L.)

The vessel *Ixia* was chartered to carry a cargo of coal from Swansea (Wales) to Constantinople (Turkey). The charterparty contained a clause by which the vessel was at liberty to "call at any ports in order for bunkering or other purposes or to make trial trips after notice". The terms of the charterparty and the Hague Rules were both incorporated in the issued bill of lading. During the voyage, the vessel was turned about five miles off its course to enter the St. Ives harbour in order to land two engineers who had been taken on board for the purpose of testing her fuel-saving apparatus. The ship did not return immediately to the customary route but remained too close to the dangerous coast of Cornwall and ran aground resulting in the total loss of the vessel and cargo . The charterers claimed damages for the value of the cargo on the ground that there had been an unlawful deviation from the contracted route. The shipowners contended, firstly, that the accident was due to a peril of the sea, and secondly, that the deviation was "reasonable" and therefore it did not constitute a breach of the contract of carriage.

***Held (for the charterers):* i)** The perils and accidents of the sea exceptions are qualified by the provisions as to deviation, and such exceptions will only exempt the shipowner from responsibility for damage if they arise from or in the course of a "reasonable" deviation.[192] **ii)** However, the departure of the present case was not a "reasonable deviation" as required by the art IV(4) of the Hague Rules. (Lord Atkin) A deviation *"may be reasonable, though it is made solely in the interests of the ship or solely in the interests of the cargo, or indeed in the direct interest of neither: as for instance where the presence of a passenger or a member of the ship or crew was urgently required after the voyage had begun on a matter of national importance; or where some person on board was a fugitive from justice, and there were urgent reasons for his immediate appearance. The true test seems to be what departure from the contract voyage might a prudent person controlling the voyage at the time make and maintain, having in mind all the relevant circumstances existing at the time, including the terms of the contract and the interests of all parties concerned, but without obligation to consider the interests of any one as conclusive".* **iii)** Deviation is a question of fact. *"Taking all the facts into account,…the coasting course directed by the master was not the correct course which would ordinarily be set*

*in those circumstances. It is obvious that the small extra risk to ship and cargo caused by deviation to St. Ives, was vastly increased by the subsequent course. It seems to me* (Lord Atkin) *not a mere error of navigation but a failure to pursue the true course from St. Ives to Constantinople which itself made the deviation cease to be reasonable".*

**213**

**Star S.S. Soc. v. Beogradska Plovidba**
*(The Junior K)*
1988, 2 Lloyd's Rep. 583 (Q.B.)

The dispute occurred between a shipowner's firm of brokers and a respondent charterers company. Both parties agreed on some but not all the terms of a charterparty to be signed on the Gencon form. The last document sent was a telex recapitulating the terms which were accepted by both parties. That telex was sent after a short period of negotiations; it was headed "recap fixture sub details" and concluded " sub dets Gencon cp", which stated it was to be subject to details. The day following the recap telex, the respondents withdrew from the negotiations. The shipowners treated this conduct as a repudiatory breach and filed a claim for damages against the Respondents.. The question before the court was whether the respondents were entitled to withdraw with impunity from the negotiations at the "recap fixture sub details" stage.

***Held (for the respondents):* i)** The claimants did not satisfy the burden of proof that a binding contract had been formed. It was understood that there is no con-

---

[192] But see *Photo Production Ltd. v. Securicor Transport Ltd.*, and also sec. 1(2) of the Carriage of Goods by Sea Act 1971 and art. IV(4) of the Hague-Visby Rules.

tract at the mere "recap telex subject details" stage. The words "subject details" were interpreted by Steyn J. as a stipulation *"that there was to be no contract until agreement had been reached on the details of the Gencon charterparty"*. **ii)** The claimants' argument that damages were recoverable based either on the principle of good faith in negotiations or of the doctrine of the promissory estoppel failed. The duty of good faith was subsumed under the civilian concept of culpa in contrahendo and thus the judge found no reason to apply such duty under English Law. With regard to the doctrine of estoppel, the words "subject details" prevented the agreement from being a firm and unequivocal representation which is necessary for an argument based on an estoppel theory to succeed.[193]

**214**

**STAR SHIPPING A.S. V. CHINA NATIONAL FOREIGN TRADE TRANSPORTATION**
*(The Star Texas)*
1993, 2 Lloyd's Rep. 445 (C.A.)

In Nov. 1989 the plaintiff disponent owners time chartered their vessel *Star Texas* to the defendant Chinese charterers. The charterparty contained the following arbitration clause: "35. Any dispute arising under the charter is to be referred to arbitration in Beijing or London in defendant's option". Pursuant to the charter, the *Star Texas* loaded a number of containers

---

[193] This decision contrasts with the American view. The U.S. Court of Appeal has established that a fixture "subject details" is a legally enforceable contract *(The Cluden, 1982, A.M.C., 2321).*

of chemicals in China but, in the course of the voyage, she was required to return because one container was leaking. The othe return voyage and sought payment of the hire from the charterers accordingly. As the charterers refused payment, the owners issued a writ for service out of the English jurisdiction. The charterers applied to set aside the service under O. 12 rule 8, and alternatively, applied for a stay under sec. 1 of the Arbitration Act, 1975. The owners replied that sec. 1 was not applicable because the arbitration agreement of cl. 35 was null and void since it implied a "floating proper law," a concept foreign to English law.

***Held (for the charterers):*** (Lloyd, L.J.) *"We have not been referred to any case which decides that a floating curial law invalidates an arbitration clause. Nor can I see any good reason why it should. It must be possible, indeed it frequently happens, that an arbitration clause provides for one or other of two or more venues. Nobody has suggested…that that makes the arbitration clause void for uncertainty or otherwise unworkable. It makes good commercial sense that the law governing the arbitration procedure should be the law of the country where the arbitration takes place, unless, which is unlikely, the parties have agreed on some other curial law. The objections which apply to a floating proper law do not apply to a floating curial law. A contract without a proper law cannot exist. It is, as has been said, no more than an abstraction or a piece of paper. But an arbitration agreement can exist perfectly well without it being known at the time the arbitration agreement is entered into what law will govern the arbitration procedure."* On these grounds, the charterers were entitled to a stay of the

English legal proceedings pursuant to sec. 1 of the 1975 Act.

## 215
### State Trading Corporation of India Ltd. v. M. Golodetz Ltd.
### 1989, 2 Lloyd's Rep. 277 (C.A.)

On Dec. 11, 1985, the sellers sold c.&f. a cargo of sugar afloat to the buyers. Under the contract, the buyers were to open a letter of credit within seven days i.e. on or before Dec. 18. It was also agreed that the carriage should be effected under a "direct sailing vessel" from the loading port to India. Pursuant to the contract, the sellers agreed to provide a performance bank guarantee in respect to their obligations connected with the sugar cargo. There was also a countertrade provision whereby the sellers had to buy other unspecified goods from the buyers for 60% the value of the sugar within the following six months. In that connection, sellers were to give a further 3% countertrade guarantee on or before Dec. 18, 1985. It happened that, in fact, the vessel called at Hong Kong to change crew and to take on lubricants. On Dec. 18, 1985, the vessel was involved in a collision and a fire occurred on board. The vessel sunk and became a constructive total loss. The sellers had opened the guarantee but not the countertrade guarantee, and the buyers did not open the letter of credit. The sellers insisted that the buyers should nevertheless open the letter of credit and referred the dispute to the Refined Sugar Association, who ruled in the sellers' favour. The arbitrators found that the sellers' failure to open the countertrade guarantee was not a repudiatory breach of the contract whilst the buyers' failure to open the letter of credit was a breach of a condition which amounted to a repudiation. The buyers appealed the award.

***Held (for the sellers):*** **i)** The sellers' obligation concerning the countertrade guarantee was not a condition of the contract the breach of which went to the essence of the contract. (Kerr, L.J.) *"[T]here is nothing in the contract which made the timeous performance of that obligation a condition precedent to any other provision of the contract or to any other action which STC (i.e. the buyers) would thereupon take in the ordinary course of business. In particular, the opening of the countertrade* (guarantee) *was not expressed to be a condition precedent to STC's obligation –admittedly in the nature of a condition- to open the letter of credit within seven days; It was not a condition precedent to anything under the express terms of the contract, and I can see no reason for concluding that it had this character by implication."*[194] **ii)** Even if their lordships' view was wrong (which was not) and the sellers' obligation to open the countertrade guarantee was a condition of the contract, the result was admitted to be the same. On that hypothesis, the reasoning of Kerr, L.J. was as follows: *"On the assumption that both parties were in breach of condition, so that each of them could have treated the other as having wrongfully repudiated, neither lost its right to claim damages for breaches by the other irrespective of which of them brought the contract to an end. On either basis both parties were*

---

[194] See *Photo Production Ltd. v. Securicor Transport Ltd.*, at our point (iii).

*relieved from the performance of future obligations while remaining liable for past breaches. So, even if the contract had been brought to an end by STC, assuming their right to do so, they would still not have had any defence to the claim for damages –equal to the price of the goods- for having failed to open the letter of credit"*. Accordingly, the award of the arbitrators was upheld.

## 216
### STETTIN, THE
### 1889, 14 P.D. 142 (P.D.A.D.)

A consignment of barrels of oil was shipped on board the *Stettin* under a set of two original bills of lading issued "to Mendelsohn or assigns". The shippers retained one bill of lading and forwarded the other to their agents to secure payment of the price. When the ship reached the port of discharge, the master accepted to deliver the oil to Mendelson without production of the bill of lading. The shippers then sued the shipowners for conversion.

***Held (for the shippers):*** (Butt, J.) *"According to English law and the English mode of conducting business, a shipowner is not entitled to deliver goods to the consignee without the production of the bill of lading. I hold that the shipowner must take the consequences of having delivered these goods to the consignee without the production of either of the two parts of which the bill of lading consisted."*[195]

---

[195] See also *Lickbarrow v. Mason, Sze Hai Tong Bank v. Rambler Cycle Co.,* and *Barclays Bank Ltd. v. Comissioners of Customs and Excise.*

## 217
### STX PAN OCEAN CO. LTD. V UGLAND BULK TRANSPORT A.S.
### *(The Livanita)*
### 2008, 1 Lloyd's Rep. 86 (Q.B.)

The owners chartered the vessel Livanita on a NYPE form for "one time charter trip via St. Petersburg, Baltic/Conti to the Far East with duration 60/70 days without guarantee…within below mentioned trading limits. The charter contained a safe port warranty, but it contained no exclusions other than entering any ice-bound port. However, it contemplated the possibility that the ship sailed behind ice-breakers. Following the loading of a cargo of 37,058 m of steel coils at St Petersburg, the vessel left for Dunkirk. Ice-breakers assisted the vessel to the outbound convoy area. The hull of the vessel was damaged by ice during the outbound passage in convoy. Owners alleged that the charterers breached the safe port warranty and claimed damages.

***Held (for the owners):*** It was not alleged nor was there any evidence that St Petersburg was "known to be unsafe" at the time of the charter. The fact that the named port may typically be affected by ice does not lead to the conclusion that the port is unsafe, particularly when the charter itself contemplated sailing behind icebreakers, which are employed in the usual safe use of the port in winter. Langley, J. said: *"There is no inherent inconsistency between a safe port warranty and a named loading or discharging port".* Yet, was the owner still entitled to rely upon the safe port warranty if he knew, or should reasonably have known, that the named port was unsafe at the time the charter was entered into? Langley, J. replied: *"…there was no evidence that either party knew or ought reasonably to have anticipated anything about the likely conditions at St Petersburg more than the other, nor that either knew or should reasonably have known that St Petersburg was unsafe at the time the charter was entered into, nor that it was unsafe as sought to be alleged in Ground 3". "… [T]he issue of what owners knew or should reasonably have known about the unsafety of St Petersburg was not raised before the tribunal. That is sufficient to dispose of these grounds of appeal."*

**218**

**SVENSKA TRAKTOR V. MARITIME AGENCIES (SOUTHAMPTON) LTD.**
1953, 2 Lloyd's Rep. 124 (Q.B.D.)

The plaintiffs (Svenska Traktor Aktiebolaget) were the consignees of fifty tractors loaded on board the MV *Glory* in Southampton (England) for a carriage to Stockholm (Sweden). The bill of lading covering the shipment was signed by the master on the printed form of the defendants (Maritime Agencies Southampton Ltd.) and was subject to the Carriage of Goods by Sea Act (COGSA) 1924. It contained a clause numbered 76 stating: "Steamer has liberty to carry goods on deck and shipowners will not be responsible for any loss, damage or claim arising therefrom". The defendants were time charterers of the ship under the charterparty form of the "Baltime 1939". Of the 50 tractors, 34 were stowed below decks and the balance

of 16 on hatches no. 1 and 2. No statement was contained in the bills of lading saying that any particular goods were being shipped on deck. On her voyage to Stockholm, the vessel encountered heavy weather, with winds of up to 5-6 on the Beaufort Scale, resulting in one tractor being swept overboard and two others being damaged. The master issued a protest for perils of the sea as soon as the vessel reached Stockholm. The shippers at all material times regarded the defendants as the owners of the ship and the consignees, as plaintiffs, brought an action against the owners for damages.

***Held (for the plaintiffs):*** (Pilcher, J.)
**i)** Did COGSA 1924 apply to the captioned shipment? Section 1 of COGSA provided that the Hague Rules "shall have effect in relation to and in connection with the carriage of goods by sea in ships carrying goods from any port of Great Britain or Northern Ireland to any other port whether in or outside Great Britain or Northern Ireland". Further Art. 1(c) of the Rules set out that "'Goods' includes goods, wares merchandises and articles of every kind whatsoever, except live animals and cargo which by the contract of carriage is stated as being carried on deck and is so carried". In light of the COGSA rules, the shipment from Southampton to Norway of goods not stated as being carried on deck (even if actually so carried) is subject to COGSA 1924 and to the scheduled Hague Rules. **ii)** Were the shipowners entitled to rely on cls. 76 of the bill of lading? *"The clause or sentence is thus in two parts, and in my view it is reasonably clear that the second part of the*

*clause offends and must offend against Art. III, Rule 8, of the Schedule to the Act and cannot be relied upon by the shipowner; the two portions of the clause under consideration are connected by the conjunction 'and' without any stop. The second part offends against the Act and the first part does not."* **iii)** Were the shipowners authorised to carry the tractors on deck? At common law, the shipowner will only be authorised to stow goods on deck (1) by an established custom binding in the trade at port of loading, to stow on deck goods of that kind on such a voyage; and (2) by express agreement with the shipper. The effect of deck stowage not so authorised will be to set aside the exceptions of the bill of lading and to render the shipowner liable for damage happening to those goods. In this case, however, by the effect of the first portion of the cls. 76, it was held that *"the shipowners had liberty to ship cargo on deck subject always to their obligations under Art. III, Rule 2, properly and carefully to load, handle, stow, carry, keep and care for the goods in question".* **iv)** Did the shipowners comply with their duties of Art. III(2) of the Hague Rules? On the facts, Pilcher J. held: *"I am content to rest my conclusion with regard to the insufficiency of the lashing of this deck cargo on the fact that the ropes connecting the tractors to each other were insufficient in size or strength and were not sufficiently tended".* **v)** Were the shipowners allowed to rely on the exemption contained in Art. IV, (2)(c) of the Hague Rules? As per Carver's (Carriage of Goods by Sea, 9th ed., p. 185) "the carrier is liable unless he can prove affirmatively (i) that he has taken reasonable care of the goods

while they were in their custody, *and* (ii) that the loss or damage falls within one of the immunities specified in Art. IV(2)". On the evidence before Pilcher, J., *"the master seems to have encountered exactly the kind of weather he expected to encounter and exactly the type of weather which in his view might easily result in the loss of deck cargo, even though properly stowed and secured; ...I think that this tractor was lost owing to the lack of care in its original lashing and in the subsequent tending of the lashings by which it and the other two tractors on No. 1 hatch were secured".*

**219**

**SZE HAI TONG BANK LTD. V. RAMBLER CYCLE CO. LTD.**
1959, A.C. 576 (H.L. & P.C.)

A consignment of bicycle parts was shipped by the respondent manufacturers from England to Singapore. A bill of lading was issued to the manufacturers requiring delivery "unto order or his or their assigns". Its clause 2(c) provided that the carrier's responsibility was to be ceased "absolutely after the goods (were) discharged from the ship". When the ship arrived at Singapore, the port agents agreed to deliver the goods to the intended consignee. Instead of a bill of lading, a written indemnity was surrendered which was issued by the receiver's bank in favour of the carrier, his servants and/or agents. The manufacturers never happened to obtain payment from the actual receiver of the goods. As shippers, they elected to sue the carrier for breach of the contract of carriage and conversion. The carrier brought the receiver and the indemnifying bank into the court proceedings. The bank admitted liability as long as the carrier was held liable by the courts. The Court of Appeal of Singapore decided against the carrier, who decided not to appeal. The bank did appeal arguing that the carrier had a valid defence in cl. 2(c) of the bill of lading.

***Held (for the manufacturers):* i)** Unless the law or custom of the port of discharge provides otherwise, the carrier is generally obliged to deliver the goods to the person who surrenders the bill of lading and is entitled to possession under it. *"There is in Singapore a practice whereby the ship's agents will always release goods without production of the bill of lading providing they are protected by an indemnity, and in this case the appellant bank gave the indemnity."* **ii)** Clause 2(c) did not protect the carrier since he delivered the goods without production of the bill of lading to a person other than that entitled by the bill of lading. (Lord Denning) *"If such an extreme width were given to the exemption clause, it would run counter to the main object and intent of the contract. For the contract, as it seems to their lordships, has as one of its main objects, the proper delivery of the goods by the shipping company, 'unto order or his or their assigns', against production of the bill of lading. It would defeat this object entirely if the shipping company was at liberty, at its own will and pleasure, to deliver the goods to somebody else, to someone not entitled at all, without being liable for the consequences. The clause must therefore be limited and modified to the extent neces-*

*sary to enable effect to be given to the main object and intent of the contract."* The carrier was found liable for conversion and for fundamental breach of contract.[196]

**220**

**Taokas Navigation S.A. v. Komrowski Bulk Shipping KG**

[2012] EWHC 1888 (Comm) (C.A.)

The parties entered into a charter for 11-13 months trading via safe ports from delivery at Hakodate Dock (Japan). Clause 94 of the Conwartime form 2004 of the charterparty provided "the vessel, unless the written consent of the owners be first obtained, shall not be ordered or be required to continue to or through any port, place, area or zone (whether of land or sea) or any water way or canal, where it appears the vessel her cargo, crew or other persons on board the vessel, in the reasonable judgement of the master and/or the owners may be or are likely to be, exposed to war risks". After delivery of the vessel, the charterers' instructions for the first voyage were to proceed to Hoping (Taiwan), to load a cargo of cement clinker for discharge in Mombasa (Kenya). The owners refused to perform the voyage instructions and relied upon the war risk clause in the charter, having regard to the risk of piracy in the Indian Ocean. Acts of piracy had been reported across the costal waters of East Africa. Due to the owners' refusal, the charterers had to charter an-

---

[196] But see *Photo Production Ltd. v. Securicor Transport Ltd.* in respect with the doctrine of fundamental breach. Other cases involving the issue of conversion are *The Ines* and *The Sormovski 3068.*

other vessel to perform the voyage at the cost of USD 815,000. The question was whether, on the true construction of the charter, the owners' refusal was contractual or not.

***Held (for owners):*** The court found that there had been no material change in the risks of proceeding with that voyage between the date of the charterparty and the date of the charterers' order. It also noted that Kenya was within the trading limits agreed in the charter. However, clause 94 of the Conwartime 2004 form provided that the owners might refuse to proceed to a place if they considered it dangerous on account of a war risk. Besides that, Conwartime 2004 did not contain a requirement that the relevant war risk had to have escalated since the date of the charterparty.

**221**

**TELFAIR SHIPPING CORP. V. ATHOS SHIPPING CO. S.A. AND OTHERS**
*(The Athos)*
1983, 1 Lloyd's Rep. 127 (C.A.)

On Feb. 16, 1977, the vessel *Athos* was chartered on the New York Produce Exchange form for a period of min. 22 max. 24 months with an option to renew for a further 22-24 months. Clause 5 of the charter provided that the owners' had the right to withdraw failing punctual payment of the hire "or on any breach of this charter-party". Clause 35 stipulated: "Charterers to reimburse owners…for extra War Risk Insurance following receipt of invoices and supporting vouchers on payment of next hire". In Jan. 1978, the

vessel was mortgaged. The owners agreed with the mortgagees that the vessel was to be covered, inter alia, for war risk insurance by the Hellenic Mutual War Risk Association (Bermuda) Ltd. The agreement provided that that Association could specify any zone as additional premium area and such premium would be required for the vessel to trade within that zone. In Dec. 1979, the charterers advised the owners to bring the vessel to a port in Iran. The owners' agents sent a telex requiring payment of an additional insurance premium and the charterers protested the sums required as being excessive. The owners' agents advised of withdrawal should the additional insurance premium were not paid by the time the next hire became payable. Payment of the hire due reached the owners' bank on May 20 i.e. before the due date of May 25, but no additional premium sums were received from the charterers. Two days later the charterers received from the owners all the "invoices and supporting vouchers" as required by clause 35. The owners ascertained that the insurance premiums were unpaid on the due date of payment and instructed the bank to repay the balance of hire to the charterers. Following earlier threats of withdrawal the vessel was finally withdrawn. The charterers issued a writ against the owners claiming damages for wrongful withdrawal on the grounds that the words 'on payment of next hire' of cls. 35 meant the date when the hire was effectively paid (i.e. May 20). Since at that time the "invoices and supporting vouchers" had not been received by charterers, -they argued- the insurance premium became payable by the next hire payment (i.e. June 25). On the contrary, the owners contended that cls. 35 meant the date the hire was due (i.e. May 25) and that at that date the invoices and supporting vouchers were already in hands of the charterers.

***Held (for the charterers):*** **i)** Were the charterers in breach of clause 35? (Neill J.; affd. by Kerr L.J.) *"…the words in cl. 35 imposed an obligation which arose following receipt of the relevant documents to pay the additional premiums at the same time as the next payment of hire was paid. The performance of the duty to reimburse was expressed to be concurrent with the payment of the next hire".* Their lordships preferred the charterers' construction of the words in cls. 35. Hence at the time the owners withdrew the vessel the charterers were not in breach of their duty to reimburse the extra war insurance premium to the owners. **ii)** Which was the precise meaning of clause 5 of the charter? The interpretation of the words "on any breach" differs from that in The Tropwind. *"I (Kerr, L.J.) there held that they did not cover a breach of the obligation to pay additional insurance premiums within a reasonable time, there being no fixed time as in cl. 35. I suggested in The Tropwind that the words 'on any breach' might possibly apply to some unjustified refusal by the charterers to make some payment, other than hire which is of course expressly dealt with. But…I would not regard the situation in the present case as one of refusal. It was a bona fide dispute as to the amount payable, and ultimately both sides were held to have been wrong in their contentions. On the construction of the charter as a whole I would conclude that such a situation falls within the printed arbitration clause and*

*not to have given to the owners an immediate right of withdrawal…"*[197]

**222**

**T**HEMEHELP **L**TD. V. **W**EST AND **O**THERS
1996, QB 84 (C.A.)

The buyers agreed to purchase the sellers' business for GBP 1.600,000. Of the total price, a portion was payable on completion of the contract and the balance through three subsequent instalments. The third, and largest, instalment was secured by a performance guarantee issued by a third party (the "guarantor"). The guarantee contemplated default by the buyers and entitled the sellers to make good the buyers' default within a certain limit. If that occurred, the guarantors would be allowed to be indemnified by the buyers. Soon after the first of the deferred instalments was paid, the buyers alleged fraudulent misrepresentation by the sellers based on concealment. The purchase price had been negotiated on the assumption of the sellers' profit projections, which happened to include a promised demand from a major client of the business. The buyers alleged that, at the conclusion of the contract, the sellers were aware that the client had decided

---

[197] Kerr L.J. *"Whatever may be the right answer, cl. 5 is unsatisfactory and requires reconsideration from the point of view of what Owners and Charterers really wish to be their respective rights and obligations in the context of the Owners' right to withdraw the ship, thereby effectively endangering any New York Produce charter on a rising freight market."* See also *The Antaios*, where Lord Diplock clarified that the words 'on any breach of this charter' only applied to repudiatory breaches.

to order all future supplies from a competitor. The buyers started proceedings seeking the rescission of the contract and damages. The sellers, in turn, declared the buyers in default and sought the enforcement of the performance guarantee from the guarantors, who were not a party to the action. The buyers applied for an interlocutory injunction to restrain the sellers from enforcing the guarantee.

***Held (for the buyers):***[198] Their lordships decided that, although a performance guarantee is generally autonomous and independent from the main transaction associated with the guarantee, and, as a matter of principle, it is not to be interfered with on grounds extraneous to the guarantee itself, they nevertheless had jurisdiction to grant an injunction restraining the beneficiaries of the guarantee (i.e. the sellers, in this case) from enforcing it provided that the beneficiaries' fraud in the main transaction was proved. Since the buyers showed a seriously arguable case of fraud and the court was satisfied with the evidence brought, the buyers were entitled to the interlocutory injunction. Accordingly, the sellers' appeal was dismissed. The broad

principles of the decision were set out as follows: **i)** (Waite, LJ) "*In a case where fraud is raised as between the parties to the main transaction at an early stage, before any question of the enforcement of the guarantee, as between the beneficiary and the guarantor, has yet arisen at all, it does not seem to me that the slightest threat is involved to the autonomy of the performance guarantee if the beneficiary is injuncted from enforcing it in proceedings to which the guarantor is not party.*" **ii)** (Balcombe, LJ) "*If, on a claim for damages for fraudulent misrepresentation, it is possible to obtain a Mareva injunction to restrain the defendant from dissipating his assets so as to prevent any judgment that may subsequently be obtained from being worthless, I can see no reason of policy or principle to prevent the court from interfering at the earlier stage and freezing the assets, in this case the amount of the guarantee, in the hands of the bank, and thus obviate the risk that the Mareva injunction may come too late or that the sellers, who are now resident out of the jurisdiction, may not obey it*".

<hr>

[198] Evans, LJ, dissenting: "*...in my judgement, the injunction is contrary to legal principle and the appeal should be allowed. In summary, the two essential reasons are (i) the contract remains binding, even if the buyers' allegation that they were induced to enter into it by fraudulent misrepresentation by the sellers is sufficiently proved; and (ii) there is no finding or evidence that fraud exception defence will be available to the banks, if payment is demanded under the guarantee; Granting an injunction such as the present in these circumstances is also harmful...to the integrity of the banking system and to standards of commercial morality which the courts should uphold*".

**223**

**TOEPFER (ALFRED CO.) V. LENERSAN-POORTMANN N.V.**

1980, 1 Lloyd's Rep. 143 (C.A.)

This was a sale of Canadian rapeseed between German sellers and Dutch buyers. The agreement was on c.i.f. terms and incorporated the contract form of the Federation of Oils, Seeds and Fats Association (FOSFA) providing inter alia the following clause: "Payment: net cash against documents and/or delivery order on arrival of the vessel at port of discharge but not later than 20 days after date of bill of lading...". The bill of lading was dated Dec. 11, 1974, but the arrival of the ship was delayed without fault of the sellers as the vessel had run aground and had to be repaired. Finally, the sellers received the bill of lading from the carrier by Jan. 1975 and presented delivery orders on the ship in Feb. 1975. The buyers rejected the documents on the ground that the time for their presentation had expired. The sellers treated that rejection as repudiation and claimed for the contract price of the goods.

***Held (for the buyers):*** In a commodity contract such provisions as to the time of shipment were prima facie conditions. The payment clause imposed not only an obligation on the buyers as to pay within the stipulated time but also an obligation on the sellers to present the documents within that time; these were correlative obligations and rights. Therefore, the buyers had rightly rejected the documents. However, if no time had been stipulated for the tender of documents or the payment of the price, the sellers should tender the documents within a "reasonable time". As a conclusion, when the stipulated time (or reasonable time, where such stipulation is absent) has expired, provided that time is usually of the essence of the contract, the innocent party is entitled to treat the contract as repudiated.

**224**

**TOEPFER, ALFRED CO. v. CONTINENTAL GRAIN CO.**
1974, 1 Lloyd's Rep. 11 (C.A.)

German Bbyers (Toepfer) agreed to purchase a quantity of wheat from US sellers

(Continental Grain). The contract of sale incorporated the London Corn Trade Associated Form no. 27, which contained a clause drafted as follows: "Quality: n° 3 Hard Amber Durum Wheat of US origin-quality/condition final at loading per Official Certificate". Pursuant to the terms of that clause, the cargo was inspected at loading by an official inspector. He took original samples and certified the quality was of "grade and kind 3 Hard Amber Durum Wheat". The buyers paid against tender of usual documents, which included a bill of lading and the inspection certificate. Then they re-sold the cargo to Italian sub-buyers, who also paid cash against documents. When the Italian sub-buyers took delivery of the wheat, they found it was not in accordance with the contractual quality requirements. The sub-buyers claimed against the buyers, and the buyers did the same as against the sellers. In the course of the dispute it was proved and accepted that there had been an error in the certificate of quality and that the inspector had been negligent. The goods were not, in fact, of the contract quality as they were not of the kind "hard". The arbitrators to whom the dispute had been referred awarded for the sellers. It was held that the buyers' claim for damages should fail because the certificate at loading was agreed to be final and conclusive. The buyers appealed contending that the certificate was conclusive only as to the numerical grade, for the only part of the words "No. 3 Hard Amber Durum Wheat" which could be regarded as referring to quality was the part indicating the numerical grade, i.e. "No. 3".

***Held (for the sellers):*** i) (Lord Denning, MR) *"The 'description' of the goods often*

*includes a statement of their quality. 'Quality' is often part of the description. In this very case the word 'hard' is a word both of quality and of description. If a certificate is final as to the quality 'hard', it is final as to the description also. The quality and the description cannot be separated. Finality as to one means finality as to the other. I hold therefore that this certificate, in certifying that this wheat was "No. 3 Hard Amber Durum Wheat" was certifying the quality of the wheat."* **ii)** The commercial purpose of a "quality final at loading" clause is to avoid disputes as to quality and to achieve finality in this respect once a proper certificate of inspection has been issued and tendered. A mistake by the inspector does not invalidate the certificate, which remains binding as between the seller and buyer and all down the chain. (Lord Denning, MR) *"It must be remembered that numerous persons act on the faith of the certificate, such as the buyers, sub-buyers, bankers lending money and so forth. Good sense requires that the finality of the clause should be upheld by arbitrators and the Courts in full."* **iii)** (Lord Denning, MR) *"Whenever two persons agree together to refer a matter to a third person for decision, and further agree that his decision is to be final and binding upon them, so long as he arrives at his decision honestly and in good faith, the two parties are bound by it. They cannot re-open it for mistake or error on his part of for any reason other than for fraud or collusion..."*[199] On the facts of the case, there was no evidence of fraud or collusion so that the buyers were left with no remedies against the sellers. They could only direct their claim against the inspector for negligence.

**225**
**TOEPFER G.M.B.H. V.
TOSSA MARINE CORP.**
*(The Derby)*
1985, 2 Lloyd's Rep. 325 (C.A.)

The ship *Derby* was time chartered on the New York Produce Exchange form. The charterparty provided in line 22 that "Vessel on her delivery to be ready to receive cargo…and in every way fitted for the service" with full complement of crew. The vessel, which was Cypriot and employed Filipino crew, did not hold an I.T.F. blue card (to indicate that the crew's pay and conditions and manning levels met the standards of the International Transport Workers Federation). The trading limits under the charterparty were stipulated to exclude areas in which the I.T.F. was known to be active, but failed to exclude Portugal. While the vessel was at the Portuguese port of Leixoes, an I.T.F. representative discovered that she did not hold the blue card and stopped her for 21 days, the period which enabled the owners to reach an agreement with the I.T.F. During this period, the vessel was off-hire. However, because of the delay the charterers were unable to perform a sub-charter and lost profits. They claimed damages against the owners alleging that the owners had failed to deliver a seaworthy vessel "in every way fitted for the service" since she did not hold the blue card.

---

[199] *Arenson v. Arenson,* 1973, 2 Lloyd's Rep. 104, at p. 107; quoted by Lord Denning MR in the case before him.

***Held (for the owners):* i)** The activity of the I.T.F. is mainly targeted to ships flying flags of convenience and/or employing third world crews. The standards sought are not based on requirements of the law of the vessel's flag or the countries the vessel may call, but on rates of pay and manning conditions agreed with seamen's trade unions of western countries. Vessels of such features may be "blacked", either by inducing the crew to go on strike or by persuading the local stevedores to boycott the vessel until an agreement with the I.T.F. is reached. **ii)** It was held that, although the Derby was off-hire, the charterers had to pay the stevedoring charges for the 21-day-period at Leixoes. The words of the line 22 NYPE ("in every way fitted for the service") constitute an express warranty solely of the physical state of the vessel. It is true that some authorities showed that their meaning, as that of the term seaworthiness, is wider in two respects: the first, in that they provide also for a sufficient and competent crew,[200] and the second, in that such words require the vessel to carry certain documents (i.e. deratisation certificates) required by the law of the vessel's flag or local port authorities.[201] Nevertheless, an I.T.F. blue card does not fall within either of these categories. The words of line 22 NYPE relate only to the physical state of the ship, and, on the facts, there is no reason for an enlargement of the scope of such words to cover the rates of pay and conditions of employment of the crew settled by an extra-legal organisation such as the I.T.F.

<hr>

[200] See *Hongkong Fir Shipping Co. Ltd. v. Kawasaki Kisen Kaisha Ltd.,* where similar words ("she being in every way fitted for ordinary cargo service") were used in the Baltime form.

[201] See *The Madelein, 1967, 2 Lloyd's Rep. 224.*, where the law of India required a certificate of deratisation and the charterparty clearly stated the vessel to be "… furnished with everything needful and necessary for such a ship, and for the voyage…".

## 226
## TORVALD KLAVENESS A/S v. ARNI MARITIME CORP.
*(The Gregos)*
1995, 1 Lloyd's Rep. 1 (H.L.)

A time charter on the New York Procedure Exchange form was agreed for the vessel *Gregos*. The charterparty stated a hire period of min. 50 to max. 70 days at charterers' option; redelivery to take place at an authorised European port. The vessel was delivered on Jan. 8, so that redelivery became due by Mar. 18 at the latest. On Feb. 9, the vessel was in a port on the Orinoco river and the charterers instructed the master to proceed to the next port to load some cargo for carriage to Fos. At that time, it was reasonable that redelivery occur on or before Mar. 18. On Feb. 12, a vessel went aground and obstructed the mouth of the river. As a result, the owners were unwilling to proceed with the voyage to Fos and treated the order as a repudiatory breach. An agreement without prejudice was entered on Feb. 29 and the vessel finally proceeded with the voyage on that date. The vessel was delivered eight days late. In the dispute, the issues were: (1) Whether the legitimacy of the voyage was to be judged at the time of the vessel's departure (the owners' view) or at the time the order was given (the charterers' view), (2) Whether there was a repudiatory breach which entitled the owners not only to refuse to comply with the order but also to discharge the charter?

***Held (for the owners):*** **i)** The charterers' orders were given and considered reasonable in advance of the time of performance (that is, the date when the vessel is sent on voyage). However, their validity or reasonability might be altered with the passage of time, that is, from the date of the order to the date of performance. In that sequence, the order, originally valid and permissible, became illegitimate. The correct date for the "legitimate last voyage test" is no doubt the performance date.[202] **ii)** The obligation to redeliver on time was found by their lordships to be an innominate term rather than a condition, and therefore, in the present case, a short delay in redelivery would not justify the termination of the contract. The shipowner's submission that redelivery after the final terminal date was a breach of condition of the contract which entitled the shipowner to discharge the contract must be rejected. **iii)** (Lord Mustill) "But it is plain from the facts stated by the arbitrator that the charterers had no intention (of redelivering the vessel before the final date), and that the critical time would pass without any valid orders being given. The charterers' persistence in the original order, which had been rendered invalid by the changed circumstances, showed that they did not want to perform their duties under the charter terms. Therefore, charterers showed an intention to be no longer bound by the charter limits, and this constitutes an anticipatory breach which goes to the root of the contract and which, in turn, entitles the owners to treat it as a repudiation."

**227**
**TRADAX EXPORT S.A. v.
ANDRE & CIE. S.A.**[203]
1976, 1 Lloyd's Rep. 416 (C.A.)

Some 660 tons of US soya bean meal was sold c.i.f. Rotterdam, shipment to be in June 1973. The contract incorporated GAFTA Form 100. Under clause 9, the contract provided that, in case of force majeure, the date of shipment would be extended by the sellers up to eight days as from the last contractual date. Clause 21 excused the seller from fulfilling his duties when the authorities of the country of origin prohibited the export, so that the contract would then be cancelled. Clause 22 provided that, in the event of force majeure, the shipper was entitled to an extension of a maximum of 1 or 2 months, at the buyers' option. Floods in the Mississippi wreaked havoc on the soya bean meal exports. The US Government imposed an embargo on the export of that product, but later allowed exporters a quota of 40% of their contractors' obligations. Few days later, the US Government increased the quota over 40% if the

---

[202] See also *The Democritos*, where the order was also rightly given at first, but by the time the vessel set sail on the final voyage, it was evident that the voyage was not to be completed in time, and so became illegitimate.

[203] This is one of the so called *Soya Bean Meal* cases.

sellers had soya bean oil-cake "en route to port, or in port earmarked for loading". The sellers originally claimed an extension under clause 22, but were still unable to provide the 131 tons of remaining cargo within the extended period, and subsequently claimed cancellation under cls. 21. The shortage prompted a great rise in the market price. The buyers claimed damages based on that market price.

***Held:*** **i)** Which is the effect of cl. 22 and 21? (Lord Denning, MR) *"A prohibition of export is well within the term 'force majeure'. It comes within both cl. 22 and cl. 21. But in some cases it may only cause 'delay' in shipment: in which case the shippers can operate under cl. 22, and claim an extension; in other cases a prohibition of export may 'prevent fulfilment', in which case cl. 21 operates automatically to cancel the contract without more ado. In order to see whether it is within cl. 22 or cl. 21, it is necessary to inquire whether the prohibition of export only 'delays' the shipment or whether it 'prevents the fulfilment' of the contract".* **ii)** Ought the sellers have bought goods afloat so as to fulfil their contract? In ordinary c.i.f. contracts, Lord Denning responded affirmatively: *"If shipment is delayed by force majeure or prevented by prohibition of export, the seller is not excused if he could have bought goods afloat to perform the contract.[204] But it is different when the seller in a string has already made arrangements to ship the goods by himself or by some shipper higher up in the string. If those arrangements are already in existence…the seller can rely on cl. 22 or cl. 21, as the case may be. He is not bound*

*to buy afloat so as to fulfil his contract".[205]* An opposite decision would create a situation of "large numbers of buyers chasing very few goods and the price would reach unheard of levels". **iii)** Was the case within the scope of clauses 22 and 21? The burden was on the seller to prove the facts bringing the case within the appropriate clause. (Lord Denning MR) *"If he relies on cl. 21, he would have to prove that the shipper, at the head of the string, had goods ready to ship and that shipment was prevented by the prohibition of export; similarly, if the seller relied on cl. 22, he would have to prove that the relevant shipper had goods ready to ship and that shipment was delayed."*

**228**

**Tradax Export S.A. v. Dorada Compañía Naviera S.A.**
*(The Lutetian)*
1982, 2 Lloyd's Rep. 140 (Q.B.)

The vessel *Lutetian* was chartered on the New York Produce Exchange form for a period of 36-40 months at charterers' option. The vessel was delivered to the charterers on July 18, 1979. Clause 5 of the charterparty established monthly payment in advance and established the owners' right of withdrawal in the event payments were not punctual and regular. Clause 15 provided that "… in the event of loss of time from … drydocking … preventing the full working of the vessel, the payment of hire shall cease for the time thereby lost…". Clause 31 provided that

---

[204] See *Lewis Emmanuel & Son Ltd. v. Sammut*

[205] See *Fairclough, Dodd & Jones Ltd. v. Vantol (J.H.) Ltd.*

the owners should give appropriate notice three working days before exercising the option of withdrawing and would not exercise such right in the event charterers had paid the hire within the three day period of notice. In July the following year, the vessel was drydocked at Palermo due to mechanical problems and the off-hire period formally started on July 8, 1980. A message was sent by the owners informing the charterers that the vessel was expected to sail again on July 21/22. The message was sent late on the evening of July 17, but it was not seen by the charterers until the following morning, on Friday, July 18, which also happened to be the due date of payment as per the terms of the charterparty. On that same day, the charterers instructed their bank to make the transfer but the owners did not receive payment until Monday, July 21. Hire was wrongly calculated for the period from July 18 to Aug. 18, with a deduction for fourteen days off-hire corresponding to the ten days already consumed (July, 8-18), plus the four days expected to accrue (July, 18-21/22). Since the owners did not receive payment on July 18, they sent notice of withdrawal that evening on the same day. The owners withdrew the vessel on July 24 arguing that the charterers had failed to make payment on the due date, and that the charterers had no right to make deductions for anticipated off-hire. The vessel was re-offered to the charterers at a higher rate of hire. The charterers then claimed damages.

***Held (for the charterers):*** (Bingham J.) **i)** Was the hire payable on July 18? *"… charterers under this form of charter-party are obliged to pay a monthly instalment of hire in advance on the due date for payment if the vessel is then on hire, even if it is known or expected that there will be a period within the month covered by the advance payment when the vessel will be off-hire; …it is in that event permissible, and common practice, for the hire paid in respect of the period of off-hire to be deducted from the next monthly hire payment".* However, if on the due date of payment the vessel is off-hire, it was held that the charterers' duty to make payment in advance of the next monthly instalment is suspended until immediately before the vessel is again on service. **ii)** Did an underpayment of hire legitimate the owners to withdraw? On the evidence, the charterers calculated incorrectly the hire due. Although their conduct was bona fidae, it was as a valid ground for withdrawal.[206] *"The duty of calculating the sum due rested on the charterers; if they calculated incorrectly, they cannot rely on their own legal error to escape the contractual consequences."* This question was thus decided in favour of the owners. **iii)** Were the charterers entitled to make a deduction for the anticipated off-hire period? The words of cls. 15 do not entitle the owners to be secured by payment in advance in respect of hire which they could never earn. *"…a provision for payment in advance does ordinarily relate to money which the recipient will, or at least may, be entitled to retain and it is surprising if an owner is entitled to receive in advance money which he and the charterer have every reason to believe*

---

[206] But see *The Nanfri*. Bingham J. clarified: "The present case is not one of set-off but of calculating the sum due".

*he can never earn"*. **iv)** Was the notice of withdrawal premature under the terms of cls. 31? Clause 31 is an anti-technicality clause which prevents the owners from withdrawing the vessel unless three days' notice has been given to the charterers. The due date for payment was July 18. Under cls. 31 the owners were not entitled to give notice of withdrawal until the due date for payment had passed i.e. not before July 21 close of business (because July 19 was a Saturday), but they did so on July 18. *"I hold that the owners' notice was given prematurely and so was invalid; notice could not be given until Monday, July 21; and since the charterers were entitled to three clear days' notice, the vessel could not properly be withdrawn on Thursday, July 24, when the owners purported to do so."*[207]

### 229
#### TRANSGRAIN SHIPPING B.V. V. GLOBAL TRANSPORTE OCEANICO
*(The Mexico 1)*
1990, 1 Lloyd's Rep. 507 (C.A.)

The vessel *Mexico 1* was chartered for a carriage of bagged maize. As this was to be only a part of the cargo, the charterers gave the shipowners the right to complete the capacity of the vessel with other cargo. Under a subsequent agreement, the vessel also carried a second cargo of beans for the same charterers. Both of the charterers' cargoes were overstowed by parts of the shipowners' completion cargo and, as a result, neither cargo was fully accessible when the vessel reached the discharge

---

[207] See *The Afovos.*

port. The vessel tendered notice of readiness on Jan. 21. The notice was apparently accepted by the local charterers' agent, but it was plainly invalid when given since the overstowage did not allow the proper discharge. The cargo of maize became fully accessible on Feb. 6, with the cargo of beans becoming accessible on Feb. 19. However, both cargoes were not discharged until Feb. 19. The shipowners argued that laytime automatically began on Feb. 6, when the vessel became ready to discharge. The charterers conceded that laytime began to run when discharge actually commenced.

***Held (for the charterers):* i)** If the notice of readiness is defective when it is given due to the vessel not being an "arrived vessel" or because the vessel is physically or legally unready, then that notice will remain defective for all purposes. Unless the charterparty provides otherwise, there is no mechanism of law whereby it can become effective when the situation leading to the defective notice of readiness has ceased to exist. The shipowners' argument that the notice became automatically valid and effective as soon as the overstowed cargo was accessible was not accepted. *"I* (Mustill L.J.) *find it impossible to say that the taking of this wrong step* (i.e. an invalid notice) *is somehow to be deemed as the taking of the right step."* **ii)** An invalid notice cannot start laytime running. If no further valid notice is served, laytime will not start to run unless it can be inferred from the conduct of the charterers either that the contractual terms of laytime commencement have varied, neither that there has been a relevant waiver or estoppel so that the parties accepted that laytime should start to run accordingly. In the absence of waiver, therefore, laytime did not start and, before it could start, a second notice of readiness had to be served. **iii)** The acceptance of the defective notice by their agent was irrelevant (in terms of precluding the charterers' rights) since the acceptance was given in reliance upon the master's implied assurance that the ship was ready for discharge.

**230**
**Transfield Shipping Inc. v.**
**Mercator Shipping Inc.**
*(The Achilleas)*
2008, 2 Lloyd's Rep. 275 (H.L.)

On 22 Jan. 2003 the MV *Achilleas* was chartered on the amended NYPE form for a period of about five to seven months at a daily hire rate of USD 13,500. The charterparty was extended by an addendum dated 12 Sept. 2003 for a further period of about five to sevem months at a rate of USD 16,750, the latest date of return being 2 May 2004. On Apr. 20 charterers gave owners notice of redelivery between Apr. 20 and May 2. On Apr. 21 owners chartered the MV *Achilleas* to Cargill International SA (Cargill) for four to six months at a daily rate of USD 39,500 and a laycan between 28 Apr. and 8 May. Yet on May 5 the vessel had not been redelivered, owners sought an extension of the canceling date with Cargill and agreed to an extension until May 11, but with a reduction in hire of USD 8,000. The ship was finally delivered to Cargill on 11 May. Owners then sought damages from charterers for USD 8,000 per day and, alternatively, for the difference between the charterparty and the market rates. The matter was referred to arbitration and owners' primary claim was admitted.

***Held (for owners):*** Their lordships upheld the award and revisited the ordinary rule of damages. Per Lord Hoffmann: *"The findings of the majority arbitrators show that they considered their decision to be contrary to what would have been the expectations of the parties, but dictated by the rules in Hadley v Baxendale as explained in C Czarnikow Ltd v Koufos (The Heron II) [1967] 2 Lloyd's Rep 457; [1969] 1 AC 350. But in my opinion these rules are not so inflexible; they are intended to give effect to the presumed intentions of the parties and not to contradict them". "... [T]he implication of a term as a matter of construction of the contract as a whole in its commercial context and the implication of the limits of damages liability seem to me to involve the application of essentially the same techniques of interpretation. In both cases, the court is engaged in construing the agreement to reflect the liabilities which the parties may reasonably be expected to have assumed and paid for. It cannot decline this task on the ground that the parties could have spared it the trouble by using clearer language. In my opinion, the findings of the arbitrators and the commercial background of the agreement are sufficient to make it clear that the charterer cannot reasonably be regarded as having assumed the risk of the owner's loss of profit on the following charter. I would therefore allow the appeal."* Per Lord Walker of Gestingthorpe: *"What mattered was whether the common intention of reasonable parties to a charterparty of this sort would have been that in the* *event of a relatively short delay in re-delivery an extraordinary loss, measured over the whole term of the renewed fixture, was… sufficiently likely to result from the breach of the contract to make it proper to hold that the loss flowed naturally from the breach or that loss of that kind should have been within [the defaulting party's] contemplation".*

## 231
### TRANS TRUST S.P.R.L. V. DANUBIAN TRADING CO.
### 1952, 2 QB 29 (C.A.)

Trans Trust agreed to sell to Danubian Trading Co. a quantity of steel. The former was to purchase the steel from a Belgian firm and the latter had committed itself to resale the steel to an American company. As the Belgian firm was not in a position to provide the money necessary to obtain delivery of the steel, a third company (i.e. the manufacturers of the steel) had given to the Belgian firm an option to buy the steel. Neither the Belgian firm, Trans Trust nor Danubian Trading Co. had the financial means to obtain delivery directly from the manufacturers. By the contract of sale between Trans Trust and Danubian Co., the latter undertook to procure a letter of credit to be opened by the American company in favour of the Belgian firm (who in fact depended on the credit in order to get the steel).[208] Against this backdrop of contracts, there

was a rise in the market price for steel and, although Trans Trust extended the time for the credit, the credit was never opened by the American company. In view of that, Danubian Trading Co. repudiated the contract with Trans Trust which then claimed damages and loss of profit for Danubian Trading Co.'s breach of contract.

***Held (for the plaintiffs):*** **i)** The clause of a sale contract whereby the buyer must open a letter of credit at a specified time is usually a condition precedent to the performance of the contract, i.e. to the delivery of the goods. On the contrary, if the parties agree that the contract itself shall be subject to the opening of the letter of credit, if no credit is provided, then there is no contract between the parties; in this hypothesis, the letter of credit is a condition precedent to the formation of the contract. In both cases, if the buyer fails to provide the credit the seller is therefore discharged from further obligations, but only in the first case he is entitled to claim damages from the buyer. In the present dispute it happened that Danubian Trading Co. agreed literally that "a credit will be opened forthwith (immediately)", so that the condition was precedent to the performance and not to the contract itself. Because the condition was not fulfilled by Danubian Trading Co., Trans Trust was discharged from further performance and was entitled to nominal damages. **ii)** Although damages were the result of the impecuniosity of the sellers (i.e. Trans Trust), they were also entitled to include their loss of profit in their claim. This is because it was foreseeable by the buyers that the sellers were to lose

---

[208] In synthesis, the scenario was as follows: manufacturers gave the Belgian firm an option to buy; the Belgian firm sold to Trans Trust; Trans Trust sold to Danubian Co.; and Danubian Co. sold to the American company.

their option on the goods if no credit was provided and that they were not in a position to sell those goods elsewhere in the market. **iii)** As to whether the sellers are also entitled to be indemnified for any damages they may have to pay to the Belgian firm, the court held that this point was not in the contemplation of the parties when they entered into their contract. The buyers did not know that the Belgian firm depended on the credit in order to obtain the goods themselves. In this respect, damages of this kind were found unforeseeable and too remote to become recoverable.

**232**
**TRASPORTI CASTELLETI SPEDIZIONI INTERNAZIONALI SPA V. HUGO TRUMPY SPA**
16.03.1999, Case C-159/97
(European Court of Justice)

In Mar. 1987 goods were shipped out of Buenos Aires (Argentina) on board a vessel operated by Lauritzen Reefers for a carriage to Savona (Italy). Bills of lading were issued and signed by the agents of Lauritzen in Buenos Aires with the following pre-printed clause on the back: "The contract evidenced by this bill of lading shall be governed by English Law and any disputes thereunder shall be determined in England by the High Court of Justice in London according to English Law to the exclusion of the Courts of any other country". The signature of the shippers appeared on the face of the bills between the particulars of the cargo and a written reference to the reverse side of the bills. Some of the goods were damaged during the discharge and the consignees in Milan (Trasporti Castelleti) commenced proceedings against the ship agents (Hugo Trumpy), who were based in Genoa. An action for compensation was brought before the Tribunale di Genoa. The ship agents contested jurisdiction based on the clause on the bill of lading conferring jurisdiction to the Courts in England. After the Corte d'Appello di Genoa, the Corte Suprema di Cassazione dismissed the appeal because the signature of the shipper could not necessarily be deemed to imply consent to all the clauses of the bills of lading. The court ruled out the possibility that an agreement conferring jurisdiction in writing had been made under article 17 of the Convention of 27 Sept. 1968 on Jurisdiction and Enforcement of Judgments in Civil and Commercial Matters (the "Brussels Convention"),[209] which prescribed: "If the parties, one or more of whom is domiciled in a Contracting State, have agreed that a court or the courts of a Contracting State are to have jurisdiction to settle any disputes which have arisen or which may arise in connection with a particular legal relationship, that court or those courts shall have exclusive jurisdiction. Such an agreement conferring jurisdiction shall be either: (a) in writing or evidenced in writing, or (b) in a form which accords with practices which the parties have established between themselves, or (c) in international trade or commerce, in a form which accords with a usage of which the parties are

---

[209] As amended by the Convention of 9 October 1978 on the Accession of Denmark, Ireland and the United Kingdom.

or ought to have been aware and which in such trade or commerce is widely known to, and regularly observed by parties to contracts of the type involved in the particular trade or commerce concerned". The Corte Suprema stayed the proceedings and referred a number of questions to the European Court of Justice for a preliminary ruling.

***Held (after the opinion of the General Advocate P. Léger):* Question 1:** Whether art. 17, in so far as it refers to the notion of "practices" (usages) whilst using the term [in the Italian version], necessarily requires that the consent of the parties to the jurisdiction clause be established. *"The answer to the first question must therefore be that the third case mentioned in the second sentence (c) of the first paragraph of Article 17 of the Convention is to be interpreted as meaning that the contracting parties' consent to the jurisdiction clause is presumed to exist where their conduct is consistent with a usage which governs the area of international trade or commerce in which they operate and for which they are, or ought to have been, aware."* **Questions 9, 4, 5 and 8:** By these questions the national court seeks to ascertain the countries in which a usage must be found to exist, the process by which it comes into being, the forms in which it must be publicised, and the consequences to be drawn, as to the existence of a usage in this area, from actions challenging the validity of jurisdiction clauses inserted in bills of lading. *"The answer to the ninth, fourth, fifth and eighth questions must therefore be that the third case mentioned in the second sentence of the first paragraph of Article 17 of the Convention is to be interpreted as follows: (i) The existence of a usage, which*

*must be determined in relation to the branch of trade or commerce in which the parties to the contract operate, is established where a particular course of conduct is generally and regularly followed by operators in that branch when conducting contracts of a particular type. (ii) It is not necessary for such a course of conduct to be established in specific countries or, in particular, in all the Contracting States. (iii) A specific form of publicity cannot be required in all cases. (iv) The fact that a course of conduct amounting to a usage is challenged before the courts is not sufficient to cause the conduct no longer to constitute a usage."* **Questions 2, 11 and 10:** By these questions, the national court is asking what is specifically required for there to be a "form which accords" within the meaning of art. 17 of the Brussels Convention,[210] in which circumstances the jurisdiction clause may be considered grossly unfair or abusive, and whether it is acceptable to rely on a usage which would derogate from mandatory statutory provisions adopted by a Contracting State as regards the form of jurisdiction clauses. *"It is…for the national court to refer to the commercial usages in the branch of international trade or commerce concerned in order to determine whether, in the case before it, the physical appearance of the jurisdiction clause, including the language in which it is drawn up, and its insertion in a standard form, which has not been signed by*

____________

[210] It asks more precisely whether the jurisdiction clause must be contained in a written document, bearing the signature of the party stipulating it, with the signature itself being accompanied by a reference to the clause, whether that clause must stand out prominently from the other clauses and whether the language in which it is drawn up must be related to the nationality of the parties.

*the party not involved in drawing it up, are consistent with the forms according with those usages… Therefore, the usages to which Article 17 refers cannot be nullified by national statutory provisions which require compliance with additional conditions as to form. The answer to the second, eleventh and tenth questions must therefore be that the third case mentioned in the second sentence of the first paragraph of Article 17 of the Convention is to be interpreted as meaning that the specific requirements covered by the expression 'form which accords' must be assessed solely in the light of the commercial usages of the branch of international trade or commerce concerned, without taking into account any particular requirements which national provisions might lay down."* **Questions 13, 14 and 12:** By these questions, the national court seeks to ascertain, first, which party must be aware of the usage and whether his nationality is relevant in this regard, next, what degree of awareness that party must have of the usage and, finally, whether any publicity must be given to the standard forms containing jurisdiction clauses and, if so, in what form. *"The answer to the thirteenth, fourteenth and twelfth questions must therefore be that the third case mentioned in the second sentence of the first paragraph of Article 17 of the Convention is to be interpreted as meaning that awareness of the usage must be assessed with respect to the original parties to the agreement conferring jurisdiction, their nationality being irrelevant in this regard. Awareness of the usage will be established when, regardless of any specific form of publicity, in the branch of trade or commerce in which the parties operate a particular course of conduct is generally and regularly followed in the conclusion of a particular type of contract, so that it may be regarded as an*

*established usage."* **Questions 3, 7 and 6:** By these questions, the national court seeks to ascertain whether there are, under art. 17 of the Convention, any limitations as to the choice of court. It asks whether it is necessary for the parties to choose a court having some link to the case, whether the court seized may review the validity of the clause as well as the intention of the party which inserted it, and whether the fact that the substantive provisions applicable before the chosen court tend to reduce that party's liability may affect the validity of the jurisdiction clause. *"The answer to the third, seventh and sixth questions must therefore be that the third case mentioned in the second sentence of the first paragraph of Article 17 is to be interpreted as meaning that the choice of court in a jurisdiction clause may be assessed only in the light of considerations connected with the requirements laid down in Article 17 of the Convention. Considerations about the links between the court designated and the relationship at issue, about the validity of the clause, or about the substantive rules of liability applicable before the chosen court are unconnected with those requirements."*

**233**

**TRANSWORLD OIL (USA) INC. V. MINOS COMPANIA NAVIERA S.A.**

*(The Lent)*

1992, 2 Lloyd's Rep. 48 (Q.B.)

Bills of lading were issued for two consignments of oil, both of which named the Abu Dhabi National Oil Co. (Adnoc) as shippers and Banque Paribas, London, as consignees. The first bill of lading acknowledged the receipt of 802,607 barrels of Murban crude and was dated 25 Aug.,

1986. The bill was endorsed by Banque Paribas "Deliver to the order of Banque Indosuez, New York" and re-endorsed by Banque Indosuez "Deliver to the order of Transworld Oil America Inc". The second bill of lading acknowledged the receipt of 450,522 barrels of upper Zakum crude oil and was dated 25 or 26 Aug., 1986. The bill was endorsed by Banque Paribas "Deliver to the order of Transworld Oil (Houston) Inc.". and re-endorsed by the latter "Deliver to the order of Exxon Company USA-Transworld Oil USA, Inc." There were shortages on outturn at discharge, and the cargo interests made claims shortly before expiry of the one year limitation period. A writ was entered without listing the name of Transworld Oil America Inc., the company to which the Murban crude had been sold due to an error by the cargo underwriters and the attorneys involved. Owners' points of defense included the fact that the company named on the writ, Transworld Oil (USA) Inc., lacked title to sue, and that the claim was time-barred. The issues before the court were: (i) Does art. III, r. 6 of the Hague Rules afford a substantive defence to the owners in respect of a claim brought by Transworld Oil America Inc.? (ii) Should leave be granted to amend the writ to add Transworld Oil America Inc. as claimant?

***Held (for the owners):*** (i) In regard to the first issue, Diamond J. first considered that *"all that is necessary is that a suit must have been brought to enforce the claim within the one year period. For the suit to qualify as one brought to enforce the claim it must…be one to enforce a claim in respect for loss or damage arising under 'a contract of carriage' as defined in art. I(b) of the Convention and as also re-ferred to in art. II. Provided that the suit has been brought in time and has been brought to enforce a claim arising under the particular contract of carriage in question, then prima facie the carrier is not discharged from lia-bility under the rule".* The Judge continued that he thought a suit would not become a "non-suit" merely because it was brought in the name of a party who ultimately lacks title to sue and thus he would have ruled that art. III, r. 6 does not provide a defence to the owners had there been no authority on the meaning of art. III, r.6. However, art. III, r. 6 is not free from authority and the court, constrained by precedents, ruled that, *"as the suit brought within the year was brought by a party which had no title to sue in respect of the Murban crude, art. III, r.6 affords a substantive defence to the owners in respect of a claim brought by Transworld Oil America Inc".* **(ii)** It was submitted on be-half of the cargo interests that in the event Transworld Oil America Inc. is barred by art. III, r. 6 from pursuing a claim, the court nevertheless has jurisdiction under R.S.C., O. 20, r. 5(3) to join that com-pany as plaintiff in the action and that such a joinder would overcome the time bar and that the court should exercise its discretion to allow the amendment. In ref-erence to "The Aries" *Tanker Corporation v. Total Transport*, 1977 1 Lloyd's Rep. 334, where it was noted that art. III, r. 6 is a special kind of time bar which extinguishes the claim, rather than one which, as most English Statutes of Limitation, bars the remedy while leaving the claim itself in existence, the court noted that the claim of Transworld Oil America Inc. ceased to exist on 9 Oct.1987 and that it would be surprising if the claim could be resurrect-ed in 1992 by means of an amendment to the writ and points of claim. Furthermore, the court outlined three reasons why leave should not be granted to amend the writ. First, the Rules of the Supreme Court do not and cannot confer power on the court to override substantive time bars. Second, that leave to amend the writ should not be granted as the amendment would not relate back to the date of issue of the writ but would take effect only from the date of the amendment. And third, granting leave would override a defence under art. III, r. 6 and would be contrary to the scheme of the Hague-Visby Rules. Furthermore, although the court found that the cargo interests could bring themselves within the wording of O. 20, r. 5(3), and if there were jurisdiction under the rules of court for amendments to be made which have the effect of overriding a substantive defence arising by reason of art. III, r. 6, such amendments must be made promptly. Because the plaintiffs made their application three and a half years after expiry of the one year time bar, the court would exercise its discretion against granting leave to join Transworld Oil America Inc. as plaintiff in the action.

**234**
**TRIAD SHIPPING CO. V. STELLAR CHARTERING & BROKERAGE**
*(The Island Archon)*
1994, 2 Lloyd's Rep. 227 (C.A.)

In 1979 the *Island Archon* was time chartered to Stellar Chartering & Brokerage (the Time Charterers) under the New York Produce Exchange Form. Clause 8 provided, inter alia, that "the Captain (although appointed by the owners), shall be under the orders and directions of the charterers as regards employment and agency". In June 1980, the German sub charterers ordered the ship on a voyage to Basrah in Iraq. After discharge there, unfounded claims were brought by the Iraqi receivers and by the authorities. These claims were mainly due to the chaos and disruption existing in Iraq at that time. The Shipowners, Triad Shipping Co., had to provide a guarantee to release the ship and some delays were caused thereby. As a result, the shipowners claimed an indemnity from the time charterers for the loss and delay suffered. The main question of the appeal was whether the Shipowners were entitled to the indemnity even though the time charterers, by ordering the ship to proceed to Basrah, were not in breach of the terms of the charterparty.

***Held (for the shipowners):*** **i)** Were the shipowners entitled to the indemnity? (Evans, L.J.) *"...the shipowners are entitled to rely upon an implied right to be indemnified against the consequences of complying with the time charterers' order to proceed to Basrah and deliver cargo there, notwithstanding that it was an order which the time charterers were entitled to give and the shipowners were bound to obey. There is an express finding that the losses claimed were the direct consequence of complying with the order and on this basis the shipowners are entitled to succeed..."*[211] **ii)** What is generally the scope of such an indemnity? (Evans, L.J.) *"...even when there is an express indemnity, time charterers are not liable for all consequences which may result from compliance with their order; first, the shipowners may*

---

[211] See also *The Athanasia Comninos.*

*themselves have been at fault; secondly, … the shipowner remains responsible for the safe navigation of the ship.*" **iii)** Were the shipowners responsible for accepting the charterers' orders? (Evans, L.J.) "*…the Iraqi system was well known only when the vessel was ordered there in June/July 1980, and the Iran/Iraq war which may have been responsible for the problem did not begin until September 1980. In these circumstances, the shipowners' failure to guard against the difficulties over a year before cannot provide grounds for barring their claim*" **iv)** Should an indemnity be generally implied when a master is placed under the orders of the charterers but no corresponding express indemnity is given? (Evans, L.J.) "*…the implication is justified, in my view, first by 'business efficacy' in the sense that if the charterer requires to have the vessel at his disposal, and to be free to choose voyages and cargoes and bill of lading terms also, then the owner must be expected to grant such freedom only if he is entitled to be indemnified against loss and liability resulting from it, subject always to the express terms of the charter-party contract; and secondly by the legal principle underlying the 'lawful request' cases*[212]*…in other words, an implication of law.*"

**235**

**TRUCKS & SPARES LTD. V. MARITIME AGENCIES (SOUTHAMPTON) LTD.**
1951, 2 All E.R. 982 (C.A.)

Six trucks and other automobile parts were shipped from Southampton (Eng-

land) for carriage to Montreal (Canada). A set of bills of lading was drawn up and signed by the master of the ship. The carrier retained the original bills of lading against payment of a balance of an account which was due by the shippers. The original bills were sent to the ship agents in Montreal with instructions to hold them until the agents in Southampton sanctioned their release to the buyers. The shippers paid the freight in advance but not their outstanding account. When the ship arrived at Montreal, the buyers asked for delivery claiming that they were the owners of the goods. Delivery was rejected by the carrier and the buyers filed an affidavit to their solicitors stating that they were the purchasers of the goods. They brought an action against the carriers and applied for an interim mandatory order to deliver, either the goods or their equivalent value, plus damages suffered for their detention. The carriers contended that, since the buyers were not the holders of the original bills of lading, they lacked sufficient title to obtain an order for delivery from the court. The question was whether the affidavit, which contained a mere assertion by the purchasers of their status, was sufficient evidence of title to grant a mandatory order for delivery.

**Held (for the carriers):**[213] (Denning L.J.) "*I do not know whether the plaintiffs have paid anything for those goods. I should doubt whether they have. If they are wise and follow the ordinary commercial practice, they will not pay except against the bills of lading, and,*

---

[212] *Sheffield Corporation v. Barclay,* [1905] A.C. 392 (H.L.).

[213] Hodson L.J. dissenting.

*if they have not paid, it is unlikely that the property has passed to them.*[214] *There may be an agreement for sale, but no passing of the property. I think we cannot allow strangers to the contract of carriage to claim the goods at this stage without the production of the bills of lading; whether the property has passed or not, in my opinion, they (the Buyers) ought to produce the bills of lading duly endorsed in order to make a good title at this stage…"* (Lloyd-Jacob J.) *"The evidence discloses that there are documents of title, the bills of lading, duly executed and held by the Montreal agents of the shippers conditionally on Hamilton's (as shippers) account, and a decision affirming title at this stage may create grave injustice to (some person or persons acquiring a title through the bills of lading in ignorance of the circumstances with which this action is concerned."* On those grounds, the mandatory order directed to the carrier to deliver the goods was denied.

**236**
**TSAKIROGLOU & CO. LTD. V. NOBLEE THORL, GMBH**[215]
**1961, 1 Lloyd's Rep. 329 (H.L.)**

Both parties entered into a sale contract of Sudanese groundnuts to be shipped at Karthoum on c.i.f. Hamburg terms. The contract contained the following clause: "…in all cases of force majeure preventing the shipment within the time fixed, or the delivery, the period allowed for shipment or delivery shall be extended by

not exceeding of 2 months. After that, if the case of force majeure is still operating, the contract shall be cancelled". The sellers booked space on a vessel on Nov. 1, 1956, but the Suez Canal became obstructed the next day as a result of military operations between Egypt and Israel. In view that the route via Cape of Good Hope was much longer and more expensive, the sellers argued that the contract was frustrated. They did not justify their frustration argument with the increase of freight but with the fact that the voyage via the Cape was commercially impracticable and fundamentally different from the customary route.

***Held (for the buyers):*** **i)** Was there an implied term that the goods should be carried via Suez? Their lordships responded negatively to that question. Contrary to the sellers' submission, in the absence of express terms to the contrary, there was generally no implied obligation in c.i.f. contracts to pursue the voyage through the customary route. In addition to that, there was no evidence that the parties herein cared for the route so chosen when they entered into the contract, and no perils (e.g. possible deterioration of cargo or loss of a seasonable market) were even alleged in relation to that route. The only condition of the contract of sale regarding the carriage was that the goods had to be loaded within a certain period. All other issues relating to the carriage belonged to the contract of affreightment only, to which the buyer was not party at all. **ii)** Was Suez the only practicable route? No. It is not the date of the contract but the time of performance which determines

---

[214] See the requirements of section 1 of the Bills of Lading Act 1855, at that time fully in force.
[215] Also known as one of the *Suez Canal cases.*

what is practicable (or reasonable) under the particular circumstances. The opposite view would be correct only if the sale contract had included an exception saying "unless at the time of performance there is no customary or usual route". In any event, the answer will depend on the circumstances of each case as contemplated by section 32(2) Sale of Goods Act 1893. **iii)** Was the contract frustrated? Again, the answer was negative. Shipping via the Cape did not obligate the seller to fulfil duties fundamentally different from those to which the seller originally agreed. Obviously, the contract of affreightment was altered thereby and so were terms of the insurance and the freight, but this is not itself a sufficient ground to allege frustration unless astronomical figures or fundamental alterations arise (which was not the case). Performance became more expensive but not impossible. (Viscount Simonds) *"It is a question of law whether a contracted has been frustrated, and it is commonly said that frustration occurs when conditions arise which are fundamentally different from those contemplated by the parties; but…an increase of expense is not a ground of frustration; the doctrine of frustration must be applied within very narrow limits."*[216]

---

[216] In the Court of Appeal, Harman L.J. stated the general view of the English courts as to the legal construction of frustration: *"Frustration is a doctrine too often invoked by a party to a contract who finds performance difficult or unprofitable, but it is very rarely relied upon with success. It is, in fact, a kind of last ditch, and, as Lord Radcliffe says in his speech in the most recent case (Davis Contractors v. Fareham U.D.C., 1956, A.C. 696), it is a conclusion which should be reached rarely and with reluctance".*

## 237

## UNIFERT INTERNATIONAL SAL v. PANOUS SHIPPING CO. INC.

*(The Virginia M)*
1989, 1 Lloyd's Rep. 603 (Q.B.)

The vessel *Virginia M* was chartered on the Gencom form dated Jan. 16, 1981. The charter was for the carriage of calcium ammonium nitrate from one safe berth Constanza to one safe berth/port in charterers' option Nigeria. Clause 22 of the charter provided: "The cargo to be discharged at the rate of 600 metric tonnes per weather working day of 24 consecutive hours." Since the cargo amounted to 9500 tonnes, the laytime available at the discharging port exceeded fifteen weather working days. The vessel was powered by old machinery consisting of a boiler which provided the steam necessary to run her auxiliaries. That boiler was fed with fresh water (about 20 tons/day). On Mar. 8, 1981, the vessel arrived at the nominated port of discharge with only 15 tons of fresh water remaining on board. It was clear that, with that quantity of water, the vessel would not be able to discharge the entire cargo at the time notice of readiness was tendered. The question under dispute was whether notice of readiness was valid. The owners submitted that the vessel ought to be ready merely to start the discharge for the notice to be valid. The arbitrators awarded in favour of the owners and the charterers appealed the award.

***Held (for the charterers):*** (Hobhouse, J.)
*"The readiness required is readiness to discharge the whole of the cargo that is the subject-matter of the charter-party. It does not suffice that the vessel is ready to discharge some*

*of the cargo if she is not ready to discharge the remainder. If the vessel having proceed into a berth and having discharged some cargo has to stop and take on fresh water or bunkers either at that berth or another berth, that is not consistent with the vessel having been ready to discharge nor is it consistent with the criteria laid down in the authorities,[217]…it is hard to see how a vessel which consumes about 20 tons per day fresh water can be ready for discharge when she only has 15 tons of fresh water remaining on board."*

## 238
## UNITED CITY MERCHANTS V. ROYAL BANK OF CANADA, VITROREFUERZOS AND BANCO CONTINENTAL S.A.
*(The American Accord)*
1982, 2 Lloyd's Rep. 1 (H.L.)

A Peruvian company (the buyers) purchased from an English firm (the sellers) a glass fibre manufacturing plant for USD 662,086 f.o.b. London for shipment to Callao (Peru). Payment was agreed through a confirmed irrevocable transferable letter of credit subject to the UCP (1974 Revision) of the ICC. At the request of the buyers, the purchase price (comprising the cargo value and the freight) was doubled in the invoice with a view to evade Peruvian exchange control regulations. The buyers opened the credit at a Peruvian issuing bank (Banco Continental), which then appointed the confirming bank (Royal Bank of Canada). The credit was effective by sight drafts against delivery, that is inter alia, of a full set of bills of lading stating a

loading extended date of Dec.15, 1976, at the latest. The goods were ready for shipment at the beginning of Dec., but the loading vessel (The *American Accord*) lifted the cargo on Dec. 16, 1976 (one day after the latest date required by the credit). The loading brokers, acting as agents of the carrier, issued a set of "received for shipment" bills of lading dated Dec. 15, 1976, and handed them to the sellers upon payment of freight. The confirming bank rejected the bills on the grounds they were not "on board" bills of lading and they were returned to the sellers. The loading brokers then issued a fresh set of "on board" bills of lading dated Dec. 15, 1976. The false date was inserted by an employee of the loading brokers, but the sellers seemed not to be aware of this fact. The amended bills were presented to the confirming bank, which again refused to pay on the grounds that the shipment date had been forged. The sellers brought an action against the buyers and the two banks. The appeal concerned the sellers' action against the confirming bank only. There were two issues before the court: (i) whether the confirming bank was exempted from issuing payment due to the forged loading date on the face of the bills; and, (ii) whether payment was alternatively precluded by virtue of art. VIII(2)(b) of the Bretton Woods Agreement, which established that all contracts which were contrary to the exchange control regulations should be unenforceable in the territories of any country member to the agreement.

***Held (for the sellers):* i)** (Lord Diplock) *"The bill of lading with the wrong date of loading placed on it by the carrier's agent was far from being a nullity. It was a valid*

---

[217] See *The Tres Flores.*

*transferable receipt for the goods giving the holder a right to claim them at their destination, Callao, and was evidence of the terms of the contract under which they were being carried; …what rational ground can there be for drawing any distinction between apparently conforming documents that, unknown to the seller, in fact contain a statement of fact that is inaccurate where the inaccuracy was due to inadvertence by the maker of the document, and the like document where the same inaccuracy had been inserted by the maker of the document with intent to deceive, among others, the seller/beneficiary itself?"* On these grounds, it was held that the confirming bank had no legitimate defence to refuse payment. The bank was obliged to pay, in spite of its knowledge of the fraud, because the fraud was made by a third party without knowledge or consent from the sellers. **ii)** As to the Bretton Woods issue, the portion of the invoice price which was added just for the purposes of evading Peruvian currency was not enforceable by virtue of art. VII(2)(b). Payment of the other half of the invoice and for 100% of the freight were indeed fully payable to the sellers. They were entitled to payment of that money since it originated from a genuine sale of goods.

**239**

**United Nations/Food and Agriculture Organisation v. Caspian Navigation Inc.**
*(The Jay Ganesh)*
1994, 2 Lloyd's Rep. 358 (Q.B.)

The vessel *Jay Ganesh* was chartered for the carriage of rice from 1/2 safe berths Bin Qasim (Pakistan) to various ports in West Africa. The charter was on the World Food Programme voyage charter form (known as Worldfood charter) and provided the following (cls.8): "At loading port before tendering notice of readiness the owners…shall ensure that all holds…are clean, dry and free from smell and in all respects suitable to receive the cargo to the…charterers' satisfaction". and (cls.9) "Laytime counting. If the notice of readiness has been tendered while the vessel is at or off the port (at the waiting for berth place)…the laytime shall commence to count and shall count as if the vessel were in berth…" The vessel gave notice of readiness on Aug. 10, 1990. There was no berth available. On Aug. 28, she was inspected by the charterers' representatives. Thereafter, the master was ordered to clean the holds and remove an infestation of insects. On Sept. 7, the vessel shifted from the anchorage into berth. It was inspected again and again the master was instructed to fumigate the holds. It was not until Sept. 9 that the vessel was considered fit to load. The owners claimed demurrage contending that the laytime started to run on Aug. 10, but subject to a deduction of about 2 ½ days for the time between berthing on Sept. 7 and being fit to load on Sept. 9. The charterers argued that the notice of readiness was invalid and with no effect, and that laytime should be counted from Sept. 9 onwards.

***Held (for the shipowners):*** When the master gave notice of readiness to load on Aug. 10, he honestly believed that the vessel was physically ready to load even though, in truth, she was (at that time unknown to the master) infested with insects. Therefore, regarding the overall effect of the clauses 8 and 9 of the charterparty, the shipowners were entitled to recover demurrage (minus the deduction) and the notice of readiness was still valid and effective. (Colman, J.) *"The overall effect of cll. 8 and 9 is accordingly, that this form of charterparty requires that the charterers must pay for waiting time at the anchorage when they have not provided a berth, but that if the vessel then causes delay after arrival in berth because she was not in truth then ready to load or discharge, that loss of time is to be borne by the owners."*[218]

## 240
## UNITED TRADING CORP. S.A. V. ALLIED ARAB BANK LTD. AND OTHERS
### 1985, 2 Lloyd's Rep. 554 (C.A.)

The plaintiffs were regular suppliers of foodstuffs to a company (Agromark) controlled by the Iraqi Ministry of Agriculture. In former cases, the terms of the sale contract required the plaintiffs to secure their obligations by procuring performance bonds in favour of Agromark. On receipt of the plaintiffs' performance bond, Agromark would open an irrevocable letter of credit in favour of the plaintiffs. These guarantees were all confirmed by Agromark's bank, the Iraqi Rafidain Bank, at 10% of the total value of the contract. All the guarantees were opened by the plaintiffs through their own bankers, Allied Arab Bank, which in exchange required an indemnity from them. Rafidain Bank itself always required a coun-

ter-indemnity from Allied Arab Bank as a condition for issuing the guarantees. The war between Iraq and Iran broke out on Sept. 22, 1980, and that gave rise to delays in the performance of the contracts. The time limits of the performance bonds were extended upon the request of Agromark, which then began to call in the performance bond referred to in earlier contracts which indeed had been performed. The plaintiffs took the view that Agromark's demands made in relation to earlier performance bonds were fraudulent, and sought an *ex parte* injunction restraining Allied Arab Bank from seeking payment from the plaintiff's indemnities.

*Held (for the defendants):* **i)** (Ackner, L.J.) *"...although the plaintiffs have provided, on the available material, a seriously arguable case that there is good reason to suspect, certainly in regard to some of these contracts, that the demands on the performance bonds have not been honestly made, they have not established a good arguable case that the only realistic inference is that the demands were fraudulent; The evidence of fraud must be clear, both as to the fact of fraud and as to the bank's knowledge..."* **ii)** (Ackner, L.J.) *"The plaintiffs took the commercial risk that the performance bonds might well be called in dishonestly by Agromark. When the plaintiffs gave the banks instructions to extend the time limits of the performance bonds, the plaintiffs as was conceded, intended to claim that any call on the performance bonds during such extended period or periods would be fraudulent. Needless to say, the plaintiffs did not disclose their intentions to the bank."* Accordingly, the plaintiffs were not entitled to maintain the injunction.

---

[218] See *The Linardos.*

**241**
**UNIVERSAL CARGO CARRIERS CORP. V.**
**CITATI**
1957 2 QB 401 (Q.B.)

A vessel was chartered for a carriage of scrap iron from Basrah (Iraq) to Buenos Aires (Argentina). The charterparty was on the Gencon form, which contained duties for the charterers drafted in the following terms: (5) "Cargo to be brought along-side…Time to commence 1 p.m. if notice of readiness is given before noon and at 6:00 a.m. next working day if notice given during office hours after noon. The notice to be given to the shippers…Time lost in waiting for berth to count as loading time…". (7) Demurrage to be at the rate of $1,000 per day…". (11) "Lay days not to commence before July 5, 1951…". The ship reached Basrah on July 12, 1951, but the charterers failed to nominate an actual shipper. The ship was sent to the buoys and remained there until July 18, three days before laytime was due to expire. On July 18, the owners decided to cancel the charter as no cargo had been provided for. On July 23, the vessel departed under the orders of different charterers and subject to a different charterparty. The owners sought damages contending that the charterers' failure to nominate a shipper or a berth or to provide cargo were breaches of conditions, and amounted to a repudiation of the charter which entitled the owners to cancel before the laytime had expired. The charterers counterclaimed for wrongful termination by the owners.

***Held (for the charterers):*** (Devlin J.):
**i)** As to the obligation to nominate a ship-per: *"Under a charterparty in this form the laydays begin to run, in effect, from the time the vessel is ready to proceed to her berth, irrespective of whether or not a berth has then been nominated or whether notice of readiness has been given".* **ii)** As to the obligation to nominate a berth and to provide cargo: *"Since no time is mentioned in the contract within which these obligations have to be fulfilled, the law implies a reasonable time. All these obligations…are preliminary to loading. The obligation to load has a time prescribed for it in the charterparty; loading must be completed within the lay days and the charterer is in breach of contract if he fails so to do. The time therefore within which the preliminary duties are to be performed is to be calculated by relation to the time prescribed for the main duty; the result is that the nomination of the berth and the provision of the cargo must be made in sufficient time to enable the vessel to be completely loaded within the lay days".* **iii)** As to the obligation to load: *"On July 18 the lay days had not expired, but the charterer had by his dilatoriness put it out of his power to comply with the term that he must complete the loading by July 21"* Devlin J. considered irrelevant the question whether this was to be classified as an anticipatory breach of an express term (of finishing loading on July 21) or as an actual breach of an implied term (of not doing anything that could deprive the power to fulfil one's duties). **iv)** As to the nature of the breaches: Devlin J. held that none of those breaches were conditions. The obligation to load within the lay days, as well as the so-called preliminary duties, are warranties breach of which results only in damages. The owners were not entitled to rescind the charter on July 18. However, that does not mean that the vessel must be indefinitely on de-

murrage in exchange for damages paid by the charterer. Devlin clarified: *"When the delay becomes so prolonged that the breach assumes a character so grave as to go to the root of the contract, the aggrieved party is entitled to rescind"*. Therefore, owners must generally wait until the laytime has expired before rescinding the charterparty should the charterers fail to provide a cargo. Even after the expiry of laytime, owners are not entitled to withdraw the ship unless it is clear that the charterers have no intention to load or the delay is such so as to frustrate the contract. Charterparty-no cargo…delay-right of owners to rescind.

## 242
### VARDINOYANNIS V. THE EGYPTIAN GENERAL PETROLEUM CORP.
*(The Evaggelos Th)*
1971, 2 Lloyd's Rep. 200 (Q.B.)

By a time charterparty dated Nov. 2, 1968, the tanker *Evaggelos TH* was let to the Egyptian charterers for trading in the Red Sea (which at all material times was a war zone) or elsewhere. The charterparty provided, inter alia, under clause 12 that: "The Cargo or Cargoes shall be laden and discharged in any dock or at any wharf or place the charterers may direct, where the vessel can always lie safely afloat…". Clause 16 of the charteparty provided that: "…The charterers hereby indemnify the owners from all consequences or liabilities that may arise from the Captain…complying with their or their Agents orders". The charterers agreed to contribute to the payment of the war risks premium in addition to the charter hire. In June 1969 the charterers ordered the vessel to proceed to

Suez. There was a cease fire between Israel and the Egypt, who were occupying the Suez Gulf and the Canal. The vessel called at Suez for discharge, but a few hours later hostilities between Israel and Egypt resumed. The vessel was fired upon and became a constructive total loss as a result of the Israeli attack. The owners declared arbitration and claimed damages from the charterers for (1) breach of clause 12, (2) breach of an implied warranty to limit the vessel's employment to safe ports, and (3) claimed indemnity under clause 16.

***Held:*** (Donaldson, J.) **i)** With regard to the words "always lie safely afloat" of cl. 12, the learned judge said: *"For my part, I think that it is concerned exclusively with the marine characteristics of the discharging place, and requires that the vessel shall at all time be water-borne and shall be able to remain there without risk of loss or damage from wind, weather or other craft which are being properly navigated… The claim under this head therefore fails".* **ii)** As to the implied warranty,[219] Donaldson, J. said: *"For my part,*

---

[219] *"Again, a charter may leave the choice of loading (or discharging) places entirely to the charterer, subject to some limitation as to the geographical range within which his choice must be exercised. In such cases, it is common practice for owners to insist upon an express limitation to safe places within the range. If this is done, the place must not only be safe when the ship is ordered to it, but safe when she arrives at it, although a temporary obstacle which will merely involve the ship in non-frustrating delay will not render the place unsafe. If the ship reasonably enters an unsafe place on the orders of the charterers and suffers damage as a result of such compliance, the charterer is liable. Safety in this context is not confined to physical safety. It extends also to political safety; But what if the charterer is given the right to nominate the loading (or discharging) place and there is no express qualification as to its safety? Is such qualification to be implied?"*

*if I were faced with a simple charter which provided that the vessel was only to go to such port or place within a specified range as might be nominated by the charterer and there load a cargo, I should have no hesitation in implying a qualification that the port or place had to be safe;…the implied term should in my judgment be limited to a warranty that the nominated port of discharge is safe at the time of nomination and may be expected to remain safe from the moment of the vessel's arrival until her departure…If, despite the fact that the nomination meets these requirements, the port is unsafe when the vessel arrives, no breach of contract is committed by the charterer, but the ship is not obliged to enter the port"*. As the arbitrators had not found that the port of Suez was unsafe when the vessel was ordered to go there and when it arrived, the charterers were not in breach of contract. **iii)** As to the question whether the proximate cause of the damage to the vessel was the charterers' order to proceed to Suez, and thus whether the charterers' indemnity should be made effective under cl. 16, the award should be remitted to the arbitrators to decide this issue.

**243**

**Vargas Pena Apezteguia y Cia Saic v. Peter Cremer GMBH**
1987, 1 Lloyd's Rep. 394 (Q.B.)

A cargo of cottonseed expeller was sold f.o.b. *Asunción* to German buyers. The sale contract stated that the cargo was to contain "15% max. fat" The letter of credit was opened contemplating the "15% max. fat" condition as per the certificate of quality to be tendered among the documents. If the stated percentage were surpassed,

the credit stated that the cargo was "rejectable at buyers' option". The buyers never objected to that clause. The market price of the goods suffered a serious fall at that time. Upon the sellers tendering the documents through their bank, the buyers sent a telex rejecting them on the ground that the certificate of quality indicated a higher content of fat. However, in the same telex, they stated they had some difficulties in rejecting f.o.b. goods being afloat and that, guided by the need to mitigate damages and having regard to a falling market, they accepted the goods for resale. According to their message, the goods were indeed sold to a third party. The sellers received only part payment on resale of the goods and claimed the balance of the contract price from the sellers.

***Held (for the sellers):*** (Saville J.) **i)** As far as the right of rejection of the goods is concerned, Saville J. said: *"In my view the buyers did not exercise this right, but on the contrary must be taken to have accepted the documents when they sold the shipment…A clear and unequivocal rejection is one where buyers indicate they want and will have nothing more to do with the goods"*. The judge found that the buyers' telex could not be taken as a valid message of rejection, and that the act of resale of the goods was inconsistent with the ownership of the sellers under section 35 of the Sale of Goods Act, 1979,[220] and therefore should be treated as

---

[220] Saville J. distinguished his decision from *Kwei Tek Chao v. British Traders and Shippers Ltd.* (involving a c.i.f. sale) because in the case before him the Buyers' loss resulted, not from the loss of the right to reject the documents, but from the market fall at the time the Buyers resold the goods.

an acceptance by the buyers. **ii)** The conduct of the buyers was not a reaction to the breach of the fat content term, rather *"by the fall in the market which was quite unrelated to the breach in this case and the buyer's desire to secure themselves with regard to what they asserted were their rights; In such a case to award damages where the documents have been accepted on the basis of the difference between the contract and the market prices at the date of the breach is to award damages that simply do not flow from the breach".* [221] **iii)** As for the buyers' reservation of their rights when they accepted the defective documents, the judge held that they *"can only reserve what rights they have if they choose to accept the documents with knowledge of the breach, then the rights they have are the rights attached to that case, and not those that would exist if they had taken a different course of action".*

### 244
### Vita Food Products v. Unus Shipping Company
1939, 63 Lloyd's Law Rep. 21 (P.C.)

A cargo of herring was shipped from Newfoundland ports to New York on board the ship *Hurry On*. Bills of lading were issued and signed by the superintendent on behalf of the ship acknowledging receipt on board of the goods in apparent good order and condition. The ship ran into bad weather and grounded off the coast of Nova Scotia (Canada). The goods were unloaded, reconditioned and

forwarded by another ship to New York. After delivery, the receivers sued the shipowners for the damaged condition of the goods, salvage and other expenses. The action was brought before the Courts of Nova Scotia and it was the Privy Council which later heard the case on appeal from the Supreme Court of Nova Scotia. It was admitted that the loss was due to the master's negligence in navigation. The shipowners pleaded that they were entitled to rely on the exemption contained in the Hague Rules, which formed part of English law. The receivers contended that the choice of English law failed in so far as there was nothing to connect the contract in any way with English law. Clause 7 of the bills included a general exemption from liability for loss or damage due to negligence of the shipowners' servants at or after the commencement of the voyage, or due to unseaworthiness provided that due diligence was proved. The same clause provided that the contract was governed by English law, which incorporated the Hague Rules by virtue of the Carriage of Goods by Sea Act 1924. Clause 22 called for, save as so provided, the then unrepealed Canadian Water-Carriage of Goods Act 1910. Apart from that, the Newfoundland Act 1932 provided in Section 1 that the Hague Rules should apply to all shipments from Newfoundland "subject to the provisions of this Act", and which in Section 3 of the Act established that all bills of lading issued in Newfoundland should contain an "express statement" that the contract was subject to the Act. Sections 4, 5 and 6(3) of the Act contained certain provisions to which the Rules were subject. However, it happened that the bills of lading did not

---

[221] But see *Kleinjan & Holst NV Rotterdam v. Bremer Handelsgesellschaft mbH Hamburg.*

contain such an "express statement". On that basis, the receivers alleged that, since Sec. 1 provided that the Rules should have effect "subject to the provisions of this Act", the Rules could not apply to a bill of lading unless the terms of Sec. 3 were complied with.

***Held (for the shipowners):*** **i)** As to the true construction of sections 1 and 3 of the Newfoundland Act: "*…the words 'subject to the provisions of this Act' merely mean in this connection that the Rules are to apply but subject to the modifications contained in Sections 2, 4, 5 and 6(3) of the Act;*[222] *In their lordship's judgment, Sec. 1 is the dominant section. Sec. 3 merely requires the bill of lading to contain an express statement of the effect of Sec. 1*". The omission of the "express statement" of Sec. 3 did not make the bills illegal or void. **ii)** As to which was the proper law of the contract: "*It is now well settled that by English law (and the law of Nova Scotia is the same) the proper law of the contract 'is the law which the parties intended to apply*'". In a question of conflict of laws, their lordships held that the English rule was that the intention of the parties was the proper test to apply provided that two requirements were met: (1) that their intention was expressed bona fide and legal; and (2) that there was no reason for avoiding the choice on the grounds of public policy. Contrary to the receivers' allegation that English law was in no way connected to the contract or the parties, their lord-

ships said: "*Connection with English law is not as a matter of principle essential. The provision in a contract (e.g. of sale) for English arbitration imports English law as the law governing the transaction, and those familiar with international business are aware how frequent such a provision is, even where the parties are not English and the transactions are carried on completely outside England*". **iii)** As to the alleged illegality of the bills of lading because Sec. 3 of the Newfoundland Act had not been complied with: "*The inconveniences that would follow from holding bills of lading illegal in such cases as that in question are very serious. A foreign merchant or banker could not be assumed to know or to inquire what the Newfoundland law is, at any rate when the bill of lading is not expressed to be governed by Newfoundland law and still less when it provides that it is governed by English law*". Once decided that the proper law was English Law and that the bills of lading were accordingly valid, their lordships took the view that the shipowners were entitled to rely on the exemption of error and negligence in navigation contained in the scheduled Hague Rules.

<hr>

[222] For the statutory application of the Hague-Visby Rules see *The Hollandia*, where their Lordships said: "*The Act of 1971 deliberately abandoned what may conveniently be termed the 'clause Paramount' technique employed in section 3 of the Act of 1924…*"

## 245
### VITOL S.A. v. ESSO AUSTRALIA LTD.
### *(The Wise)*
### 1989, 2 Lloyd's Rep. 451 (C.A.)

A cargo of 29,000-31,000 tonnes of premium motor spirit was sold c.&f. Hobart and Melbourne during the Iran-Irak war in 1986. Under clause 12 of the contract, "Title and risk: passes at vessel's manifold flange at load port". The c. & f. sellers nominated the vessel *Wise* which was accepted by the buyers. Subsequently, the sellers sent a message stating that they could not ship the minimum contractual quantity of 29,000 tonnes. The contract was then amended to allow shipment of only 27,500 tonnes. A further message was sent by the sellers stating that, in fact, the quantity shipped amounted to only 26,895 tonnes. After that message was sent, the vessel was hit by an Exocet missile during her voyage through the Gulf. A "without prejudice agreement" was entered into entitling the buyers to reject the cargo if it was not delivered by Mar. 30, 1986, in which case, the price for the cargo would be switched to the f.o.b. market price in the Gulf on the date transhipment of the cargo was completed. The sellers sued the buyers for the price of the goods, or alternatively for damages. The buyers formally abandoned the voyage and contended (1) that title and risk associated with the cargo remained with the sellers and (2) that failure to deliver the cargo on the contractual date entitled them to reject the delivery.

***Held (for the sellers):*** **i)** (Mustill L.J.) *"The purpose and effect of the without prejudice agreement was to confine the argument on the existing rights, in relation to which the interim arrangements for the delivery and payment were to be 'without prejudice' to those already in dispute when the arrangement was made".* **ii)** Where the goods are unascertained, as in the case of shipments of bulk, and various parts of the bulk are sold to different buyers, the property does not pass to these buyers until the various portions are appropriated to them. This is so even if the parties have agreed in the contract that the property shall pass upon the cargo being loaded on

board.[223] **iii)** However, the buyers were not entitled to reject the cargo on the ground that the quantity actually shipped was less than the contractual quantity: at no time had the buyers represented that they would raise the issue of the shortfall in quantity. (Mustill L.J.) *"I consider that the conduct of Esso, taken as a whole, and including their participation in formulating the terms of the without prejudice agreement, was such that they cannot fairly be allowed to rely on their new point. Whether the principle which leads to this conclusion is expressed in terms of waiver or estoppel does not seem to me of great importance. They were in possession of copy documents which made the shortfall obvious. Two weeks later, they advanced three propositions, none of them founded on the shortfall. More than two weeks later still, they were ready to sign an agreement which defined the dispute in terms of those three points (only)..."*

**246**
**VITOL S.A. V. NORELF LTD.**
*(The Santa Clara)*
1996, 2 Lloyd's Rep. 225 (H.L.)

Vitol S.A. purchased from Norelf Ltd. a cargo of propane on c.i.f. terms. The contract expressly incorporated the Incoterms 1990, Clause A8 of which required the sellers to tender the bill of lading to the buyers promptly after loading. Payment was to be made within thirty days of the bill of lading date. Delivery of the cargo at destination should be done between 1 and

---

[223] But see new sections 16, 20A and 20B of the Sales of Goods Act 1979 (as amended, 1995).

7 Mar., 1990. It happened that throughout Mar. 1991, there was a serious downturn in the regional market for propane. On Mar. 8, 1991, the *Santa Clara* loaded the cargo under the sellers' orders. On that date, the buyers sent a telex rejecting the cargo and repudiating the contract since, as they said, the ship was too late to meet the contractual delivery period. The sellers did nothing to perform the contract (including non-tender of the bill of lading) and re-sold the cargo at a price lower than the contracted for price. Some months later the sellers claimed about USD 1 million in damages based on the difference between the contract price and the resale price. The dispute was referred to arbitration and it was determined that the buyers' rejection of the telex constituted an anticipatory breach, and that the sellers' apparent failure to take any further steps to perform the contract constituted sufficient communication of acceptance of the buyers' repudiation. On appeal, the main issue for decision was whether the sellers, merely by failing to perform the contract, accepted the buyers' repudiation of the contract.

***Held (for the sellers):*** (Lord Steyn) "*For present purposes, I would accept as established law the following propositions: (1) Where a party has repudiated a contract the aggrieved party has an election to accept the repudiation or to affirm the contract…(2) An act of acceptance of a repudiation requires no particular form: a communication does not have to be couched in the language of acceptance. It is sufficient that the communication or conduct clearly and unequivocally conveys to the repudiating party that that aggrieved party is treating the contract as at an end. (3) It is rightly conceded…that the aggrieved party need not personally, or by an agent, to notify the repudiating party of his election to treat the contract as at an end. It is sufficient that the fact comes to the repudiating party's attention…; a failure to perform may sometimes signify to a repudiating party an election by the aggrieved party to treat the contract as at an end.*"Judgment for the sellers.

**247**
**VTC v. PVS**
2012, EWHC 1100 (Q.B.)

This is a section 69 arbitration appeal concerning the construction of a Shelltime 4 charter in a dispute about the state of the vessel's tanks on arrival at the loadport. The vessel had been chartered on an amended Shelltime 4 Form for about ten years. She was sub-chartered to load a cargo of gasoline at Rotterdam (Netherlands) for discharge at various destinations in Mexico, the USA and the Caribbean. The laycan was 18-20 Dec. 2010. Whilst en route to Rotterdam, a 12 mm crack in the port side slop tank was discovered by the crew. This could not be repaired before the cancelling date, for which reason on 17 Dec. the sub-charterers decided to cancel the sub-charter. At 22:00 hours on 20 Dec., the vessel arrived in Rotterdam, where she undertook two days of repairs and was ordered to the UK West coast to load another cargo. Charterers deducted USD 455,432 from hire alleging breach of clause 64 of the charter, which read as follows: "Owners warrant that vessel will arrive at each load port with all cargo tanks, pumps and lines suitable to load the intended cargo as per charterers' representative and/or independent surveyor's satisfaction which always is subject to tank cleaning/squeeging clause 102. All damages, time lost and costs incurred due to non compliance will be for owner's account and deducted from monthly hire". Clause 102 of the charter contained information about of the vessel's description, including details of the slop tanks.

***Held (for owners):*** Charterers' view was that the reference to "all cargo tanks" in clause 64 was meant to include the vessel's slop tanks. The court disagreed. Yet, even if the "cargo tanks" had been intended to include the slop tanks, there were still no findings that the slop tanks were intended to be used as cargo tanks or fell within that description. The court upheld the arbitrators finding that there was a difference between cargo tanks and slop tanks. The owners would only be in breach of clause 64 if the vessel arrived at a loading port and her cargo tanks were actually found not to be suitable to the satisfaction of the charterer's representative or independent surveyor. As a matter of fact, when the vessel arrived at Rotterdam the sub-charterers had already cancelled the charter and the cargo tanks were not even inspected. There was, therefore, no breach by the owners.

**248**

**WAREN IMPORT GESELLSCHAFT KROHN & CO. V. TOEPFER (ALFRED C.)**
*(The Vladimir Ilich)*
1974, 1 Lloyd's Rep. 322 (Q.B.)

A quantity of Thailand tapioca was sold c.i.f. Hamburg incorporating the Grain and Feed Trade Association Form no. 100. Under clause 10, this standard con-tract provided, inter alia, that: "(e) Every such Notice of Appropriation shall be open to correction of any errors occurring in transmission, provided that the sender is not responsible for such errors... (g) When a valid Notice of Appropriation has been received by buyers, it shall not be withdrawn except with their consent". Once shipment was effected, the sellers sent the buyers a telex stating the goods were shipped at Bangkok on board the "*Vladimir* (or better name)". The buyers replied that they would reject the tender because no vessel named *Vladimir* had loaded at Bangkok at that time and hence the appropriation was "uncontractual". The sellers then amended the original appropriation with a telex stating that, under the clause "or better name" they amended the name as *Vladimir Ilich*. The buyers again rejected the shipping docu-ments on the ground that the clause "or better name" referred only to probable writing mistakes. The buyers took the appropriation as invalid and treated the sellers' conduct as constituting an antic-ipatory breach.

***Held (for the sellers):*** (Donaldson J.) **i)** The first question was whether the original appropriation was valid or not. *"It is important to remember that an ap-propriation is a matter of contract not of performance. That comes later. Accordingly, validity depends upon form and timing and not upon substance or factual accuracy. The appropriation was made within the proper time and was not defective in form".* There-fore, at that stage, the appropriation was valid. **ii)** The mention "or better name" did not deprive the appropriation of its essential certainty and it has commonly been accepted in the ordinary trade. It has no other effect than the limited right to correct errors in transmission within the scope of cls. 10(e).[224] The appropriation remained therefore valid. **iii)** As to the conduct of the buyers, Donaldson J. said that *"the buyers cannot reject a notice of appropriation as invalid…and later reject the documents because they do not comply with it"*. If they had accepted the notice and had waited until the tender of documents, they would had been entitled to reject the documents because they would have showed a vessel other than that stated in the notice. However, as the buyers rejected the notice immediately, they impliedly gave the opportunity to the Sellers to send a fresh amended notice in time. Thereafter, the buyers were faced with a valid notice of appropriation and a tender of documents which was indeed in compliance with that notice. *"The buyers were not entitled to reject the tender as being uncontractual; the alleged right to cancel based on the rejection never arose. Accordingly, the buyers' cancellation was premature and was itself a repudiation which the sellers accepted by re-selling the goods."*

**249**
**West Tankers Inc. v. Allianz
Spa & Anor**
[2012] EWHC 854 (Comm.)

The underlying dispute was between the Allianz SpA, underwriters of the charterers of the MV *Front Connor*, and West Tankers

Inc., the vessel's owners. The dispute related to damages out of a collision. The charterparty contained an arbitration clause pursuant to which any dispute should be heard by arbitration in London. While the arbitration was on-going, Allianz brought a claim against West Tankers before the Tribunale di Siracusa in Italy for the same incident. West Tankers sought an anti-suit injunction from the English Court to restrain Allianz from pursuing their action in Italy, which was in conflict with the arbitration agreement. The injunction was set aside by the European Court of Justice. West Tankers then asked the arbitral tribunal to award damages against Allianz for breach of the arbitration agreement as a result of bringing court proceedings in Italy. The question was if, under the principle of effective judicial protection, the arbitral tribunal was deprived of jurisdiction to award equitable damages.

**Held:** Since arbitration falls outside the Regulation (EC) 44/2001, the jurisdiction of the arbitral tribunal is not constrained or limited by the principle of effective judicial protection. The arbitral tribunal was not deprived, by reason of EU law, of jurisdiction to award equitable damages for breach of the obligation to arbitrate.

**250**
**Whistler Int. Ltd. v. Kawasaki Kisen
Kaisha Ltd.**
*(The Hill Harmony)*
1999, 2 Lloyd's Rep. 209 (C.A.)

Cosco, owners of the vessel *Hill Harmony*, let her on a time charter to the plaintiffs Whistler. During the currency of the

---

[224] See *Kleinjan & Holst N.V. Rotterdam v. Bremer Handelsgeselsgesellschaft G.m.b.H.*

charter, the ship was sub-time chartered by Whistler to the defendants Kawasaki on the New York Produce Exchange form. The defendants, in turn, sub-sub-chartered her to Tokai Shipping Co. Ltd. for a time trip charter of 30/35 days covering a voyage from Vancouver (Canada) to Shiogama (Japan) also under a NYPE form. The NYPE form incorporated the Hague-Visby Rules and contained, inter alia, the following clauses numbered 8 and 55 respectively: "8. That the Captain shall prosecute his voyage with the utmost despatch, and shall render all customary assistance with ship's crew and equipment. The Captain…shall be under the orders and directions of the charterers as regards employment and agency". "55. In the event of loss of time …caused by… reason of the refusal of Master or Officers or crew to perform their duties…the hire shall be suspended…and direct expenses incurred including bunkers consumed during such period of suspension shall be for owners' account". Before the commencement of the charters, the vessel had suffered severe heavy-weather damage on a northerly trans-Pacific route from San Francisco to Japan. During the currency of the charters, the charterers (Kawasaki and Tokai) ordered the Master to take the shorter northern Great Circle route on her way to Shiogama. The master, however, resisted such order and sought to proceed by the more southerly course with a resulting increase in time and bunker's consumption. Tokai deducted hire and claimed the extra bunkering cost to Kawasaki. Kawasaki, in turn, did the same to Whistler and the dispute was referred to arbitration. The award was appealed. The issue for decision was whether Whis-

tler was in breach of cls. 8 NYPE form because the master allegedly failed "to prosecute his voyage with utmost despatch" and/or he failed to follow the "orders and directions of the charterers as regards employment and agency". Whistler challenged the charterers' claim on the basis of art. IV(2) and (4) of the Rules.

***Held (for whistler):*** i) As to the alleged breach of the "utmost despatch" obligation: (Potter, LJ) "*The obligation of the master/owners was to proceed with the 'utmost despatch' (which in my view adds nothing to the concept of reasonable despatch) from port to port or other nominated destination without deviation, i.e. by the direct route or by a route which, though not direct, was a usual and reasonable route. They were also obliged to operate the ship in accordance with the charterers' orders as to its employment. However, neither obligation displaced the right and responsibility of the master in matters of navigation and, in particular, to decide upon the course or courses to be followed when prosecuting the voyage as properly defined, having regard to weather conditions and other hazards of navigation*". ii) As to whether the orders and directions were as regards "employment" or "navigation": (Potter, LJ) "*On the basis that it is common ground that the charter-party contemplates a dichotomy between orders as to employment and navigation, orders of the charterers as to a particular course to be followed should not be interpreted or treated as tying the hands of the master in respect of a decision taken by him as to the navigation of the vessel; … the appropriate categorization of the charterers' additional directions as an order as to employment or an order as to navigation* *must be a matter of fact and degree in the circumstances of the case; however I do not accept that it is solely a question of fact…it is a fixed question of fact and law; It seems to me that…the master took the decision to set and follow the course which he did on the grounds that he would thereby avoid the danger of bad weather and possible damage to the ship as a result, that was indeed…a decision taken (and there is no suggestion that it was not bona fide taken) for the safety of the vessel and, as such, was a decision as to navigation."* **iii)** As to the applicability of art. IV(2)(a) of the Hague-Visby Rules: The exemption afforded by art. IV(2)(a) is apt to apply to acts or decisions of "navigation" which are made either before or after the vessel has left port. So it happens in this case, where the decision was taken in the course of the voyage planning, to steer a particular route bearing in mind the forecasted weather.

# Analytic index

Numbers referred to in each item are meant to be the numbers allocated to each case by the author.

## Negociación intercultural. Estrategias y técnicas de negociación internacional

*Domingo Cabeza, Pelayo Corella, Carlos Jiménez*
Una herramienta imprescindible para gestionar los procesos de negociación en entornos internacionales.
336 págs.; 17 x 24 cm. Color. ISBN: 978-84-15340-79-9.

## Las reglas Incoterms® 2010. Manual para usarlas con eficacia

*Alfonso Cabrera Cánovas*
Un manual práctico con la respuesta a todos los interrogantes que surgen en el uso de las reglas Incoterms para el comercio internacional.
234 págs.; 17 x 24 cm. Color. ISBN 978-84-15340-10-2.

## Gestión aduanera en la Unión Europea. Normativa de la UE para el comercio exterior

*Pedro Coll*
Un manual sobre la normativa aduanera de la Unión Europea para realizar operaciones de importación o exportación, tanto si se opera desde la propia UE como si se hace desde terceros países .
160 págs.; 17 x 24 cm.ISBN: 978-84-15340-60-7.

## Regímenes aduaneros económicos y procesos logísticos en el comercio internacional

*Pedro Coll*
Desarrollo operativo de los regímenes aduaneros económicos que pueden aplicarse en cada circunstancia y de los procesos logísticos en las operaciones de compraventa internacional.
256 págs.; 17 x 24 cm.ISBN: 978-84-15340-32-4.

## Inglés náutico normalizado para las comunicaciones marítimas

*José Manuel Díaz Pérez*
Práctico manual que presenta el vocabulario normalizado de navegación, así como las frases normalizadas para las comunicaciones marítimas establecidas por la OMI.
144 págs.; 17 x 24 cm. ISBN 978-84-15340-07-2.

## Gestión financiera del comercio internacional

*Josep M.ª Casadejús*
Una herramienta para conocer en profundidad los aspectos comerciales y financieros del mercado internacional.
272 págs.; 17 x 24 cm. ISBN 978-84-92442-84-3.

## El desorden sanitario tiene cura. Desde la seguridad del paciente hasta la sostenibilidad del sistema sanitario con la gestión por procesos

*Rajaram Govindarajan*
Un sistema para la prevención, el análisis y la corrección de los principales problemas en la sanidad pública.
200 págs.; 17 x 24 cm. ISBN 978-84-92442-56-0.

## Shipping & Commercial Case Law

*Albert Badia*
250 leading cases of the High Courts of England & the European Court of Justice.
292 págs.; 17 x 24 cm. ISBN 978-84-15340-84-3.

## Gestión y liderazgo en una empresa de seguros

*Simón Mahfoud y Digna Peña*
Una experiencia de gestión, con una visión completa del sector asegurador, de su estructura, su funcionamiento y sus aportes a la economía.
160 págs.; 17 x 24 cm. ISBN 978-84-86684-75-4.

## Personalización masiva

*Blas Gómez*
Las claves del nuevo horizonte empresarial en la producción y los servicios: la personalización masiva (mass costumization).
144 págs.; 17 x 24 cm. ISBN 978-84-86684-68-6.

## Gestión medioambiental en la industria

*José M.ª Suris*
Claves para hacer sostenible y rentable la gestión medioambiental en los procesos industriales y la distribución de productos.
248 págs.; 17 x 24 cm. ISBN 84-86684-33-1.

## Los abordajes en la mar

*Carlos F. Salinas*
La respuesta a todos los interrogantes que surgen en la prevención de los abordajes.
Incluye Reglamento actualizado.141 ilustraciones a color; 208 págs.; 17 x 24 cm. ISBN 84-86684-25-0.

## La cadena de suministro

*IESE-CIIL; Coordinador: Federico Sabrià*
Los modelos y herramientas necesarios para planificar y optimizar la gestión de la cadena de suministro.
208 págs.; 17 x 24 cm. ISBN 84-86684-27-7.

## Logística de la carga aérea

*Carlos Vila López*
Manual de los procesos y procedimientos documentales para la gestión logística en el transporte aéreo de mercancías.
224 págs.; 17 x 24 cm. ISBN 84-86684-22-6.

València, 558, ático 2.º  08026 Barcelona – Tel. +34-932 449 130 – marge@marge.es – www.marge.es

## Transporte ferroviario de mercancías
*Miguel Ángel Dombriz*
Las claves de la eficiencia de los servicios ferroviarios, en qué condiciones se deben contratar y qué elementos inciden en sus costes y su operatividad.
246 págs.; 17 x 24 cm. Color. ISBN 978-84-15340-80-5.

## Transporte en contenedor
*Jaime Rodrigo de Larrucea, Ricard Marí, Álvaro Librán*
El proceso de transporte del contenedor, su manipulación en terminales, el régimen jurídico y la casuística de daños y averías que pueden afectarlo.
338 págs.; 17 x 24 cm. Color. ISBN 978-84-15340-67-6.

## El transporte por carretera
*José Manuel Ruiz Rodríguez*
Un manual con todos los conocimientos que necesita el profesional del transporte por carretera.
232 págs.; 17 x 24 cm. ISBN 978-84-15340-01-0.

## Logística hospitalaria
*Borja Ozores*
Claves y tendencias de las operaciones logísticas en el sector hospitalario: calidad en la atención sanitaria y reducción de costes.
138 págs.; 17 x 24 cm. ISBN 978-84-15340-66-9.

## La seguridad en los puertos
*Ricard Marí, Jaime Rodrigo de Larrucea, Álvaro Librán*
Cómo implantar planes de seguridad y protección en instalaciones portuarias y buques según el código de la Organización Marítima Internacional (OMI).
288 págs.; 17 x 24 cm. ISBN 978-84-15340-48-5.

## Centros logísticos
*Ignasi Ragàs*
Planificación, promoción y gestión de los centros de actividades logísticas.
264 págs.; 17 x 24 cm. Color. ISBN 978-84-15340-41-6.

## El Convenio CMR
*Francisco Sánchez-Gamborino, Alfonso Cabrera Cánovas*
El contrato de transporte internacional de mercancías por carretera.
252 págs.; 17 x 24 cm. ISBN 978-84-15340-33-1.

## Logística inversa en la gestión de la cadena de suministro
*Domingo Cabeza*
Cómo generar valor económico, respetar el medio ambiente y contribuir al desarrollo sostenible.
152 págs.; 17 x 24 cm. ISBN 978-84-15340-58-4.

## Soluciones logísticas
*Francisco Álvarez Ochoa*
Manual con casos prácticos para optimizar la cadena de suministro.
218 págs.; 17 x 24 cm. ISBN 978-84-92442-96-6.

## El transporte internacional por carretera
*Alfonso Cabrera Cánovas*
Un manual para la contratación y gestión del transporte internacional por carretera y su adecuación a las reglas Incoterms 2010.
160 págs.; 17 x 24 cm. ISBN 978-84-15340-06-5.

## Gestión del transporte
*Jaime Mira, David Soler*
Manual práctico para la gestión integral del transporte de mercancías.
320 págs.; 17 x 24 cm. ISBN 978-84-92442-97-3.

## El contrato de transporte por carretera
(Ley 15/2009)
*Alfonso Cabrera Cánovas*
Manual práctico para aplicar la ley que regula en España el contrato de transporte de mercancías por carretera.
160 págs.; 17 x 24 cm. ISBN 978-84-92442-94-2.

## El seguro de las mercancías en el transporte
*Albert Badia*
Manual práctico para resolver dudas y conocer en profundidad el ámbito del seguro de transporte de mercancías por vía marítima, terrestre y aérea.
320 págs.; 17 x 24 cm. ISBN 978-84-92442-28-7.

## Capacitación profesional para el transporte de mercancías por carretera
*José Manuel Ruiz Rodríguez*
Un manual para conseguir el certificado de capacitación profesional de transportista de mercancías, nacional e internacional.
360 págs.; 17 x 24 cm. ISBN 978-84-86684-76-1.

## Diccionario de logística
*David Soler*
Más de 3.500 conceptos relacionados con la logística y la cadena de suministro con su traducción al inglés.
378 págs.; 14,5 x 21 cm. ISBN 978-84-92442-24-9.

## Logística urbana. Ciudad y mercancías
*Institut Cerdà*
Políticas de movilidad y soluciones de gestión de la logística urbana para las empresas y los organismos públicos.
164 págs.; 17 x 24 cm. ISBN 978-84-92442-14-0.

## Abandono de buques y tripulaciones
*Domingo González Joyanes*
Un estudio sobre las repercusiones sociales, económicas y medioambientales que provocan el abandono de buques y sus tripulaciones, incluyendo su problemática procesal con la aportación de casos concretos y un estudio de todos los agentes involucrados.
256 págs.; 17 x 24 cm. ISBN 978-84-92442-23-2.

## Capacitación profesional para el transporte de mercancías por carretera (hasta 3.500 kg MMA)

*José Manuel Ruiz Rodríguez*
Un manual para conseguir el certificado de capacitación profesional autonómica de transportista de mercancías.
226 págs.; 17 x 24 cm. ISBN 978-84-86684-99-0.

## Almacenamiento de materiales

*Mariano Pérez*
Como diseñar y gestionar almacenes optimizando todos los recursos de los procesos logísticos.
320 págs.; 17 x 24 cm. ISBN 84-86684-59-5.

## Operadores logísticos

*Andrés Mira*
Claves y perspectivas de los servicios de los operadores logísticos.
160 págs.; 17 x 24 cm; tapa dura; a color.
ISBN 84-86684-56-0.

## Calidad total y logística

*José Presencia*
Cómo alcanzar procesos logísticos eficientes mediante la gestión de la calidad total.
160 págs.; 17 x 24 cm. ISBN 84-86684-24-2.

## Logística del automóvil

*Federico Sabrià*
Claves operativas y estrategias de producción de los fabricantes de automóviles.
128 págs.; 17 x 24 cm. ISBN 84-86684-26-9.

## El transporte marítimo

*Rosa Romero*
Todos los conceptos y procesos para la gestión del principal modo de transporte en el comercio internacional.
192 págs.; 17 x 24 cm. ISBN 84-86684-15-3.

## Subcontratación de servicios logísticos

*Josep A. Aguilar*
Cómo desarrollar una operación de outsourcing en la gestión logística integral.
144 págs.; 21 x 29,7 cm. ISBN 84-86684-13-7.

## Transporte internacional

*Josep Baena*
Manual didáctico con los principales conceptos y elementos del transporte internacional y su vinculación con el comercio exterior.
64 págs.; 17 x 24 cm; a color. ISBN 84-86684-17-X.

## Logística e intermodalidad

*Luis Montero*
Manual didáctico con los conceptos básicos de la logística y la intermodalidad en el transporte de mercancías.
64 págs.; 17 x 24 cm; a color. ISBN 84-86684-18-8.

## Logística y marketing geográfico

*Fernando S. Amago*
Geomarketing para tomar decisiones visualmente.
224 págs.; 21 x 29,7 cm. ISBN 84-86684-08-0.

## e-Logistics (II)

*Miguel Ángel Pesquera*
Los fundamentos del comercio electrónico en la gestión de las cadenas logísticas.
160 págs.; 21 x 29,7 cm. ISBN 84-86684-09-9.

## e-Logistics (I)

*Ángel Ibeas*
Las claves de la gestión del transporte para alcanzar un alto servicio con el menor coste y la mayor competitividad.
144 págs.; 21 x 29,7 cm. ISBN 84-86684-06-5.

València, 558, ático 2.º 08026 Barcelona — Tel. +34-932 449 130 — marge@marge.es — www.marge.es